One of the most dominant and dramatic personalities at the United Nations from 1947 to 1962, Krishna Menon also was a major figure in the shaping of Indian foreign and domestic policy. Yet little of substance has been written about him—mainly because he has been in political eclipse since 1962.

In 1964–65, Michael Brecher, Professor of Political Science at McGill University, conducted a series of tape-recorded interviews with Krishna Menon on widely ranging themes, and the main part of this book, an edited version of that dialogue, is a valuable and fascinating commentary on world and Indian politics, being at once a primary source for scholars and, by retaining as far as possible the conversational flavor and tone, a reflection of Krishna Menon's complex personality. In response to Professor Brecher's questions, Krishna Menon expounds, in typically candid fashion, on the workings of the Indian Parliament, the basic tenets of India's foreign policy, his country's relations with Pakistan and Burma, its policy of non-alignment, its place in the British Commonwealth, and its stands on the issues of the Korean War, the Suez crisis, the Hungarian Revolution, and the disturbances in the Congo. His reflections on Jawaharlal Nehru constitute a significant portrait by one who may have known that statesman better than any of his other colleagues did.

In the second part of the book, adding historical documentation to the information he gained in the interviews, Professor Brecher incisively analyzes both Krishna Menon's view of the world and its impact on India's foreign policy.

In an appendix for the specialist—a content analysis of the interviews—Janice Gross Stein traces the major themes of Indian fore͏ attitudes t͏ dealings wi͏

D1261441

INDIA AND
WORLD POLITICS

*Krishna Menon's
View of the World*

INDIA AND WORLD POLITICS

*Krishna Menon's
View of the World*

MICHAEL BRECHER

FREDERICK A. PRAEGER, *Publishers*
New York · Washington

BOOKS THAT MATTER

Published in the United States of America in 1968
by Frederick A. Praeger, Inc., Publishers
111 Fourth Avenue, New York, N.Y. 10003

© 1968, in England, by Oxford University Press
London, England

Library of Congress Catalog Card Number: 68-16083

Printed in Great Britain

TO MY
MOTHER AND FATHER

PREFACE

THIS book, like an earlier one on decision-making—*Succession in India* (1966)—is the result of recent field research, in 1964-5 and for shorter periods in the winters of 1966 and 1967. Its origins are twofold. The first object was an attempt to secure Krishna Menon's reflections, as vital source material for a larger work on India's Foreign Policy System now in progress; the second was a need to test an idea about the nature of decision-making in foreign policy. Reading and reflection, and discussions in a university seminar, had suggested a close link between élite images and policy acts. More pointedly, they had given rise to the proposition that the choice among policy options derives from decision-makers' perceptions of their State's environment and its desirable roles in international politics. It followed from this hypothesis that a key, if not the master key, to understanding the Foreign Policy System is the World View of the small coterie of men within each State who make foreign-policy decisions. Krishna Menon's place in that Indian élite for fifteen years (1947-62) offered an unrivalled opportunity to explore this idea in depth.

The dialogue began as one informal interview on the origins, rationale, and assessment of Non-Alignment. It developed into seventeen hours of taped, extemporaneous interviews covering twenty-one themes or events, most of them in world politics since the Second World War. The first series was held in Mr. Menon's home in New Delhi almost every day for three weeks in November–December 1964. Supplementary interviews were conducted in May 1965, in order to fill gaps that became apparent from the transcript of the initial discussions. The completed draft of the dialogue was edited by Mr. Menon early in 1966, during my return to India to observe the second succession contest. It was further edited by me in the autumn of that year, special care being taken not to alter the content or meaning of Mr. Menon's articulated images. The analyses of his View of the World were prepared during 1967 and were based on Mr. Menon's edited version of the dialogue, that is, on his considered thoughts about the topics under investigation.

There are three closely related segments in this volume. The first comprises the candid recollections and reflections of the most influential decision-maker in India's foreign policy during the Nehru era, apart from Nehru himself, and a prominent figure in world politics generally, from 1952 to 1962. Menon has never written memoirs: at the outset of the dialogue he remarked, 'Please don't ask me for dates—I have no records'; and on more than one occasion he deprecated autobiography, on the grounds that it distorts reality. Thus his reconstruction of events, in which he played a crucial role, provides a primary source on international politics during a tumultuous era. On some issues Menon's account corroborates those of other participants, wholly or in part. His recollection is at variance with others on certain topics. And, on still others, he has added either a new dimension or hitherto unknown material. In short, these fragments of induced memoirs contribute to the understanding of an outsider delving into the labyrinth of decision-making.

The second part of this book attempts to break fresh ground in foreign policy studies by providing a systematic analysis of Krishna Menon's View of the World and its impact on India's foreign policy. It focuses on one of six components of a Foreign Policy System—Élite Images or Psychological Environment—and is designed to illustrate the link between decision-makers' perceptions and policy choices. As such, it may be viewed as a pilot project for other foreign policy studies of this type; these, in turn, are part of larger works on the whole Foreign Policy System in which the writer is presently engaged, one on Israel, the other on India.

The third section takes the form of a content analysis of Menon's View of the World and was prepared by a Political Science colleague, Professor Janice Gross Stein. Directed primarily at International Relations specialists, this paper reveals the analytical value of this statistical technique of foreign policy analysis. It also sheds some light on what has seemed to many a wasteful debate over the relative merits of quantitative and non-quantitative methods of political analysis: there is a place for both—and a need for both. In this instance, the two methods proved to be complementary, not contradictory, or even at variance; their conclusions were remarkably similar, though stated differently.

This book owes much to various persons and institutions:

Mr. V. K. Krishna Menon, who readily consented to a wide-ranging, extemporaneous dialogue on tape, covering many controversial topics in world and Indian politics over a period of twenty years; for the candour of his reflections; for the privilege and pleasure of friendly debate with a talented intellectual in politics; and for permission to publish the dialogue. I regret the fact that Mr. Menon found it necessary to delete or soften some of his more forthright judgements of men and events, but this has not, in my judgement, altered the main thrusts of the dialogue or its value for persons interested in international politics;

the late Professor Charles O. Lerche, who inspired the Foreign Policy Project at the American University's School of International Service, which provided a Grant-in-Aid of Research on India's foreign policy, in 1963–4;

the Rockefeller Foundation, whose Travelling Fellowship in International Relations made it possible for me to spend a year in India gathering materials on India's foreign policy;

the John Simon Guggenheim Memorial Foundation, which sponsored my research into Israel's foreign policy in 1965–6 and thereby enabled me to return to India in the winter of 1966 to continue this project;

McGill University, which granted me a two-year leave of absence;

the McGill Centre of Developing Area Studies, for providing an atmosphere conducive to Social Science Research on developing States and for enabling me to return to India briefly in 1967;

Mrs. Ann Douglas, who worked selflessly and with great skill over many months to transcribe the dialogue from tape to paper, and who typed two complete drafts of the transcript;

Professor Blema S. Steinberg, a Political Science colleague, who read the entire manuscript with care and made many valuable suggestions; and

Miss Ena Sheen, of the Oxford University Press, London, who added a sure editorial touch to many obscure points in the dialogue and contributed much to its readability.

My wife, as always, provided encouragement and assistance of various kinds throughout the long gestation period of this book. The dialogue is essentially unchanged from the version edited by Mr. Menon. Part II, containing the interpretation and analysis of his View, is the author's responsibility.

MICHAEL BRECHER

Montreal
December 1967

CONTENTS

PART I

DIALOGUE

1. Non-Alignment

B I would like to begin, Mr. Menon, with some questions on non-alignment. Who conceived the policy? What was your role in this? What was Mr. Nehru's role? In short, could you go back to the origins of non-alignment and its foundations?

M Even if nobody conceived it, non-alignment was more or less a residue of historical circumstances. In 1945, immediately before India got her independence, it was all 'one world'; but by 1947 it was 'two worlds', and we, for the first time, had to make up our minds on the issue, how we would function and what we would do. We would not go back to the West with its colonialism; and there was no question of our going the Soviet way; we did not even know them much. And with the attaining of our independence we desired not to get involved in foreign entanglements. All these things entered into it. But it is not as though we sat around the table deciding how we should non-align ourselves! There were two blocs. Both the Prime Minister [Nehru] and I exclaimed or thought aloud *simultaneously*, 'why should we be with anybody?'

B But the word 'non-alignment' itself: who conceived this and when?

M That, I used much later—spontaneously. I think it was at the United Nations but I couldn't say for certain. We were being ridiculed about being 'neutral'. I said then, 'We are not neutral; we are non-aligned. We are not aligned to either side, we are non-aligned.' In fact, the Prime Minister didn't approve very much of the word at the beginning, but it had quickly gained currency.

B It was, then, at some meeting in 1950?

M No. No. It was later than that. I don't think you will see the word 'non-aligned' used that early—to the best of my recollection. I think it was probably used some time in '53–'54; that is my recollection, but you had better check up on that. But the word 'non-alignment' was first used at the United Nations.

B Mr. Menon, you would agree, I think, that in any foreign policy, non-alignment or other, there is bound to be a combination of 'national interest' and idealist considerations. One wonders, in the Indian case, to what extent non-alignment was considered to be an instrument of the 'national interest' and to what extent it was simply a projection of Indian ideals—or to what extent both were involved?

M I don't know about ideals. There was, as I told you, the inevitability of it. Secondly, there was the fact of independence itself. What is non-alignment? It is merely independence in external affairs. What are external affairs? They are only a projection of internal or national policy in the field of International Relations.

B Would you go so far as to say that non-alignment is the logical extension of nationalism?

M Logical extension of nationalism, yes, and of the conflict between nationalism and military blocs, the fact that we had little in common with the *raison d'être* of the blocs; with the West, because to us the West meant Empire.

B But is it not true that, as Mr. Nehru and you conceived a foreign policy for India, non-alignment was thought of as the most efficient path to economic development?

M Yes, but I don't think anyone thought about it that way at the time, because the question of foreign aid and things of that kind, which are so prominent today, did not figure in our minds very much. We didn't think back from economics to politics.

B So there was no direct material factor in the origins of non-alignment. This was to come much later?

M Much later. You will also find that Panditji's[1] utterances on this matter at that time must have appeared to Americans very abrupt. I remember one occasion, when George Allen was [U.S.] Ambassador here; somebody had exported from here to China Rs. 50,000 worth of some clay product, used in the making of gas mantles. In the normal course of export we

---

[1] A term of endearment for Pandit Nehru, commonly used by Indians from all walks of life.

don't even have to know about such things; merchandise, you know. But apparently this is classified as atomic material. And this gentleman, a good friend of ours, came to make representations to the Prime Minister. 'This cannot be done under the Battle Act', he said. 'Whose Battle Act?' he was asked. They [the U.S.] wanted us to take it off the ship at Colombo. 'We export what we like.' That was the position of India at that time.

B Apart from non-alignment as the core of India's foreign policy, did you, in the early stage at any rate, think of it as something that could make a genuine contribution to international peace?

M I did, but to what extent the Prime Minister did, I don't know. I had an idea of what you might call the theory of it, but his mind didn't work like that.

B How precisely did his mind work on these questions?

M He would pick up something which by intuition appealed to him and make use of it. What is more, if I said something and he adopted and repeated it, that is all that the world would know about it. I will tell you something interesting as an example. I was a student for a long time, but I haven't got his [Nehru's] experience in most matters—I was Professor Laski's only student for ten years, the one Honours student. I said to him [Nehru] at one time: 'There is a difference between our national development—our nationalism and Western nationalism—in this way: in the West economic development came first and political independence came afterwards, in the sense of universal franchise, by the pressure of the working classes and so on; but here we have had a full fledged political revolution first—everybody is equal—and economic development has to come afterwards.' Ours is the reverse process, which will result either in instability or the death of democracy and the growth of Hitler Fascism, or in just plain but progressive decay.

B Is this Indian process characteristic of all Afro-Asian countries?

M No, it only became so later. We were the only one to be non-aligned. Burma came soon afterwards and then all the other countries that emerged from colonialism. This proves my thesis: it is part of historical circumstances. What I said [about political and economic development] is also true of African countries, theoretically. African countries have adult franchise: take Egypt or Ghana; but it doesn't work the same way as over here. It doesn't work here either as fully as it should. It exists here mostly on paper because new democracies tend to be largely caucus-ridden. I would like to be frank with you: for example, the position is that I may be able to get elected for practically any constituency in this country.

B And the reason for that is?

M Perhaps I have a certain mass appeal.

B But you used the term 'caucus-ridden'; what does that mean?

M I must explain this to you. It is like this. I can stand for any constituency under the Constitution; shall we say I can win in almost any place,[1] but can I get selected for any one of them? The selection is done by the Caucus, not even by the central caucus, but by the local caucus. Why, even in your Canada to a certain extent this could happen. You may be in every way an eminent national figure, but there will be some local fellow who is a carpenter or a priest or whatever he is, who has a pull on the local people. That is how it works over there; but over here, the local caucus would have a big say; that is to say, they can collect some supporters and bar your selection. But that could be overruled. Last time [1962, in North Bombay] they tried it on me; it didn't work.

B Isn't the Pradesh Selection Committee [of the Congress] the crucial body for selecting candidates?

M Yes and no; that is, only partly so; they can be overruled, but you cannot use a steam-hammer for all these purposes. They can say, 'Well, Krishna Menon is a wonderful fellow.' That's what some of them said to the Prime Minister last time. 'Why should he bother about Bombay? He can be selected for any place; anybody will have him.' He said, 'If anybody will have him why don't you have him?' I had the majority of votes in the Bombay caucus itself; that makes a difference, do you

[1] Menon was defeated in the Fourth General Elections, Feb. 1967, when he ran as an Independent in the North Bombay constituency. He was defeated once more in a by-election in the same constituency two months later.

see. But they [some of the local bosses] tried to put out that the local committees were not happy in this matter; because, they said, some local people must have a chance, and so on. I fought on the basis that I didn't recognize those local attitudes in parliamentary elections. It would be a good thing, I told the Prime Minister, if he were elected from the South. He agreed theoretically but he was very much attached to the U.P.[1] I'm not exclusively attached to any part of India.

B Well, perhaps that is because you went away from India at an early age and lived abroad for a long period.

M Yes, but even before that, when I was a boy, I was like that; not attached exclusively to Kerala, though it is my home place. No, I like Kerala—it is a beautiful place—but I have no exclusive passion for it.

B Whereas he, by contrast, had a feeling for the U.P.?

M He always used to say 'my province'. I told him, jocularly, 'as Prime Minister you can have no province'.

B May I go back, Mr. Menon, to your interesting observation about the difference between Indian democracy and democracy in Egypt and Ghana. How would you contrast non-alignment as it operated in the Indian case with what Nasser and Nkrumah call 'positive neutralism'?

M That was a different phraseology. Nkrumah, particularly, didn't want to use 'non-alignment'; we had used it. He was fighting for something called 'positive neutralism'. I am afraid I ridiculed it with banter. Then, in Belgrade [1961, Non-aligned Conference], 'non-alignment' became established. Non-alignment, in a sense, is an ugly word. It's negative but becomes positive when you use it in the way we do!

B But was there no difference in the way that Egypt and Ghana looked at their role in the world?

M I imagine so, but not in their relation to the power blocs. They probably did not see non-alignment in the beginning as a moral force or as an instrument of world peace. Now, I think, they know better; Nasser understands it more, and well, I think. He is far more intelligent, far more honest, and a much bigger

---

[1] The United Provinces, now known as Uttar Pradesh.

man than some people think. I have a great regard for him and faith in his integrity.

B But would you not say that in both cases narrow national interests loomed much larger in their enunciation of 'positive neutralism' than in India's?

M That may be so in a way. In the case of Africans it was more a kind of 'Africanism'.

We said from the very beginning that non-alignment was not just a policy of a nation but one of those things that the world requires; otherwise the world remains divided into two camps opposed to each other. There must be something, an 'area of peace', I called it, not territorially, but politically, diplomatically, morally, etc.

B So an 'area of peace' is to be distinguished from what came to be called a Third Bloc?

M Third Bloc, never! The Third Bloc is a foolish idea. How can there be a Third Bloc?

My understanding of non-alignment is that it cannot be a Third Bloc, for a bloc means power and a Third Bloc to be effective must have at least two and a half times the power of one bloc! That will never happen and if it did it would be a superbloc dangerous to mankind. Secondly, Third Bloc also means superior economic power. This [an area of peace] is a policy of independence and peace; that is, materially speaking, a weak man's policy. In a sense, now that I think about it, it is like Gandhi's non-co-operation. In his weakness he invented an instrument which was stronger than anything else.

B Non-alignment helped India achieve a degree of influence in the world which was quite disproportionate to its power, far beyond its military and political power. I wonder whether this was in your mind and in the minds of Nehru and others at the time?

M It emerged in that way. Panditji, even more than I, was anxious to keep away from their [bloc] conflict. 'Why should we get involved?': that was, in general, his reaction. But India acquired that degree of influence for several reasons, not only because we were non-aligned (one wants to be objective about this—whether you may think it is egoistic or otherwise): (1) *People trusted us.* My worst enemy would not say that I would cheat him. At the U.N. the Americans would tell me quite frankly what their position was; so would the Russians, and I would not communicate with either about the other. Americans never really thought that I was in the Communist lobby; nor did the Russians think I was in the Imperialist lobby; they may have said so sometimes. We established a degree of respect with them because they believed we had integrity. (2) *We never hesitated to vote against one side or the other.*

Also, there was the fact that *we were not frightened of the American strength at the U.N.* Nehru allowed me—in effect, he put me on—to draw their fire. They have said some very sharp things about him too: it's all very well to pay tribute now that he is dead, but the abuse they hurled at him at various times was quite considerable. I had to take the brunt of it, and the American attack in many cases is not in the open field. Their attack is always outside and often has no relation to facts. For example, in the whole of my experience in America, which was about ten years, I had never once commented on American internal policy, except on Little Rock and that was expressing understanding of the Americans' position, but they keep on saying that I am against America. I was dealing with world affairs, and it happened that the United Nations was located in New York. But among the masses of the American people, and I met lots of people there and had contacts with them, I encountered no personal hostility—except in odd cases. They are like that, even today, friendly and appreciative. For instance, many of the Americans who have come now [to Delhi] for the Lawyers' Conference, they all rang me up and appeared very happy to meet me. I am not flattered by it as I know that has always been the true position.

B One of the interesting features about non-alignment was the degree to which India served as a mediator. Was mediation a necessary, integral part of non-alignment? Did it grow logically?

M It grew, and I found that somehow or other I fitted into it. It came with Korea. There was the Korean War and a dead-lock, so we started on this. I will talk to you some other time on this Korean business [see chapter 3]. I started on Korea when I was High Commissioner in London. I have a reputation in the world at the present time that I have no ideas of my own, that I only communicate them. Is not that so? I remember *Look* magazine printing one hundred photographs of prominent Indians, and there was mine there; and people like Maulana Azad.[1] They were regarded as the policy-makers, and Krishna Menon—he made no original contribution, they said. He was a communicator or spinner of words, or something to that effect. This was the role I accepted for myself because it was the only way to play it.

Mediation came about for these reasons: (1) the two blocs talked themselves into a deadlock; (2) nobody wanted to destroy the U.N.'s prestige—some may have wanted to, but not at the cost of war; (3) there wasn't anybody able to feel a way out. For example, when the French walked out [of the General Assembly], nobody could bring them back. We did so.

B This was the Algerian case?

M The Algerian case, and we practically found ourselves in possession of the U.N.!

B What I am trying to get at here is this: in theory, would you argue that a non-aligned state would have to engage in mediation or, alternatively, that only a non-aligned state could be a mediator?

M I think it was very much the latter. Except that the Americans often, when anything came to fruition and to some result, liked to take it over themselves.

B Is it not true that in the Suez case [1956] it was Canada, an aligned state, that was a mediator?

M No; that is what Pearson[2] tells everybody. I had the greatest difficulty in getting the Egyptians (I telephoned Cairo from New York and so on) to accept Canadian units in the U.N. Force; they did not want British helmets there; they said, 'they are British'.

---

[1] Veteran Congress leader, dean of India's Muslims, and Minister of Education in the Government of India from 1947 until his death in 1958.

[2] Lester Pearson, then Canadian Secretary of State for External Affairs, later Prime Minister of Canada.

B But what about the idea of the U.N. Emergency Force itself?

M Well, I cannot talk to you about that. It was the same thing as Paul Martin[1] saying that he got the sixteen nations in [to the U.N. in the 'package deal' of 1955]. He walked out that evening in despair, just before we succeeded.

Pearson had a pronounced dual personality: one aspect of him was the idealist, a very decent kind of person, while on the other side he was a chip off the old block. Thirdly, he was a civil servant. I had a great deal of personal affection for him and I believe he had some for me, but not as much as I had for him. And I thought at one time that Canada would be a kind of 'aligned non-aligned' country. India was instrumental in putting the Canadians on the U.N. [five-member] Disarmament Sub-Committee with this idea in mind. They themselves thought they would play that part, but they soon made themselves a fourth Western power in it [aligned with the U.S., U.K., and France]. Economics take precedence over everything else.

B But are you also saying that mediation is a role that can be played only by a non-aligned state?

M No. It depends on circumstances, on who you are mediating with.

B But if two great powers are involved, if the two blocs are involved, is it only a non-aligned state that can mediate?

M It is history, isn't it?

B I am asking you.

M But how else can it be? I think the man who helped to promote this use of our non-alignment the most was Anthony Eden, because he grasped the importance of the conception of some sort of formula whereby this Korean deadlock could be resolved; that's number one. Number two, he realized more than anybody else that the Americans would tie themselves up into a long war. And I suppose he thought privately, these are youngsters, they don't know anything; they are inexperienced

---

[1] Head of the Canadian U.N. Delegation in 1955–6 and, later, Secretary of State for External Affairs.

people. And so it surprised even me, after I had made the speech on Korea [in the General Assembly in November 1952], to see that the U.S. would not commit themselves to be with us. I had no written speech; I spoke for about an hour on Korea. And then Eden came out publicly welcoming our initiative.[1] Acheson[2] visited Canada two days afterwards. There he cursed the British and said this is a 'parting of the ways'. Acheson gave an ultimatum to me at the U.N. and said, 'this is our last word'; and he gave me a piece of blue-tinted paper containing his terms! And then, when they saw that my proposal was going through, they put their arms around us (metaphorically). This 'poisonous' embrace served to antagonize the Russians.

B What was the Russian reaction to this initiative on your part?

M Russia's reaction for a long time was to say nothing against our proposal [Menon's proposal regarding prisoners-of-war] because they didn't quite know which way the Chinese were going to jump. And while we didn't claim to speak for the Chinese, the Chinese had given us a great deal of encouragement to go on in this way. China at that time proclaimed that they had accepted the Geneva Convention [on prisoners-of-war], but Stalinist Russia persuaded them at the last moment not to accept our proposals.

B There are two more points on non-alignment that interest me. As you look back over the years since 1950, what do you regard as the main accomplishments of non-alignment as a foreign policy for India? Was it prestige?

M No, it established India, not as a major power but as an important quantity in world affairs. Secondly, it prevented us from becoming a satellite state. Even today the Americans are trying to rope us into their orbit.

B That you attribute to . . . ?

M To non-alignment. Thirdly, I should say it has on several occasions put a brake on war—though the Indo-China problem

---

[1] See the General Assembly Proceedings for that period.
[2] Dean Acheson, then U.S. Secretary of State.

is still in a bad state, largely thanks to the United States. It also showed a way for the newly independent countries. Otherwise, they would all have been pushed around this way and that way, and the balance of power would have played a very much more important part in new Africa.

B So you were really pioneering for all the new states of Asia and Africa?

M Don't put it that way. They gravitated that way, didn't they? We didn't do it; they did. There was only U Nu's Burma who agreed with us in the beginning, but gradually they all gravitated; Indonesia next, and then the rest. In Africa and Arabia too. There [in the Arab world] the Israel problem always complicates everything. But they, too, found that in the Suez business we were with them. So this is a contribution of non-alignment in world affairs.

Fourthly, I think non-alignment enabled us to strengthen ourselves, too. It gave us a considerable degree of self-confidence, inner strength, things of that kind. It has been built up into a philosophy. I believe it also enabled us to establish relations with China, whatever may have happened afterwards. It prevented, in my opinion, deterioration in regard to our relations with the Soviet Union. It certainly did not give us 'leadership' over non-aligned people. This is where our own people misunderstand non-alignment. Non-alignment is not a bloc and is not a quip.

I say that a non-aligned nation must be non-aligned with the non-aligned, if you can put it that way! Otherwise, where is independence? It may be that a common view about Suez or a common view about the Congo [1960 ff.] or about other things may all lead us into one lobby, but we don't by definition go there; affinity may take us there. That is the essence of non-alignment. And that is why, when some people here say, 'why haven't all the non-aligned people stood up and shouted against China', I tell them, 'they have their own policy, they have their own independence'.

B Then, in terms of the principles of non-alignment, the attitude of many African and Asian States towards the India-China border dispute makes perfect sense?

M Of course it does, even if not to us, but given the fact that these States are independent, it does. But it would not make any sense if they were doing it because they were afraid of China.

B Which they are in many cases.

M In some cases. Or it may be because they are playing Russia against China in their own countries; there are 'Chinese-Communist parties' and 'Russian-Communist parties' in these areas.

B Non-alignment, as you pointed out at the beginning, grew out of the historic fact that there were two blocs when India emerged into independence. Does that mean that once the conflict between the two blocs recedes non-alignment ceases to have any kind of operational meaning?

M No, I don't mean that, but other conditions come about. A newer situation arises. But the basic position of independence need not change.

B My point is this: in the post-Cuba, October 1962 period, or the post-China-India Border War of 1962, does non-alignment continue to have the same appeal?

M In my opinion, apart from the national excitement, disappointment, and anger in India, the China clash, if anything, only reinforces non-alignment. Where would we be today supposing we were aligned with America?

B There are some people who would argue that you would be better off, that you would have benefited even more than you have.

M We might have been atom-bombed. I don't know if it would have been atom bombs.

B Do you think the Chinese would have resorted to strategic bombing, including major Indian cities?

M And we would have started it because the Americans would have said to us, 'well, go and bomb China'. If you are in doubt about it, read Bowles's[1] speech at Bhopal [November 1964]. I

---

[1] Chester Bowles, U.S. Ambassador to India, 1951–3 and 1963– .

don't say these things out of prejudice, you know. And I don't say I sit down and think them out with a cold towel over my head. Somehow or other these things come to my mind.

B Non-alignment, then, has become more than just a policy.

M Non-alignment is not inflexible. In a sense, it is true, there are always variations. But they are not deviations; they are ghosts! [i.e. distorted by propaganda].

B An interesting way of putting it. Well, let's leave non-alignment.

2. The Commonwealth

B May we now turn to the Commonwealth, Mr. Menon, especially India's decision in 1948–9 to remain in that club? How would you define Mr. Nehru's role?

M The crucial role the Prime Minister played in this matter was in allowing negotiations to go on; secondly, in placing confidence; thirdly, in taking on the opposition; in the preparation of opinion here, and things of that kind. He never concerned himself with the minutiae or anything of that character. And I took very good care not to embarrass him. The language I used in all these matters was extremely restrained.

B But he did have insight into the main thrust of the policy?

M Yes, of course, very much so; not of individual policies, no, but the broad policy. That is to say, we had no future, either politically or morally, as an armed power, able to intervene in this place or that place. And he had the notion, in later years, that this was the way to maintain both our independence and our dignity.

B And for the rest he allowed you pretty well *carte blanche*?

M Yes, but I always told him of anything new or important.

B Were there not others also involved in that sense?

M That I could not tell you. Every telegram I sent was to the Prime Minister, not to the [Indian] Foreign Office.

B I see; so this was almost a communication system outside the Foreign Office.

M No, *he* was the Foreign Minister.

B But you dealt at the level of the Prime Minister only?

M I wouldn't do it in any other way in any case because I would have to have dealings with Foreign Ministers abroad.

If tomorrow I were sent out, I would deal with the Prime Minister or the Foreign Minister.

B But Indian Ambassadors send reports to the Secretary-General[1] or Foreign Secretary.[2]

M Not in my time on matters of this kind. In England, I rarely negotiated with the Commonwealth Secretary; I always talked with the Foreign Secretary.

B And your reports back to Delhi?

M I sent them to the Prime Minister, except any technical thing that required attention at the Office. But he showed them telegrams [his senior career officials]. They were all marked 'Personal', for the simple reason that if you didn't mark them 'Personal' they were distributed to everybody.

B The next point I want to come to is the whole question of 'the formula', and the Indian decision to remain in the Commonwealth.

M My recollection is rather vague on some of these things.

B Let me try to stimulate your memory on these matters because I think it is important.

M You see, during the last two years [1962–4] the Prime Minister had become very much of a blanket for the Right, so to say; he was not a Rightist himself but he became in effect a protection for them, when I was away from his Residence. And I would never go and hang around; not because of pride— I just didn't think it right or fair to him.

B But do you feel that the problems India is confronted with at the moment are inherited from these two years?

M I don't think anyone knows the enormous amount of defence potential and diplomatic potential that we built up in past years.

[1] Senior official in the Indian Ministry of External Affairs from 1947 until the abolition of the post on 30 November 1964.
[2] Second ranking officer in the Ministry of External Affairs from 1947 to 1964; thereafter, the senior official in that ministry.

B Why was it not utilized?

M Now you are going into things much too deeply. You see, when everything is said and done, I am in the minds of some of these people still a 'foreigner'. During the whole of the Commonwealth period [1948–9] some said I was an Englishman!

B But they said that about Panditji himself.

M Not so much.

B Even in the obituaries, in the recollections, his attachment to things English was stressed.

Mr. Menon, to begin this second stage of the discussion, I would like to explore the whole issue of India's relations with the Commonwealth, beginning with the critical decision made in 1948–9 to remain a member. At that time you were High Commissioner in London and played a very important part in this episode. May I put a series of specific questions here? I would like to know what your own role was, specifically; I would like to know what Mr. Nehru's attitude was; the attitude of Mr. Attlee; the role, if any, that was played by the King; the attitude of other members of the Commonwealth who were present at the 1948 Meeting—these and related questions, if you could think back to them?

M I think it is incorrect to say that the critical date was 1949 because this went on for a long time—ever since and even before the declaration of the Republic. Basically, it was in one's mind. You remember that the demand of India, her insistence, was that she should be a Republic and be totally independent. This was one of the difficulties in speeding up the Independence Act [of 1947] in the British Parliament. There were also technical difficulties. Have you seen *Mission with Mountbatten*?[1]

B Yes, I have.

M Well, he puts it rather cynically: 'Krishna Menon claims the credit', or something of that kind. I claim no credit. I said to Mountbatten that the best way was for him to persuade our people to accept immediate Dominion status, but not as an

---

[1] The diary of Alan Campbell-Johnson, Press Attaché to Lord Mountbatten as Viceroy and Governor-General, 1947–8; it was published by Robert Hale in 1951.

instalment on the way to independence. They could proclaim independence themselves, without going to Westminster. For Westminster to pass a Republic Act would be difficult; it would have to be a new type of legislation. But to make a Dominion under the Statute of Westminster was no problem, and the Statute of Westminster permits you to go out [secede], do what you like; and so the first stage was a Dominion for that reason, apart from practical considerations and the guarding of our own interests. India having been made a Dominion, the question became transformed. Basically, we were a Republic; that is to say, as far as we were concerned the Republic position was the key position. As early as 1945 the Prime Minister asked me to make a draft of the preamble to the Constitution and my draft was made in the context of Pakistan remaining in and the residual powers resting in the States; so that preamble said that India is a Union of States. Now that has been altered. But I had no doubt in my mind that whatever might happen in the far future we had to maintain what was then erroneously called the British connection.

B Why did you have no doubt in your mind?

M I don't know.

B Were there concrete factors which led you to believe this?

M There were a large number of things.

B Could you elucidate them?

M There was the factor of stability. It was probably a way of keeping out others, intruders. Looking back, I didn't think about it at the time; at least at that period American infiltration [into India] was less.

B But in your mind it was primarily an intangible, almost an emotional link?

M Not quite emotional in the sense that it would appear to a Canadian or an Australian, but I thought of practical things.

B Were there also strategic or economic factors involved?

M No. I didn't go into all that at the time; I found it was better for our stability.

B Did Mr. Nehru share this attitude to the Commonwealth at that time?

M Subconsciously, yes; but he was not going to break his neck over it. I think it is true that at one time I was the only person who wanted it, the one single person who wanted to keep membership in the Commonwealth.

B When did the Congress High Command enter the picture?

M The Congress High Command at that time meant Vallabhbhai Patel[1] and Pandit Nehru. And Vallabhbhai Patel was an intensely practical man; if he said 'yes', people here were not going to create difficulties. The Prime Minister also was a practical man, in the sense that he had no dogma inhibitions. Apart from that, independence had come, and they knew that it was independence. There was no question of any limitation, apart from the King being the Head of the Dominion, and all that. The Statute of Westminster had speeded up things in such a way that, constitutionally, a Dominion was independent; but for psychological purposes, there is something in a Republic which makes independence complete, if you like.

B Are you saying that both Panditji and Patel were well disposed?

M Yes, but they didn't make any speeches or anything. They gave me to understand—as Panditji put it to me—that 'Vallabhbhai would have no objections'; I think Gandhiji also had no objections. Probably in their private minds there was, perhaps, a dread of the unknown. And at that time there was inhibition or reticence on the British side as on our side. Attlee expressed no opinions; none of the Labour Ministers put on any pressure to keep us in the Commonwealth.

B Were they bending over backwards because of their knowledge of your sensitivity or did they simply have no interest?

M No, I think they had a great deal of interest but they did not want anyone to say they took away with one hand what they

---

[1] Deputy Prime Minister of India and 'strong man' of the Congress until his death in 1950.

gave with the other. They were quite willing to have us if we wanted to come.

B What about the law officers in London?

M They were bad; I will come to that in a minute. And so, you had Mountbatten, Stafford Cripps, Lord Jowitt, the Foreign Office lawyers, as far as I can recollect, on that side. They were all quite clear that you could not have a Republic in the Commonwealth; there can be no such thing as Commonwealth citizenship; you are either alien or you are native; this was the Foreign Office lawyers' position. In fact, I remember an occasion at No. 11 Downing Street; Sir Stafford Cripps was then Chancellor of the Exchequer and Lord Jowitt was Lord Chancellor. Lord Jowitt said: 'It's impossible; you cannot be a Republic', in those words. He was not being abusive; he just said, 'it's quite impossible'! Stafford was also there. Of course, Stafford Cripps had a capacity for adaptation that allowed him, when things were going against him, to waive his objections; Mountbatten and Cripps are like that. Mountbatten had no particular objection to a Republic, but his conception of a Republic was a crowned Republic; he thought the Union Jack could be put in the middle of our flag, somewhere. He is not a political person, you know, though he is intelligent. Actually, in his position, he would have the credit and the responsibility for a lot of things. He had hunches and intuitions and he has a great personality and prestige from the war.

B What was the attitude of the King to this whole question?

M That, I am afraid, I cannot talk about, except to say that if the King had been difficult it would have created an obstacle. You have asked the crucial question. There was an occasion— this much can be said—when it was made quite clear that he would not be an obstacle. There were no long discussions between us. There was some difficulty in that way which had to be taken into account. The King played an important part in the Commonwealth issue but not by providing a formula or anything of that kind.

B Was there much opposition in the U.K. itself, beyond the Government?

M There was no 'opposition', but difficulties. It was a kind of 'squaring the circle' that was being sought. This went on for nearly eighteen months. We tried various things at that time. At one time I had suggested that the King should be the 'First Citizen' of this country, and for this purpose, in each Commonwealth State, the King would be the First Citizen of the Commonwealth. Now, I don't know who it was, I believe it was Attlee, who said, 'Oh no! First Citizen, that sounds like Robespierre', or something of that kind, 'and it would not go down.' Of course, he knew English psychology, from that point of view, better than I did. I am not quite sure it would not have worked: the President of the United States is the First Citizen. I didn't say the King should be called the First Citizen—he would be the First Citizen as King, that was the idea at that time. But I could not do more than mention it. You know, I hadn't the same kind of status among these people as Ministers had because at that time I was not even a High Commissioner.

B Would it be correct to say that, on the Indian side, the decision was taken by Panditji and the Sardar?[1]

M —and Gandhiji. Gandhiji agreed with the decision. It was the same with Kashmir [the decision to send troops in October 1947]—Gandhiji nods!

B So in that sense it was a triumvirate at work.

M Oh, yes. I pursued the matter for months. I told Nehru, and he said, 'yes, if you can—I have no objection'. So it was a question of squaring the circle. Then I think I brought around Cripps, and he said, 'yes, we can do something'. Then I went and told Nehru what Cripps said. And then, on my side, I had to be clear about what was the minimum requirement.

My idea at that time was that there must be a common citizenship, not a common citizenship in the sense of a United States but that we should not be alien to each other, though there should be a distinction between aliens and Commonwealth citizens. The second point was reciprocity. You find it again in *Mission with Mountbatten*—there should be simple reciprocity. That was largely because of South Africa. This was our other trouble: how could we remain in the Commonwealth

[1] Patel.

with South Africa also in. So I said, each Commonwealth country has its own immigration and citizenship laws and there has to develop a pattern of reciprocity. At that time South Africans couldn't come here to India. I put three principles: one was common citizenship; another was reciprocity; the third principle was independence—afterwards it became irrelevant as we were independent. These three principles were discussed and there were talks at Mountbatten's house at Broadlands, at Downing Street, here, there, and everywhere. Actually, I was really a busybody in this business, and the Prime Minister kept saying, 'oh! get on with it, do whatever is possible and don't give it up', or words to that effect.

B Who actually drafted the document that came to be known as 'The London Declaration' of 1949?

M That was done between Norman Brook[1] and myself.

B And the crucial phrase of the King's role in the Common-wealth?

M That was done at the Downing Street table. It happened this way. The document was there. The Prime Minister [Nehru] had first asked that the Statement be drafted by Sir Girja Bajpai.[2] Bajpai produced a draft which talked about 'freedom is the life blood of the Commonwealth', the King is the link, and all that—a Balfour type of declaration. The Prime Minister tore it up. He said, 'how will people take all this'. So it came to me. He gave it to me so that there should be no flaws of that kind in it. So I drafted something. Then the Prime Minister and their Prime Minister [Attlee] decided, 'we had better look into it'. So Norman Brook and I sat down to draft it. And then it came to the table at the Conference.

The difficulty was that the British were not willing to say, 'you should stay in or we will give you a different status'. We *had* become a Republic. Having become a Republic, we were willing to say to the Commonwealth that, if they had no objection, we would like to stay in the Commonwealth. So you see that, India having proclaimed herself a Republic and expressed

---

[1] Then Secretary of the British Cabinet (now Lord Normanbrook).
[2] Secretary-General of External Affairs, Government of India, 1947-52.

the desire to remain associated with the Commonwealth, the others also accepted. This is the formula we produced.

That was not the difficult part of it. Too clever by half, I had made no mention of the King or the Crown at all in the Declaration! It would have made no difference if the word 'King' had not been put in the Declaration, but Pakistan was quite anxious to put a spoke in the wheel. They wanted to say, 'if you want to be a Republic you bloody well keep out'. That was their idea; in that way to create difficulties. We were the important factor at this Conference; at all Commonwealth Conferences. And whether any British Tory put him up to it or not, one can't say, but suddenly, in the course of the discussion, Liaquat Ali[1] said, 'What about the King; we cannot have a Declaration of the Commonwealth without a King!' So we all looked at each other. I am not quite sure but I think the Prime Minister [Nehru] at that time became stone cold. And then I produced these words, 'as such'. So the King at one time said to me in jest, 'what am I now—As Such?'

This question of the Head of the Commonwealth came in like that. Now the moment you make the King Head of the Commonwealth, within the existing Commonwealth constitutional ideas and practice, we accept the Crown as Head of India. That we could not have. So I said, 'We are a free state, the Crown is a *symbol* of this Union and, "*as such*", the Head of the Commonwealth.' This 'as such' came after half an hour of going backwards and forwards. It was not the British so much. The South Africans were on our side in all the discussions. Really, it was Pakistan that made the difficulty. They tried to push us out. That particular part of the formula lasted half an hour. But the entire discussions went on for over an hour and a half. I think it took nearly a year before it dawned on all concerned that it would be possible. I think Attlee must have given instructions to the Cabinet Secretary to find or accept a way.

Then you asked about the Foreign Office lawyers. There came a time when, Lord Jowitt having raised the legal difficulties, the British Government said our Foreign Office lawyers were making difficulties in regard to 'alien' and 'foreigner'. The Foreign Office were the people concerned with matters of citizenship and treaties, etc. I was by then High Commissioner

[1] Liaquat Ali Khan, Prime Minister of Pakistan, 1947–51.

and the Prime Minister said he would send Sir B. N. Rau[1] as a legal authority. So we went together to the Foreign Office. The conversation was between Rau, myself, Foreign Office officials, and lawyers. We were about five or six there, and the Foreign Office was adamant, very legal: 'this can't be done, that can't be done, there is no such thing as Commonwealth citizen'. I kept quiet for some time and then said, 'what do you mean, it cannot be done—we are the people to make it possible'. They looked at me as though I was a schoolboy. The discussions went on for three or four days and were inconclusive. B. N. Rau was more like them, an Indian High Court Judge, Indian Foreign Office man, and so on. He didn't make any difficulties but he felt it was impossible to have an intermediate status between citizen and alien. He agreed more or less with the [British] Foreign Office legal view. So the conversation concluded with my saying, 'this is not a legal question, it's a political question'.

B And we must find legal formulae.

M Yes, that is right—'a political question, and I think we must leave it to the Heads of Government', or words to that effect. And so we went no more to the Foreign Office. But I said the Foreign Office must make a report and the document must not be drafted by lawyers. True, I might be a lawyer, but not in that sense.

On the British side the persons who were most helpful in this business were, to the best of my recollection, Lord Addison and Lord Ismay. Lord Addison was a very fine man; he was Commonwealth Secretary and an elder statesman; and, no doubt, he told Attlee that it would be all right, or words to that effect. I had great difficulty. I could not look as though we were anxious about it because I would get into trouble over here, and the British wanted to know what we would do. The people who were concerned on that side were Attlee, Cripps, Lord Jowitt, and Lord Addison; I don't think the Foreign Minister came into it. It was Bevin at that time. I saw him once or twice but I don't think he ever understood this position.

B I wonder if I might ask two further general questions about the Commonwealth. There have been a number of occasions

---

[1] Sir Benegal Narsing Rau, Constitutional Adviser to the Indian Constituent Assembly, 1946–9, and Permanent Representative to the U.N., 1949–51.

since 1949 when people in this country talked about the desirability of leaving the Commonwealth because of one crisis or another. In your recollection was there ever any really *serious* consideration given at the highest level of the Indian Government to withdrawal from the Commonwealth; and, if so, when?

M No. There was the difficulty about the U.K. Citizenship Bill. I was in England at the time and the best I could do was to get it put off. But by the time it came into effect the autonomy of the two countries had become more established.

B I am thinking more particularly of the periodic outbursts over Kashmir and the Suez crisis.

M 'Get out of the Commonwealth' is one of those cries that you always hear, same as in Canada I suppose.

B But was it ever seriously considered at the level of the Prime Minister or the Cabinet?

M No, no, no. It has just been taken for granted; this is not a serious issue with us. It may come some day, but the line we have taken is this—that the Commonwealth is independence plus not independence minus. Secondly, it is not hurting us; I have said many times that by being an equal member of this society we have influence in the Commonwealth; you know, that is quite true. When I was High Commissioner they did practically what I asked them. It depends on personalities to a certain extent. We had influence in the Commonwealth, and even the speed of the independence of the British colonies had some relation to this matter. It made the position of the Labour Government a little easier because the diehards couldn't say, 'see what you have done'.

I must say, in this Commonwealth business the man who was most emotionally moved was Winston Churchill. I wasn't there, but when he talked to me later tears rolled from his eyes. The Prime Minister [Nehru] went to see him out of courtesy after it was over, at his [Churchill's] house. And the old boy—he thought there was more in it than appeared. Tears rolled down his cheeks. To him, India remaining in was as if the prodigal had come home or something of that kind! He was very deeply moved.

It was not as though one had everything in one's head, as to how to work all this out; it came by trial and error on various points at various times. And Stafford [Cripps] had good personal relations with me though we fell out a little during the Cripps Mission period [1942] because I think he behaved badly. Probably he didn't understand—he tried to beguile us, and that didn't work. If you asked me thirty years hence, 'what was your main contribution', and if I were not inhibited, I would say, 'it was not the formula—it was not this or that or the other but merely not giving up'. If I hadn't taken any initiative things would have fallen through because the principals wouldn't talk to each other, and the principals were of the view, 'drop it, well and good'. That was the position. But they all really wanted it; the main thing therefore was to keep it alive. I knew very well I would get no thanks from the British, because there were people who thought that it was the beginning of the end of the Commonwealth, because I had produced the Republic formula. In fact, one of the High Commissioners told me at the end of that meeting, 'you have finished the Commonwealth, my boy'.

B You mentioned something about South Africa's attitude. What about the attitude of countries like Canada, Australia, and New Zealand?

M Canada was helpful; Australia was more 'Kingish'; New Zealand said they would make no objection. They were all anxious; they were all happy to have us.

B Provided a suitable formula was found?

M Yes. For a long time the Australians called this the British Commonwealth of Nations; we called it the Commonwealth of Nations. Nobody raised an issue about it. In a practical sense we approached this problem very much the way the British do. We didn't make an issue of it: 'you can say what you like; we say what we like'. I believe at some stage there was some suggestion that each must interpret this in his own way. That was the general idea.

B One last point on the Commonwealth, Mr. Menon. You mentioned earlier that the time might come when India might consider withdrawing.

M I don't think it will come as withdrawal in that sense. I think the time will come when it will become too onerous for Britain; it has come already. The Commonwealth is getting worn down: immigration laws, the Canadian agitation on Quebec with practically no consultation. When India becomes a big major country the present position cannot remain.

B Is there any single provocative action which might be taken that would lead an Indian Government to say this connection is no longer to her advantage?

M It might happen if, for example, they did something that we cannot bear about Rhodesia.

B But you don't anticipate a break occurring in the near future?

M No. The time may come when the Commonwealth will not have its present meaning. It's already more like a junior United Nations! After the Balfour Declaration [1926] it was one thing; then, after the Statute of Westminster [1931], it was something else. When people ask me what do we get out of it, I say, 'what do we get out of the United Nations?'

SUPPLEMENTARY INTERVIEW, MAY 1965

B We are now moving into an era where men like Nehru and many more who had strong attachments to the United Kingdom are no more. One wonders whether this means a probable change in the relationship of India to the Commonwealth. More specifically, does it not become increasingly likely that the bonds between them will lessen steadily? Secondly, what in your view will keep India in the Commonwealth in the coming decade?

M I think there is a fallacy in the first part of your question. It is a mistake to think that the Commonwealth tie was created just because some of us were Western-educated or something of that kind. It certainly cannot apply to Sardar Patel. It was mainly because of (*a*) the fact that we had an existing connection and (*b*) the realization that the Commonwealth relationship would not mean any derogation in our independence. The third reason, certainly in my mind, was that we would be less prone to be absorbed into other combinations. Furthermore, it had advantages for both sides and it would be a corrective to the pressures and tendencies of racial and reactionary policies on the part of the Western members. All these things came into it consciously or otherwise. Actually, it was not so much of a sit-down, considered proposition. We were there within the Commonwealth, and if we wanted to go out there must be a good reason for it. The objection to the British connection was the subjection and inequalities on which it was based and worked.

A few people who have always been against the Commonwealth will continue to be. Also I think a great many people are unwilling to accept the connection when antagonism or adverse reactions to us come from the West. There is an anti-West reaction owing to their policies, particularly *vis-à-vis* Pakistan. We are not prepared to talk about association with the U.S., do you see. Therefore these critics, whatever the cause, find an excuse to blame it wholly or partly on the British. It gives them a sense of having done something. The British lend themselves to it because, quite unnecessarily, they hang on to the Americans and identify themselves with U.S. reaction. What is more, the only outlet they have is being vociferous about the Commonwealth. But having said that much, let me tell you this.

We are speaking about things as they were ten or twelve years ago. It is, if I may say so, an incomplete way of thinking to regard the Commonwealth entirely from here or between India and Britain. The Commonwealth has changed: first of all, by the emergence of African areas as independent African nations; secondly, by our declaration of a Republic, which at the time was considered a specifically Indian insistence or waywardness. This course has now been adopted by every new member for all practical purposes; and, in fact, even by one of the former white Dominions. The others may not be formal Republics, in the sense that the Head is still called a Governor-General. They accept the Crown as part of their constitution and the Governor-General as its representative. But he is virtually a President. The third change is that Britain and the Dominions, under newer world and European conditions, have formed other ties or want to form them: (*a*) in NATO and all the alliances that came out of it; and (b) in the Common Market and things of that kind. In the old days they were talking more about sentiment. The newer Britain is not tied up with all those things, either on the Tory side or the Labour side, in the face of other determining circumstances. However you or I may feel about it, there have been rapid and considerable changes in the once great Empire. And whatever one may say on the platform or in relation to one's own country, it makes one sad for people in Britain who have not readjusted themselves. It is no use their having moonshine about the Commonwealth; it is not yet realized by them that Britain is a small country like Sweden.

In the beginning the Commonwealth in the minds of some was only a word that was a concession to Imperialism; it was really an Empire; the Empire has almost come to an end. A leadership has not arisen in the Commonwealth, either in terms of persons or in terms of groups or ideas. The Prime Minister [Nehru] did a certain amount, but we have not made a positive link because the particular leadership has always remained in Britain. Monarchy has never had the same thrill-giving quality here as in the United States, though some foreign people think it is the other way; Canada and India are not moved much by royalty. Australia is, but she doesn't count much in terms of making any impact. These are the factors that have to be taken into account. Secondly, the affinities in the Commonwealth were governed by a degree of intimacy. Now that has disappeared with the large number of new nations that have come in, of great virility. All that old world rounded-off with fine language doesn't exist any more. To this you must add the fact that, in spite of the recognition that the Commonwealth must be resolved into its component factors, at every stage it has been too little and too late. Look at what goes on in regard to Aden or the 'East of Suez' operations. Now it is British Guiana. Again the same old resistance, the same 'divide and rule'; that is to say, on the Imperial side, which includes all of you [white members]. There is no conscious effort to deliberately liquidate colonialism and liberate yourselves from colonial ideas.

B May I interrupt for a moment. I am thinking of the situation ten or fifteen years hence when a whole new generation of Indian politicians comes upon the scene. This will be a group

which will no longer have the educational ties to Oxford,
Cambridge, and the like, in a situation in which the psychological
and communication roles played by English decline. The attachment, the awareness, the formal tie with the British will lessen
all across the country. This then will be a political élite which
is more traditionally Indian. Will these people feel the same
way about the Commonwealth as your generation?

M As I said earlier, there is an initial fallacy here. It is not our
feelings of that kind that will prove to be conditioning or
determining factors. We were not tied to the Commonwealth
in the same way, in the same sense, that Australia was and is;
yet we took the initiative after we became a Republic, after we
had established ourselves as an independent nation. So that is
not the tie. It is more rational, pragmatic, and sensible factors.
Secondly, it depends upon the changes that have taken place
in the Commonwealth. For example, if all the African countries
are going to remain in, and the other Asian countries as well,
would it be to the advantage of India to step out? If Indian
development had gone on, without the interruption that took
place [the Chinese invasion], it is quite likely that in ten years'
time India would have been economically, militarily, and otherwise a much more powerful country. Then, the balance of
forces in the Commonwealth might become shifted. Thirdly—
this is purely speculative—supposing this country at least kept
up the pace towards socialism, which may or may not be
possible, then a new tie might arise. It is conceivable that
American imperialism and the juxtaposition of the blocs would
then be realized by more people to be an adverse factor. The
moderate kind of westernism that the Commonwealth represents would be an antidote—in the same way that Canada
remains in the Commonwealth largely because of the common
frontiers with the United States. There are such a large number
of circumstances in this matter unconnected with India.

You are laying a great deal of stress on the people who went
to Oxford and Cambridge. How many people went to Oxford
and Cambridge and how many of those had any influence on
constitution-making? Very few. That was not the reason for
the link. I think it was largely a matter of common sense. I have
said so many times. We don't think we can lose anything by it, if

we are of equal status and are members of the Commonwealth on that basis. As a Canadian you probably read a little more into the Commonwealth relationship.

Basically, therefore, this depends a lot upon mutuality of interests. Britain will throw Canada overboard and us overboard if she cannot survive, shall we say, without the Common Market. Similarly, we have various requirements, economic and other; the better behaviour of the British in regard to these matters will affect the issue. On the other hand, if the drift in this country towards permitting itself to be economically dominated continues, this will probably become a competition between the Americans and the British. It is all a matter of speculation of course.

You asked me a further question. Another factor may be the English language, you said. Now anybody would be a fool who would forecast the future of language or languages in this country, but it is conceivable that there may be a rebound from present reactions. It may take ten years or fifteen years. We may come to recognize that one out of every six persons in the Soviet Union is learning English. We may recognize that Ethiopia has adopted English as a second official language though it had nothing to do with Britain nor was in subjection to the British Empire. It is quite possible that ten years may be a sufficient period to bring about this realization, but English is not the main thing in this matter. English is necessary for us so as not to be an antediluvian nation because we cannot be isolated from modern and world currents of thought. That is partly why the Russians are learning English.

B Mr. Menon, the over-all assessment that you have given me is that, regardless of the absence or presence of sentimental attachment by the élite of the next generation, India's continuation in the Commonwealth is almost a certainty.

M No, I didn't say that. I said it depended upon other circumstances as well, such as the attitude of other Commonwealth countries and the erasement of racial discrimination. Supposing, for example, Britain emerges as a kind of standard-bearer in the fight against racialism; that would certainly strengthen the tie. Similarly, if Britain goes into the Common Market, that would be another factor in the opposite direction. If, for example, the proposal for a Commonwealth Secretariat materializes, it would probably break the Commonwealth. This is only my view. The other danger is that the moment we include countries that were not formerly part of the British Empire or in its special orbit, the Americans will horn in. This is what has happened with the Colombo Plan. It will become a Western alliance or Commonwealth NATO; or it will become either an ineffective forum or an area of conflict with countries like Indonesia (or others in the Colombo Plan), which means projections of other ideas and approaches.

3. Korea 1950–1954

B May we go on to Korea, Mr. Menon. You said something about this the other day, but I would like to deal with it more systematically. First of all, in the early days of the Korean War the Indian Delegation at the U.N. remained uncertain as to its attitude and did not in fact support the second Security Council Resolution [27 June 1950] immediately.

M In my view neither North Korea nor South Korea committed 'aggression'; as Korea was one country they were 'aggressing' into each other. The United Nations, which at that time was the United States, caught the North Koreans at the time when these fellows went south [North Koreans crossing the 38th Parallel]. They were both moving into each other in the sense that neither of them regarded the other as a separate country. I believe the whole of the Korean business was an understanding—I don't use any stronger word—between Trygve Lie[1] on the one hand and the Americans on the other. Otherwise why should he call a Security Council meeting on a Sunday morning without proper notice.

So far as we were concerned, what happened was, the Indian Observer on the pre-independence [U.N. Korean] Commission, K. P. S. Menon,[2] sent reports about the aggression of a kind which his own colleagues didn't agree with. I was taken aback when we subscribed to this Resolution on Aggression.[3]

B Going back to June 1950, after three days Sir Benegal Rau . . .

M Rau was India's representative on the Security Council and, as in the Foreign Office discussions [on the Commonwealth], he rather took this textbook view of things.[4] The Russians

---

[1] Secretary-General of the United Nations, 1946–53.

[2] Foreign Secretary, 1948–52, and Ambassador to the U.S.S.R., 1952–61.

[3] The Resolution of the Security Council, 25 June 1950, referred to a 'breach of the peace', not 'aggression', an important distinction under Article 39 of the U.N. Charter.

[4] The 'Secret and Personal Correspondence' between Nehru and B. N. Rau during that period reveals that Rau acted wholly on the Indian Prime Minister's instructions. The text of this correspondence is in B. Shiva Rao, 'Nehru and the

weren't there. Our contact with them at that time was prac-
tically nil. There was the fact that our man had reported from
Korea, which should not have counted for much. I was in
London—it was often like that when such things happened. It
was one of those things on which I put my view strongly to the
Prime Minister. Then we watered down India's attitude to the
U.N. role in Korea.

B What was the point of this? Having agreed to the Security
Council Resolutions, why did India not then become a full-
fledged participant in the U.N. Command?

M There are two or three reasons. I believe I had perhaps more
influence on policy at that time than anybody else.

B Including Panikkar?[1]

M Panikkar was our Ambassador in China. I do not know how
much he had to do with foreign policy as a whole. I had a great
deal to do with Foreign Affairs even when I was in London.
I think the Prime Minister said once or twice that India House
[London] was a sub-Foreign Office. He was quite amenable to
it because I was not doing anything contrary to his wishes and
it was not as though I made the decisions. But having become
involved, we had to mend our fences. It dawned on us that we
were landing ourselves in a major war. We were becoming part
of the [Western] bloc. At that time non-alignment, in fact
though not in name, had become our policy.

B Was Rau merely a spokesman in the Security Council?

M Yes; he was very much like that, an official type of representative, but a very decent man I should say, very painstaking
and liberal-minded.

B You said there were various factors leading India to go
slowly.

M Yes. First of all, we didn't want to become involved in a
major war abroad because that was against the whole of our

U.N.: Korea; China's Admission; Kashmir', *The Statesman Weekly* (Calcutta),
11 Dec. 1965, pp. 6–7.

[1] K. M. Panikkar, who had just arrived in Peking as the first Indian Ambassador
to the People's Republic of China and who is generally regarded as a major
influence on India's early China policy.

idea that Indian troops should not be sent out for fighting purposes. Secondly, by that time it had dawned on us that there was such an institution as Parliament and we should consult it. To a certain extent India's policy was muddled for a brief period, but to a certain extent also we were playing safe, and to a certain extent it was a practical solution. Indian units were there for ambulance purposes and they took the risks of war.

B Was the Indian Government profoundly affected when, in October 1950, U.N. troops crossed the 38th Parallel?

M Yes.

B What was the feeling in Delhi at that time?

M Very bad. I pointed out that the 'Chinese Volunteers' had come in as the result of the Americans crossing the 38th Parallel and the fear that they would cross the Yalu River. The Prime Minister also took this view and spoke publicly about it. They distorted what I said: the American propagandists said that I had said they had bombed Manchuria; I hadn't said any such thing.

B You told me earlier that India did not support the Resolution of the General Assembly, in January 1951, which termed China an aggressor. At what stage did you and, more generally, the Indian Government get involved in a search for a way out of the impasse in the Korean War?

M When I arrived at the U.N. General Assembly in the autumn of 1952, the Korean position was that an Armistice Treaty with sixty-two clauses had been drafted. There was an agreement between both sides on all but two, and the two were the crucial ones; those two were connected with repatriation [of prisoners]. The crucial problem was the repatriation business. Mrs. Pandit[1] was leading the delegation; I was No. 2. At the last minute I was pushed in there, and she said to me, 'you had better handle Korea'; she didn't think the Korean problem would blow up then in the way it did. I have the unfortunate luck that whenever I take on something it becomes big. I tried

[1] Sister of Prime Minister Nehru, President of the U.N. General Assembly in 1953 and later High Commissioner to the U.K.

to get meetings with the Asians and Africans—who would not agree. There was not much that we could go on. So one had to find a basis on which to proceed.

The basis I invented at that time—I think it's correct to use that term—was the Geneva Agreement in regard to Prisoners of War. I had some familiarity with it because, as High Commissioner, the Government of India had asked me to send representatives to the Commission of this Convention in Geneva [1949], and though I was handling that matter from a distance, it was fresh in my mind. I said, if we can bring it down to some formula on a basis which has a wide moral appeal it must be an international agreement in regard to the treatment of POWs. I said in my speech at the U.N., in regard to the prisoners, it should neither be 'push nor pull'. The Geneva Agreements should be the basis.

The Americans had put down what was called the 21-Power Resolution. They were very angry. Frontal opposition it would have been easy to crush, but when you produce another rail on which you can ride quite comfortably over the obstacle, the people who don't want to cross the obstacle get very angry! The 21-Power Resolution totally held the field when we entered it. It must be said that I had the support of the Commonwealth —including Australia—in the attempt to break the deadlock, not because they liked my face but because they were getting pretty tired of war. In spite of the Armistice Agreement being drafted, people were being killed every day. I was also—though I knew little about war—moved by this sort of thing, killing people, killing people all the time. The Chinese had made the mistake of thinking that the best strategy was to tie up the Americans on the peninsula; it looked as though they could have pushed the Americans into the sea near Pyongyang—no, they didn't do that. They wanted to keep them engaged! America is a powerful country; in time they pushed forward and the Chinese massive assistance [to North Korea] was not like the attack on us. We were but a handful of people, relatively speaking [against the Chinese in 1962]. This was the basis of the Korean Agreement.

B You said you had the Commonwealth with you, but there was the alternative 21-Power Resolution.

M The Commonwealth were with the 21-Power Resolution but they were still willing to be of assistance.

B What finally broke the barrier, do you think, to get your resolution accepted?

M Because it was a reasonable one, and they thought it was ingenious.

B The Americans did?

M No, no, the British did. The Americans were against it.

B But they had to be brought around.

M I think the Americans found that I had broken the unity of the Western group. They said so. They thought I was a vicious Machiavellian person. I really think the main reason was that everybody was getting tired of the war. Secondly, the deadlock was a thing to be got over if there was to be an end to the Korean War. We were not negotiating an armistice; that had already been done. There was a draft. Thirdly, the Canadians played a helpful role. This matter was handled by Paul Martin. The main role he played was to push me rather than push the other side. I had to amend my own resolution two or three times in some details under his pressure. I brought the period of explanation down to three months, for instance, which created difficulties for me but did not affect the basic principles. In fact, they told me from Delhi, after I had got agreement, that it need not have been done. We added two clauses—by that time I had come to the conclusion that the thing was to get an agreement —and one or two amendments which were quite unnecessary were agreed to by me. I believe myself that Canada feared that the thing might break down altogether. It was probably Paul Martin's first entry into this business. Mr. Pearson was not handling it.

B You have said nothing at all about the Soviet role in all this except what you mentioned the other day. What was the Russian attitude to the Korean War from the very outset? Were they involved from the beginning, do you think?

M No. My view is that they were not involved and that they had no intention at any time of becoming involved.

B Do you think they were annoyed with the Chinese?

M No. I think they hadn't minded the Chinese fighting; *they* didn't want to fight.

B They were determined then to stay out?

M It looked like it. I had no inside knowledge. Their view was that it was United Nations intervention in Korea.

B I know that was their official view.

M That was their view. Their view was that America was trying to make the 38th Parallel a permanent division in the hope of taking the whole of Korea by first dividing and weakening the country; that, I think, is still their view; there is something in it. I don't think the U.N.'s [military] intervention helped to solve the Korean problem. Both Hammarskjöld[1] and Trygve Lie were wrong, Hammarskjöld more wrong than Trygve Lie, in regard to the Congo [1960–1]. I think the official Russian view [on Korea] was their real view. In this [Menon's resolution] they didn't want to call us names at any time, though I believe they did try to browbeat me. I had a talk with Vyshinsky[2] one whole afternoon.

B Was it you who were responsible for the creation of the Neutral Nations Repatriation Commission (N.N.R.C.) and its composition?

M Yes, but we didn't say that we ought to be there. I said there should be an equal number from both sides, with a neutral chairman, and the Russian view was always fifty-fifty, so that there would be a deadlock or a bilateral solution. It was not as if they produced a committee of four and we produced a fifth. I said their general approach was fifty-fifty, while we said that the only way to deal with this is, as with general arbitration, to have an equal number from each side and a neutral chairman. The Russians would not look at it at that time. It was only in the last stage that Vyshinsky made a speech [in the General Assembly] attacking it—'this is a rotten resolution'—he didn't like doing it, but there it was. Then came the adjournment.

---

[1] Secretary-General of the United Nations, 1953–61.
[2] Soviet Foreign Minister at the time.

I moved that this question be considered as soon as the U.N. met again the next year. Lester Pearson was helpful—he was President [of the U.N. Assembly]—and he was one of those people who played a part in this. The Assembly agreed; then from somewhere there were some questions on phraseology which had to be vague if they were to be acceptable. So I put in the words 'as appropriate' or something of that kind; now it appears in a good many U.N. resolutions. That was how it came about. India emerged as somebody in the U.N. Here was Korea deadlocked, no settlement taking place. We seemed more or less pitchforked into a very important controversy around the area of Korea at that time.

In all these matters, while we must know where to draw the line, there must be a sense of concern in somebody's mind. Lester Pearson had to be on the Western side. It's no reflection on him when I say that he had his limitations. Whatever happened he could not get away from the United States. Against this personal limitation, he was a very friendly person and he made for himself a name as a statesman. They [the Canadians] didn't like us entering into every question. In my opinion, Canada didn't play a United Nations part. In all questions in which they were not particularly involved they simply voted with the Americans. But they did exercise very considerable influence on the United States—not on these questions, but on various other questions.

B Can you think of any questions in which Canada's influence on the U.S. was noticeable?

M Not on the basic big things; but at various stages Canada had a great influence in the sense that the United States generally did not want to isolate themselves from Canada and vice versa. Had Canada gone a little more our way, she would have been non-aligned—on the side of the West.

B Was that as true of Canada's role when Pearson was in charge as when Diefenbaker became Prime Minister [1957–62]?

M Under Diefenbaker I don't think Canada figured very much or as much in the United Nations.

B You think its influence declined?

M You had representatives from Canada, Green[1] and people of that kind. Green was difficult but nice.

B But he did not carry the same weight.

M He carried weight because he was Canada. He was not very close to us, polite and all that—while Pearson, until a later stage, wanted to get on. He said often we were always ready with a solution. The one thing you should not be at the U.N. is too previous with your solution! You should have it in your head or on paper—it's a good thing if somebody else puts it in or co-sponsors it. We are lucky with our initials so that we don't ever come first in a group of sponsors.

B You would never take the initiative in that form?

M It looks like it. If the historian looks at the whole record he would probably think differently.

B Let me get back to the N.N.R.C. In your judgement, how did it function? Was it a credit to India? Was Thimayya's[2] role one that India could be proud of? Did the Commission perform its function well?

M There were periods when Thimayya appeared to take too much the American view but there were periods also when the Commission functioned with firmness. The United States gave no real assistance and practically tried to break it up. There were a lot of cruelties performed [in the POW camps]. I don't think we acted with sufficient firmness in some cases. Thimayya had three people shot dead in a critical situation. It was a great act of firmness. Whenever it was merely soldiers' business, he did well; the rest of it was instructions given from here; some of the cables I drafted myself. We did turn down what he said more than once if we felt he had no statesmanlike understanding of things. He had a personality in the British sense; he had built up a name, and on one occasion, when the South Koreans

[1] Howard Green, Secretary of State for External Affairs in Diefenbaker's Cabinet.

[2] General G. S. Thimayya, Commander of the U.N. Custodian Force in Korea, 1953–4, later Chief of the (Indian) Army Staff, Chief of the U.N. Force in Cyprus, 1964–5, and the best-known soldier in independent India. He died in Cyprus in 1965.

created a demonstration and threatened to cross the camp, he said, 'if you move we will shoot you'. They did move, and he had three men shot down immediately.

B Was that Commission a good model or precedent for the Commissions that were to come later in Indo-China?

M It helped. Our difficulty was to get the Chinese to accept Canada.

B But the basis of the Commission in Indo-China was the Korean experience.

M Not so much the Korean experience as the idea of one [from the West] and one [from the East] and one [neutral]—there must be a neutral chairman; and we had difficulty because everybody thought we were trying to get the job for ourselves. Ultimately they could not find anybody else.

B Was Panditji satisfied with the way in which the Commission worked in Korea?

M He was never satisfied with all the details, but I think he was happy that it performed a role for peace—and he was quite willing to pull up Thimayya. We didn't interfere with the smaller things, though we knew that within the Commission there were differences. The U.S.A. were doing a lot of things to pull people this way and that way and there was suspicion that some people were influenced by China and all that. But by and large it functioned. But ultimately it didn't complete its tasks.

B It did not?

M Ultimately a whole lot [of prisoners] went to Formosa, which they should not have done. Perhaps you would say, historically, what does it matter? after all, it stopped the war.

B I think this is what the historians of the future will say about it.

M It may be. In a certain way we deluded ourselves and other people that we stopped the war. But the Americans, by assisting the prisoners under the custody of the Commission to go to Formosa, broke faith. They behaved very badly.

B It was soon after the end of the Korean War that India became involved in still another important conflict, that of Indo-China.

M To a certain extent. These things come in this way—because we were a new country we had no Foreign Office traditions, we had no officials who could say this or the other or apply the brakes, and so on. The Prime Minister also had a habit of coming and giving some instructions to somebody and leaving it there for them to carry on. He allowed initiative. And Mrs. Pandit, without knowing that it would be a big thing, said, 'you take Korea'; and I said, 'I will take Korea and leave me with it'. She said she didn't want to have anything to do with it.

B Did you have *carte blanche* all through the Korean affair?

M On the Korean affair I had to, it was my item, but I told her what was happening. I believe at one time the delegation voted against an adjournment which I wanted. The Americans didn't want it, so Mrs. Pandit didn't want it either. But I said, 'No.' I fought for an adjournment and I stood by it. So she went around to the British and asked them to vote against us, which they did, but the adjournment was carried by three votes.

B That is a rather unusual case surely?

M Yes, but the British—Selwyn Lloyd[1] it was, I believe—said, 'what am I to do, you please come and tell me'. And I said to him, 'you do what you like. You will be defeated.'

[1] U.K. Representative to the U.N., later Foreign Secretary.

4. Geneva Conference on Indo-China 1954

B In the case of Indo-China, Mr. Menon, the earliest Indian involvement was a six-point statement which Nehru made in Parliament in February 1954.

M He asked me to draft it.

B Why did India become involved in the Indo-China conflict?

M Because it's Asia, it is peace.

B And by that time it had almost become a habit?

M Well, not habit. It was our concern in a true sense. Imperialism, China, the French were there; this part of the world was concerned. It could lead to war, things of that kind.

B But India's involvement was of a very different kind, since you were not formally invited to the Geneva Conference.

M Well, I think perhaps we didn't stand on dignity; we just stood on the doorstep and tried to be helpful. We were not taken into the Conference because the Americans would not have us. Everybody else would have welcomed us, including Canada. The British would not take any initiative, but they probably would have liked to help; and they welcomed us and accepted our assistance all through. There were complications; if we were in, then other people would also have had to be in. The U.S.A. didn't want us at the [simultaneous] Korean Conference either.

B Do you think that this initiative in Panditji's speech, the one you drafted, played an important role in bringing about the Conference?

M That I cannot say beyond that it might have done so. The Geneva Conference on Indo-China came as an aftermath to the Korean Conference. The matter came up in the Korea business. Everybody there said, 'let us treat this separately'; I was not in the Korean Conference at all. I got Nehru's permission or somehow or other I went on a trip—to Geneva as a visitor. I was going somewhere else. I got a call from Anthony Eden and I met him in Paris at their Embassy for two or three hours. I think it was at that time that the British said definitely to the Americans that they would not agree to the [U.S.] aircraft carriers going to the Indo-China area. Dulles wanted to wage war.

B This was also the time when the British were opposed to the creation of the South East Asia Treaty Organization (SEATO) before the Geneva Conference was concluded?

M My impression was that the British would not permit the South East Asia [Manila] Conference to eventuate. In fact that was why they kept on saying, 'before the [Geneva] agreement was dry they [America] formed this'. It's quite true. I cannot say they gave me a written document, but the impression the British gave me was that the South East Asia Conference was dead, that it would not be an obstacle.

B Can you tell me about the Geneva Conference itself? Although you were not a formal participant, I recall that you were present in Geneva.

M I was there for three months—for the whole of the time—and I believe that no day passed without my seeing each one of the leading participants, sometimes two of them.

B Tell me first about the role of Mendès-France.[1]

M The difficulty at that time, towards the end, was M. Bidault.[2] He had feelings about the French Empire collapsing. He was that way. When the change came in France, Mendès-France came over to Geneva and was extremely friendly to me. I told him that the main thing was that there must be a time limit; so he announced on his own that this matter must be settled by the 20th of May which, like the Mountbatten Plan [for the partition of India, 1947], had its advantages and disadvantages. It's a long story. Having agreed to that, he told me, 'we must come out' [of Indo-China]. What really decided the issue was Dien Bien Phu and the defeat of the French.

---

[1] Pierre Mendès-France, French Premier at the time.
[2] Georges Bidault, French Foreign Minister at the time.

B And the Americans, surely Dulles did play a role?

M Oh, very much so. Fortunately for us Dulles was not there the whole time; Bedell Smith[1] was more helpful.

B Why were the Americans so opposed to a settlement whereby the French would withdraw?

M Because of this theory of stopping Communism, being against Russia, being against China, jealous of us, jealous of the British. After all, the British had stopped the American intervention in Indo-China at that time. And what is taking place now [U.S. intervention in Vietnam] would have taken place more overtly in 1954 . The aircraft carriers were ready to go and I must say that Eden's firm attitude stopped it—and a war.

B How would you appraise the British role at the Geneva Conference?

M I think their role was constructive, but we assisted them a great deal. I think we smoked out the position—North Vietnam, etc. The difficult people initially were the Chinese. Also there was the Cambodian delegation, which at that time had a different complexion. Then the question arose, who were they negotiating with? They were negotiating with the French on a question in which the *Indo-Chinese* were concerned. The French signed; the main problem was to get the French out of Indo-China. It was a kind of agreement which perhaps was not formally correct or conventional.

B What about the Russian role?

M I think the Russians were very helpful and constructive. I must have seen Molotov twenty or thirty times.

B They wanted a settlement?

M Not any old how, but they wanted a settlement.

B Why were they so keen?

M Basically the Russians are against war, but if I said that, probably I would be in a tight spot—even Molotov didn't want

---

[1] General Walter Bedell Smith, then Under-Secretary of State and head of the American delegation to the Geneva Conference in Dulles's absence.

war at any time. The thing is that the Russians were really against war; after all, they suffered greatly the last time.

B But did Molotov play a strong role, a constructive role?

M Yes, a constructive role, but I don't know to what extent. Even initially he was constructive. I found him easier to handle than even the British.

B And Chou En-lai himself?

M Chou En-lai was like a typical English radical. My conversations with him probably went on for two, three, or four hours each time, because, with the two translations, there were four speeches!

B Was he rigid or was he flexible?

M He was flexible. The difficulty was with regard to the Pathet Lao. He felt later that, had we been a little more forthcoming then, perhaps the Laotian troubles of today [1964] would not have arisen.

B Would you say that Chou En-lai had as much freedom of action in negotiation as you had on the Indian side?

M He seemed to have even more. He was the Chinese Government.

B But to what extent was he acting on instructions from Peking?

M It didn't look like it. I found no inhibitions—I could go in at any time and talk at any time. Of course, there were officials there all the time.

B But he made a favourable impression on the Conference?

M Oh, yes. The Americans did not admit it. He wasn't a Gromyko, Molotov, or anything of that kind, as they were ten years ago. He did not make any speeches that were aggressive and he certainly was a person who helped [me] in bringing the North Vietnamese around. The North Vietnamese were the real parties to negotiate with and I appeared to strike up a good friendship with Pham Van Dong.[1] Mind you, the North

[1] Prime Minister of North Vietnam and Head of her Delegation.

Vietnamese and the Chinese are not as close as people think. But there were various characters: there was our friend Casey[1] from Australia; he came in and thought he would play the same role as I was playing and he asked to see me.

B What about the lesser powers at the Conference; for example, the less-involved countries like Canada? Did they play any role?

M Ronning[2] was there and was very helpful. He understands the Chinese; in fact he is regarded as too pro-Chinese. Ronning is a decent fellow and he played a good part. He had not at that time become Ambassador. I used Ronning or, rather, Ronning used me, both with China and the British. Canada's role was constructive, but the Chinese didn't trust them.

B This leads me to the working of the Commissions in Indo-China, where India and Canada were intimately involved. These Commissions have been operating for ten years now. Do you think that in any one of the Indo-Chinese States the Commission has played a vital role in terms of the intentions of the 1954 Geneva Agreement?

M In the early part they did. The Canadians were always against us; the Poles were sometimes against us. We sometimes voted with the Canadians against the Poles and at other times vice versa.

B But is not that a natural give-and-take among three parties?

M Not altogether. The trouble in Laos is due to Canada. At one time, about five or six years ago, the Laotian Government came totally under the influence of the United States. They took the view, 'we are independent, why should the Commission be here'; Canada played up to it, and I had great difficulty in finding a formula with Ronning to prevent the Commission from being fully terminated. Ultimately we had the Commission located outside Laos. After Diefenbaker's Government came in [1957], it was quite hopeless. Green had some ideas of helicopters painted white. He talked a great deal about this in the

---

[1] R. G. Casey, Australian Secretary of State for External Affairs at the time.
[2] Chester Ronning, later Canadian High Commissioner to India, 1957–64.

Second Conference at Geneva in 1959.[1] He thought the heli-copters would settle the whole issue! Canada was always looked upon at these conferences as a balanced country of the West but she was very much distrusted by the Chinese, in spite of Ronning.

B As a result of this Laotian involvement?

M No, I had great difficulty in persuading Chou En-lai to accept Canada on the Commission. Ultimately in Geneva he agreed after many talks. I had the further difficulty of not being able to tell Canada this, because they would have been very upset and would not have joined the Commission at all. And there was no other country to which the other side would agree. This co-chairman idea was my invention—the only way to get this thing going was to get the Russians and the British to be co-chairmen. It all sounds simple today but it was very difficult in those days. I had this advantage: as I was not a principal I was not attacked in public, except in gossip, because I was not making any speeches. But I acquired a very bad and un-deserved reputation, as a kind of Machiavelli or something like that.

B Can you tell me about the working of the Commission in Vietnam itself; did that suffer from the same kind of friction?

M Oh yes. In Vietnam our representative, Mr. M. J. Desai,[2] was beaten up at one time by the Vietnamese. The Americans were believed to be in it. In Vietnam, America was very mis-chievous.

B This is one of the few areas where the Canadians and the Indians, in close involvement, did not get on too well. To what do you attribute this?

M By and large we worked well together.

B In the Commissions?

M Canada—you won't mind my saying so—can never forget that she is a protectorate of America.

---

[1] See the Reports of the Conference.
[2] Later, Secretary-General of External Affairs, Government of India.

B Do you think this expresses itself in specific policies?

M Oh, yes.

B Yet you say that Canada and India worked well together on the Commissions.

M Yes, because we are both liberal countries—we have no axes to grind. Canada is not imperialist like Britain. She has no superiority feeling about us. There were all these individuals like Pearson and Ronning who were good, decent people.

B You don't think that the Indo-China experience marred the relations between India and Canada?

M At one time it had become very difficult, because they were extremely unreasonable. They were playing the American game. We said so. Ultimately, but for Ronning, it would have become a crisis. They asked me to invent a formula but, having done so, I don't think they honoured it.

5. Bandung 1955

B I would like now to hear your account of the Bandung Conference.

M The Colombo meeting [1950] was a Commonwealth meeting, and I think if anybody could claim an initiative in this it is the Australians. In order to give the Commonwealth some life, they said, 'let us have a meeting; it need not be in London'; so there came the Colombo meeting. Ernest Bevin was then Foreign Secretary; if there had been no Labour Government it probably would not have taken place; so it came to Colombo. Senanayake's[1] ego went up. Percy Spender,[2] although he was not a front-rank statesman or anything of that kind, I think hatched this Colombo Plan idea. We were not unkeen; we just went, that is all. But when we went there, naturally, things changed. When the Colombo Plan members got together, Indonesia was out. Soekarno probably wanted something all his own. We were talking about Asia, Asia, Asia, and they were talking about Australasia. From the Colombo Conference [1954] came the Bandung affair. It was really the Colombo Powers, as they were called at that time, with Indonesia, that took the initiative for what became Bandung.

B It met at Bogor first?

M Yes. The Colombo Powers and Indonesia got together. Then we had the meeting at Bogor. This was the key meeting regarding Bandung. At Bogor things nearly broke down. It was only at 4 o'clock in the morning that we got an agreement. Pakistan raised some obstruction and I put up formula after formula to meet them. At the thirteenth or fourteenth formula, the Prime Minister [Nehru] said, 'we cannot go on like this'. They [Pakistan] were obviously obstructing it; they wanted to run the Conference themselves. I said to the Prime Minister, 'this is an international discussion, you cannot go to bed', and then

---

[1] Don Stephen Senanayake, Prime Minister of Ceylon at the time.
[2] Australian Secretary of State for External Affairs at the time.

I said to him that he should ask for an adjournment for a couple of hours. I talked to U Nu[1] and asked him to speak to the Pakistanis; and so the Conference adjourned for two hours while the Pakistanis and Burmese had a talk; we finally came to an agreement.

The Burmese were difficult at first. They said, 'we won't come without Israel'. We said our position is the same but we have got to carry the Arabs with us. We will do whatever the Conference agrees but we will vote for an invitation to Israel. And we were three to two, Ceylon, Burma, and India for, and Pakistan and Indonesia against; but Pakistan was the leader. They made propaganda against us and issued leaflets terming us a pro-Jewish country. We said that the Bandung Conference must be on a geographical basis. We said Australia should be asked, and ultimately Australia was accepted as an observer.

Number one, Bandung came out of Colombo; number two, Bandung came out of economic aid and the Colombo Plan. But we were from the very beginning against the idea of building up continental compartmentalism if it meant detracting from world unity. The U.N. has now made all these regional organizations. In my opinion, it's not a good thing.

We met at Bogor to plan the first Afro-Asian Conference. It was mainly Asian then. Bandung was suggested by the Indonesians; they wanted it in Indonesia; we didn't ask for it here. We have never had a conference here. Colombo would have been better. In regard to Bandung, the day before the Conference our Prime Minister and the Indonesian Prime Minister got together with those persons who had earlier prepared the Agenda of the Conference. Pakistan was not there at that time. I said to the Prime Minister privately, 'this won't do'. Then Pakistan arrived and smashed up the whole thing. So we had to begin all over again.

Sastroamidjojo[2] was elected Chairman of the Conference. He was not a good chairman. He was a very difficult man, not clear-headed; he could not understand procedures. Everybody got so sick of things. We proposed—I suggested—Prince Wan[3] as Chief of the Drafting Committee. That was a good stroke

---

[1] Prime Minister of Burma at the time.
[2] Prime Minister of Indonesia at the time.
[3] Thai Representative to the U.N. at the time.

because he was right-wing and acceptable. Then came this Declaration of Principles, and we had God's own trouble there, in the Committee. We appointed Nasser as Chairman of that Committee. Nasser was a good chairman but Pakistan made hell. She wanted to bring in something under American inspiration. Chou En-lai was very reasonable; he was sitting next to me and we were practically consulting each other. Ultimately, he said he was not going to be insulted at this Conference—he would not have it. They pushed him and pushed him and pushed him a great deal on various things. Nasser asked him to stay; we all asked him to stay. He stayed and we finally got an agreement. That was how the phrase criticizing 'colonialism in all its manifestations', which I suggested, emerged. But then Nasser had some difficulty or a sense of lack of completeness about part of the formulation. You will find two points out of the ten in the Declaration that are contradictory or almost contradictory.

B But you agreed to the general condemnation of colonialism just to get agreement?

M No. That would be a very wrong way of putting it. We were always prepared to condemn colonialism. But what Pakistan wanted was to condemn Russia—the American position that Russia is imperialist, that Hungary is a colony and so on. Our position is that countries in the U.N. cannot be regarded as colonies.

B That is a highly legalistic position.

M No, not at all. Hungary is one of those questions on which the world outside distorted what we said at the United Nations [1956]. America decided to do so as part of her anti-Russian propaganda. Our attitude on the Hungary item at the United Nations is one of those things on which I don't apologize. Nobody who talks about it has read our speeches at the General Assembly. What is more, the Indian Resolution on Hungary was carried by two votes more than the other one [the Western Resolution sponsored by Pakistan and Cuba]. This is never mentioned. Our position is set out in the Resolution which we sponsored with other countries and which was adopted by the Assembly. We would not support the Red Cross Resolution

because the Americans tacked on a condemnatory clause. It
ceased to be a 'humanitarian' resolution as was contended.[1]

To return to Bandung, Pakistan's Prime Minister said they
didn't want the Five Principles [Panch Sheel]. It was pure
small-mindedness—so in the committees different countries
added new clauses and finally it became Ten Principles!

B What about Chou's role at Bandung?

M It was very good and helpful. Chou's role at Bandung and
at Geneva [1954] was that of a good liberal who wanted a settlement.

B You don't see this as part of a general Chinese strategy in
South and South-East Asia?

M No, no. I think China has changed since then; that is my
opinion.

B What was its aim at that time?

M Chou wanted to be an Asian—and to be accepted as such—
and to play the role of a statesman. Nobody was saying anything at Bandung to which he could object. We were all for
China; why should he antagonize us?

B Was Panditji convinced at that time that this was all Chou
En-lai was interested in?

M I don't think Panditji was ever convinced that anybody was
ever wholly with him or anything like that; he would be a fool
who thinks so. But Panditji knew that China should be admitted into the United Nations and was a great country. He
was very active in regard to this at that time; there was nothing
to object to in China's position then. Ronning was there too;
you can ask him. Very few people knew what was happening
inside the Conference; even the Prime Minister knew very little
because Mr. Dutt[2] was nowhere near these things. He was
occupied and had to be away from the Conference Hall. I told
him what was happening and he wrote down what I told him.

B Do you feel Bandung was a successful conference, given the
context in which it was held?

---

[1] See ch. 8 below, Hungary 1956.
[2] S. Dutt, India's Foreign Secretary at the time.

M Bandung was successful in the sense that it presented a front of Asian unity. We were always against repeating 'Bandung' in a hurry as some wanted because we were afraid we would undo the good done there. It was the high point of Asian unity.

B Were you convinced then that it was a façade or front?

M No, we were not too keen to rush it because we didn't know what would happen; but having entered on the project we made the best of it. You see, conferences have to be taken more or less in the British way; the British had great skill in these matters—they don't use it nowadays. But other countries, particularly the Commonwealth, tried to reduce this amorphous organization into something very strict and formal. Out of the white Commonwealth, in relation to the Commonwealth itself, Canada is the only country, and perhaps New Zealand, which takes a flexible view. Australia is rather more rigid in her ideas of Commonwealth relations. So she tried to put up Commonwealth Secretariats and often proposed an establishment of Commonwealth institutions. It won't work. I have always said that. Lord Bryce proposed the idea of a Commonwealth Secretariat. It had no takers. It remained an informal 'family gathering'.

B Were there any actual agreements arrived at at Bandung in terms of settling problems between the Thais and the Cambodians and things of that kind?

M There was a settlement in regard to Chinese nationals in Indonesia. There were a lot of Kuomintang flags out, you know. We were the conciliators between the Indonesians and the Chinese; we got a formula agreed to on this question. China regards all people of Chinese origin in other countries as Chinese nationals.

B But your feeling is that Chou En-lai's intentions were genuine?

M Yes. The Indonesians agreed that all Chinese who retained Chinese nationality were of the People's Republic of China. They would be treated as foreigners; and the others who were Chinese by blood and race, but did not claim or accept Chinese nationality, were Indonesians. The Indonesians agreed to this and Chou En-lai also agreed to it. But he didn't implement it afterwards: they still have 'Overseas Chinese'.

B How long did the Bandung spirit continue as a force in Asian and International Affairs?

M We were not so very effusive about it, but some people were; the Indonesians kept on, 'Bandung, Bandung, Bandung', and the Russians supported both Bandung and the Indonesian effusiveness about it in the beginning. The Americans were against the idea; they tried to kill it—until it emerged and succeeded. Then they simulated enthusiasm. They sort of 'came to scoff and remained to pray'—the same as with the Korea Resolution [leading to the cease-fire]. One of the people who was very useful at the beginning but afterwards became not so enthusiastic was Sihanouk,[1] a very young man who has since gained much experience.

B Did Bandung serve as a logical starting-point for the Belgrade [1961] and Cairo [1964] Conferences?

M Not in a constitutional or organizational sense; I don't think it would be true to claim that. They were independent meetings but they had a common factor in their organs, purposes, and ethos.

B You don't seem to attach much importance to the Bandung Conference?

M I am sorry you get that impression—as you know I was not quite a spectator there. But it was more psychologically and emotionally an Asian event. I don't think it was more. But important, I don't know; in the long term of history this event will not be too insignificant.

B Could you trace it back to the original Asian Relations Conference which was held in Delhi in 1947?

M That is what some of your people write, but it hadn't anything to do with it organizationally. But the Asian Relations Conference also helped the birth of Asianism, perhaps more so than recognized. I think Bandung came partly out of Colombo [Colombo Conference 1954] and partly because the Indonesians

---

[1] Prime Minister of Cambodia at the time and later Chief of State.

wanted it; they were feeling that we should establish an Asian
Secretariat and other such permanent institutions. They had
somewhat grandiose ideas. Later Nkrumah[1] and Soekarno often
projected several ideas which reflected this view.

SUPPLEMENTARY INTERVIEW—MAY 1965

B Could you tell me what role Panditji played at Bandung?
Was he active? Did he stand out as the dominant personality
there at that time?

M The Bandung spirit was Nehru; there is no gainsaying it.
I think Soekarno from Indonesia took, and is entitled to, some
credit for pursuing the idea and bringing about Bandung. We
ourselves were not quite sure how it would go; the Westerners
were against it. Certainly Nehru was the spirit of the Bandung
Conference—not by any running around, but by his great
personality and his catholicity of outlook. He was a quietening
element. He was a kind of elder statesman and an experienced
elder statesman at that. At that time he held that position in
the eyes of most individuals who came to Bandung, except
those from Pakistan. Pakistan was the only country who said,
'well—who is India?' At the same time neither Nehru nor even,
in a smaller way, Soekarno dominated it.

It was ten years ago, when every Asian country realized that
solidarity was a good thing for them. Now each one wants its
own kind of solidarity! I was speaking at a recent meeting of
some of the historic differences in Europe, the nationalism that
has developed among small units which came together, and in
the process of such coming together there had been armed conflicts and rivalries. If you compare that with Bandung, what
has happened is this: nations came together in spirit as well as
in person. There was something called the 'Bandung spirit' and
so the conflicts that took place outside the brotherhood—or
whatever you would like to call it—now take place inside. The
conflict is a historical malaise, that is all I can say. In fact,
Bandung did take place in circumstances that resulted in a
'Holy Alliance'.

[1] Kwame Nkrumah, Nationalist leader of Ghana, later Prime Minister and
President of Ghana.

B There were reports from various people who were present that Chou En-lai played the leading role and occupied the centre of the stage. Is that true?

M I don't want to minimize Chou En-lai as an individual or anything of that kind. Chou—shall we say—'played', as he wanted Bandung to succeed, because he would be part of it in a big way. Chou En-lai was, however, introduced to everyone by me; he played a good liberal and useful role except in a very few instances, for example, with the Pakistanis. When the latter became very difficult in a key meeting presided over by Nasser, then he said, 'we cannot go any further'. Chou En-lai's role, both there and at Geneva in 1954, was that of a good liberal and something of a conciliator. But he, himself, did not take great initiatives. I don't say Chou was a kind of younger brother to us, but he co-operated. We found him very useful.

I would not have believed at that time that he would be the Prime Minister of a country that would invade India. We had little difficulties and so on, but I would still have anticipated that he would have opposed large-scale fighting.

B A British writer claims from unimpeachable sources that, soon after the Bandung Conference, Peking sent a letter to Karachi indicating a desire for good relations with Pakistan, despite her membership of SEATO, etc.; furthermore, that the Chinese indicated in this letter that they expected a deterioration in Sino-Indian relations. Now this was 1955. On the basis of your knowledge of the Chinese and of Bandung and what happened in the middle and late 1950s, is it possible, in your judgement, that Peking was playing a double game with India and Pakistan.

M From subsequent events it looks like that. There is no doubt that to Chou En-lai, even at that time, it was quite clear (and we were able to accept the fact) that China was a large country and that if she was trying to play the role of Asia she was not going to put Pakistan outside it. At no time have Chou En-lai and the Chinese actually subscribed to our position on Kashmir in the way that the Russians have done. But they have not subscribed the other way either. Chou En-lai, no doubt, because of the Chinese Muslims, wanted to keep in with Pakistan, but obviously China's prevarication on Kashmir in the days of Sino-Indian friendship was more sinister than we had reason to think at that time. I don't know of any letter; it is possible. But I very much doubt that the Chinese would put it in writing to show that they were anticipating trouble with India because, though we had trouble with them in 1952 and so on, they always said there is no great difference between us. Knowing how these countries work, it's quite likely that someone had written to Pakistan; but I would not be able to accept that in 1955 they would write an official letter to Pakistan because they would know Pakistan would publish it and China was wooing India with a vengeance.

B To conclude this discussion on Bandung, how would you assess its impact on world events from 1955 onwards?

M Let us take the plus and minus factors. First the minus factors: there are today Asians fighting Asians; this is taking place not only between Pakistan and India but between Indonesia and Malaysia, between China and India, and so on. There is suspicion of China in various countries whose names I need not mention. That is one minus factor. Another is that China, in trying to be a 'harmonizing' element, is trying to canvass and dragoon people and nations. I am glad to say that, in spite of what the newspapers say, she is not cutting much ice in Africa or anywhere else for that matter.

Another minus factor is that Imperialism rears its head or attempts backdoor entries. One was between Britain and France and Israel against Egypt. Another is the trouble in Cyprus. The third is the Belgian position in the Congo. There are more. All this and the whole of the complexes in Africa are the attempts of empires to come through the backdoor. All this amounts to attempts at economic domination by the U.S. over Asian countries and of powerful economic interests seeking privileged positions in other people's countries. These are some of the minus factors. And the result is that you have a sizeable instalment of trouble in the war in Indo-China. We feared the Bandung spirit would become eclipsed by it and by Chinese expansionist activities and propaganda.

Now we come to the 'plus' factors. First of all, as I said, Bandung was like Geneva and Locarno [1925]. These are old expressions now; people don't even know where Locarno is, whether it is in Italy or in Switzerland, but still Locarno is a spirit. It was an asset so far as it went. Bandung has become a world-known name. If you ask a lot of Canadians where is Bandung they wouldn't know, but probably they would know it is in Asia, or even in Indonesia. At any rate there is a Bandung spirit. I don't want to make it emotional but it is one positive gain. The second 'plus' is that Bandung was largely Asian. The Afro-Asian Committee got set up, though we [India] are not taking as much part in it as some of the other countries. At the time of Bandung, colonialism was still a contestant, but now the liquidation of colonialism is an accepted doctrine. It is realized that the clock cannot be put back. It is part of the United Nations' resolve that colonies should cease to exist.

B It is virtually a completed process now.

M I wouldn't say that. But it's certainly acquiesced in, yes, certainly accepted as a principle, and that is a great thing. There is probably a bit of a move towards anti-racialism but it is largely on paper; it takes a very long time to live down prejudice. These are the gains; also a certain amount of increase in economic ties between nations.

The gain since Bandung has also been that the Western attempt to fill what is called the power vacuum in the Middle East has receded. The United States started this doctrine of a power vacuum, and others joined her. Others wanted to get into the Middle East. Now there is no ghost of a chance of America or any foreign countries dominating the Middle East. The Western bloc was beaten in Lebanon; it had to side with the anti-colonialism forces in the Suez issue; it was not able to control Kuwait oil or anything of that kind. So I think so far as things stand at present, expansionism in the Middle East has taken a beating, except in Saudi Arabia. Therefore, since Bandung there is a prospect of new types of social and economic and other policies emerging in the Middle East and the advantage of greater solidarity and progress. People don't study enough about what happens in the U.A.R. A great many things are happening there. A great socialist advance is taking place; 90 per cent of U.A.R. industry is nationalized.

Since Bandung, also, the African independent nations have

come into existence. Thus, these are the 'plus' and 'minus' factors. But on the whole I fear 'Bandung' has come to a stop for the time being, thanks largely to China—her hostility to India, her conflict with the Soviet Union, and her interference in Africa and Latin America. The present postures may have to undergo some major transformations. In the last twelve months, however, I assess that the capacity of China to make mischief is somewhat less; I realized that when I went to Cairo and met a lot of African people from all sorts of places. An unexpectedly large number of nations wanted the Soviet Union to come into the Algiers Conference.[1] One thing is apparent and that is the maturity of Asia. I mean, ten years ago, to speak of an Asian power sounded far-fetched. Today there are so many independent nations in Africa and Asia. A time may come when Europe becomes one with Asia and Africa.

[1] Scheduled for June 1965; it was postponed to October 1965 and proved to be abortive.

6. Suez 1956

B May we turn now to the Suez Crisis, Mr. Menon?

M That was one of the few things which made Anthony Eden so bitter. First of all, Anthony Eden always thought Nasser was a kind of junior Egyptian Mussolini or Hitler; he always talked to me like that. Nasser was a blind spot with Eden. Then came the Suez Canal and, in regard to the Canal, Egypt said this was a totally Egyptian waterway. The Egyptians said, 'we have a right to nationalize it'; they didn't ask anybody. And you will see from the speeches of the Prime Minister [Nehru] that he said 'they were right to do so, but I would not have done it that way'. That was one of the Prime Minister's usual ways; he would often say, 'there are so many things about Russia I don't like!'; he would say it on every necessary occasion in order to keep his balance. In what other way the Egyptians could have done it, I don't myself know. I think they acted within their rights and courageously in nationalizing the Suez Canal.

B Was there no advance knowledge in Delhi of Cairo's plans?

M No. Not at all so far as I know. Why should Egypt have told us about it if it was their national affair.

B Was there any annoyance because of this?

M No, because we took it as their business. In fact, if you ask me now, I believe we would have been embarrassed if they had told us beforehand. There was no discussion at Brioni[1] on this matter because the Egyptians are so conscious of their nationalism they would not discuss it with us at that stage. They nationalized the Canal. The British banked on the idea that the Egyptians would never be able to take ships through the Canal. But this was one of those fictions that had built up. More ships passed through that canal during the period of the interregnum than during any corresponding length of time before, which

---

[1] Conference of Tito, Nehru, and Nasser in July 1956.

angered the British very much; some of the European pilots
had been bought over!

The Egyptians said that it was nobody else's business, it was
an Egyptian waterway. But they always admitted there was an
international factor in it. We put up the formula for them—
that they would carry out the obligations of the [Constantinople]
Convention of 1888. That put them in the right. Nasser accepted
that basis long before all the other things happened. We took
the position at one time, and I think I said it in London [first
Conference on Suez in August 1956], that we were equally concerned with the Convention of 1888, for we were part of the
British Empire when the Convention was signed. As a successor
State to Britain's Indian Empire we were as much a signatory
to 1888 as Britain or anybody else. So we put forward the 1888
position. We proposed certain things at different times, all on
this basis. One was the recognition of the right of ships to go
through the Canal in accordance with the Convention of 1888;
I will come to Israel afterwards. Secondly, that Egypt would do
its best to improve the Canal; this was Eden's chief apprehension; he said 'they will take all the money [dues] and do nothing
for the Canal'. A third was no discrimination. There were five
points in all.

At first the Egyptians weren't too happy about it all, but
fortunately we developed closer and good relations with them,
particularly with Nasser personally. India didn't make the
mistake, when Nasser came in, of saying it was a *coup d'état*. We
had been friendly with Neguib[1] also, but Neguib didn't fill the
bill as things developed in Egypt—God knows what happened
to him; anyway it was their business; why should we interfere?
We recognized Nasser and the régime and did not look on it as
a break from established relations. I found him extremely simple,
straightforward, and willing to learn from experience, but very
determined and courageous.

He nationalized the Canal. The question arose, would it be
by expropriation or otherwise. We said, 'whatever you do, don't
do it that way [expropriate], the world won't like it'. I gave
Nasser the instance of foreign enterprises in Russia, where Stalin
said—or is supposed to have said—'if we were to do this all over

[1] General Mohammed Neguib, first head of Egypt's Revolutionary Council
after the ouster of King Farouk, 1952–3.

again we would not have confiscated them', or words to that effect. We said, 'expropriation, you will not get away with'. We also said, 'under the Constitution we cannot expropriate even our landlords, we pay compensation'. It may be wrong or shortsighted, but there it is. Therefore we could not stand up in public and say we will support expropriation. Nasser fortunately said, 'we will pay the shareholders at the current rate—the market rate'. Now that was a big thing for him to do, at that time. So we proclaimed to the world that Egypt will pay compensation; why then can she not nationalize? If Egypt can nationalize her shipping why cannot she nationalize her canal? It all turned on 1888: I think Dulles played a double game here; probably he talked about it one way to us and to the British differently. He was the person who actually killed the London Conference. We could have got an agreement in London if the United States played the role that she had to and did play afterwards, at the United Nations.

B You could have got an agreement on the basis of your five-point proposal?

M At that time, yes. The Americans did not want us to put forward a proposal at all at the London Conference. For a long time I didn't put forward any counter-proposals to those of Mr. Dulles, hoping that because Dulles proposed the creation of a 'Canal Authority', which would be a kingdom of its own, it would get nowhere. We knew this as we knew the Egyptians; they would not take it. The Americans thought they could get away with it. I remember meeting Dulles at his house at Regent's Park, and he talked to me very sweetly as though he and I were saying the same thing; I believed him. He double-crossed me on this; otherwise he was a more or less straightforward fellow. I got on very well with him then and in later years. On Indo-China he was frankly difficult, but direct—not quite direct, but direct enough.

So the position in regard to the Canal was: (*a*) there would be compensation; (*b*) there would be something said about keeping the Canal in good condition; (*c*) there would be mention of 1888—there would be no discrimination; (*d*) Egyptians would work the Canal. And at one time we suggested to them that there might be an 'independent' Canal Authority, but without prejudice to Egypt's sovereign rights as under 1888. They agreed to that. The Egyptian Government would set up a Corporation; it would not be a Government Department.

B It would be like a British Crown Corporation?

M Yes. Naturally it would be dominated by the Egyptian Government. It would, however, be a corporation run on a commercial basis. Secondly, Egypt said they had no objection to a Users Committee; whether it would be advisory or otherwise was left vague. This was distorted by Dulles. What we got the Egyptians to agree to, and which the British spoiled, was very much better than what the Anglo-Americans finally got.

One day I came back from Cairo and then wanted to return the next day because they wanted me there after I had reported to the Prime Minister. I said to Nasser that I could not proceed further without at least informing Nehru, who said, 'how can you go back the next day, you only came yesterday'. We were a little concerned as to what people would say. Panditji was very sensitive to public opinion in that way and also unwilling to get involved—because this was serious business. I felt it would be more serious if we did not do whatever was possible—and succeed. For myself, I anticipated this war [Suez, October–November 1956], but the Prime Minister never believed—there is no harm in saying so—that the British would send troops. He had great faith in British common sense. I said to him, 'You don't know them as well as I do. You don't give them credit adequately for their generosity, equally you don't take into account their imperial methods—it's in their blood; the British will invade them.' He said, 'What nonsense are you talking; in the twentieth century, in the fifties, is anybody going to invade anybody?' He fully believed this, which prevented my conveying effectively the urgency involved. So I could not go back the next day. At last I persuaded him and two days afterwards I returned.

In the meantime more than a little change had taken place. The British were becoming tougher; Eden's allergy to Nasser grew. But the worst was yet to come. I had talks in London with the British after seeing Nasser. Selwyn Lloyd was handling the matter at Foreign Office level. I was seeing him and Eden once or twice a day, and for the first time in my experience of

Eden—a very well-mannered man who would not say anything rude—I found him impatient, unwilling to listen. I told him, 'the best bet you have for settling with Israel is Nasser', because I knew at that time that Nasser was disposed to look at these things rationally and at least not to precipitate the situation. I knew that there were Jewish officers in the Egyptian Army but they were Egyptians and, personally, Nasser was no anti-Jew nor showed any anti-Jewish feeling; he was even in touch with Ben-Gurion. The British spoilt all that because they still thought of the Egyptians as 'natives'. Basically that was their trouble. In regard to Eden the trouble was this Mussolini complex—his conviction that Nasser was a Fascist.

One evening, the day before I was to leave for Delhi, I was at No. 1 Carlton Gardens [the official residence of the British Foreign Secretary]. Selwyn Lloyd told me that the formula I had put up was agreeable to him; but he said, 'I cannot say "yes" to you because, after all, I have to get the [British] Prime Minister's O.K., but you may take it that it will be all right. You come to New York' (by that time the issue had gone to the Security Council) 'by the time I get there.' I came to Delhi and was in the same trouble as before: the Prime Minister said, 'why go again so quickly?' So I had to wait. We were not members of the Security Council nor involved in any official talks at the time.

I arrived in New York two days later. In the meantime Hammarskjöld, who now intervened, had objected to my five principles and had put up a further one. This one (which became the third clause), something about international control, was the crux of the trouble, and upset the balance of the original five. Nasser would not accept it, though Fawzi,[1] in direct negotiations with Hammarskjöld, acquiesced. His interpretation was different. I had been trying to avoid this. Fawzi was like Hammarskjöld—I never knew precisely what he was saying; perhaps he believed that vagueness would help him; Hammarskjöld was the same way. So Fawzi had agreed to Hammarskjöld's change and this led to a difference of opinion between Fawzi and me. But after all, it was his country! In those days Fawzi had not yet reached his present eminence; he was an able but very harassed man, a good man and very friendly, but

---

[1] Dr. Mahmoud Fawzi, Egyptian Foreign Minister at the time.

he came from the old stock of diplomats and was afraid of war.

It's my belief—this may be egoism—that had I reached New York the same time as Selwyn Lloyd this development could have been stopped. When I arrived I found a different Selwyn Lloyd, partly because he hadn't agreed with his chief [Eden] on the lines we had discussed at Carlton Gardens, though he could not say this to me. Then, I believe in public speeches and certainly privately, he mentioned that we were interfering! And so you will find in Eden's 'Squaring the Circle', or whatever it is called,[1] a reference to 'the aviatory Mr. Krishna Menon'. This was not what he thought at Geneva in 1954. I believe little things count sometimes—the right moment and all that. By that time Suez had got into a bad way. When British troops landed in Egypt, Nehru was the most shocked man. He said, 'what is the use of my talking about changes in the world, it's like the old days'. But we stuck to this: there must be compensation, not expropriation; Egypt must repair the Canal. Finally, the scheme as it came out incorporated these provisions.

Then came the complication of Israel. It appeared insurmountable; after having a private conversation with Nasser, I could not see any way out. I knew well that in no circumstances could any Arab country do other than Nasser was doing. Neither he nor anyone else could get the population to agree to the idea of ships going through the Suez Canal with an Israeli flag flying. It may not be rational; it may not be politically sensible; but then they have this feeling; what can you do? But we got Nasser to agree at first that Israeli goods could go in other ships. Israel, quite rightly from their point of view, was not having any subterfuge. I asked Nasser, 'what is your position in law?' He said, 'we are at war with Israel and we are not going to allow enemy ships to go through'. He was right.

B But the U.N. Security Council had declared that the Nasser contention that Egypt was at war with Israel was invalid.

M Yes, I know. I do not have to defend him but I am saying that that was his position; I think the U.N.'s contention was wrong. In any case, said Nasser, we cannot have Israeli ships

---

[1] *Full Circle*, the first volume of Eden's memoirs.

going through, and I talked to him about anti-semitism. He said, 'it's nothing to do with that; Israel is part of Imperial business—going back 2,000 years to claiming Palestine on theocratic grounds'. Of course, we were all against Zionism before Hitler—this included well-known Jewish intellectuals—I won't go into the Zionist question now.

So the Israeli position had to be squared. I said, 'This is not a question of the British, it's not a question of Israel. You will have to convince the Americans and you will have to convince the world at large that there is some legal basis for this.' He agreed and repeated his contention that Egypt was at war with Israel. I had to find a compromise and I said, 'you have accepted 1888 and have not shifted from it and therefore any question arising about the 1888 Convention should go to the World Court'. To my surprise, Nasser accepted this; 'let the World Court decide', he said, because he was quite sure of his position. So when I got that I thought we had the basis of a compromise. I specifically asked him if Israel was excluded and he said, 'no; anybody who has a case may go there; I challenge Israel to go to the Court'; that was his position. I think he was able to do that because he had no anti-Jewish feeling personally, and part of him was a statesman even then, and he wanted a settlement.

Throughout the negotiations on a Suez treaty—'the instrument' as I christened it (it was my draft)—we went backwards and forwards. Nasser would not sign a treaty. He said, 'why should I sign a treaty about my own territory?' So I devised the word 'instrument' to substitute for treaty—he didn't haggle about it and accepted the distinction! I said there would be an 'instrument' something like the Instrument of Accession with our Princes[1] in India. An instrument is perhaps more than a treaty. He agreed to deposit it at the U.N. as treaties are deposited. He was always trying to find a way out.

The draft instrument went to the United Nations. Then came the talk that the Egyptians were thinking of building another canal. That also acquired international significance—that is to say, they said they would increase the facilities for traffic in both directions. We practically carried the burden of the

---

[1] The device whereby India's Princes acceded to the Union of India after 15 August 1947.

Egyptian campaign at the U.N., and Lodge[1] and I were working there closely together. Cabot Lodge said at one time, 'I want
to go and speak to the Arab delegates', but I said to him, 'I fear
they won't see you.' However, I tried my best; after a week or
so I finally persuaded them to let him come to one of their
meetings. It's always forgotten by people who write columns
and memoirs, but Lodge said publicly on various occasions
that we had pulled the Americans out of trouble more than
once at the U.N. So did Wadsworth[2]—later.

B What period are you referring to?

M This was in regard to the withdrawal of British troops from
Egypt [December 1956, January 1957]. They started saying it
will take so much time to leave. So I got up and said, 'how does
it take longer for troops to come out than to go in?'

B How did Mr. Nehru feel about the French and the Israeli
involvement?

M He thought that Israel was very foolish, but we were only
really concerned with the British and French. We don't think
that the Israelis did right, but they were only trying to get their
own back in a difficult situation. We knew that the Egyptians
would be defeated but we were not bothered about it because
we knew that the defeat would not matter very much—the
invasion proved their main asset! Then came the burning of
Port Said by the British, and there were a lot of atrocities. And
the Egyptian soldiers were not up to much. It was Farouk's
army, not the army of today.

B Was it your evaluation that the French or the British took
the initiative?

M British, British, British.

B And the French role was . . .

M The French it appears were prepared to settle. Even after
all this was over—a year or two later—I told the British that
Nasser would sooner give them preference than the French in
the restoration of normal relations. He was willing to do so; the
British wouldn't play. After a great deal of difficulty we got
them to send back Humphrey Trevelyan as Chargé d'Affaires

[1] Henry Cabot Lodge, U.S. Representative to the U.N. at the time.
[2] James J. Wadsworth, U.S. Deputy Representative to the U.N. at the time.

[to Cairo]. The British were very pigheaded about this. Nasser was quite prepared to deal with them on the issue of the banks [nationalization]. He said, 'we are quite prepared to give the British preference over other people'. He had hopes that they would recognize the changes in the world and he had undisputed political authority in the country at the time.

The British for some time behaved as though we were the bad ones. They soon discovered for themselves that such was not the case. Pierson Dixon[1] told me one day at the U.N. that they were in the doghouse; nobody would talk to them, even the Commonwealth countries were cold. Not even the Canadians were with them; they were almost boycotted in the place during the worst weeks. He said to me that I was the only one of the leading delegates who would talk to them. My political sympathies were not with them; I knew it was part of the Imperial business—the last phase—though everybody was shocked at the idea that in the fifties there could be a colonial war—for it was nothing else. They didn't tell us anything about landing troops. They were mounting their troops in Cyprus; we protested privately. I believe the Canadians were told about this but we weren't. And Mountbatten said to me that he was very unhappy about it all.

B What about the American role after the Anglo-French landing?

M In my opinion the Americans changed over for two or three reasons: they saw that in the U.N. the Latin Americans were with us; Dulles was very angry that the invasion had taken place without his consent; and he also reminded Eden what he [Eden] had said about Indo-China in 1954; Eden would perhaps deny this. It's quite true that Eden had stopped the American invasion then and he was getting tit for tat. The Americans didn't like being thwarted. In 1954 America hadn't yet been weaned; she was still learning her diplomacy, that was the impression I had. You must think back in these terms; in those years the Americans looked to the British for the way to talk in the diplomatic world. Anyway, Dulles was very angry that they had done this on their own, without American counsel and assistance. They did it without even telling the Americans

---

[1] Sir Pierson Dixon, British Representative to the U.N. at the time.

because they knew they would have been stopped. But what really frightened the British was Khrushchev.

B Could you tell me about the Soviet involvement?

M There was no involvement. He simply said, 'we have got rockets'. But I have no doubt that if the war had gone on the Russians would have gone in on the Egyptian side—though there was no understanding between the Egyptians and the Russians. The Russians looked upon it as an imperial war, the same as Cuba [in 1962]. They had no intention, I think, of using rockets; but they said that if this is an imperial war with rockets, we have them too. The English popular press, for example the *Daily Mirror*, played up the 'we have rockets' speech of Khrushchev.

B Do you think that the Russian Note was the decisive factor in the British withdrawal or were there other factors?

M It was one of them.

B What about the role of British public opinion?

M A decisive factor? No! British public opinion, Commonwealth public opinion, were almost entirely against the invasion. I say 'almost' because Australian governmental opinion was an exception. The man who played the biggest foolish role in this was Robert Menzies, Prime Minister of Australia. You can imagine the pigheadedness of Imperialism. After the London Conference they appointed a Committee to negotiate but really to tell Nasser where to get off, Robert Menzies leading it; I imagine he was appointed by the majority at the London Conference on British initiative. Imagine sending Menzies to the Egyptians! When asked, I said to the Committee, 'The Egyptians will receive you, they are courteous people like us; but you won't get anywhere'. Menzies went to lay down the law to them; they asked him to go away. I followed Menzies to Cairo, and Eden objected to that. I didn't go before because the British would have said that I had come to get in the way of Menzies; also we did not want to get in the way of Menzies. I knew how they would deal with him; I had to smooth out the bad impression left by him before I could get the Egyptian side in a talking mood. I think they might have got on better if they had sent somebody else, Lester Pearson for example (I don't think he was asked because Canada didn't come into it) or Nash;[1] Menzies was the worst man to have selected. They did that deliberately. Dulles was with them because Dulles had his own plan which Menzies was carrying; it was still the 'imperial phase'. But for the fact that the British had cleverly manœuvred the Americans into this, the subsequent position might have been different. They were afraid the Americans would not agree to war. The British probably thought that after the Menzies phase the United States would play along with them.

B Did Eisenhower play any role?

M Not that I know of. But there did not appear to be any differences on the U.S. side in the U.N. discussions. The U.S. was with the British, or the other way round, in Hammarskjöld's phase at the Security Council when they together introduced the third clause I mentioned and eventually precipitated a breakdown and invalidated our efforts.

B Did Dulles have *carte blanche*?

M Eisenhower never played any potent role except in the Korean War, when he said, 'I will bring the boys back'. But he was the man who prevented the negotiations with China when I came back from Peking in 1955 and there was hope of bringing China to talk to the U.S.

B But all through Suez Dulles had a free rein?

M Yes, I believe so. If Eisenhower had any role it was to say, 'we don't want war', that's all.

B Could you tell me about the United Nations Emergency Force—how it came into existence and who played the key roles?

M In the announcing, in the moving of the Resolution in the Assembly, Canada did—as with the Sixteen-States Admission Resolution [the 'package deal' in 1955]. But the Sixteen-States Resolution was worked out by us jointly. The political work was Indo-Soviet. Panditji intervened from here with Moscow at

[1] The Rt. Hon. Walter Nash, later Prime Minister of New Zealand.

a crucial stage after a total breakdown just prior to the next and successful effort.

B Could you tell me about that first; where was that worked out, was it here in Delhi or in New York?

M We had been talking to the Russians about this Admission issue for several years. They had begun to say, 'we will do something about it'. Then, ultimately, it broke down.

B I have seen reports that when Bulganin and Khrushchev were in Delhi in 1955, the Prime Minister spoke to them about this the day before they left.

M I did send telegrams about it. I asked the Prime Minister to speak to them and he mentioned it.

B But was it at that point that the Russians changed their position somewhat?

M Well, yes. It wasn't a 'change' but they would not go the whole hog. We kept on talking to them at New York, even after the breakdown. Ultimately they agreed with me to go as far as the [Security] Council. But they would not accept Japan, because of the Kurile Islands. It could be said to be a change because they would not accept the whole of the Canada–India position. And our friend Paul Martin said, 'I have done everything I can; now they have let us down'. In fact he could not be found after the breakdown; we had to wake him up, I believe, at midnight to move the Resolution, which the Russians agreed to, leaving Japan for talks with the United States. Martin was not going to join in this—he was very sensitive in regard to American sentiment. The actual Resolution was put down by Canada and ourselves. Canada had a separate Resolution and we knew that that would complicate matters, so we got around them and put in a joint Resolution. We handed the business over to Canada for moving in the Assembly because Paul Martin believed he had worked it all out. Lester Pearson would have been easier in a situation of that kind but Paul Martin was handling it; he was friendly with me personally. So he took it over. It was called the 'Canadian' proposal, though this had been going on for five years. The previous year we had tried to stop [the impasse] becoming a total breakdown by a Good

Offices Committee. After Stalin's death we got Russia to revise their position on the grounds that they were keeping a lot of Asians and Africans out, and so on. The decision was taken in Moscow itself, I think.

Then came the Japanese issue. I remember lunching in the delegates' dining-room with Gromyko and someone else. Normally the Russians didn't come and sit with the commonalty of members and visitors in the public dining-room in those days but now we went to an unreserved table and sat down and talked it through, and I got them to agree. The difficulty then became Outer Mongolia. China would not agree to Outer Mongolia; therefore the Russians said they would not agree to Japan. What was the trouble? The trouble was that the Americans weren't willing to put sufficient pressure on the [Nationalist] Chinese to withdraw their veto. They said they did but I don't believe it. So the Chinese vetoed Outer Mongolia.

B Outer Mongolia was a *quid pro quo* for Japan?

M Yes; Outer Mongolia was the crux of the difficulty and so, ultimately, the Russians vetoed the whole thing. That is my recollection. Then I had to produce a formula to postpone the entry of Japan; from seventeen it came down to sixteen new members. The Japanese were very upset. I had to persuade a Japanese friend not to raise objections, and he was reasonable, so we postponed Japan for a year. We had some talk about the Kurile Islands [with the Russians]—what they would do and what they would not do. So the Japanese, who didn't agree, kept quiet. The Americans had been persuaded to agree, without Japan [coming in], and about 10 o'clock at night we at last got an agreement. The Russians said they wouldn't object to a Sixteen-Power solution; that is all we wanted then. We had one advantage—we didn't seek any kudos. If we had wanted our name on the Resolution, perhaps it might have created delays and new difficulties.

B Now, to go back to UNEF: are you saying that this was a similar situation?

M Yes. The Egyptians were always quite unwilling to admit troops, from any country. The problem, however, was that the Israelis would not agree to any settlement which would not offer them what they thought was protection. The Americans would not agree to giving direct protection. And we suggested a Boundary Force at that time; you will probably find in my speeches talk about a Boundary Force. The name 'Boundary Force' came into my head because we had one here [in 1947]— with very sad results, but still the name was there. We moved no resolution. Mr. Pearson was thinking along the same lines. He proposed his United Nations Emergency Force—but his original proposal was a police force, which would make people behave. Ultimately what came out was a force to keep people apart and prevent conflict.

Then, who would be in the Force? The Egyptians said, 'if you [Indians] are there we will have no objections'. The Canadians wanted to be in it; Pearson was dead keen on it; he said, 'other-wise there will be no Emergency Force'. I said the Egyptians just would *not* agree, whatever he might say. At last I tele-phoned to Cairo from the U.N. and talked to Nasser himself. He said, 'with these British helmets?' (apparently the Canadian Army wear British helmets); I said, 'these people [Canada] are ex-colonials', but he replied, 'no, no, they are NATO; under no circumstances can we have the Canadians.' Pearson was the heart of NATO, you know. And I tried the next day and the next day and the next, and finally Nasser said yes. That is the way the Canadians came in [to UNEF]. I mentioned [this incident] to Pearson and he didn't like it. He thought it was cutting down their dignity for me to have spoken like that and so on. At one time Egypt suggested that the Canadians should not wear these helmets. Somebody even raised the question, why should they wear British uniform. Well, I said, no Canadian Army would allow the taking away of its uniform, and ulti-mately it was settled. I had the same difficulty with Chou En-lai.

B You mean in the Indo-China Commissions?

M With him it was not so much the British; it was NATO. I regretted that Pearson had unnecessarily gone heart and soul into NATO. Why? What was Canada's interest in NATO? It was purely personal, I thought at the time. He became a kind of pundit to NATO. After all, how can you say to China and the Soviets that he was 'neutral' when he was the boss of

NATO? This was our difficulty. We knew that he was a liberal
—a conservative liberal but a liberal. But NATO was always
intruding. He could not talk without mentioning NATO most
times. He was more NATO than Spaak was at that time. It must
be said to his credit, though, that it was not the same NATO in
those days. I think the idea was that it should be a European
organization rather than a world organization. Then they
talked about putting teeth into NATO and so on. Pearson was
certainly a liberal. He would avoid war if left to himself, and
if he had had the power he would have exercised it over the
Americans. They listened to him at least, so I thought. We
respected him and I was very fond of him.

7. Israel, the Arabs, and India

B The Israelis were the last to withdraw from Sinai. What pressures operated on them?

M Nobody waited on their consent. They resisted pressures; they were very difficult, but they knew they would have to withdraw—they were somewhat like bad schoolboys, you know. They said, 'we have won the war; we have been through the Sinai desert' and so on. Then they brought up the Suez Canal and discrimination—all kinds of things like that. They had a case for freedom of navigation; they had no case for invasion. I think the Israelis lost by joining the French and British. The invasion angered Asia and Africa; it placed them in the role of allies and abettors of Imperialism.

B But you think they had a case so far as free movement of Israeli ships through the Canal was concerned?

M There is a case against them here also; the invasion didn't help any! Which Arab government could permit the Israeli flag in their home waters, even in the name of freedom of navigation? The Arabs would not agree to this; a red rag to a bull is the Israeli flag. It may be the fault of the Arabs—but no Arab government, no Egyptian government could agree to Israeli ships going through the Canal. The Arabs claim that they are at war with Israel. We tried some way to help solve the Israeli problem—conditions were more suitable for them before the Suez invasion. Nasser was at least willing to listen to what we had proposed.

We have not had any talks with Israel. At the United Nations I have often met Mrs. Golda Meir, Mr. Eban and other Israeli diplomats—we exchanged the usual courtesies. I cannot say that I talked to them about the Israeli problem, much less made proposals. Nasser might have agreed to talk to Mr. Ben-Gurion—before he attacked Egypt in the Suez days; he was the one Arab statesman who might have done so. It could have started a dialogue. This is only my guess. At Bandung the

Arab delegates agreed to the United Nations Resolution—the partition resolution of 1947. This meant the recognition of the existence of Israel and could, perhaps, have been a starting-point, if the Israelis had taken advantage of this Afro-Asian initiative. Facts, particularly the fact of Israel's aggression and taking the Negev Desert, had made the resolution out of date as a reflection of the existing situation. If Israel had found it possible also to accept that resolution, some dialogue could have begun. It was argued by some people that Egypt's inva-sion of Israel in 1948 repudiated the U.N. resolution. This kind of argument does not help much. If Egypt had committed an abortive invasion in 1948, Israel had taken the Negev, also not given to her by the U.N. So Israel's title is made to rest on occupation as a result of war.

In this issue, Jewish sentiment the world over is involved. So are Arab passions; even more so, because Palestine was lost and large numbers of refugees who are in camps were from Palestine. The Arabs say it is their homeland. On the other side, it was first the Jewish national home and later the State of Israel. The Arabs say that the refugees have been pushed out of their homes. When compensation is spoken of, the displaced say 'we want our homes'. They also argue that the Arabs inside Israel are discriminated against. We have not offered to discuss the issue between Israelis and Arabs. But one had the feeling before Suez that some dialogue could have begun. The attack and the invasion of Sinai, the partnership in Imperialist war, killed it. I have not seen much point in discussing it with the parties.

B Does this suggest to you that the conflict will go on in-definitely?

M Indefinitely? Who can say? I do not, however, see any immediate solution. The situation for a *détente* is worse today than it was before the Anglo-French-Israeli war against Egypt.

B Can we go back to the Indian position on the Arab-Jewish problem right from the beginning? I wonder why it took India two years or more to recognize Israel and why, even after seventeen years, you don't have any formal diplomatic relations?

M We decided upon Israel being recognized from the begin-ning; I have always taken the view that whatever country is recognized by the U.N. should be recognized by us. Whether we should send ambassadors or not is a different matter. Initially there was no question of sending an ambassador or minister; there was no deliberation in this. We don't send ambassadors to a lot of countries. If we had sent an ambassador at that time there would have been no difficulty.

B Mr. Menon, you say that you advocated recognition on the grounds that the U.N. had recognized Israel. What was Mr. Nehru's view? Was his attitude to Israel largely geared to his desire not to alienate the Arabs?

M Yes, to an extent. He was very sympathetic to Israel but said, I remember, at Bandung, when an Israel ambassador met him coming through Burma, 'I cannot argue this logically or on reason; this is the position: the Arabs will not attend if Israel is invited.' In fact, we asked for Israel to come to Bandung, but Pakistan and Indonesia vetoed it; Burma, ourselves, and Ceylon supported it. The question was whether Bandung would meet or not. Even Indonesia might have been persuaded at that time, but Pakistan made use of our attitude to Israel's presence at Bandung in propaganda with the Arabs. Since then there has been the Israeli invasion of Egypt.

B And the Arabs threatened to boycott Bandung?

M They did not threaten. The Arabs would not have come.

B Are you convinced of that?

M Oh, I'm sure. The Arabs wouldn't come to dinner [with Israelis]; the Arabs won't sit anywhere with them.

B Yes, we saw that in Delhi a little while ago [the Lebanese Ambassador to India walked out of an official Government of India party in October 1964 because of the presence of an Indian professor who was a member of the Indo-Israel Cultural Society].

M The only place where the Arabs sit with the Israelis is the U.N. That is why I said to the Prime Minister, 'the Israelis are in the U.N., we must recognize them'. I did not see any reservation in that.

B What harm do you think would have resulted from India establishing diplomatic relations with Israel?

M The Arabs would have disliked it.

B But so many other States have done this and not suffered?

M But we are in a difficult position because of Pakistan and our own anti-Imperialist views. Pakistan does nothing but she makes anti-Israeli speeches. And the Israelis, if I may say so, are maladroit. Despite opposition, I was not against their Consulate in Bombay. I knew we also have Consulates in East Germany. But should a Consul come and make political speeches here, as the Israeli Consul did in Delhi in November 1964? They are propagandists temperamentally, the same as the Arabs. Arabs will not make speeches without mentioning Israel and no Israeli can make a speech without attacking the Arabs.

B Do you think developments in recent months have delayed the normalizing of relations between Israel and India?

M There will be no 'normal' relations between Israel and India until the world situation changes. The Russians can afford to have somebody in Israel because they are a big power. We have got Pakistan on our borders, and the West supports Pakistan, and we cannot go and create more enemies than we have at the present moment. The one very good friend we have in the world is Nasser. We have also taken certain positions about Israel's attack on Egypt.

B Is Nasser being a 'best friend', for example, on the border dispute with China?

M Yes.

B Has he ever supported you on Kashmir?

M Oh, yes, Nasser is a friend to India; he is a very decent person. With Nasser Israel could have done a deal, but Ben-Gurion did not rise to the opportunity. In fact he embarked on the Sinai campaign while they were having friendly talks, in which he had told Nasser that he would not make difficulties for the Egyptians: Israel would not play cuckoo in the nest when they were being attacked by the West.

B You think this was the great divide in Israeli-Egyptian relations?

M I think that if Israel had not been involved in the Suez War it would have been better. I don't say that Egypt would have recognized it but things would have been easier.

B But in the Arab world is Nasser the one most likely to come to terms with Israel?

M He would have been once, but not now. I remember the talks we had. The Arabs should never have recognized Israel taking over the Negev Desert, but some compromise could have been reached; the Egyptians were the most reasonable of the Arabs, you know. There is anti-Semitism, it is said, in Iraq. I don't know how it is now, but until the Suez business there was no discrimination against the Jews in Egypt; they could get down from aircraft at Cairo. We diverted our planes from Basra because the Iraqis would not allow Jews to alight there as transit passengers. We have always been clear on this racial question and we have always taken it up with the Egyptians. They said, 'It is not a racial question, it's an imperial question; why is Israel here? Only because the imperialists placed them there; how are they here in defiance of Arab nationalism? The Palestinians have been displaced.' I think that if the British and the Americans hadn't butted in some solution would have been found. The Israelis would have been Jewish-Arabs. The Israelis, now, who are they? They are mostly Europeans, Americans, not Arabs. The Arabs say that Palestine is an Arab land.

B Firstly, they are Jews. And, for the record, at the moment almost 50 per cent of the Jewish population of Israel originates from Africa or Asia.

M Fifty per cent? So it's an Asian country! And the Arabs are badly treated in Israel. I believe that the Arabs may be using their refugees for propaganda also; on the other hand, they have been dispossessed. It's one of those questions where there is no easy solution, you see. Israel was at first a Churchillian conception, a National Home—what do the Jews gain, apart from sentiment, from this National Home? It's really a kind of a hothouse State; all the money comes from elsewhere; but it is too late now to say anything. So it will settle down somehow or other.

To stop war is the only purpose of UNEF. It has been in difficulties at various times; if the Indian troops were not there it could not have survived. We have very good relations with both sides. The Israelis were very difficult at the beginning. And it must be said to Nasser's credit that without his assistance UNEF would not be there, because it is based in Egyptian territory.

B What about the long-range political effects of the Suez War in 1956, in terms of the British position, the American position, etc.?

M It has given Nasser a position in the Middle East which is an advantage in the long run. It has meant a retreat of empire from that part of the world. It certainly increased the prestige of the U.N. at that time. It also showed the Asiatic peoples that they could pilot a ship through the Canal!

The best I could get on the Israel question in the Suez negotiations was the agreement about the reference to the World Court. And I am quite certain that Nasser agreed to this knowing its implications. I told him, 'If they have any sense they won't go even if you go, because their case is weak; besides, they would consider it an infringement of their sovereign rights. But you must admit the acceptance of international law.' I said, 'you cannot do it in any other way'. But in those decisions Nasser didn't question my judgement or rectitude—I don't know what he would do now. He practically agreed to what we said as it was a way out without loss of principle.

B Did Suez tend to give the Soviets a breakthrough in the Middle East?

M Nasser was then very much putting the Soviet Union on probation because he is anti-communist. He is a Muslim at heart—not a fanatical Muslim—and he won't have any communism in Egypt.

B Did the Arabs welcome the U.S. attitude to the Suez War?

M At that time, with limitations. Defeat in the war didn't upset them. That is what I told Prime Minister Nehru during the war with China in 1962; what did the Egyptians do? They didn't panic.

SUPPLEMENTARY INTERVIEW—MAY 1965

B During our earlier interviews, Mr. Menon, you expounded certain views on the Arab-Israeli conflict. Recently some astonishing reports appeared about your remarks at a 'Palestine' Conference in Cairo. What I would like to know is whether or not the reports are accurate? The essence of the reports is that you drew a sharp analogy between Israeli 'occupation' of so-called 'Arab lands' and China's occupation of Aksai Chin.

M I didn't say that. I said the position in regard to Israel and the occupation of Arab territory was of the same kind as that in regard to Kashmir. I did not say, at any time, as was reported by one of the newspapers here, prompted by Western propaganda, that the Arabs should go to war with Israel. As you know, even in regard to Kashmir, the position I have always held is that we must not surrender sovereignty but that we should not take war initiatives even to assert our rights over occupied territory.

B You were reported to have called on the Arabs to unite and bide their time until they could throw the Israelis into the sea. That is hardly a peaceful approach.

M No, what I said was that they had not handled the United Nations resolutions properly—after all, the Israelis had been warned many times by the U.N. You cannot say that, if you drive out people from their homes to make room for others. . . . And the United Nations resolution, in the beginning, was that the refugees had the option of either compensation or repatriation. But I said there should be no violence. Israel started the war. The United Nations resolution also said that there should be no racial discrimination. All this sort of thing I did say and believe. I said that Palestine could become an Arab nation but I felt the Arabs thought I was overdoing it. I spoke very strongly against anti-Semitism, but according to Israeli writers ghettoes existed inside Israel itself. I was not prepared to subscribe to the view that because Israel had come into existence, therefore the country should not be an Arab land. There is no reason why Palestine should not be an independent state with all such Jews that are there. It should not be an outpost of an empire.

B But according to press reports, you spoke in terms of the liquidation of the State of Israel.

M I didn't say anything about that; somebody else did, but I didn't. But I think that it cannot be left like this and I think it is wrong for it to be used as a pawn by anybody else.

8. Hungary 1956

B I would like to return now, if I may, to India's policy on the Hungary Question and to get your reflections on this very controversial issue.

M Our view of the usefulness and function of the United Nations has been that action should be taken there and that the U.N. should concern itself with such matters and in such ways as would lead to some helpful result. The U.N. should not be used as an instrument of the Cold War. In the Hungary Question the United States—the U.K. too—was most shamefacedly using the U.N. as an instrument of the Cold War.

We said and voted that the question should be debated. Our view then and today was that the Hungarian uprising in the beginning was a national revolt, not in the sense of a territorial revolt but national in character, and that it should be met by as conciliatory and just methods as were possible. Secondly, we said that it should not be allowed to develop into or lead to the outbreak of a world war. Thirdly, the way to deal with it was not to isolate the Hungary Question in respect of the use of foreign forces and to point your finger of scorn but to demand that all foreign occupying forces should be withdrawn from Europe. It wouldn't be possible to insist on the Russians withdrawing their [foreign] force from Hungary, except of their own free will, without requiring that the American, the British, and the French withdraw their troops from Germany, because Hungary was merely the base on which they were stationed. The troops were part of the Soviet [foreign] occupying troops. They might have been used or were used in suppressing Hungary, whatever the reasons were. This idea, that they were primarily there as part of the forces [Soviet and Western] after the world war and were a component of the Cold War complex, was not appreciated. Here lay the root of the evil.

Next, the question having been inscribed, we never opposed this inscription. We suggested, however—and this is proof of its Cold War propaganda—that, like all major questions, it should go to the appropriate committee of the General Assembly. As you know, the committees of the U.N. are not small cliques; they are replicas of the General Assembly. One reason was that debating would be more businesslike and reasonable; there would be speaking and counter-speaking with deliberation. Having debated it in the committee, it would come to the Plenary Session. This is how all items are normally debated at the U.N. But the U.S. made a major issue of this procedural point. They assumed the item should go direct to the Assembly and they specially pleaded that it would save time. In fact, it took more time that way! Everybody knew it would. The American desire was only to give the one side a grand slam in the Assembly. That is the background.

The basis of our approach was: first, our background in regard to national sentiments and the maintenance of foreign forces; second, our desire not to use the U.N. for 'fisticuffs'; and third, we were against the use of force or unnecessarily forceful language! Even among ourselves—you look at the South African Resolution we sponsored year after year—you don't find the use of the word 'condemn' anywhere. This was our general background.

Now what was the background of the West? The entire Western opinion and facts were derived not only then but even today from refugees. Nobody went to Hungary. For two or three years Mr. Leslie Munro[1] had been paid a salary and had been appointed chairman of a committee in order to collect information from people who gathered in New York. Second, it was based on the presumption that Hungary was wrong in any case, or Russia was wrong, and this was an opportunity to make a fight and show them up. Also, this was part of the effort to stop the expansion of communism. Now, how do you prevent the expansion of communism in a communist state except by foreign intervention? It was like Mr. Casey[2] telling me when he came to Geneva [1954] that he wanted to be introduced to Pham Van Dong [of North Vietnam]—to talk him out of communism! You find all these queer characteristics in international relations when you get new people in high places. The Western

---

[1] New Zealand Permanent Representative to the U.N.
[2] R. G. (now Lord) Casey, Australian Secretary of State for External Affairs at the time.

approach in this matter was to punish Russia, not to get anything done to alter the situation in Hungary. They didn't want
anything done. I will prove it to you in a moment. Furthermore,
they wanted a public debate not a private confabulation, even
a few committee discussions. This is the background.

The main thing is the facts. What are they? The facts on
which the charges were made and the debate rested are news-
paper accounts, refugees' stories, people being thrown out of
their homes and things of that kind. I will take them one by
one. The main one is the basic factor of the refugees. The
prosecutors had to 'convince' in a predetermined way. The
refugees were at hand. The prosecutor confessed afterwards,
when things cooled down, that some of these things were quite
unconfirmed; nobody knew who these informants were; the
numbers and figures given proved to be all wrong. It was all
just atrocity stories, not a thing to bring before a court of law,
not the sort of thing that should come up at the U.N. It's all
right to speak about it at a political party convention. Secondly,
you cannot expect us to take the same line as the prosecutors
did, to make the U.N. a forum for the Cold War. There was one
more factor: they would not take into account the fact that,
whether they liked it or not, Hungary was a member-State of
the U.N.; she had a voice there. Now what was the West
saying? They were saying that Hungary was a stooge of the
Russians—and the very same people were holding the China
seat [Formosa] there. We took the view that so long as Hungary
was a member of the U.N. you could not talk of her as a colony.
They could have expelled Hungary; then they could have
talked. They didn't do that; they wanted to keep Hungary in.
You cannot have it both ways. What is more, Hungary had its
Foreign Minister at the General Assembly and she conformed to
all the main criteria of a State, especially the habitual obedience
of its people, however that obedience was said to be obtained.

What did we do? I proposed that Hammarskjöld, the Secretary-General, should make inquiries. The Assembly agreed that
he should make a report on people's feelings and conditions in
Hungary. The meeting then adjourned. Even the adjournment
was manipulated and it came amazingly quickly. The renewed
meeting was the next day or the day after—I had meanwhile
been continuously in touch with the Secretary-General. It was

not as if I went only to the meetings or met only with the Hungarians; with the Hungarians we had a certain amount of influence because of our objective position. They were willing to respond to our wish for information because they knew the state of public feeling. The Secretary-General made a statement to the Assembly that he was in no position to make a report; he said he wanted more time. That was the substance of his talk to the Assembly in open session. I took the view that if you appoint a tribunal or an individual to report on a particular matter under dispute, then you cannot pass resolutions on the substantive issues until he has reported, unless you prove to yourself or are convinced that the delay is deliberate, is *mala fide*. Isn't it so? And so I said, 'we have asked the Secretary-General to report; then let him report, and when he has reported then we can say whatever we like and take whatever action we want'. The whole Western tactic and objective was turning on the position that somebody must get into Hungary; India should use whatever influence she had with the Hungarians direct, not through the Russians, to enable the Secretary-General to go there. Well, believe it or not, the Foreign Minister [of Hungary] agreed that they would invite the Secretary-General to go there and see things for himself. We had a great deal of difficulty in obtaining this agreement. I had introduced the Foreign Minister to a number of our U.N. colleagues and he said, 'in view of the *Indian* position we will agree, but the Secretary-General should come on our invitation'. So I spoke to the Secretary-General, and he was very happy about it. But the Hungarians said, 'We cannot give a date just now, but we won't create any unnecessary delay; we will discuss with the Secretary-General and we will fix a date that is convenient to us; if it's inconvenient to him then we can re-consider it.' I was comparatively happy about this.

I spoke to the American delegation, too; unfortunately Cabot Lodge was not at the meeting that day but the Americans also appeared comparatively happy. I spoke to Wadsworth who thought it was a good arrangement; but he was number two in his delegation. He did not have the same public obligation to make vitriolic speeches as the leader of the delegation [Lodge] had, whether he believed them or not. They had bred this McCarthyism which is basic to American thinking. Once you start hatred you cannot control it; it's a Frankenstein monster. Anyway, the position was as I have set it out; there isn't one word of inaccuracy in this.

In the meanwhile Pakistan had taken a hand. At that time Pakistan was not taking any interest in U.N. affairs; she didn't count for very much there, unless Zafrullah[1] or someone like that came. But she took a hand merely to embarrass us. She drafted a resolution that was highly objectionable, and she got Cuba to second it—Batista's[2] Cuba. The Pakistan–Cuba draft came up. We hadn't even put in our draft resolution yet: Hammarskjöld had not yet reported. Secondly, we had got an agreement with Hungary to enable the Secretary-General to go there; I got the Foreign Minister [of Hungary] to say that on the rostrum. But the Americans, that is Cabot Lodge, broke it all up, to the surprise even of his own delegation. While I was speaking on the rostrum, in walked Cabot Lodge—he had come late, about 3.30 in the afternoon. He knew nothing of what had happened or of the conversation I had had with his delegation. I don't know where he sat down while I was talking; in any case he didn't consult although he was very friendly to me. My relations with him were very good then, and are now. He then walked straight to the platform and delivered a tirade—the usual one. The main substance of it was: 'We are not interested in all this, the Hungarians must say here and now when the Secretary-General can go. They must announce a date, and there is no question of negotiations.' He made that speech; I knew that the balloon had gone up and nothing could be done.

Hungary then stiffened. Here and elsewhere my surmise is that the Hungarians must have thought we had great influence with the Americans; and every time we did something like this, even if it was at the Americans' request, we always ran the risk of last-minute bust-ups. Cabot Lodge knew this—he never does anything personally that is not gentlemanly. But [Adlai] Stevenson, he was ill-mannered after he came to the U.N. He has no sense of propriety or a United Nations sense. He has nothing; he is merely an 'intellectual' with a swelled head.

[1] Mohammed Zafrullah Khan, long-time Foreign Minister of Pakistan, afterwards Judge of the International Court of Justice and, later, Pakistan's Permanent Representative to the U.N.

[2] Col. F. Batista, strong man of Cuba before Castro obtained power.

I was very sad about this incident because I had spent up to the early hours of that morning trying to persuade the Hungarians to do this. I had got my Asian-Africans all lined up. Cabot Lodge went up to the rostrum and said, 'we support the Pakistan–Cuba resolution'. They put down their two names to it. They made it a Cold War issue. We then put down our resolution. Ultimately, after several days, both of these resolutions went to a vote, which is what, in fact, nobody talks about. My recollection is, and the only place I find it is in that book on Indian diplomacy,[1] that our resolution was passed by two votes more than theirs. Both were passed by the U.N.—which is one of those things that happen. Then how can one say that Indian policy was not approved by the U.N.? Indian policy was embodied in that resolution and it was passed with four votes against and some abstentions. But the positive votes were as many as or more than for the Pakistan–Cuba draft.

It is not fair to leave it like that because that is not the whole of the story. We voted against the other resolution because it contained a provision for conducting an election in Hungary by the U.N. without the Hungarians being a consenting party. And we said Hungary was a member-State and it would be just like landing troops in the Congo without the Congo Government's consent [1964]. The U.N. is not a super-State; it can't go ahead and conduct 'elections'. I even went to the extent of taking this piece out—just those few words about the elections. I said I wanted these separately voted on and I warned the Assembly of the complications of such a resolution. I won't mention countries but I will say that some countries who said they would vote with us got cold feet because of American propaganda and they abstained. Our amendment, to remove the reference to U.N. elections, was by a procedural device used to further the American position. The Americans exercised their right. At that time I went to Cabot Lodge and told him, 'We will even abstain on this [Pakistan–Cuba] resolution if you let these words go, if you take them out. Even then we would not vote for it because there are other objectionable parts, but we will abstain.' They didn't realize at that time that the Congo would happen. I cannot say I anticipated the paratroop landing [in December 1964], but I still believed that the Empire [Belgium]

---

[1] Ross N. Berkes and M. S. Bedi, *The Diplomacy of India* (1958), 104.

would try to come back in various ways; Imperialism doesn't die
at a stroke like that. The U.N. would go through a period of
destruction either physical or moral, and the Belgians and the
Americans would come again, to rule over liberated territory
until bloody murder comes around or the world changes. This
is my private view. You may say, 'you are an awful cynic', but
there it is. So I voted against the [Pakistan–Cuba] resolution.
It's only fair to say that I had no instructions. I had a free hand,
and some people even asked me, 'why do we want to vote
against it, why can't we abstain?' I said either we have a
conviction or we haven't.

B You mean some people in your own delegation?

M Yes, in my own delegation and some others. I said either we
have a conviction or we have not; we cannot go back on our
basic objections. Therefore, we voted against it.

We voted against another resolution also moved by the U.S.
in regard to sending Red Cross assistance. First, the Red Cross
could not go there without the Hungarian Government's consent. The resolution was only a political stunt. It was an indirect
way, a dishonest way, of dealing with that matter. That was not
the main reason I put forward. If you read that resolution, it
was not a Red Cross resolution—a Red Cross resolution would
be non-political, wouldn't it? It starts off by condemnation of
Hungary, that is to say, they tacked on their cold war stuff to it
and spoke aloud about so-called humanitarian reasons. You
hear a great deal about rescuing foreign women [in Stanleyville, the Congo, December 1964] but what about all the
Africans killed by the foreigners? What about Lumumba?
What about the Indian troops who were killed in Katanga?
I feel shivers about it; I was responsible for sending them there,
and the interventionists had them slaughtered. You think I am
anti-West, but I happen to know things that you don't. I have
no bitterness, though I may speak emphatically. So this is the
Hungarian story.

And then they put out a lot about double standards and that
Krishna Menon is a communist. This is their final expedient
always. What is there in this, you tell me? First of all, how can
any responsible people want to pass a resolution on an issue
still under inquiry. It wasn't a question of months and weeks.

And they killed an agreement that had been made—one which the Russian delegation perhaps hadn't wanted the Hungarians to accept, and at that time Hungary and Russia were very close. But the Hungarians were not willing to ask the Secretary-General to go the next morning. How can anyone object to a reasonable way of fixing a date?

Let us assume for the sake of argument that the Hungarians were not sincere. But if they went up to the platform and said, 'you can come', the United Nations and particularly the prosecuting people would have scored a point. They could have pursued that; they didn't do it. They brought Hungary up year after year. After the first year the sessions dragged on; it was a kind of ritual with the West; year after year they brought it up in the same way. Sir Leslie Munro was appointed head of an investigation; it is one of those things that happen at the United Nations. Frank Graham[1] sits there on Kashmir, this gentleman on Hungary. They are borne on the U.N. payroll. I don't mind telling you, Hungarian refugees—not Kadar's[2] people, but others—who came to see me at the U.N. and held demonstrations outside, were friendly to me, not antagonistic at all. They knew I had spoken about Hungarian nationalism. I am not referring to the so-called 'Friends of Free Europe'; they appear to be paid propagandists [Americans]; but there were other groups who were very friendly. Our detractors made capital out of it; they hurled abuse and misrepresented things every way they could. Newspapers wrote nasty things; they used all their machinery over here to embarrass the Prime Minister and to blackguard me.

But Pandit Nehru felt very strongly on it. He said, 'he [Krishna Menon] has not said anything that is contrary to what I have said or against our policy'. He had the telegrams. I dare say, if the Prime Minister had been present, probably he might have abstained. On the other hand, he might not have abstained. Even if we had abstained it would have made no difference because the West were determined to make a scapegoat of us on account of our non-aligned position and the strength that the Asian-African group was gaining. Our position

[1] Dr. Frank Graham, U.N. Representative on the India–Pakistan Question since 1951.

[2] Janos Kadar, Prime Minister of Hungary at the time.

on Colonialism, Co-existence, and Disarmament also was not to their liking.

B You say you had no instructions, so that in your mind you had a free hand to act on your own discretion?

M Yes; not only in my mind. I had no instructions in the sense that I had no instructions on this particular matter. I had the confidence of the Government.

B Might I digress by asking whether you had instructions generally at the United Nations?

M Oh, yes. In the absence of a particular instruction I voted according to my discretion. The Delegation held frequent meetings. Government's basic policies were not in doubt. There were necessary references to the Prime Minister.

B But in general, as a Representative to the U.N., did you have instructions on a great many issues?

M Not on specific issues generally. There is always a brief on the agenda items. When I wanted instructions I sent a telegram to the Prime Minister setting out the case and suggesting how and what should be done; in fact, more or less informing him what our instructions should be. He would usually send a telegram back and say, 'I generally agree with your analysis. You must use your discretion.' No Representative functioned in the way I did; I functioned as a Foreign Minister would at the U.N. and the Americans and other people knew it. Sometimes, to gain time, I would say, 'I want time for instructions', which I was entitled to say. And they often laughed.

B You made a point, Mr. Menon, about the far-reaching implications for the U.N. and other countries, and for India itself, of the resolution calling for elections in Hungary conducted by the U.N.

M I know what you are getting at, but Kashmir was not dominant in my mind; it was one of the things. Other people told me about it. But I revolted against the idea of the United Nations intervening in elections, as well as against the suggestion that the position I took was because of Kashmir. The idea of calling Czechoslovakia a colony is preposterous; one could call Canada a colony, couldn't one? After all, Canada has hardly ever voted against the United States, though I believe Green did once. It is two independent member-States, whatever the reason, acting in the same manner.

B What other implications are there in your view? Is this a case in which sovereignty becomes an absolute value?

M No. It really means that the U.S. is to decide when there is to be an election anywhere. It is interventionism. Secondly, to the U.S. Hungary was a Cold War affair, although the issue was being debated on other ostensible grounds.

B And Kashmir didn't loom large in your thinking?

M No. Our views on Kashmir are well known and stand unalterable. It does not loom large in my mind as far as the U.N. is concerned, because we don't agree with whatever resolutions they pass. I did say in Parliament the other day, 'if all the nations in the world said that Kashmir must belong to Pakistan, are we going to give it up to them?' So what is the use of all this. And it won't stop there; it will lead to a bloody revolution in this country. I sometimes feel that if I have done anything in this land at all in recent years, it is to clarify people's minds and tighten up our people on Kashmir. Nobody will give it up.

No one who has criticized India on Hungary has read the records. Even the people at the U.N. were not present at some of the meetings because the Hungarian sessions, after the first two or three days, had become a dreadful bore. There were no new ideas—only that 'Carthage must be destroyed', do you see. And I want to repeat that you will find in the first submission we made that we were the only people who gave facts and figures, in accordance with the information we then had, about the atrocities—the Russians did not forgive us for that and I think they were right because we had given out figures which were not really correct, which afterwards proved to be exaggerated.

B One point that comes to my mind is that the reaction against India's policy on Hungary in the U.N. was not confined to those whom you would consider traditional critics, people hostile to India in the United States and elsewhere. Within this country itself there was very substantial criticism from a wide section of the public, from Parliament, political parties, from the Press, etc. How does one explain this?

M Very simple, because how does this country get any information?

B Mainly from the news agencies.

M Quite. And who are the news agencies?

B These are Western, that is true.

M They get it from the news agencies—they don't read the United Nations papers to which I have referred. The articulate people here are our political opposition. They would try to discredit the Prime Minister or to attack me and also show up that I am a particular friend of the Prime Minister. To attack me is also to gain a certain amount of publicity. And then there are people who are communist-baiters and there are the communists. If I wanted to be a communist on account of conviction I would openly be a communist. I would not masquerade as a Congressman. Those who insinuate this are seeing others in their own image.

B Is it true, do you think, when you look back on the Hungarian episode and its effect on India's position in the world, that this marked a turning-point in the respect in which India is held by a number of States?

M Not at all. I don't know where you got that idea from. This is the first time I have heard it. If it was so, so much worse for the world that you speak of. I have given the facts as they are. Secondly, I don't think it made any difference. You talk about Hungary; some people talk about Tibet in the same way. We are sympathetic to the Tibetans; we somewhat provoked China by having the Dalai Lama treated here as though he was a ruling monarch. But that is our affair. It may be wise or it may not be wise, but our public opinion and our sentiments in the matter tended that way. It was one way of showing our protest against the violation of human rights and so on. What arguments did we use? We did not say China was right. We said it was not going to do the Dalai Lama any good. It's not going to settle this problem and also China is not at the door. Now this year I am told some people want us to support the [Tibetan] sovereignty resolution [in the U.N.]. I think it would be very bad. It would look a bit small-minded, after so many years now suddenly realizing that human rights have been violated. But China's continued conduct justifies our revision of attitudes.

9. Congo 1960

B During the discussion on Hungary, Mr. Menon, you made some reference to the Congo, particularly your role in the dispatch of Indian troops as part of the U.N. Congo Force. This leads me to raise some questions about Indian policy on the Congo, going back to the summer of 1960. What considerations prompted the Indian Government to involve itself to such an extent in the Congo, especially at a time when it was confronted with so many problems on its own borders with Pakistan and China?

M We sent troops to the Congo because the U.N., rightly or wrongly, had got itself involved. We think it's necessary for its survival and the world's! And the United Nations had got itself into a very bad mess over there. Therefore, at that time, the only thing that could save them was the presence of troops— and nobody else who had any troops was willing to send them.

B You say that the U.N. became involved in the Congo rightly or wrongly, but is it not a fact that it became involved initially because Lumumba[1] asked it to become involved?

M Now you are asking me to talk about the Congo at very great length.

B I am indeed.

M But for that I must have documents—for this reason: we were not members of the Security Council, and you are now speaking as you did on the Korea business. You should take the events in order, not go backwards and forwards until you catch the situation in the way you want. I have forgotten the sequence of it now; Lumumba did ask the U.N. at that time, but he did say in subsequent letters also . . .

B I remember the sequence very well, Mr. Menon, if it's relevant.

---

[1] Patrice Lumumba, first Premier of the independent Congo.

M Let us leave Lumumba out of it for the present. Let me say that this may not be a Government of India view, but personally I think it was very wrong to send army troops to the Congo from the beginning and as an untried step.

B Why was it wrong?

M I don't know who advised it. It had never been done before. Only a State can wage war. The U.N. were sending their forces to keep people in order; the U.N. has not reached that stage of keeping world law! I believe myself that Hammarskjöld thought that all he had to do was send some troops and in three weeks the whole thing would be over. He was wrong.

B What would have happened if the U.N. hadn't sent troops?

M Well, perhaps there would have been civil war, short or prolonged. This was what eventuated anyway. I thought at the time, and think so now, that the United Nations should have tried various other things in the Congo before sending troops. It should have called the Belgians to order in the first instance.

B And then, Cold War involvements in Africa?

M Not necessarily. The situation would not have been worse than what developed. The United Nations should have concerned itself with the Congo but not allowed it to become a scene of war and strife.

B The Soviets would have moved in and the Americans would have moved in.

M I think the move of sending troops to the Congo at that stage, without using any negotiation, was a mistake. But we took the position as it was. I would have first exhausted all machinery in the way of negotiation. No Asian or African countries were involved; we were not in it at that time. It was purely a Security Council action which really meant it was simply Hammarskjöld's position. As things developed, the U.N. policy in the Congo was conditioned by the Western bloc. America carried most of the financial burden and other countries in some places tried to become interventionists.

B At the Government of India end, who took the decision? Was it the Prime Minister's decision to send troops?

M That was about two years afterwards. Naturally and rightly, we would send them because the U.N. had asked for them and it was heavily involved. Without assistance the U.N. position in the Congo would have been difficult. The first troops were not combatant troops.

B That is correct. But India then decided to send the Brigade group.

M We never thought of sending combatant troops at first. At that time we would not, because, even though the Prime Minister didn't say so, he had the same view as I had: 'Where is all this going to—waging war everywhere; and who was the U.N. to go into Central Africa, knowing nothing at all, to wage war on African peoples?' It was a grievous tragedy that occurred as events proved. The U.N. shouldn't have done it; the policy failed and brought on Katanga and Tshombe—not our troops, no, but the U.N. policy in the Congo. Having had the experience of Korea, they should have carried the Russians and others along with them and then perhaps the whole of the U.N. could have got on with it as a joint and more peaceful enterprise. Also, they should have taken into account the fact that they were dealing with Africa and most of the States were new. And then there was nobody at the U.N., Hammarskjöld included, who appeared to have thought out the implications.

B Let me put the question this way: what do you think were the consequences of the U.N. involvement in the Congo?

M I think it has weakened the United Nations, which has set a bad precedent. The U.N. Congo Force is not like UNEF; it's not even like the Korea Command. The Korea Command only used the U.N. as a cover.

B And UNEF?

M UNEF is merely a boundary force; it is not a fighting force. Our men haven't even got any arms, only side-arms.

B But the Congo Force was not a fighting force until December 1962?

M Ours wasn't a fighting force in the beginning; the Indian Brigade group which was sent later, was. What is more, there is a difference between the Israelis and the Arabs, two contending parties fighting with equal arms, and the Congo. The Congo, from a certain point of view, was like a civil commotion. How can you say it was a fighting force when the first thing the United Nations had to do, or did, was to confine the Congolese Army to barracks?

B You mean the U.N. had strict orders not to engage in actual military operations unless they were attacked?

M Our men took all the bullet wounds in their chests and didn't return the fire in the early phase. Even later they protected the hospitals. It has not been recorded anywhere. The hospital was in military danger—there were ninety men who were badly injured or killed at one time.

B What Indian national interests were served by India sending troops to the Congo?

M I think the Prime Minister thought Hammarskjöld had taken a step which, whether wise or not, had to be supported. I think he was mistaken in the wisdom part because he had no personal acquaintance with the Secretary-General, except when he came here. I knew Hammarskjöld better and I think he was a good man but he was a limited person. And I am afraid Hammarskjöld often placed too much stress on his capacity to use words which meant two things at the same time. Thirdly, he had no knowledge of Africa, though great sympathy and concern. I haven't either, but I have a certain amount of 'mental knowledge'. Unfortunately, he presumed he had it; it's my own feeling that he miscalculated the time and the course it would take. Ultimately it became a Western operation and caused splits in Asian and African opinion.

I believe he thought that in a few weeks' time the whole thing would be settled! It was something akin to the cease fire line in Kashmir; we would never have agreed to that cease fire line—nobody would—nor to all these arguments about plebiscite, if we had known it was going to go on for ten years. This was not regretted then as it was regarded as a thing to be done immediately. I was away in London at that time, but if I had been there I would have suggested a different time limit; now it is always used against us, although only by misinterpretation and disregard of the decisions, assurances, and pronouncements of the United Nations itself.

B Time limit to the offer of a plebiscite?

M No, no; there is no offer of a plebiscite. I mean the whole of the business.

B What was the reaction of African States to the dispatch of Indian troops to the Congo? Did that win you friends or lose you friends?

M No, I don't think we lost any friends. We might have created jealousies. . . .

B I am puzzled by your conception of the proper role of the U.N. You have given me the impression that the U.N. has a function as a negotiating body and nothing else. You do not say that the U.N. must ultimately become the kind of institution that can put out a fire in different parts of the world. Isn't this the legitimate function of the U.N.?

M This is a professor's outlook.

B Perhaps.

M But I think you corrected yourself by using the word 'ultimate'.

B But I am still left with the problem—if there occurs in any part of the world a massive outbreak which has the possible danger of consequences far beyond the Congo, who, then, should take action?

M It cannot be done by war, especially in the present circumstances. That could lead to a world war.

B But you think the chaos in the Congo could have been worse?

M Chaos in the Congo would perhaps have been better avoided by other methods.

B Mainly negotiations?

M Yes, mainly negotiations and conciliatory processes without ambivalence. What is more, the U.N. errors of omission and commission in the Congo were largely responsible for the developments which culminated in the murder of Lumumba. We should have stood behind the nationalist forces instead of weakening them.

B But you are assuming that the nationalist forces were strong enough to function on their own?

M I know they were all equally weak compared to older nationalist movements. After all, what forces were there? Why, up to 1959 they didn't even have a public meeting in the place. The Congo movement welled up in a short period.

B Quite. Therefore, it seems to me that the Congo was almost a classic illustration of a political vacuum in the world.

M It was not that; that is too simple. I personally believe that with high-level and consistent negotiations and persistent work —unfortunately the U.N. have not got the personnel for it—it should have been possible to create a different situation in the Congo. And even if it sent troops, it should have been more like UNEF, not like what it became. Also, in UNEF we kept the great powers, like the United States, at a distance; we wouldn't agree to great-power involvement. That was one of the conditions under which we went there.

B What was your own appraisal of the various measures in the response of different powers to the difficulty in the Congo—America, Belgium, France?

M The Western group are basically responsible [for the tangle]. And it has come out more and more that there had been difficulties technically between the U.S. and the U.K., because the U.K. thinks the Congo is their preserve on account of their interests in copper. . . . They are changing now, of course, and they don't always agree with the Americans. Equally, there have been phases of American policy: first of all, the Americans at that period had one guiding light and that was how to blacken the Russians. You cannot proceed in these matters only in that way. They got the Congo Government to pull out the Russian presence in other parts of Africa and all that kind of thing. The U.N. passed these resolutions and there was much steam-rolling business. We are not in the Security Council. America had every right to regard herself as one of the two big powers, but she is not herself suited to be the major intermediary in the world.

B What about the French and Belgians in all this?

M The French are imperialists; the French gave the Katangans aeroplanes. The Belgians wanted to stage a come-back by the back door. The *Union Minière* was a military base; the atrocities performed on Lumumba became nobody's business. I don't say Lumumba was a saint or anything like that; he was just like all of us, but events made him a national leader and symbol. And he certainly was the ablest of them all.

B Were the Soviets not involved in the Congo at all?

M If it had been rightly done, the Soviets would perhaps have said, 'don't send arms' and they would have proposed negotiations with them. On the other hand, if their arms had gone, the position would have been different. It is difficult to speculate what would have been the situation.

B But were they not involved in recognizing the Gizenga[1] regime?

M That is all later. They were first for Lumumba, the same as everybody else. Then the Americans changed, and Lumumba was said to have gone over to the communists. He was murdered in circumstances, to say the least, that have yet to be cleared up. The U.N. made so many military mistakes in the Congo from the very beginning. They confined the Congolese Army to barracks, stupidly as it turned out—the U.N. behaved like a poor principal of a girls' school. Then the U.N. brought them out on a U.N. day for a parade!—let them loose—how could they put them back? That was the beginning of the trouble.

I think there are two things you should read on the Congo, the Security Council proceedings and the Dayal Report. Dayal[2] was a conventional I.C.S. officer, a very decent fellow; he was very pro-American and I believe he is not anti—even now. The U.N. sent him there—Mr. Hammarskjöld thought him very

---

[1] Antoine Gizenga, self-appointed successor to Lumumba, with headquarters in Stanleyville.

[2] Rajeshwar Dayal, a senior Indian diplomat who served as the U.N. Secretary-General's Permanent Representative in the Congo, 1960–1.

good. We didn't ask for him; we would not have done so for more than one reason. You can take it from me that we never interfered with Indian personnel we placed at the disposal of the U.N. We regarded them as on deputation, as international personnel.

B You mean those who are actually employed by the U.N. or seconded to the U.N.?

M Yes. Committees are different; but those employed by the U.N., we never touch; we never give them instructions.

B Would you say that the Dayal Report came as a surprise to you?

M Not to us but to the Americans and some others. I was agreeably affected, not surprised, that he was so courageous. He would have brought about an agreement with the other side given a fair chance and an approach of integrity by all concerned—but he had no support there. The intrigue came to the surface at that time; they, the interested parties, were using the Congo the same way as they were using Hungary, with even less justification. We had agreed to the admission of the Congo [to the U.N.]—all of us had agreed to bringing all the African States in. Under the old style the Russians would not have agreed to the French colonies because they were really not free.

B Why do you say they were really not free?

M The Frenchmen sat next to them and told them how to vote. Things have changed since, thanks to African assertions.

B In the U.N.?

M Yes, apart from Mali and later Senegal, and later you could add Guinea. Some of these States didn't want to become independent—they were forced by de Gaulle's bluff, after Sékou Touré[1] called it! Therefore, having given self-determination to one, the French had to give it to everybody.

We agreed to all the African States coming in, on the understanding that, with regard to the Congo [Leopoldville]— because there was this trouble—we would admit them (and the Russians were very reasonable about it) but would not seat

[1] President of Guinea.

the Government [in the U.N.]. This went on for some time, until December 1960. Then the Americans fought tooth and nail to defeat our Congo Resolution. They moved theirs against ours and won by five votes; those votes were the French-African votes. That altered, perhaps, the situation in the U.N.; otherwise the Congo business would have been settled differently. They brought Kasavubu[1] to New York without telling anybody, by aeroplane on a Thursday, and set him up somewhere in the building. Then, on Friday I believe, they suddenly produced him. Neither the Russians nor we could walk out or shout anything. He was the Head of a State; the man must stay. Had he been the Prime Minister some would have walked out or protested, but he was a Head of State. He was told by the U.S. not to make a political speech but once on the rostrum he made a terrible political speech. We listened and didn't say anything. They brought him back and they made it all an issue. They twisted every arm they could; at 6 o'clock in the evening they got a vote on the recognition of the Kasavubu Government as the Government of the Congo. We were prepared to regard him as Head of State, everybody would, but not as Head of the Government of the Congo. This was neither the Constitution [of the Congo] nor the agreement at the U.N. when Congo was admitted.

B Did the Indian Government's attitude to U.N. involvement in the Congo change over the three or four years? Did it become more disenchanted with the way the U.N. was handling the issue?

M We never functioned in that way, 'if you don't do it my way I will not support you'. But we had reason to feel concerned. There was the Dayal Report. There was the way Katanga was dealt with. Our troops were deployed by the U.N., not always to the best advantage.

B Did the Prime Minister feel rather unhappy about the way the U.N. was functioning in the Congo?

M He thought the thing had been messed up but, as I told you, he had a certain amount of regard for Hammarskjöld.

---

[1] President of the Congo.

Hammarskjöld came and spoke about it here quite a lot, and the Prime Minister agreed to send a battalion.

B The decision was in fact made by Cabinet?

M The Prime Minister made the decision. He would have consulted his colleagues, I have no doubt he did, for the sending of troops would have to be at the final stage a government decision. But I said we cannot allow a single battalion to go. All he wanted was, 'troops should be sent'. I was at first against it and then we discussed it privately, and I said, 'if we want them to go, they will go but, in that case, a single battalion cannot go, it will be massacred and we cannot be responsible for it'. So he then said, 'all right, let us send a brigade group'.

The transport of troops was done by the United States. There were delays, but the people who took them were very friendly —the captains of the ships and so on. I went to see them off at Bombay and Palam.[1] We sent troops because the U.N. had got itself into a mess. And also we didn't want to see Tshombe[2] succeed. We were against the secession of Katanga—that was one reason why we sent troops. We didn't take sides with Gizenga or anyone; if we had been taking orders from the Soviets, as often insinuated, we should have been supporting Gizenga. We were friendly with him when he came to see us. But we were against Tshombe; we knew that he was a Belgian stooge; it was the come-back of the Empire. We knew all about *Union Minière*. We attacked him on that and we allowed our troops to go to these places and face the music, but the deployment and arrangements were such that it could not be called the best military strategy; our men—poor devils—had to do more or less what the U.N. directed. They were U.N. troops. They had to do the best they could.

[1] New Delhi's international airport.
[2] President of secessionist Katanga, later Prime Minister of the Congo.

10. The United Nations

B The discussion on the Congo, Mr. Menon, leads me to a new question, namely, the work of the United Nations. I am interested in your assessment of Secretaries-General, of the Secretariat, the Security Council, the General Assembly, the impact of the new African States in the U.N., and a host of other themes. I would like to take these in turn if I may.

You were able to observe the three Secretaries-General —Trygve Lie, Dag Hammarskjöld, and U Thant. What do you think of these men?

M I didn't know Trygve Lie too well because I didn't go to the U.N. then, except in 1946 and then in 1952, the year he was going out. I think probably he had a good grasp of the machine, but he didn't show too much skill in diplomacy. I believe he was much influenced by Norway's internal politics, by the inhibitions which arose from the controversies between the Second and Third Internationals, and other things of that kind.

B Are you suggesting that internal politics in Norway affected the way in which he functioned in the United Nations?

M Probably in his own mind, with the result that very soon he became a participant on the Western side. The Second International tended to be more anti-communist than anti-capitalist. Communism is not only a doctrine or an economic philosophy; it's also the creed of the governing power in Russia, and we have to remember that the Soviet Union is a powerful State. One has to take this into account, isn't that so? I mean, you don't have to be a Catholic to respect the Vatican!

I saw a good bit of Hammarskjöld. His election came as a surprise. He was nominated by the French representative on the Security Council: they were having difficulty in finding anybody at all.

B Wasn't Pearson a candidate?

M Yes and no. We backed Pearson and he would have got it but for NATO. The Russians had no personal objection to

Pearson. We had some discussions about him, but I felt they could not vote for him because of NATO. For Pearson is regarded as NATO personified. That was his mistake. Otherwise he would have made a good Secretary-General.

Everybody was exhausted, various people had been considered and then the name of Hammarskjöld was put up and everybody agreed. Nobody knew him or had heard of him, no one could pronounce his name, but anyway, there he was. Personally, I found him friendly and eager. But I doubt very much whether in the years to come his impact will appear to have been like that of Sir Eric Drummond, Secretary-General of the League of Nations. Of course, conditions have changed today, and people don't accept anybody as big.

B What contribution did he make to the U.N.?

M According to him, he reorganized the Secretariat—although personally I think it was reorganized on bad lines altogether. He brought in one or two new ideas which he believed to be good, but which I think were pernicious in their effect. One was called 'the U.N. Presence'. This was merely an expansionist idea and the U.N. was pushed in everywhere. That led him into trouble with Africa and China. I had the greatest difficulty in persuading Chou En-lai to release the American fliers [1955] on account of Hammarskjöld.

B What were his other new ideas?

M He was good in the sense that his heart was with Africa. Although he was rather conservative in outlook he projected Africa in his reports, particularly in the report he wrote two years before he died. I didn't know his personal emotional reactions. I did not have much opportunity of knowing him at close quarters although I suppose I knew him as well as any other delegate at the U.N. I didn't hang around him. I went to see him when I wanted to see him or when he wanted to see me. However, we became very friendly.

B Was he respected among the delegates at the U.N.?

M Yes, any Secretary-General is respected up to a point; but he was not a kind of elder statesman; nobody regarded him in that light.

As for Mr. Thant, he has had many opportunities and he tries to do his best. I have not been at the U.N. much since his appointment.

Hammarskjöld was popular with the French. He knew them. I think that in the earlier part of his tenure he stood up to Western pressures. The Russians were firm with him when there were differences of opinion with the result that he became more and more isolated. I think his last two years were rather unhappy.

B But you don't see him as creating a lasting effect on the U.N.?

M No. Although history may write him up that way.

B But you, as a man who for many years served at the U.N., do not see him like this?

M But I wouldn't count! What difference would it make what I felt about Hammarskjöld? You are asking me and I am telling you; what inference you care to draw is your own business.

B You began to say something about U Thant.

M U Thant was a member of the Burmese delegation. We were all pleased when he was elected. He was not regarded as a prospective Secretary-General but he has grown somewhat after being there. He has unqualified American support. Yet he tries to maintain independence.

B Has he impressed delegations from non-bloc States?

M I don't know about the last two years, but before then he did not show great independence. People did not know what to expect because before this U Thant was more a formal kind of delegate. Nobody ever thought of him as a future Secretary-General. At first, the British took him up, put out his name, and nobody objected. It had to be someone from Asia; India would not be considered. It was a difficult time. U Thant is a Burmese and it was a good choice.

B I would like to know what you think about the General Assembly, which no doubt you know best. The Assembly has gone through various stages some of which were due to the increase in membership. How would you compare the work of the Assembly in the early and middle 1950s, when there were fifty to sixty members, and the period after 1959–60, when the membership doubled?

M It was more attractive when it was smaller of course! Certainly Asian and African people were more effective as a group. During the last two or three years [1960–2] my visits to the U.N. became briefer but earlier I was more or less living there [1952 to 1960]. I think that after the entry of so many African States the Afro-Asian group developed like this: such groups as the Arabs, Africans, Asians started and one of our officials, contrary to instructions given to him, made the mistake of sort of helping to formalize these groups—having Drafting Committees and Chairmen and all sorts of formal organization. That created trouble. Then you had the newer people who wanted the group to be a bloc and who had very positive views. At one time the Afro-Asian group was probably the most significant group in the Assembly and this lasted four or five years at least.

B When was this?

M Before it became the large group that it is now. When the African States came unity became more complex. For example, Nigeria and Ghana did not always agree, while Egypt is an African country and wanted to be with the African group as well as Asia. The various members had to be persuaded into forming a new set of relationships within the wider Afro-Asian group.

B Was it the Asians or Africans who dominated the Afro-Asian group?

M The Africans I think, although there were no defined group lines or conflicts. We were all conscious of the need for Afro-Asian unity and of our common problems.

B Did the Africans dominate by sheer numbers?

M No, no: they would not talk to *me* like that. They were friendly and considerate, though there were always differences in approach.

B But did they greatly outnumber the Asians in the group?

M Yes. But it wasn't a question of voting or being divided into two camps. Take Quaison-Sackey [Ghana] who became President [of the General Assembly]; he treated me as a younger person would. I was older and had been in the place too long. We never tried to compete for things or assume a position of leadership.

B How important were the other groups within the Assembly structure?

M Before the Afro-Asian group became significant, the U.N. was mainly under U.S. leadership which was in conflict with the Soviet group most of the time. It was really the U.S. which was in control because of the twenty-one Latin American States who were then all in the American orbit. Then after a time the Latin Americans themselves split and though they appeared to be one group they were in fact really two; of these, one was more with us; Mexico, for example, very often stated her position quite independently and there were certain countries—I cannot recall them now—who were always anxious to be independent of pressures.

I don't think the Africans will make their best contribution for some time. I mean that when this colonial business is over and done with they will become more involved in world concerns. What line will they take then? It is interesting to speculate. Perhaps they will go on with economic development; perhaps they will break up; perhaps they will become subservient. But Africa will never be the same again despite nostalgic imperialists and do-gooders.

B Did the Commonwealth have an active group at the U.N.?

M Commonwealth members met each week with the British taking the Chair, but the group never agreed on anything very much. The meetings were certainly friendly and useful for exchanging views. But there were no Commonwealth decisions. India was always in a minority, usually of one; sometimes we might get someone to come along with us—the Canadians or later Ceylon or Ghana. Meanwhile Britain has her commitments to the U.S.A. and imperial traditions while the newer African and Asian countries are anti-colonialists.

B Did the Arabs constitute a sub-group within the Afro-Asian group?

M No. The Arab group was very informal; they met and discussed common Arab matters. Egypt attended African group meetings too. There was no secrecy about these. It was all a question of finding common ground and resisting the attempts of powerful national groups to twist our arms.

B I was wondering really whether decisions taken in the Assembly were really confirmations of decisions taken within and between the groups or blocs. Would you say that the groups and blocs acted almost as political parties within the Assembly?

M No. The groups, with exceptions, were not blocs. It cannot be said that the Afro-Asians ever functioned as a bloc. I always held that we were only ambassadors; we had no right to make decisions on policy. Some of the people at the U.N. wanted to make themselves into a kind of Foreign Office! Our officials, too, tended to become like that, and that is how it got spoiled; Afro-Asian relations became more rigid and less effective. The use of a group in that way is not practical. The older countries all resisted this idea, though we never made an issue of it. We did not feel any compulsion about it. There was no whip, except in the sense that India didn't want to be isolated from the Africans.

B Did you yourself serve on the Security Council?

M No. We were on the Security Council for only two years [1949–51] and that was before I went to the U.N. I don't think there is any particular point in being a member of the Security Council. It has somewhat lost its importance, because of the American desire to isolate the Russians and the lack of Great Power consensus on it.

B When would you date the decline of the Security Council?

M From the date of the 'Uniting for Peace' resolution [1950].

B What do you think about that resolution?

M I was not there when it was being hammered out. We, too, used it or accepted its use but I think it was wrong. If you read the debates at San Francisco [1945] on the doctrine of Great Power unanimity, the most powerful exponent was the United States. I think Big Power Unanimity is a good doctrine because it's unrealistic to vote the world into war by a majority.

I think it's a pity that the Security Council's full functioning as contemplated in the Charter stands delayed. The usual view of the Security Council—the Russians' 155th veto and so on— is sheer propaganda. What does the 155th veto mean? In the early 1950s they used the veto six times in six years on each of the sixteen countries seeking admission. This is calculated as ninety vetoes. They made use of the veto to thwart Western intervention in Kashmir.

B How do you think the Soviets and the Americans look at the U.N.?

M I think the American enthusiasm for the U.N. will now decline. It has been decreasing for the last two years; they cannot get anything through as easily as they did before. Besides, anti-colonialism and opposition to intervention condition most of the members.

B But was the U.N. simply an instrument of American foreign policy for the American delegation?

M That is an over-simplification.

B And what is the attitude of the Indian delegation?

M We are a very much smaller quantity in world affairs. What policy do we want to promote for ourselves? None.

B But every State has a policy.

M I know, but what do we want out of the U.N. for ourselves?

B Pressure for economic development, the end of colonialism.

M Economic development: what is worth while is mostly bilateral.

B But even as a pressure group to hasten the end of colonialism?

M Oh yes; that, later on.

B Or in terms of the apartheid issue in South Africa?

M Yes, but all these are not national issues. They are world issues and the West is beginning to understand them in this way.

B But this is a world issue in which India has a vital interest.

M Certainly. The racial issue has always been supported by us from 1946 onwards. In 1946 we were almost alone except that Burma was with us and Pakistan too always opposed and hit the British on Indians in South Africa. She was a passenger in our boat. Since 1945 or so we called it an Indo-Pakistan issue with South Africa.

B Would you say that the Soviets and the Americans are committed to the United Nations?

M I think on balance that compared with the Americans, the Soviets after Stalin's time have been more concerned with the U.N. as a constructive force. The U.S. took the U.N. for granted. I think that before Stalin's death the Russians used it more as a way of insisting on their own point of view. They were willing to make full use of the United Nations. The Soviets have now got the U.N. tempo; they don't accept American leadership, and they are better at making bilateral dealings with the U.S. The Americans and the Russians, and even the British, don't come into the Delegates' lounge and sit down or anything like that. They are all superior people and have got private rooms in the U.N. They feel themselves to be the Great Powers. The U.N. has, however, now increasingly become an Assembly of the smaller ones.

B As you look back over the last fifteen years, what do you consider the positive contributions of the United Nations to have been?

M It survives.

B Why is that so important?

M It means things get debated; it's better to talk at each other than to shoot at each other. In that sense the U.N. has been a good safety valve and often delays crises. I believe that although there are these disagreements they, too, have their value.

I think the most important contribution of the U.N. is in the Trusteeship business, not because I am an ex-colonial but because it has helped to bring the old-style empires to an end. It has helped the emergence of Africa.

B You are saying that the Trusteeship Council plays a very useful role in hastening the end of colonialism in general.

M Yes. I think it did. The colonial field is the one in which the U.N. can show real results. I am not talking now about the social endeavours of the WHO and other specialized agencies; I don't know very much about them. They are expensively and rather inefficiently run. But they have great achievements to their credit. The Afro-Asian nations have become more involved and potent in ECOSOC [the Economic and Social Council] and its Specialized Agencies since 1957.

B Outside the field of decolonization is there any single, positive, tangible achievement of the U.N.?

M It has prevented a head-on collision between the super powers; there is little doubt about it.

B But you see it largely as a debating forum, don't you?

M No. It is not a debating forum. Much of the greater part of the work is done in the U.N. outside the Assembly. That is why the delegations that are merely institutionally minded today do not cut much ice; none of these understands the U.N. business or the U.N. manner. They think it's a matter of making speeches or giving instructions and so on. It's also a question of personalities—knowing people. It is very much like the British Parliament in this particular respect. In fact, in the Delegates' lounge—we don't use it much now—people said there was an area called the Indian corner. I never went there much, but it was a little enclave.

B What about peace-keeping operations?

M That was a dismal failure, except for UNEF. The name 'peace-keeping operations' was given afterwards to a number of *ad hoc* arrangements.

B Do you see this as an important function of the U.N. in the future?

M It is invoked only when trouble erupts. It can be a reality only when the world is disarmed. By disarmament I mean real disarmament when there is also some system of law and no danger of some powerful group or individual taking snap decisions. Some day there will be a World Government.

B This is another way of saying that in the foreseeable future the U.N. should not get involved in what we call 'peace-keeping operations'.

M If they get a general agreement they can do something, indeed anything.

The Americans and the British are taking more from the new African countries than they take from us older ex-colonials. This is largely because they have found that these new nations will take radical decisions and they are large in numbers. The African nations have strengthened the U.N. for the future.

B To go back to decolonization for a moment: would you go so far as to argue that without the presence of the U.N. as an organization, the coming of independence to Africa would have been delayed for a considerable period?

M Sure.

B It was not part of the general process that would have occurred anyway?

M You cannot separate them. The U.N. is part of that 'general process'. I do think an important role was played by the Trusteeship Council, for example in the uniting of Togoland with the Gold Coast. The liberation of the Gold Coast itself became a U.N. issue—normally it would not have—but because Togoland was there, it did. Other Trust Territories had to go also, like Tanganyika. When we were discussing Tanganyika the British would never agree to a time limit; we, too, were against a time limit for a totally different reason. We said quite frankly, 'You cannot measure these things by the clock; it's a question of how fast events develop.' We said there should be equality between the races in Tanganyika. We also said that it should become independent without intermediate stages. Even some of the Tanganyikans were shocked. Now they all believe we were right in saying there should be no time limit because the

British might have enforced it for twenty-five years! At that period nobody would have asked for independence in less than that time. But we felt that in the twentieth century twenty-five years is an age!

B What about India's own contributions to the U.N.?

M That you must ask somebody else. After all, what was the U.N. as far as India was concerned? I was very much involved with it, particularly from 1952 to 1962. How can I answer you? I may be very egoistic and vain or what not but I have a certain sense of proportion and propriety.

B I am asking you simply to reflect on your own role at the U.N. In what spheres do you feel India made a contribution?

M First of all, we behaved as though we were members of the U.N. and tried to function U.N.-wise. We functioned fully and conscientiously in every committee and we kept our benches occupied. Some said we took up every question to the point of ridicule. But that was our job as members of the U.N.

B You were oriented towards and committed to the U.N.?

M Certainly; India was and I was; yes. But I don't know how it is now in terms of life at the U.N. I don't think the U.N. will bring the millennium. Even if it did, it would not be the U.N. as we know it. It would be something else.

Looking at it now I find that it has provided opportunities for people to get over inhibitions, preconceived ideas, and so on. Take Cabot Lodge for example; he was quite a reactionary when he first came there, not only with me but with other people too. But he changed so much. He, too, had a U.N. sense; it even hit his blind spot about Russia. The U.N. has also enabled the nations of the world to understand and appreciate the Americans—American state policy is a different matter. And also the U.N. has done much to remove racial discrimination at the individual social level.

B But has it helped people to love India?

M I don't know about love. Nations should not canvass love. The U.N. has helped people to appreciate India and her outlook towards the world, particularly in the earlier days.

B Apart from your U.N. commitment, what tangible role do you think India, as distinct from you as a person, has played at the U.N.? Did it help to create the Asian-African bloc? Did it help set the tone of Assembly debates?

M I think India helped to set up the Asian-African bloc. I think it was India—I only happened to be the instrument, the target, the whipping boy, and everything else at that time.

B This was at the time of Sir Benegal Rau, about 1950?

M Yes; it was a very informal group. It was set up when there were few of us. It would have come anyhow because the new African countries came and the larger number of us would have to have had a group. I think, or hope, that in the future there will be more cohesion—flexible cohesion. There were no personal animosities there in my time. I was happy that I was very well received by the Africans and I was friendly with the South African delegation at the personal level. It's very difficult to say much about all this when one is so personally involved in it.

B But it's precisely for that reason that I put the question. Do you think there has been a change in the way in which the U.N. works since 1960?

M I cannot say, because in 1961–2 I went there for only a week; in November 1962 I resigned from the Government. People tell me that we have not the same influence with the Africans that we used to have. We have allowed jealousies to grow up, whereas we should have shown an increasing degree of magnanimity and understanding. We have lost our position but that is part of growth. Certainly you can see that in the groups that have emerged in the world. Cairo has become an international centre and not merely the capital of the Arab League.

B Were you satisfied with the work of your own subordinates year after year?

M Some of them were very good.

B Did you select them yourself or were they selected by the External Affairs Ministry?

M Well, it's very difficult to say, it depends on who. Most people, given the opportunity, can do something; you don't want any 'genius'. He would ruin us at the U.N.—that is not what is wanted. We need good men, men with dedication and a sense of proportion. We don't need self-opinionated heroes. I do not wish to name people but I have worked with people the like of whom it is difficult for any country to find. We all owe a great debt to some little-known people.

B Among the galaxy of people whom you came across at the U.N., who stand out in your memory as able performers and negotiators in the U.N. system? Who were the delegates who impressed you the most?

M Impressed is a wrong word to use when we speak of a society of nations. I was friendly; I got on well with most of them. Vyshinsky cut a great figure with people; he didn't impress me too much but he impressed the U.N. He was regarded as the best man there; in his time he was the biggest man there. Cabot Lodge grew in size. Gromyko, Kuznetsov, they are all U.N. personalities.

B Were there no British delegates who stood out, or French?

M Eden did at first but he was there for a very short time. The British delegates always left it to their officials, and later on, when they sent a Minister, it was Ormsby-Gore; he was not up to much. Most of the British delegates were average and they kept very much to themselves. The Canadians did the same, with the exception of Paul Martin. Lester Pearson was probably the best of them; he made an impact on people; but NATO spoilt him for the U.N.

B What about the Latin American delegates?

M There was a delegate called Fabrikat from Uruguay who was there from the beginning. He was liked but I cannot say he made an impact, because Latin Americans were part of the U.S. at the U.N. They put up Brazil as the big country and until recently Brazil was reactionary. So I think everybody paid obeisance; they didn't get very far. It varied from year to year, and I cannot say anyone dominated. There was the Mexican Foreign Minister who was once elected President of the Assembly; he made some impact because it was Mexico and he was politically awake. They all carried a certain amount of kudos because of their countries. Among the Arabs it was Dr. Fawzi. This was not only on account of his friendly personality but on account of his country as well. He played an important role at the U.N. especially after Suez.

B Was there any outstanding African delegate?

M Quaison-Sackey [Ghana] was the biggest of them in my time. He is President of the Assembly and an educated young man. He acquired a U.N. sense. I was close to him.

11. Goa 1961

B This morning Mr. Menon I should like to turn to the controversial issue of Goa, in which you played a very important role. May I begin by asking: why was Goa important to India? why was it necessary for India to act in 1961 as it did?

M I don't know how much I should talk about these things. Goa was important to India in the sense that it was what could be called 'unfinished business'—the ending of imperialism and the establishment of national unity. I do not know much Canadian history, but I suppose Manitoba was important to Canadians in 1907!

B This was largely an emotional question then?

M So what? But perhaps not exclusively an emotional question. If on the map of Canada you had a conquered part which was still under foreign rule, you would still take it, wouldn't you? Look at what happened about Nova Scotia. You 'took it' in a different way from the way we had to act in Goa. Must I go into this? I am a little surprised at your question. Do you really think that after we forced the British to abdicate we would let the Portuguese stay?

B I don't dispute the fact. I wonder, though, whether there were other considerations? Is Goa important strategically to India?

M No, no one thought about it that way. Every part of our mainland is strategically important, especially if it is likely to be some kind of a landing point. But this was not the main issue. I will return to this particular point in a minute. It was only on account of our peaceful tradition and the position of the Prime Minister that people were prepared to wait patiently for so long, before we ended Portuguese rule. Had we pushed them out in 1947 nobody in the outside world would have said anything at all. They would even have expected it. When the British Empire had to go from here, why should the Portuguese Empire have remained?

The question arises from some idea that Goa was foreign territory. But to us it was a matter of colonial liberation. So the world should understand that we were not acting as imperialists. The real question is whether we should have liberated ourselves with the use of force. One of those clichés that go around is that having liberated India without the use of force we ought not to have used force to liberate Goa.

B Does that suggest that you might have used force against the British?

M Well, I don't know; how can I say? Supposing that a country had been conquered and it became armed, I cannot imagine it sitting down under alien rule for long. First of all, as far as Goa was concerned, in 1947 we were preoccupied. We recognized Portugal and established diplomatic relations with her. We did not expect that the Portuguese would be so obtuse. I think it was one of the earliest countries in which we established a Mission. We thought that both the French and the Portuguese would behave themselves. The French did behave after some time—a long time. I mean, we went on with patience, more patience, and still more patience. Which other country would sit back for so many years to take sixty-four and a half villages [in Pondicherry]? But anyway we pursued the same course of patience and waiting in regard to Portugal. I myself was involved in the negotiations at various times over seventeen years. Even Gandhiji did something about this before Independence.

The Portuguese were adamant, obstinate, blind. Yet, in the final stage, we even told them—I did this myself—that before entering into the question of who has sovereignty over it, they should just come into a room for talks. But they wouldn't have it. And the way they talked and corresponded was most offensive. This was the basic position. We failed to persuade them but that was not why we moved.

The main consideration was that we were holding our own people back by force, quite literally, at the border. If we had maintained the position that we would not allow any of our people to go ahead and liberate Goa, then we would have had to shoot our own people. Some 20,000 or 30,000 might have marched into Goa—10,000 were ready to go anyway—and if they marched into Goa and the Portuguese showed fright, shot them, could our government sit back and survive? It's all very well for Stevenson to have talked high-falutin' nonsense. What is so revolting about our march into Goa? I don't understand. Governor Stevenson could not have been oblivious of American history.

B The point here is that to much of the outside world the Indian action in Goa seemed in sharp contrast with the statements made time and time again that India would not resort to force.

M We would not and did not wage wars of aggression. The Goa business is in the same category as the completion of any national struggle for unity. We had told the U.N.—I had told them myself in the previous year—that India is not pacifist. We are a State, although individually some of us may be pacifists. We had tried everything to achieve a peaceful evacuation of Goa. Ultimately a country must seek to establish its independence. They didn't take our warning seriously. We had no animus against Portugal but only against imperialism. We worked hard and voted for her entry into the U.N.

Various other questions arise. I don't claim to know what and how much was in the Prime Minister's mind; in my view Portugal was a NATO country, the oldest ally of England. The Americans would not do anything to knock sense into their ally. What did they do to persuade their friend to abandon colonialism? The United States, I believe in 1956, singled out Portugal and South Africa for the atomic club and actually voted at the U.N. for it. We fought it and won.

B Were there efforts made by the Prime Minister or yourself to get the Americans to use their influence with the Portuguese?

M Oh, yes, yes, yes. At the last moment, when the troops had already moved, the Americans came and said, 'Don't do anything for six months.' What do they think we are? But I will tell you something of how it all happened.

We still thought the Portuguese would do the right thing [leave] peacefully; it might have happened. We were tending to keep large numbers of security forces near Goa, for they were constantly violating our territory. People love to say, 'Oh,

Goa violating your territory; nobody can violate your territory. You are a large country'; but Goa was behaving like that. Also there was serious agitation in this country to liberate Goa. Oppressed Goans came to be known as refugees, and fugitives came here. Various groups of people would have walked in [to Goa] from India. We were arresting the demonstrators and putting them in prison, observing correct diplomatic practice. Ultimately, we would have had to shoot these people; if we didn't shoot them they would go, and if we let them go, the Portuguese would have shot them all. They shot our people quite a bit; they tortured them; they committed crimes which were revolting. Even a person like me who is not moved very much by atrocity stories knew very well what was happening. Inside Goa a state of anarchy had arisen. There was practically no effective government there, and I think if we had not done anything, in six months' time or less we would have had a very difficult situation on our hands. Unfortunately for us people don't believe this.

The truth of what I say is exemplified by the fact that Goa fell like a ripe plum. After all, however powerful we are in a limited area, they had an army of occupation. If they had any standing or strength they would have put up some resistance wouldn't they! They didn't fire a shot, but not because they were pacifists. They ran away. And as for their own Indian soldiers—we couldn't find one of them. They had a very considerable army, and we had evidence that they had prepared to collect arms—NATO arms. Stevenson may deny it, but they had collected a large quantity. But their administration was such that the arms consignments were not even opened.

There were several precipitating causes. Firstly, a large number of people [Indian *Satyagrahis*] were going to move [into Goa]. Secondly, there was trouble in the two enclaves that had liberated themselves before [Dadar and Nagar-Haveli]. Thirdly, inside India there were the Maharashtrians and the Catholics and others, who had their counterparts in Goa, and they were all coming together. And then, fourthly, the Portuguese started provoking us.

This is literally true, we didn't cook the story up. I know this at first hand as I was myself dealing with Goa at that moment both politically and militarily. They started provoking us by shooting at our people and by torturing some of the nationalists there. Some of them, Gandhians, took it on the left cheek, some others didn't. They shot people inside their prisons and public opinion here was outraged. At that time, either fortunately or otherwise, the Portuguese indulged in acts of war against us. One of the Scindia ships was passing through the sea channel. The Portuguese shot at that ship and they shot the people inside the ship's dining-room; this created a lot of excitement in India. The ship was not in Portuguese [Goan] inland waters but was using the waterway that Indian and other ships have used for hundreds of years. They shot our fishermen and buried them. When our ship went there and they shot at it we made up our minds that they could not do this sort of thing with impunity. And they were also violating our air space.

You see there had been talks between Pakistan and Portugal, and for the first time, two years before the liberation of Goa, the Pakistanis had begun to talk about [India's] spurious claims [to Goa]. If Pakistan hadn't taken a lead we would not have said anything about this. Goa was a bridgehead for foreign countries and the best harbour through which an alien invader could come. When our [Scindia] ship sailed through these waters and the Portuguese shot people, the Prime Minister— I won't say he was worked up—found himself in a position where he had to say that we must push these people out. But even then I was prepared to negotiate. They used the most offensive language in their correspondence, so much so that our people had begun to react in the same way. I had to stop it and had to guard against it myself. The Prime Minister would not have allowed insolent or undignified language. We could not indulge in that sort of thing. It was most unseemly and undignified.

When the ship passed through these waters and was attacked, the Prime Minister told me once, 'I am sure that the time has come; we have to stop this'. He said, 'We should push them off these islands; the Navy and others should do this.' I said, 'I can't push them off in that way; our troops would be massacred. Either you push them out altogether [from Goa, etc.] or take the kicks. You cannot just push them off this little island from outside.' This was proved right, because ultimately, when

Goa was to be taken, we landed marines and they had to scale the side of the island. Every soldier that went was killed. They were a small party. They had to scramble up a side and they were shot one by one, the way the Japanese shot down the Americans in the Pacific Islands.

B What was the Prime Minister's response to your attitude?

M He didn't like it at all. I took the maps to him and said, 'In my view we must act now'. There were good reasons for it. I said to him myself, 'These people [the Portuguese] will have to go out or we will have to say both in Parliament and to our public that we cannot use force, that we have to put up with the Portuguese Empire in India, and that the shooting of your own people will take place.' And then, I believe, another incident happened immediately afterwards. A large body of unarmed people [Indians] were preparing to go into Goa and they said, 'This time we are not going to be persuaded, and if you want you can shoot us.' We were certainly not going to open fire on them. Their cause was the Government's, too. Our C.I.D. and people of that kind informed us that Goa was in a state of ferment and that there was going to be widespread trouble and anarchy. We knew Pakistan was negotiating with them. Panditji was quite clear that the Portuguese must go. He would not put up with them shooting at our ships. But he was undecided about what steps to take.

B He left it to you?

M Not the actual policy, but the action in pursuance of the Government's policy. It was my business [as Defence Minister] to accomplish the operation. I told the people concerned to do it in such a way that there would be no kick-back, for otherwise it would be like Kashmir; we would get bogged down. I advised that it must be a quick sharp operation and not a war. You cannot strike and not wound; I knew this; I had been saying this to myself but I had to get military advice. And they said, 'However small the operation we cannot take chances on it.' They had the plans. 'You say that we should not shoot if we can help it,' they said, 'and therefore massive troops are required.' We moved in a Division because that was the most humane thing to do. We ensured our final supplies in such a way as to be sure that the U.S.A. or Pakistan would not sabotage us by cutting off or impeding our petrol supplies. We surprised everybody by accumulating fuel and whatever else was required. Otherwise the American companies might not have given us the oil, do you see; and if it had gone on for three weeks we would have been stuck.

We asked the Navy to patrol but not to shoot. It had orders to stay outside the harbour and away from Goa, in the open sea. We had information that Portuguese ships were under way and we had no desire to be blockaded or to engage them at sea; we patrolled in order to prevent naval supplies reaching Goa. However, the Portuguese Navy did not appear.

And then it was put out, I don't know by whom, that if we marched into Goa—we called it a police action—without declaring war, our ships on the high seas would be subject to the law of piracy. The Portuguese could walk on board and take everything. I told the Prime Minister quite frankly, 'If we don't declare war our ships will be searched by the Portuguese ships, and we would have to be prepared to go and shoot them.' He asked me, 'Could you take it on?' I said, 'If the Americans and the British don't give the Portuguese support, the Portuguese won't fight.' If necessary, we could have cut down merchant shipping, sea travel, and so on, and could have minimized exposure to piracy.

Nehru approved of the idea. We were prepared to engage Portuguese vessels defensively in our waters but we would not attack her ships. And the American Ambassador, Galbraith, went back and forth, hoping to manipulate things his way and making difficulties. He regarded himself as a kind of super-ambassador, like an old-time British Resident of an Indian [Princely] State. At no time have I come to a worse conclusion about anybody I have had to deal with. There are only two such people: he is one of them—largely because he was so ignorant.

B Did he attempt to put any pressure on you and the Prime Minister?

M Oh, yes, yes, yes, yes; he attempted to put pressure on us half an hour before the advance elements had moved.

B On you?

M Me! He wouldn't talk to me! I was always polite to him and indeed tried to understand him but I cannot stand supercilious people, I just stay away from them. I don't mind people being rude; I don't mind people criticizing. It was not only me; to him the whole of this country was just a little worm under his feet.

We had a Division in the Punjab all ready to go, because it was a reserve Division; we didn't touch anything else. We looked into everything. Even the Prime Minister didn't know about this petrol business [advance accumulation]; he did not have to; it was one of the many things to be done. Nobody in this country knew except a few army officers and myself.

So the Division moved. We told the Navy not to engage in any war action. Actually the aircraft carrier [I.N.S. *Vikrant*] was easily a hundred miles away, far away. Pakistan and other countries reported that the *Vikrant* was near the Goan coast ready for action! One little frigate [I.N.S. *Beas*] was sent there to stand guard outside Goan waters just to be vigilant. The Portuguese fired on her. At first we asked the Navy to take it and not to do anything. The Portuguese fired on her again, and then a naval unit went into action in what we regarded as our waters. Actually, even under the Portuguese system the waters belonged to both countries. The Navy did its duty. They could not fire shells because the Portuguese frigates were between merchantmen. We could not fire at merchantmen. Somehow or other the Navy managed it. The Air Force tried to bomb the Portuguese craft; it was not very successful, but the *Beas* shot into the *Albuquerque* and she sank like lead. The *Albuquerque* was formerly a British ship—she had just come back from refitting before she sank. The Navy took the people off. That was the only naval action in the sense of fighting at sea. The Navy, which is always straining at the leash, wanted to take the island. We said, 'All right, go ahead and take it.' They landed marines and took the place in record time. The whole of the Goan land operation was over in less than twenty-four hours. The Navy was seven hours ahead.

B You mean the Army moved only after the naval and air actions?

M No, it all happened simultaneously. The Army moved
from three different places; one column reached there far ahead
of the others. They telephoned to me here in Delhi. I said,
'you will not enter Panjim[1] during the night'—the Army were
a little angry with me I fear. Internationally it would have
looked bad entering a city at night, and secondly we didn't
know what the Portuguese Army would do to their own people.
So they stayed three miles outside the city until daybreak—
I mean literally. And if the Portuguese had wanted to resist
they would have done so. They had blown up all the bridges.
There were no communications, in fact the Army earth-moving
machinery went on and made the roads as they went. Generals
carried things on their heads. There was very little fighting.
I don't think there were more than a handful of people engaged
on either side and on both sides equal numbers were killed; it
could not have been more than ten or twelve on each side.
They talked about offering resistance until they landed troop
reinforcements from Portugal. Nothing came of it. These people
were running like rats all over the place. It was a dismal affair
that an old Power could not even put up a token resistance.
They could have handed over their swords afterwards and they
could have said, 'You are a large country. You have superior
force. You have not declared war.' No, they didn't do that.

General Chaudhuri[2]—who had done nothing, neither parti-
cipating nor planning—went to the scene to take the 'surrender';
I was disturbed because there should have been no question of
surrender in this, it was an internal matter, an internal action.
That was the line we took. He played the role he did to show
off. He should not have done that.

B What were the strategic factors?

M NATO. We had reason to think that the Portuguese were
talking with the Pakistanis. We had asked the NATO countries,
including Canada I believe, to restrain the Portuguese. Very
little was done in that way. The Americans could have stopped
them but they didn't. We had already taken all measures short
of expulsion by force. We had withdrawn our Ambassador from

---

[1] Panjim is the capital of Goa.
[2] G.O.C.-in-C., Western Command, and later Chief of the Army Staff.

Lisbon; ultimately we had to close down the Legation [in Lisbon, 1955]. We allowed the Embassy here in New Delhi to remain in order to maintain talking relations with them. I met them many times even after our withdrawal of diplomatic personnel from Lisbon. They were nice to me in personal conversation but I have nothing to regret. I do not feel that this [taking Goa] was the wrong thing to do.

We fixed a date [to march into Goa], and the Americans got hold of the news; I believe they passed it on to the Portuguese, their NATO ally. At the same time the U.S. Ambassador here was pressing us not to go into Goa or use force.

B You began to tell me something about Galbraith's activities.

M I think that from the Prime Minister's house or somewhere he must have got the date through illegitimate and unknown channels; they might have intercepted wireless messages or whatever it was. Then the Americans put pressure on us to cancel or postpone our plans. My Prime Minister said, 'Yes, we will postpone it.' He did so to give the Americans an opportunity to advise the Portuguese. We postponed it a few days.

I was disturbed but I wouldn't say anything which would disturb Panditji's mind. I said [to Nehru], 'We cannot have the Army hanging around in Belgaum [a town in Maharashtra close to the Goan border] all ready for action and nothing to do; there will be trouble. What is more, now we have shown our hand, our plan is out; everybody knows that we can beat them; another time we cannot do this.' He said patiently, 'Nothing is lost by a few days.' I took it all for apart from anything else, I always felt instinctively in such circumstances that Panditji would be right. However unhappy I felt at times I accepted what he said or did.

We fixed another date: I am afraid I did not tell even the P.M. this time because I feared he would think it his duty to tell others. He used to be free about these matters. He would at times say, 'so what!' so I didn't even tell him what day it was. He told me that it should be between such and such dates and so we fixed another date and didn't tell him until the actual morning. Actually he was quite happy about it. The knowledge of the exact date would have been an embarrassment.

He was supposed to see me at 9.30. Galbraith went to see

him at 9! I learned later that Mr. Galbraith knew through his own channels that I was seeing the P.M. The Prime Minister telephoned here and said, 'The Ambassador is here. Come a little later'—so I went at 10 o'clock. Galbraith had been trying to put pressure on the P.M. to accept his proposal. The proposal was that we do nothing for six months and the U.S.A. would see what they could do about it. The Prime Minister was probably angry but he didn't say anything to the Ambassador. He told him something to the effect that we might perhaps consider it. He gave no promise.

When he told me this, I said, 'I am very sorry: the troops have moved.' Early next morning our people were in Goan territory. It was 10 o'clock at night when I saw the Prime Minister. Our scouts had gone out and they were in the territory [in Goa] at 2 o'clock in the morning. I said, 'I am sorry, the troops have moved; we cannot pull them back now; I have no means of communication.' I cannot know even down to this day whether Nehru felt happy that the thing was off his hands or if he felt angry. I have always wondered what he thought— we having agreed—because I could not and would not pass an operation without the Prime Minister's consent.

B Was it consent or acquiescence, Mr. Menon?

M No. No. He wanted something to be done. You see, he had a complicated temperament; he didn't like the vulgarity and the cruelty of it, but at the same time he wanted the results— the liberation of Indian territory. He had never disapproved of frank positions at the U.N. He himself would express them, probably quite rightly, in his own way. He might even have said something slightly different over here, although not different in substance. I took it in that way—such things have to be understood. Somebody has got to try and draw the other people's fire. I had complete confidence that he would not do anything undignified or mean or lacking in integrity. Moreover, the country was passionately in favour of policies of this kind. So we walked in.

I think he was probably relieved when I told him that there was nothing I could do about it; fortunately, technically, it happened to be true because the scouts had gone out. I dare say that if the Americans told us, 'yes, now we have told the

Portuguese and they will get out in three months and we can give you our word', we could still have recalled the scouts. I didn't say we could not have done so but I said that they had moved, which was quite correct. The scouts had already gone out and I was not prepared to ask the Army to have them sacrificed. 'You can order them yourself,' I said, 'you have the responsibility. I will carry out what you finally decide but for the present the action has begun.' He was most anxious that it should not be interpreted in the world—and I credit him with the most charitable motives—that we were going in like conquering heroes. I didn't want it either. The Army leaders wanted me to go to Belgaum to see the troops before they went. I told him about this two or three days before the action. He frowned. I knew at once that he didn't want me to go so I said, 'All right, I am not leading the Army.' And then came the question of going to Goa after the liberation. I told him I wouldn't go there until the Prime Minister had gone and the Prime Minister's visit was put off and put off. I never went to Goa at all. I get invitations and requests even now. But I have not gone there.

B Did the decision ever come before the Cabinet?

M Oh, yes, oh, yes, but not the full Cabinet, only the elder members. Operational matters cannot be discussed in any Cabinet. I cannot recollect whether there was formal Cabinet approval or not because the Cabinet doesn't pass resolutions about matters of this kind! Everybody knew all about it but they had not been told exactly how many troops were involved or when they would move. That is another matter. I mean, even the Army may not and need not tell me, you know. But Nehru had informed all his senior colleagues, and I believe he had some kind of formal approval too. I have forgotten who gave it; to the best of my knowledge it was not the Foreign Affairs Committee [of the Cabinet]. But it was certainly known about by all the senior members of the Cabinet. And to the best of my recollection we did have a Cabinet meeting at the last stage, the morning before the advance elements left. The Prime Minister did say that this was going to happen or words to that effect and that naturally they should not say anything about it. Almost everybody agreed that we need not discuss it.

B As you look back on the Goan episode now, how would you assess its impact on India's position in the world? Did it have any lasting effect?

M None that is adverse to our strength or reputation. Afro-Asian opinion welcomed it. The only people who were concerned about it were the people who wanted to abuse us. It was welcomed in all the ex-colonial world. The British pretended to be horrified of course. The point was that if we hadn't finished the action in twenty-four hours it would have got bogged down in the Security Council. It would have been very difficult for us to defy it. Had the Security Council intervened we would not have stopped the action. We had learned some lessons. What happened to the Kashmir business? We had person after person such as MacNaughton,[1] Owen Dixon,[2] and various others who were in effect always using the machinery of international affairs against us. The nation that behaves well is always in a bad position.

B Do you think that the Goan episode and the Government of India's action had any effect on the subsequent General Election? [India 1962.]

M That is a canard put out by the United States press, probably inspired. Some of the critics said that Krishna Menon did it to gain votes in Bombay. There is only a handful of Goans in my constituency. There was nothing new in it because it was Government policy, and people around here are sensible enough to know that all this was propaganda against the Government and the country designed by interested parties to shake our firmness in remaining independent.

B I was thinking of the larger question of the effect on the Congress.

M I don't think so. It was long afterwards that the Congress met. If Nehru had done nothing I don't think it would have created opposition even then, because the Prime Minister's position was so supreme. I don't think it had any adverse effect

---

[1] General A. G. L. MacNaughton, Canadian Delegate to the Security Council, 1949–51.
[2] Sir Owen Dixon, Australian Jurist, who served as U.N. Representative (Mediator) on the Kashmir dispute in 1950.

on Congress. It might have, but very little, very little. And then the U.S. brought it up before the Security Council.

B This is when Stevenson spoke very strongly.

M Yes, he brought it up before the Security Council. And I left here after the action was over; by that time the Security Council had adjourned. It was all over. They could not do anything very much. But I knew this and I told the senior officers concerned, 'Look here, whatever happens, even if it is a forced march, there should be no delay because then we would be in trouble.' I feared that once speeches started [at the Security Council] the Prime Minister would feel that we must stop. And my fear was that the troops would have to march on just the same. The key considerations were that it should be done without bloodshed but that it must be done quickly.

Stevenson could have made a token protest; but instead of that he took it as though it was like the Anschluss [of Austria]. He made grandiose speeches. I arrived in New York to attend the Security Council if necessary, and then when I arrived at the airport there were some newspapermen all talking to me as though we were the criminals. I said, 'This is our business and not yours. You have come here for news.' The newspapermen were not seeking information which of course they had the right to do but were taking up a political and hostile attitude. One fellow got up on the platform and shook me, and I gave him a push. If anybody touches me I react before I think—it is more or less a reflex. There were various pictures of 'Mr. Menon fighting with journalists'. The airport officials had arranged for me to go away by a backdoor, but I was not going to look as if I was slinking out of the place.

I went straight to the U.N. Almost the first thing I did was to ask for an interview with Stevenson. I wanted just to call on him. He was very uppish about it, 'hoity-toity' as they call it in England. In the end he gave me an appointment. He behaved as though I was one of his employees. I went to his office across the street from the U.N. and he sat there like this, hands folded, and said, 'What can I do for you? What do you want to see me about?' I said, 'I don't want to see you about anything; I came here out of politeness; I didn't come here to argue. I thought that having come to this country and knowing that you have

certain views about Goa I should call on you as a matter of
common courtesy. Normally I have always come and called on
you.' He piped down a bit after that. But afterwards he was never
really friendly. I thought he lost his balance on this matter.

He went on making speeches and behaving without diplomatic
restraint, telling all sorts of things that were not true. That is
how I came to consider him although I had started with a
very high opinion of him. For example, he came during a
Kashmir debate and I read out what the American delegate
said in 1948, when Warren Austin had said that because
the British abdicated in India the sovereignty of Kashmir
had passed to the Union of India. They recognized Indian
sovereignty at that time, and it was the correct position. I read
it to the Security Council, and the moment I sat down he
[Stevenson] came up behind my chair and said, 'You should not
have read that out; it was in another context.' It was the same
debate yet he was saying I could not use what was in my
favour! It all arises from this idea that the whole world is but a
satellite of the U.S.A. I did not think that either my country or I
should accept it. I did not then and will not now. I know the
United States has power and often uses it for good. But I am
an Indian and it is my business to be concerned with my country's
honour and interests.

SUPPLEMENTARY INTERVIEW—MAY 1965

B There are a few loose threads in the Goan episode that
I would like to tie up. A few months before the Goan operation Nehru attended the Belgrade Conference of Non-aligned
States and there he found himself out of step with the more
militant new African States because of his declared view that
the problem of war and peace was more urgent and dangerous
than the elimination of the remnants of colonialism. Was the
timing of India's action in Goa, in December 1961 soon after
this conference, in any way influenced by what happened at
Belgrade—by the desire to strengthen India's ties with the
African States? More generally, was India's action in Goa
affected by broad considerations of her position in Afro-Asia,
especially Africa, where her long-held position of leadership was
declining?

M No. I must say, you do think up some pretty far-fetched theories. There was no question of India starting a big war. What India did during all these years was to insist that a calendar time limit should not be accepted for a colonial country giving up imperial possessions.

B There was a special seminar on Portuguese Colonialism in Delhi in August 1961. Did that seminar and the pressure of African nationalists in Portuguese colonies for support in their struggle in Angola and Mozambique influence the course of events in Goa in any way?

M But that pressure had been going on for a long long time in Africa where tens of thousands of people marched and demonstrated.

B What roles did Gopi Handoo and General Kaul play in the Goan affair?

M General Kaul planned the whole operation and went with the troops though he didn't assume command. He nominated General Candeth but as Chief of the General Staff he planned the whole operation. Handoo was our civil intelligence officer there. He was very hard-working and dedicated.

12. China 1949–1962

B Mr. Menon, I should like to move away from Goa to what is probably the most important aspect of India's foreign policy in the last fifteen years—India's relations with China.

I think it's best if we go back to 1949. I believe India decided to recognize the Peking regime at the end of December 1949. This was approximately three months after the formal creation of the Chinese People's Republic. Can you explain the reasons for the delay in recognition?

M My relations with the U.K. people and a great many leaders of both parties have been a great deal closer than people realize, and I would not say anything calculated to damage their reputation. We wanted Britain to recognize China first because they had told us that they would do so. Later Great Britain told me that it would be good if we both did it simultaneously. Burma had already recognized China because she found we were taking time over it. We were not in any race and were not seeking to claim credit. The recognition of China was an act of political maturity; not to do so would be just closing your eyes to stubborn reality.

As there were other matters to talk about, I went day after day, week after week, to see Ernest Bevin. I had long talks with him on the recognition of China. Each time he would say, 'tomorrow, tomorrow', meaning soon. He gave me a date in October and then again in November [1949]. These didn't come off. Ultimately I had to tell him, 'We cannot wait any longer and we are going to recognize China.' Both when I was continually asking him about it and finally when I told him we would go ahead I was speaking for the Prime Minister.

B You are saying that this was the principal reason for the delay?

M That was the *only* reason. The only reason for the delay was that we thought that as a Commonwealth country with particular relations with the U.K., and with a Labour Government there, we should be patient and act together. I knew that everybody except the Foreign Office was in favour of recognition. Mr. Ernest Bevin was not able to stand up to his officials in the Foreign Office. Also his conservative reactions and anti-communist feelings might have come into it. It was not so much for our benefit but rather from the feeling that the recognition should not come in by the backdoor—as I fear it did so far as Britain was concerned. If the British had done it [granted recognition] in a big way, I don't know what the attitude of Canada and America would have been. But what did the British do? To begin with they dragged their feet, ultimately they recognized China—fifteen days after us.

B Panikkar has written in one of his books that India allowed Burma, at their request, to recognize Communist China first. Is that correct?

M That may or may not be true. I have no factual knowledge of it, but it is only a question of a week or two. Burma waited for us in the same spirit as we waited for Britain.

B Did Panikkar himself play any role in the discussions leading to the Indian decision to recognize China?

M Not in the matter of recognition so far as I know. I myself suggested that Panikkar go [as Ambassador] to the Chinese People's Republic. He went and it had its value at the time, for he was a calming influence there. The decision was ours. The initiative was Panditji's. He had no doubt about it.

B You say, 'ours'?

M It was India's, centred in New Delhi.

B Does that mean the Prime Minister's?

M Yes, but not his in the sense that he was steam-rolling anyone. There were consultations and I knew all about it at every stage. We had told the British for three months or so, long before the Burmese took action, that we were going to recognize China. We kept the British informed. At that time I was told or knew practically everything that happened here [Delhi].

B One other point: it has been suggested to me that one of the possible reasons for the delay was the Prime Minister's long-standing respect for Chiang Kai-shek and Madame Chiang Kai-shek, due particularly to their sympathy for India during the war.

M That did not enter into it. Naturally he still maintained those personal feelings. He had no desire to humiliate them or anything of that kind. Their Ambassador came day after day, a kind of priest-like person, and he explained to us . . . but we would have done the same thing if by any unfortunate chance the situation had been reversed.

B And how did Communist China receive India's recognition?

M Very well. There was no question of any reserved attitude on their side; our relations were very good. Having recognized China, instead of sending an ambassador the British sent a chargé d'affaires and at first the Chinese would not have it. We had great difficulty in persuading them. After some time they accepted this but asked for an ambassador. This was one of the things which the Chinese hold against us. I believe that privately they took it for granted that we knew the British mind. I told Mr. Bevin that this [his idea of sending a chargé first] would be to bargain for the worst of both worlds but he would not listen. The man who went could have been called an ambassador but the British Government didn't want to do that. They wanted to show the Chinese that they were big people and to put them on probation or something of the kind.

B And the Chinese, you feel, were insulted by the British decision?

M I think they were certainly hurt by it and they had probably felt that we could deliver the goods.

B The first major episode that indicated all was not well with Sino-Indian relations, looking back at this in retrospect, was the Chinese occupation of Tibet in October 1950. At that time, there was a fairly sharp exchange of Notes between Peking and Delhi.

M I don't know very much about it. I don't think there was such a sharp exchange of Notes. We had never questioned Chinese suzerainty over Tibet. We were rather upset about the atrocities or the strong action taken, but at that time the Chinese had apparently told us that there were rebellions there. We asked them to go slow but so far as I know we didn't protest.

B When you did say that they should go slowly they accused you of acting on behalf of an imperialist power; I was told that the Prime Minister was terribly annoyed.

M I believe so. I don't know very much about it.

B It has been said to me that the Prime Minister, in looking at the Tibetan relationship to China, used the word 'suzerainty' rather than 'sovereignty' and that instructions were sent to the Indian Mission in Peking to be perfectly clear that India was recognizing Chinese suzerainty, and this was changed by Panikkar to sovereignty. Is that a fact?

M I don't know, I don't know. I don't think anything turns on it. I don't know what difference it makes. I don't think there is very much in it, though I had heard of the controversy. But we have always accepted that Tibet was part of China; we have never accepted this buffer State position; we had always looked upon the attempt by the British to make Tibet into a 'no-man's-land' as an imperialistic device. Even after the invasion [of Tibet in 1950], we had said that we did not regret it [India's policy]; you can see that for yourself in the Prime Minister's speeches.

There is no historical background for Tibet's independence. Tibet was never a member of the League of Nations though the British could have put her there—they put so many other countries there. In spite of what people say, so far as I know there has been no period in Tibet's history when she has been a separate State. Whatever may be the position today we had no sympathy with the theocratic reactionary Lama regime either. There was no question in his [Nehru's] mind of any rights in Tibet. We had said to China that Tibet must have autonomy. And supposing the Chinese had said, 'no, Tibet is our business', we still would have had to recognize China's claim over Tibet. That was the real problem. I was away [in London] at the time of the Tibet talks, so I was not directly involved in the actual minutiae of the affair.

My impression of Panikkar at that time was that he was doing a good job of work. Later I discovered he used some words which became the subject of controversy. He has a sound basic grounding and his experience is varied. He is very attractive— he has read a lot, and can write a history book in half an hour which I could not write in six years! We have different types of minds. I think he tried to provide an historical justification for our decision which was not really required. He also argued that co-operation and harmony between China and ourselves was for our benefit as well as for theirs—here he was quite right. It was the first time that he was an Ambassador. That is the history of the episode as far as I know it.

B It has been said to me, Mr. Menon, that during the negotiations leading to the Agreement on Tibet in 1954, Bajpai put forward the view that India ought to try to get the Chinese to recognize the entire India–China border as part of a settlement on Tibet. Is this in fact true?

M I don't think so. I never heard about it. I don't think Bajpai came into it at all. At that time the Prime Minister's view was that there should be no argument about the border; the border was there; the McMahon Line is our border. We told the Chinese several times [in the early and mid 1950s] and they never protested.

B But did they say 'yes'?

M Yes, they said that the traditional borders should remain. And when we mentioned the [Chinese] maps [in 1954, 1956, etc., showing large parts of Indian territory as Chinese], they said, 'these are old maps'. I think you will find all this in a speech I made.[1]

B Was the Prime Minister satisfied then that Chou En-lai's statements about the maps were clear and unambiguous? [on visits to India in 1954 and 1956].

M Yes. What reason had we to think China wanted to pick a quarrel with us? In fact, if China wanted any areas or concessions, we could have considered some adjustments. But we would not surrender sovereignty and submit to aggression.

---

[1] Later published as *Chinese Aggression on India*, Bombay, 1963.

China invaded our territories more than once. She occupied them in east and west.

B But there was no thought at that time that there might be war?

M At no time was there an indication that she would wage war against India. In fact, Chou had said at the time that they were not ready to meet India; therefore, we put this view [old maps] forward. These are the facts about China and her aggression as far as I know them. Chou is a decent person; I may have certain views about China but these have been forced on me by events and inferences about the factors that operate inside China.

I think that one must discuss the whole Chinese question in terms of its historical background. History will say—though there are historians and historians—that Sino-Indian relations are rooted in our past approaches to China. Equally they are now affected by the betrayal of our friendship and good faith. India's policy towards China must be looked at as one of the basic intuitions of the Prime Minister. I shared it, if I may say so, without comparing small things with great.

B During 1954 the 'Five Principles of Peaceful Co-Existence' or *Panch Sheel* were first enunciated. Who was responsible for the notion of the Five Principles? Was it Nehru or Chou En-lai, or was it someone else?

M It acquired its real importance afterwards; it was not a kind of revelation from the Book of Genesis. When we were discussing the Tibetan Treaty the way we should conduct ourselves came up willy-nilly. After all, what is the Tibetan Treaty? Tibet, including the various trade arrangements involved, was the only problem we had with China which called for regularization. We were determined not to be in anybody else's territory, and we wanted to make some practical trade arrangements. This was the basis of discussion.

The five points, as you can see, are not very well drafted. It was not as though it was a prepared formula. It emerged out of the conversations—that is all there was to it. But those five points were the things that we were already working on in our relations with others. We were talking about sovereignty, equality—all those things.

The five points really contained nothing new. Having set them out as principles which should govern our relations, I believe that both sides, but mainly the Chinese at first, started talking about the five points or Five Principles. Somebody called it Panch Sheel here. In my own opinion, it was really a kind of excrescence, it was not the starting-point. It was merely a restatement of those principles which we call non-alignment—what else!

Politically, it may not be right to put it this way. I myself didn't draft it [the Five Principles]—it would not be in its present form if I had. It might be worse or better worded or constructed but the context would be the same. It is tautological in places, repetitive, and not very well constructed. If anybody had anything to do with its formulation—I don't say its wording—it was Kaul who is now Indian Ambassador in Moscow and who was then in Peking.[1] But I think it had no particular author.

B Are you saying that the idea came mainly from the Chinese side?

M No. All I say is this: there must be some basis for our relationship and this came out in the course of conversation. It was rather like a communiqué. It was not a revelation. It was not a creed or part of a formulation of our foreign policy. Certainly it has not been part of China's foreign policy, as we have discovered to our regret.

After all, what were the main concerns of the Chinese at that time? (1) Abolition of extra-territoriality; (2) abolition of unequal treaties; (3) reciprocity; that is the way I would read it. When I saw the drafting of the Five Principles I thought it had been rather badly written. I said so to the Prime Minister, and he said, 'What does it matter; it isn't a treaty or anything, it's a preface to this Tibetan business.' Quite frankly it was only afterwards that the Five Principles emerged as a *mantra* [dictum], a slogan, a prop. It shows only that both countries required it. All this does not detract from the value of its content or minimize the impact it made on us and other countries. Those who ridicule it do so because it does not fit in with expansionism and imperialism.

[1] T. N. Kaul, later Secretary in the Ministry of External Affairs.

B How did Panditji regard the Chinese leaders?

M I think he knew Chiang Kai-shek the best. He, Nehru, was a cultured man and although he may have disapproved of policies he could appreciate personal qualities and affinities.

B Did he feel at home with Chou En-lai?

M I think so, but not in the sense that he would with Mountbatten or Kennedy, or people of that kind. I did not ask him. I think he considered Chou En-lai the best informed and the most 'liberal' of Chinese leaders.

B Would you say that Nehru regarded India and China as natural rivals for a position in Asia, or as complementary?

M He knew that our economies were not complementary. His position in regard to economics was that the development of each country was not only good for itself but good for others and the world. He had the awareness that we were both very large countries, and he often said, 'China cannot eat us up and we cannot eat her up.' Even if in the last two years of his life he had any private reservations, these were due to Chinese aggression and his reaction to a betrayal of faith. In the last two years of his life he allowed himself to be overcome by the Chinese betrayal whereas normally he would have said, 'these are all passing phases'. But he couldn't say that in public. He had an immense capacity to assess public sentiment and reactions.

B Let us return to the period of the middle and late fifties, Mr. Menon. There was already evidence from 1954 onwards of Chinese probes on the frontier, whether in Barahoti or further east, in NEFA.[1] Now, for five years, as it turned out later, the Indian Government didn't attach very great importance to this, certainly not enough importance to reveal it to the Indian Parliament. Can you explain this?

M Nothing was concealed from Parliament either before 1954 or from 1954 to 1959. We thought that these were smaller territorial disputes, not the prelude to aggression. We talked to the

[1] The North East Frontier Agency.

Chinese at various times about the intrusions and they never
said 'this is a war to the finish'. You may remember we
skirmished with them at Longju [in 1959] and that we made
them withdraw. So we sent for the old maps in order to settle
the matter as between reasonable people. Meanwhile we were
urging the Burmese to settle their differences with China. We
advised U Nu to go to Peking and end the disagreements and
he went. No one, no one, not even the Chinese perhaps believed
then that they might lead large armies into India. We never
entered Chinese territory. There were various circumstances
about which I don't wish to speak.

B There were other sources of annoyance in the late 1950s, and
I would like to know your views about these. For example, after
the Dalai Lama had been to Delhi for the first time in the winter
of 1956–7, he invited Mr. Nehru to Lhasa. I have been told that
it took something like eight months for the Chinese Government to transmit the invitation; that, in fact, they never
bothered to give the Prime Minister a visa and also that they
told him that it would not be safe for him to go to Lhasa!
Surely he must have been annoyed by this.

M He might well have been and with good reason, and the
Chinese might also have been annoyed for their own reasons.
But personally, I think that this unnecessary, emotional,
romantic idea of assumed affinity with the Dalai Lama has
been part of our sins in our relations with the Chinese. They
were quite wrong in thinking that we had any designs on Tibet
whatsoever. We, the country as a whole, did not like China's
treatment of Tibet.

B You are referring to the Tibetan Revolt of 1959?

M No. We may have given the Chinese the opportunity to
think that we were like the British and when we pleaded for
autonomy in Tibet the Chinese might have thought that we
were merely acting as expansionists. We didn't know about the
building of the Ladakh [Aksai Chin] Road until our police
patrol discovered it.

B If you had been in the position to decide, what policy would
you have adopted on the Tibetan question?

C 5594   L

M I was a member of the Government and therefore as responsible as anyone else. We should have defined our relationship to China *vis-à-vis* Tibet. We should have said, 'We regret these incidents, and we think it is in your interests to give them autonomy, but it's entirely your own business.' Sometimes we did say that, sometimes we didn't say anything, but we gave the Chinese the idea that we wanted Tibet, or that we wanted to use Tibet as a buffer State or something. The Chinese pretended to believe that we were really in the Western camp; they were not concerned about whether we were friendly with the Russians or not.

B But they could not have thought this at the time of Bandung.

M That may be true but they could say to themselves that we had taken American aid. They exaggerate the extent to which this country is slanted towards the West. The Chinese like to malign us, and taunt us, calling us imperialists and a satellite of the U.S.

B To go back to Tibet: the Chinese accused India of instigating the Revolt in 1959. What do you think about this?

M I think the accusation is entirely false, we didn't mastermind anything and had no intention of interfering.

B When the refugees started coming from Tibet was there any choice?

M I don't know. Personally I have been suspicious of some of the refugees. But if people seek shelter and succour you cannot make them go back. If we had made them return China might then have accused us of pushing their people about or of entering their territory.

B What would you have done?

M I would have made the less genuine ones go back to the border. I think some of them might have been Chinese spies and they brought disease and dirt. They needed help. As Minister of Defence pressure was put on me to take them to build roads, to give them work and sustenance, but they were not much use as labour.

B You don't think it was wise to grant asylum to the Dalai Lama?

M I would give asylum to anybody—I would give it to you if you asked for it—but I would treat you as a political asylum-seeker. I would not have said, 'go back to China to be killed'. You tell *me*, you are a professor of political science, what is asylum? Of his own free will a person moves to another country. Having moved, you don't hand him back, do you? It never occurred to us to do that. We didn't bring the Dalai Lama; we allowed him to come and we sent out government officials to meet him so that his entry would be orderly. We didn't allow him to make speeches here or to set up an *émigré* government. He may have his 'ministers', but we took no notice of them. I did not see the Dalai Lama for two years after his arrival. He is a good person, for all I know; but we should have treated him merely as a political asylum-seeker.

B How important, do you think, was India's reception of the Dalai Lama and Tibetan refugees for the Chinese?

M I am sure, though I may be wrong, that different elements in China utilized this. . . .

B So that it did provide a pretext for the Chinese invasion?

M I believe that the invasion was partly because of expansion-ism. But I have no doubt that they preferred to think that we were after Tibet.

B How do you explain the Chinese movement into NEFA?

M They did it to worry us. That is why in all these conversa-tions they hinted to us not to 'bother about NEFA but to settle on the other [Ladakh] side'. But we had both reached a position where compromise was impossible.

B Do you attach great importance to the role of Tibet in the Sino-Indian conflict?

M Yes. I am not for a moment saying that Tibet was the cause of the aggression; they used it as an excuse. . . . Basically they are expansionists.

B Mr. Menon, if you are so convinced that they are basically expansionists, why, from 1949 to 1962, did India refuse to recognize this?

M The trouble, perhaps, with us is that we believe in trust. Our policy is not to wage war on the frontier. The pressure upon me from all sides was not to increase the Army's efficiency and strength but to cut it down.

B When, would you say, did this appreciation of Chinese expansionism become evident in Delhi? Was it only after the invasion?

M Well, look, I couldn't tell you that as I don't know what you mean by Delhi.

B Delhi, meaning you, the Prime Minister, those who made policy. In other words, when did it become apparent to the leading decision makers of foreign policy in this country that China is basically expansionist and therefore represents a threat, either long-term or short-term, to India? Was it only after the Chinese invasion or was it recognized before?

M It was certainly pointed out after the trouble with the policemen [1959].[1] It was the Home Ministry's responsibility to control the frontiers. The Chinese capture of police personnel generated much feeling here.

B But is it correct to say that until October 1962 neither Pandit Nehru nor you felt that the Chinese would strike against India in a massive way in the foreseeable future?

M That is not quite correct. We knew that from 1959 to 1962 they had what I call a policy of expanding frontiers. That explains why from 1959 onwards we started moving forward and why from '59 to '62 we established ourselves in Ladakh in a parallel position to them in something like 4,000 square miles of territory, planting posts and so on. That began in 1959 and I started it myself. We repaired the Chushul airfield. Certainly from 1959, although we had not prepared for a major war, we knew that we had to build posts, etc. At the same time there was the factual recognition that you could not do any more given

---

[1] Kongka Pass incident in Ladakh, October 1959.

the financial, economic, political, and moral commitments of this country.

B The alternative at that time was a political settlement. This was being considered and various negotiations were held from 1960 onwards. When Chou En-lai came to Delhi in April 1960 what proposals were put forward? Did you ever come near to agreeing over the Ladakh question?

M The 1960 visit was spoiled by the fact that we had too many people involved in it. It was not known to what extent the Chinese came here to sort out our differences. I believe that Chen Yi[1] was a bad influence and that there were great changes taking place inside China at the time. On our side, inside the Congress and in the country, public opinion had become aroused so that it was no longer possible to talk in terms of negotiations. And the Home Minister [Pandit Pant], who had by that time acquired a powerful influence over the Prime Minister, was not in favour of negotiation.

B Did Pant become influential only in Chinese affairs or was his influence more general?

M I did not say Panditji was dependent on him. He was very attached to Pantji and relied on him a great deal.

On the 8th of September [1962] China invaded us—not invaded us—they intruded [into NEFA], and we were quite determined that we would have to do something about it; we could not let them run away with these posts; what we tried to do was the same as we had done in Ladakh for that was all we were capable of then. We should have pursued the Ladakh strategy. It would not have resulted in large-scale conflict. We did not enter into Chinese territory. There was a real danger to India.

The whole of this road-building operation had to be pushed through; the only support was from the Prime Minister. Under the Border Road Development Board we built more than 1,500 miles of roads and repaired over 1,000 miles in Ladakh and did a lot of other work as well. It was an enormous undertaking. People do not know much about this. It was a great achievement. Defence Production provided much of the

[1] Marshal Chen Yi, China's Foreign Minister.

equipment and vehicles. The performance of the Soviet transport planes, owned by Border Roads and in use for the first time, was quite marvellous.

B So, from your point of view, the building of roads and camps and the stationing of troops—the making of the Indian presence known in this area—was the maximum that could be achieved?

M Perhaps it would be more appropriate if I said that it was the maximum that could be achieved in the circumstances. But there was also the question of the expansion of the Army that we considered necessary.

B Mr. Menon, I have been reading the Annual Reports of the Defence Ministry during the period when you held that Portfolio and I would like some information about various points that emerge. In 1959–60 you proposed a reduction of more than 25 crores of rupees in defence expenditure. Given the turmoil in Tibet and the growing friction with China, why did you not suggest a substantial *increase* in expenditure instead?

M Well, first of all these budgets are not of one man's making and they are made according to the resources of the country. I have no particular recollection of it but I know very well that we had no intention of using arms over Tibet. We cannot remain an independent sovereign nation without a certain amount of defence, but anything like the amount to which we are now committed was not contemplated earlier. It may well be that unless the world disarms, in ten years' time the present allocation may appear too small.

B The more general point that emerges from this is that during the period from 1959 onwards . . .

M Just one thing more. It may be said, and this is very important, that for one rupee one was getting more than one rupee worth. We were spending money more efficiently than we had been doing in the previous years.

B In subsequent years, Mr. Menon, one finds the same rather puzzling development with regard to expenditure on the Armed Forces. For example, in 1962–3, while you proposed an

increase of 60 crores in expenditure you noted that the per-
centage of defence expenditure from national revenue declined
from 28 per cent (in 1960–1) to 24·9 per cent (in 1961–2).
Once more I raise the question—how does one explain the fact
that during a period of increasing tension between India and
China the defence expenditure declined rather than being
sustained or increased?

M You are reading it all wrongly. The general idea was to
keep defence expenditure within the limits of our economy. As
I said, we were getting more for the money we spent than we
used to get before. However, I make no secret of the fact that
we were not prepared for a war against China. That did not
mean we were going to disarm or that we were not going to
resist aggression. In fact we had been doing that in Ladakh
ever since we knew about the Aksai Chin Road. Our policy in
regard to China was one of building posts, showing the flag,
and so on, largely depending upon our hope that good sense
would prevail. We expected negotiation and diplomacy to play
their part. So far as we were concerned, there was no more
question of forcing a military decision than there was of running
in the face of aggression or attacks.

B I would like to return to the visit of Chou En-lai to Delhi in
1960. It has been said to me that you came up with a
proposal . . .

M I would rather not talk about it.

B . . . with a proposal that India might lease or make available
in some way . . .

M Please, Mr. Brecher, it is not possible to talk about that part
because there were so many negotiations and so many talks.
In any case I do not want to talk about it.

B Can you not just give me a general idea about the crucial
proposals?

M You are asking me what our policy was. I cannot answer
that because at that time we didn't have an over-all policy
except in the most general terms.

B But at some stage there must have been a clearly conceived notion of what terms of settlement with China were possible.

M Yes, but it was not possible to carry them through. You need not infer that it was our fault.

B But what, in your view, was theoretically possible?

M Look here, after all I have been inside a Government; I cannot talk about things in that way. It is tragic that two countries in Asia came into such conflict. China made it difficult to do anything else. We could have got, not a settlement but a Korean situation established, a kind of no-war relationship. The Chinese were shooting at our posts. They were provocative and aggressive and had no justification for it. They could have got whatever they wanted within reason from us at any time to our mutual advantage had they only tried to get it in a different, more reasonable way.

B Wasn't the lease idea [Menon's reported idea of a lease of Aksai Chin in Ladakh in return for a Chinese lease of the Chumbhi Valley] a possible basis?

M There may have been all sorts of ideas. Actually, the Prime Minister and I had talks on what could be done but other people, some of them senior men, although they did not veto it, said, 'Why all this now, we will see when it comes.' It was not understood that in diplomacy if you take the initiative your action has far greater effect. Perhaps they thought it was not necessary.

I believe that in 1960 China had made it very difficult for those of us who wanted to do anything. That is what I told Chou En-lai when he came here. I said, 'You may hurt us, but you hurt yourselves more; you have strengthened every reactionary element in this country and the forces of tension in the world; you have made it impossible for reasonable people to talk and seek ways of settlement.' I don't think Chou En-lai had much freedom [of action] himself. I am not even now sure that the Chinese did not think we were much more powerful than we were [in 1962]—that the whole of America would be behind us with the threat to invade China from its under belly. It may have been a foolish idea—but there it was.

B Mr. Menon, as you know, there are some students of Sino-Indian problems who are not malicious nor anti-Indian, but who believe that in those last months before October 1962 the activists were the Indians rather than the Chinese. They have put forward the thesis that the events of October–November 1962 were precipitated largely by what was called the Indian 'Forward Policy', particularly in Ladakh, culminating in the Prime Minister's statement on his way to Madras, on 12 October, 'I have given orders to the Army to throw the Chinese out'. What are your thoughts about this?

M Well, there certainly was a 'forward movement'—if you can call a movement inside your own country 'forward'. There couldn't be anything but forward movement because, if they claim every position of ours as theirs then it means wherever we are our policy becomes 'forward'. If you look at those lines [the Chinese claim lines], the 1951–2 line, '56 line, and so on, you can see that it moves! Ultimately they were claiming Ladakh and everything else. So there was a forward movement in the sense that we were active from 1959. We had our posts covering some 4,000 square miles of new roads which were being built. NEFA had begun to be pretty well guarded. The Prime Minister did not say we were prepared for a large-scale conflict.

As for this speech of his at the airport here [in Delhi], neither I nor anybody else briefed him; it was just on his own, the way he felt about it.

B What was the point of making such a statement?

M He doubtless thought it necessary to reassure the people.

B Didn't this cause some difficulty?

M The Chinese probably took it as implying powerful resistance. Shastriji went all round the country making similar speeches. Oh, there were lots of such speeches. I kept quiet—I had some knowledge of what strength we had and of what we were assuming at the time. You do not find anything like that in my speeches at the time. And I had told the Prime Minister in London [mid-September 1962] that I had instructed the Army not to allow any further incursions. That was all I could do. I accepted responsibility, because I knew what was coming.

I had prepared to resign because somebody had to. This was not a piece of heroism. Each one has his own ideas of what is right and wrong. So, even if that statement of Nehru had not been made, I think that when you say we were responsible, I have to say we were not responsible in the sense that we were taking action against the Chinese militarily or anything of that kind—we were on our territory and defending our posts as we were in Ladakh.

B Did you provide a pretext for the Chinese?

M We did not provide any 'pretexts' as you say. The main speeches were made by Shastriji in the country—the Chinese must have taken them seriously. There were [Indian] troop movements that they could see. The Chinese had only two companies on the top of Thagla Pass [Ridge], and our military advice was that we could have contained them. We were a peace-time Army and our main enemy was Pakistan. Even today, I maintain that our main enemy is Pakistan. China, even if she came here, could not stay here. But she will continue to harass us with Pakistan.

B You don't think that this kind of massive Chinese intrusion can occur again?

M It could, but they wouldn't come in and live here. Pakistan could invade and live here.

B No, but the Chinese could bite off a good bit of the frontier area.

M No, they cannot. Oh, they could come down to Bomdila as they have tried to do but there would always be trouble. They cannot invade the whole of this country. There are those who say we should not have stopped them [1962]; we should have allowed them to come down into the plains. But public opinion would not stand it.

B What about the Thagla Ridge incident [8 September 1962]? Did Indian troops take the initiative in an attempt to push the Chinese out of the area?

M That area is ours. We had a post at Dhola inside our area; the Chinese attacked it. At one time our Army thought that what they would do was only to go as far back as the Nam-katchu river. But the Chinese destroyed the bridges and advanced. All we did was to put a post there, as we had done in Ladakh. They surrounded our post and, when we started fighting, they withdrew. They went away and returned with their avalanche of men. They came back like ants on every side.

B When you look back, Mr. Menon, what do you regard as the precipitating cause of the massive intrusion of the Chinese? Was it Mr. Nehru's speech, was it the Indian troop movements, or was it some large-scale plan on their part?

M It is superficial to ascribe all this to what Mr. Nehru said at the airport. It was the cumulative effect of all sorts of things. But more than anything else, China thought it was best to launch a massive attack.

B What do you feel the Chinese hoped to achieve in October 1962, apart from gaining control over an area they claimed?

M I think they wanted to discredit India and the Prime Minister.

B Personally?

M Yes. They also wanted to get him thrown out. The Prime Minister was the best friend they had. The extremists among them were probably afraid that we might come to some agreement. They wanted to discredit our Prime Minister. They wanted to discredit India in the eyes of South-East Asia. They wanted the hegemony of Asia. They found that the Russians were friendly with us; they didn't like it.

B Did they want to undermine Indian economic development?

M Yes, they did. They wanted to show that nobody could stand up to China. They didn't give one thought to the fact that we had risked our immediate political interest in many ways and that we had always supported them. They took it all for granted.

B Do you think that Chou En-lai was a party to that kind of thing?

M I should not think so, but I cannot tell how things work in China. I found him a very decent fellow.

B Would you say the Chinese accomplished all or most of the objectives that you have just mentioned?

M I think the Chinese gained very little because what they now have is a kind of cold war.

B But did they not discredit the Prime Minister?

M They might think they have discredited the Prime Minister. They may have won in the very short term.

B Do you think that by this the Chinese won an almost unassailable position in Africa and the rest of Asia?

M I don't believe this at all. Nobody has an unassailable position in Africa. Africa has still to develop its national policies. What is Africa? States who are proud of freedom. They have troubles like anybody else. But they will not succumb to China's blandishments. Besides, China will outplay her hand. You will see.

B But you yourself said the other day that the Cairo Non-Aligned Conference [1964], if not a disaster was certainly not a major victory for India.

M Did I say disaster? All that it showed, at worst, was that they were not all willing to stand up and swear at China in the way that we wanted, in the way that we would stand up for the Arabs [against Israel]. The Chinese have influence in Africa to the extent that Africans permit; Israel has influence in Africa in the sense that she spent nine million pounds in Nigeria, and what is Israel getting for it? Nobody has influence in Africa. The Africans themselves have to build up their own influence. And quite rightly.

B Do you think that the Chinese have influence in South-East Asia?

M Yes, in the sense that they have power there.

B You don't think that the events of October–November 1962 affected the relative influence of India and China in South-East Asia?

M No, I think that even without the invasion it is still likely that China would have intruded into that territory [South-

East Asia] in the same way as Russia is doing. You see, the South-East Asia position is not only one of China versus India; China is also against the Soviet Union. The Africans may think that we were on Chinese territory. They have not said so to us to my knowledge. But sensible people do not believe this. They do not believe that we attacked China.

B I was about to ask the effect of the Chinese invasion on Nehru himself.

M I think it affected him deeply; it had a very bad effect on him. It demoralized him very much. Everything that he had built was threatened; India was to adopt a militarist outlook which he did not like. And also he knew about the big economic burdens we were carrying.

B Some people think that he felt betrayed by the Chinese.

M I think that is a wrong way of looking at it—he was far too big for that, but he felt that the Chinese action betrayed the world in the sense that it broke people's faith in the cause of Afro-Asian solidarity. But it was not as though he was mesmerized by the Chinese before the invasion or at the time of recognition. He was too realistic for that and he had both the realism and the brain of a statesman. Let it be said that the Western and particularly the United States' opposition to China originally stemmed not only from her being communist but from the apprehension that Russia and China together would form a double power at the U.N.

B But he felt that Sino-Indian friendship was shattered?

M He felt that the Chinese had done something very wrong and totally inimical to our mutual interests.

Nehru was a great man—there is no doubt about that. When you speak about small things or details, you might well say that he didn't know about this or that. But that is a totally different question. It was part of his bigness in a sense that he did not get lost or diminished by small things. He was a great man, a very affectionate person. Up to a certain point he carried everybody's burdens, but beyond that he would not go. At one stage he would convince himself that his position was necessary; in that way he was ruthless. But I don't know of any person who had the degree of warmth that he had. I was very close to him as all the world knows. But I can remember no instance where he let that personal comradeship rise above better judgement and devotion to causes.

B And during those last two years?

M I don't know how to answer that; I think that perhaps he got to a stage where he said, 'This is all I can do; I have done what I can.' I am not in a position to judge.

B And then his own illness seemed to undermine the position?

M His illness may have been caused by this or various other causes which I need not go into. I think that people who had little appreciation of world affairs and who had burgomaster minds conditioned what he could achieve.

B And you think that these people have affected Indian thinking and action in foreign affairs?

M I don't know about that. Foreign affairs cannot be isolated from national efforts, conditions, and domestic pressures.

B As you look ahead which path would you like India to follow?

M I don't think you can see anything clearly either here or almost anywhere in the world. But in India the 'clearest path' is our people. Their maturity is something that some of our leaders who have become isolated from the masses and from mass sentiments do not understand. Panditji sometimes said that the people are ahead of leadership.

B Then the alternative is continued impasse?

M At the moment it may sometimes look like that. But I think it's a great mistake to think you can write a 'prescription'.

B What about Jaya Prakash's [Narayan's] proposal [to lease the Aksai Chin to China]?

M I don't want to talk about it. I am not aware that he made any such proposal at the relevant time. He was a great leader and was significant in political affairs in the past. He is a lovable person but he put proposals in a political vacuum. People respect him. They are full of affection for him. So am I.

B Do you not see any way out of the present impasse with China then?

M We are part of the world. There is no simple and direct way out of impasses. From 1945 we have been discussing disarmament and, apart from this Nuclear Test Ban Treaty, is there any achievement? Then what is the use of talking about India and China?

Why did the Chinese withdraw? Firstly, we killed a lot of their people. It's all very well to talk, with effortless superiority, about defeats and reverses. We did inflict terrible casualties on the enemy. Secondly, they knew that once we regrouped things would happen; they were larger in numbers and therefore power, but they could not keep up this position for long without conflict. Thirdly, the Russians stopped fuel supplies to China. China had 300 aeroplanes flying against us at the time and a lot of wheeled traffic—you know there was wheeled traffic right up to nearly the top of the Himalayas and the Tibetan plateau. No fuel meant no armament. Fourthly, public opinion was against China. It's all very well to say non-alignment failed. Only two or three small countries supported China. The fifth reason was that they may have discovered that we had no desire to take Tibet and that even if we had we could not have done so. In this sense they were the victims of their own propaganda. Also, as you say, they had achieved what they wanted, namely, to discredit Nehru, to harm this country, to 'teach us a lesson' and that sort of thing.

So they withdrew. They had practically withdrawn to the areas from which they had come. The only thing is that we cannot go there unless we want to precipitate trouble. But one doesn't know how long it will remain that way. The invasion had certainly affected all of India. First of all the Chinese withdrew. They abdicated from the offensive! And one or two battles do not make a war.

I think it is an error to say that the non-aligned countries didn't support us. They supported us to the same extent that we would defend any other country in similar circumstances. What did we do when Britain invaded Egypt? We didn't go and fight the invaders. We worked in the U.N. and in diplomatic channels. I mean you cannot expect a non-aligned country to denounce China as an aggressor; China is too large a country for that. Some people did, but certainly nobody said that India invaded China.

A situation was created where it was thought desirable for us to become heavily armed. Naturally we asked the British first; they were the first to send us weapons, although this was merely a token gesture. No American or British arms have been used against the Chinese so far. It's ridiculous nonsense to say that they came to our assistance in the fight.

The Opposition exploited the chance to run down the Government. The fiercest opponents were the people who wanted to change our foreign policy to alignment with the West.

In fact I had great heart-searching when I resigned. I am quite certain that if I had said to the Prime Minister, 'I will resign' but had seen that he didn't want me to resign, I would have accepted his advice.

What had happened was more than a border incident or series of them. We had done nothing to make it a war of the size it assumed. We were not prepared for it. Left to ourselves we would have continued the strategy that had begun in Ladakh and been pursued for eight years and that had resulted in our being in 4,000 square miles of our country. We would have fought them bit by bit, and if we had been pushed back by sheer weight of numbers then we would have drawn them into less suitable territory for fighting. I am sure we could have handled the situation then.

We created a situation where we ourselves were tearing a hole in non-alignment. We should have gone all out to both sides [West and East]. Non-alignment would have become a way of being aligned with both without political subservience and pressures.

Because of defence requirements economic conditions were affected, and we started moving away from our industrial policy. I don't believe that it's possible to maintain non-alignment, by which I mean national independence, in conditions in which massive foreign aid is taken. Apart from the Prime Minister, everyone concerned not only took things but were in a hurry to ask for things. They made light of national dignity and of our capacity to do things for ourselves. They made a spectacle of themselves. There was a drift of Ministers, to the United States or England. It is not a good thing for Ministers to go around seeking aid unless they are specifically invited.

B Was there not an effort, Mr. Menon, to secure aid from both Western and Soviet blocs in that period of crisis?

M Domestically there was also an attempt to reverse everything that had been done before. Anything that Krishna Menon did or attempted to do had to be turned upside down. Therefore we drifted into a situation where we were being subservient to foreign interests and 'advice', in both military and in economic affairs. I do not mean that our military operations were at any time directed by foreigners. The quantum of military stuff which has come from the U.S. has been comparatively small, far smaller than what Pakistan has had from them.

B Did the Prime Minister think that you could take aid in this way and not sacrifice your policy of non-alignment?

M He believed so, for otherwise he would not have acquiesced. And if he had had proper assistance and information he probably would have managed it.

Defence apart, the whole economic policy showed signs of change. Panditji himself rightly took the view that it was a passing phase. We allowed a larger quantum of so-called equity capital to come in and agreed to new conditions. Our production slowed down. But more importantly there was a large influx of foreign personnel, mostly American. This has taken away our dignity and sense of self-reliance. Even before all this the American Transport Command used to have five or six aeroplanes lined up in Palam. I have no doubt at all that it was to convince the Indian people of American power. One day I said to the Prime Minister, 'What is all this? Every country should conduct its own transport even in peace time. There shouldn't be all these American military transports standing permanently in our military airport.' And he said, 'Oh no, you exaggerate it.' Then I think this PL 480[1] should never have

---

[1] Providing for massive food imports into India from the U.S., paid for in rupees.

been agreed to. I was against it when I was in the Government. PL 480 has not solved our problems but nobody will speak about it because they fear it will be said that we are ungrateful. So long as we import food in this way, although we pay for it, it has got two consequences. Firstly, a foreign country has a vast amount of our currency invested in our private industry. Secondly, crores are spent by the U.S. on their administration and propaganda so our independence becomes diluted.

B You have said on three or four occasions that in October–November 1962 India did not suffer a defeat at the hands of China. Yet everywhere in the world people believe that India did suffer defeat.

M What was the defeat? We sent a few thousand troops or so who were deployed in the Himalayan region, faced by several divisions of the enemy. They came like ants. It is quite true that the Indian troops were scattered. The army was not conditioned for this kind of war. They would not wear quilted coats: 'We would look like monkeys', one General told me.

B When you say that India did not suffer a defeat, did you mean that Indian troops were outnumbered?

M The Indian troops were certainly outnumbered. We were fighting in an uphill terrain; even the sun was against us—their snow melted and ours didn't! And we were not conditioned for that war. We were conditioned to hold posts.

B Do you think that if they had come down into the plains the war would have ended differently?

M Certainly.

B Why wasn't that kind of strategy adopted?

M Because the nation wanted the Chinese to be prevented from entering. And China withdrew instead of coming down.

B This is what the Russians did with the Germans in 1941.

M That is what should have been done here too had circumstances permitted. The choice was not available to me. In Russia there was prolonged war and it was declared war.

SUPPLEMENTARY INTERVIEW—MAY 1965

B In his book *Two Chinas*, Panikkar claims credit for having initiated talks with Chou En-lai in Peking in December 1952 that paved the way for negotiations leading to the 1954 Agreement on Tibet. What role do you yourself consider Panikkar to have played?

M I think it would be wrong to say that he initiated anything. Normally Ambassadors merely carry out policy. It is true that they also have to react to certain situations which arise. No doubt Panikkar played a helpful role. When Ambassadors retire they become out of touch with events and their memories become blurred. You always ask me, 'Why don't you write memoirs; why don't you write an autobiography?' This is how it is! Even a very honest person will find himself thinking or saying that he created the world!

B Mr. Menon, the Aksai Chin Road was built by the Chinese across Ladakh between 1954 and 1956. It was first discovered by the Indian Embassy in Peking in the autumn of 1957. Delhi was informed at the time but no protest went to the Chinese until October 1958, more than a year later. What accounts for the delay, if this was clearly regarded by the Indian Government as Indian territory?

M I have no recollection of our Embassy in Peking informing us about the Road. If they did it could only have been at second-hand or from rumours of some kind. I am quite certain that if there was a communication from Peking to that effect we would have done something. Secondly, when we speak about the Aksai Chin Road we are not thinking in terms of a throughway from New York or even a Nepal–Tibetan or Indian–Tibetan roadway, or anything of that kind. The Aksai Chin Road, whatever it is today, was a rudimentary affair at that time. It was a very flat plain, comparatively hard ground to about 10 or 12 inches in depth. If they removed the boulders and tidied it up it became almost a road. We came to know about it partly from reports from our Central Reserve Police patrols, and after a time from air reconnaissance.

B Mr. Menon, how much importance do you attach to India's policy towards Tibet?

M There may be many people who are wise after the event, but I don't think any sensible government could have done any differently or thought any differently from Panditji. Rightly or wrongly—and I think rightly—we took the view that we should treat China as a sovereign nation which had inherited the older China of the Kuomintang and the Manchus, that is to say, recognize that they have suzerainty over Tibet. We had no territorial ambitions either then or now over Tibet. Since we had an Embassy in China the right thing to do was to acknowledge that China had sovereignty over Tibet. The fact that China didn't respond in the same way was no argument for our side to behave like an empire. I still maintain that our position was entirely correct.

We used both the words 'sovereignty' and 'suzerainty'—the words mean the same thing or almost the same. There was at no time any doubt that Tibet could not remain independent in the context of world politics. The only hope for Tibet was to be an independent autonomous territory in an independent China. Our conversations with the Chinese were on these lines. They spoke of autonomy in Tibet.

It is argued that there is a moral case against China, in the sense that the Tibetans were a comparatively unarmed people. Now I maintain that it is not our business to go around the world in the way the Americans do and the British used to do, and try to save the world from communism. We lack the desire and the time, let alone the resources. So, though our stand may have been immediately disadvantageous both to us and to the Tibetans, nevertheless it was entirely correct. You might say that our trust in China was misplaced and that it didn't pay off. This only shows that China didn't behave like a civilized nation.

B Mr. Menon, I would like to refer here to the larger considerations of China's policy towards India. Are you inclined to regard this as simply a border or boundary dispute, or was China's policy towards India in the period from 1959 onwards intimately tied up both with Sino-Soviet rivalry within the world communist movement and with larger Chinese goals in South-East Asia and in the world at large?

M Neither I nor anyone else could give you a fully informed answer. I can only give you the gist of things as they come to my mind.

I don't know how old the Sino-Soviet rivalry is, but it goes back for some time. The basic point is that in practice we did not realize that whenever China has had a powerful government she has been expansionist. Secondly, the New China had come into power through violence and force and nothing else; she had been at war for thirty or forty years, and the bulk of the world's people were in sympathy with the exploits of the Red Army. Thirdly, China wanted to show both us and the world that she was the largest Asian nation.

To China, India strutting across the world stage was virtually the largest and most significant country of a non-aligned group talking on equal terms to great countries in the international field, sometimes trying to bring about compromise solutions to problems between the Soviet Union and the United States in the United Nations. Even at Bandung they found that we were introducing China to the world; we were making China acceptable. All that must have irked them.

Then, over and above all that—this is only speculation—the Chinese want foreign adventure in order to keep up their non-democratic regime and the exploitation of their own people in terms of a 'policy of power' and not a 'policy of plenty'. You must take into account that not only has China got a huge standing regular army but also millions and millions of people in their reserves. Hands who have done nothing but fight for twenty-five years are not fit for anything else. Their minds are attuned to fighting. When a man is always looking down the barrel of a gun he cannot see things in any other terms.

I cannot make up my mind about Chou En-lai, because the Chou En-lai that I had known was a decent kind of person. I suppose that to him it was his country, right or wrong. It is very difficult for me to believe that a man who appeared so sensitive to argument would be the Prime Minister of a country that invaded India. His way of talking about India was not really a party-political one; he did not always even subscribe to the views of some of his colleagues.

Now, about Tibet. If we had allowed the Tibetans to form a government over here it would not have done them any good and perhaps would have done them more harm, China's position being what it was.

B Do you think that for the leadership in Peking this was a *bona fide* border dispute, that is to say, that they genuinely felt the area in Ladakh, possibly in NEFA as well, was traditionally Chinese territory?

M No, the dispute was not genuine in that sense. They had told us that there was no dispute between us and that since they had agreed to the McMahon Line in regard to Burma, they would do the same thing in regard to us, and that there was no question of frontier disputes. Perhaps the cynic could say that even from their point of view it is no longer a border dispute because they claim nearly four-fifths of NEFA!

B What about Ladakh?

M Ladakh too. They did not even tell us that they thought there was a problem there. They now say that the word Ladakh means in Chinese 'the white plains' on account of the white stones there. Therefore they say it is Chinese! It is a puerile argument. What is more, if that is the case, why had they agreed to it all these years? Also, assuming that they did have claims, how do territorial claims allegedly based on history and maps vary from year to year? The '51, '54, '57, '58, '59 lines—an 'expanding frontier'—it is purely expansionism.

B The first serious border incident was at Longju in August 1959. What was your reaction to it at the time as Defence Minister? What was the Prime Minister's reaction? Do you see any link between this incident in August 1959 and the Khrushchev–Eisenhower talks at Camp David, i.e. the Chinese desire to undermine a developing Soviet-American understanding?

M The Chinese knew Longju belonged to us, but they also knew that part of the district in which Longju is located belonged to them—Mitiyun—or whatever it is called. At that time we didn't think of China invading us. We knew that they were not as friendly as they had been before and that they were trying to create difficulties for us. They precipitated the clash at Longju. Then they evacuated Longju. The Prime Minister,

as a conciliatory and generous gesture of peace, did not seek
our reoccupation of Longju. It was left without either country
having any actual hold there. From a military or other point of
view it did not have much value at the time.

I do not think it had any connection with the Camp David
talks except of course that the Chinese always were jealous of
the Russians and they were not going to allow Russia and the
United States alone to be the two great powers of the world.
Even today China thinks of herself as a world power.

B It has been said over and over again, from 1959 or 1960
onwards, that the army stressed to the Government of India
the serious shortage of supplies and weapons and the inability
of the Indian army to take on China in a major campaign.
I don't know how to assess this kind of report, but it seems to me
to be of some importance. The army claims that it was unpre-
pared and was not in a position to engage a major enemy in
battle. What do you remember about this?

M Our defence policy until the Chinese invaded us was
intended to resist an attack from Pakistan. It is not true that
the army or anybody else said that we had not got enough
supplies to fight China. The question didn't arise at the time.
It is quite true that not only the army but the Ministries and
various other people concerned may have asked for various
things they thought were required for national defence. But
that is a normal thing to happen in government. It is also quite
true that considering the size of our country we have a small
army. The actual size of the army from 1957 to 1962 was
quite a bit more than the planned figure.

It should not be forgotten that India had no Indian Army
before Independence. The new Army of India emerged—or
began to emerge—only in 1957. Generally any army is not
interested in 'self-sufficiency' or industry; they just say 'get
this'. As a rule they do not relate their needs to the general
economy of the country. It is quite true that in relation to the
new conditions that have been imposed on us, the army and
its resources are not sufficient.

B Mr. Menon, at various points you have referred to India
moving forward in the disputed territory from 1959 onwards.

I would like to explore the Forward Policy a little more carefully. When was it conceived? I have heard two versions: one, that it was conceived at a meeting soon after the impasse in Nehru's talks with Chou En-lai in April 1960 and a second that it was developed in the winter of 1961–2. Is either of these versions correct? Also, what was the Prime Minister's attitude to the Forward Policy? How effective was it, do you think? And do you consider that the Chinese saw it as Indian expansion in 'their' territory? In other words, how important was the Forward Policy in the process that led to the events of the autumn of 1962?

M I think the last question comes first because it was not a forward policy; for us to occupy our own areas, establish defences and so on cannot be called a forward policy. The position was that we had made our presence known in these areas, otherwise it was 'no man's land'; it is quite normal to build roads. In fact, the army did not initiate the building of roads nor build them, if you want to know. They considered that if you go too near the frontier with a road then the other side comes too near you. We started moving gradually from the areas we occupied and I think we more or less began to control 4,000 square miles of territory, some of which China would contest as theirs, the line of control moving nearer and nearer to the present line each year. There are some people who think that we attacked China or went into her territory. We did nothing of the kind; we never went into Chinese territory. And even if it was 'disputed' territory in Chinese eyes, did that justify them starting a war? For us, it was not disputed territory. It was ours.

B How would you analyse the Soviet role in the Sino-Indian conflict—from Longju and the Tass Statement of 9 September 1959, down to November 1962? Did they try to push India into a settlement? Did they offer or seem to suggest any inducements to India?

M This can only be guesswork. They were conscious of the fact that we would not come well out of it because the Soviets had no military or protective obligation to us at all. We had treated the Soviets with reserve, certainly in regard to defence, forward areas, etc. Even if we wanted to we could not go to them and say 'Now you do something about it'. So far as I know the Soviets did not regard the Chinese as a threat to India. Unfortunately for us, and I think for China, they went on thinking like this for rather too long. I think that in the long run Soviet policy had the effect of forcing the decision on China to withdraw from our territory, even to the extent that they ultimately did in 1962. But the Soviet inhibitory policies came later as they had their own difficulties.

Before the Chinese aggression started they used to tell us not to attack; I told them we would have no choice but to resist if the Chinese came into our territory. They still hoped that we would avoid a conflict. We never asked for Soviet initiative in this matter and I am not saying we should have done. But the Soviet position was one of wanting to localize the conflict. The Soviets never come in anywhere or come out against China unless they can be effective. Their effectiveness in intervening with arms or diplomacy did not appear practical at the time. In any event they were obviously not prepared to lose us. They considered that it would be spreading the war, even though the Chinese were claiming Soviet territory too. That was the Soviet position. Their support to India came later. And I have no doubt in my mind that one of the conducive factors behind the Chinese withdrawal was the Soviet unwillingness to give them support, not only militarily but in fuel and other things.

B There is one further point I want to raise before we move on to the climax of the Sino-Indian conflict. In his biography of you, published a year ago, Mr. George discusses your role and attitude in the dispute with China. Is his account accurate on the whole? More specifically, George says that when you met Chou En-lai in Delhi in April 1960 you proposed an exchange of a lease of Aksai Chin for a lease of the Chumbhi Valley. Is that correct? Is it true that Pant and Morarji Desai killed the idea? Finally, how did Panditji feel about it?

M I never provided George with any material nor did I encourage him to write the book. I have given much more to you in these talks. I have never discussed anything with anyone— I would never discuss these questions outside Government.

I am not prepared to say yes or no at this point nor am I prepared to continue talking about these issues.

B If you will forgive me for pressing these points, may I ask
what transpired during your conversations two years later in
Geneva with the Chinese Foreign Minister, Marshal Chen Yi?
There was a great deal of speculation then.

M Well, there again, you see, they were not 'negotiations' of
any kind; they were just informal talks. The Chinese General
pretended to believe that we had committed aggression.
I imagine that if he was willing and we were willing, perhaps
there would have been a little more talk. But I never said that
I was not prepared to tell you what was said or what was not
said. These things do not hurt. It was not an organized formal
conversation or anything like that. At these conferences people
meet. Chen Yi was most anxious to see me, so I invited him to
breakfast. I called on him too. He called on me three or four
times. At that time we had not reached the stage when one
could have said we were in conflict, though the Chinese were
pushing into what they choose now to call 'the line of actual
control'!

B Mr. Menon, for a long time in the 1950s and even in the
early 1960s there was a widespread assumption in Delhi that,
if any attack came, it would come from Pakistan, not from
China. Who was responsible for this belief? Was it Nehru, the
Defence Minister, or was it the Army Chiefs, or was it such
a widespread view that one could simply apply it to the Government of India as a whole?

M I think it is rather incongruous to say that the danger
'would come' from Pakistan because Pakistan has been invading us for eighteen years. I have never said one country is
enemy no. 1 and the other country is enemy no. 2. I have said
that Pakistan is a danger to us: she claims our territories and
she has taken them; she probes our frontiers and she carries on
subversive activity inside India; she means no good to us; we
cannot afford to take a generous view of her. After all, Pakistan
could have come to us then and said, 'Look, you are being
invaded by China, and we should stand together', but they
didn't say that; instead they kept our troops tied down. In

Pakistan's view the Partition [of India, 1947] is only the beginning. Her idea is to get a jumping-off ground to take the whole of India. Their minds work in this way—that it was from the Moghuls that the British took over. Now, the British having gone, they must come back. This is the attitude of the Pakistan extremists. Fortunately, the Muslims who have remained here are Indians and have stayed Indians. They have never been anything else.

B In your earlier account you referred to the Prime Minister's statement of 12 October 1962 at Palam airport, when he asked the army to throw the Chinese out. One thing puzzles me about this. I have been told by someone who was present that at a meeting on the evening of 11 October at the Prime Minister's house, those orders were actually rescinded or altered to a purely defensive posture in the Thagla Ridge area. Is this correct? If so, why should Nehru make the statement he did *after* the change in orders to the army? I am trying to get a clear picture of what took place in September 1962 before the Chinese invasion, and the events of 11 and 12 October seem to be an indication of what happened.

M I am sorry but I cannot help you. First of all it was you and not me who referred to the Palam statement. I will not comment on it. I thought and will continue to think that the Prime Minister did what any honourable man in his position would do. He had the right and the authority to speak for this country. If the Prime Minister was alive you could have gone and asked him but as it is I am not able to tell you. I think the story is inaccurate.

B You say that this is an inaccurate version?

M I don't say that it *is* inaccurate; please don't misunderstand me. I merely say that it *may* be inaccurate. I cannot tell you exactly what happened nor can I tell you why the Prime Minister said this or that and so on. Loyalty is more important than what you may consider to be my duty to posterity about which you have spoken to me.

B Mr. Menon, in referring to the early Sino-Indian incidents, you said that nobody would have imagined large Chinese armies coming into India and you added, 'that was brought about by various circumstances'. Unfortunately, we moved on before you had elaborated on this statement. Could you reflect on those circumstances now?

M I think when they first came, on 8 September 1962, their forces were not as large as they were afterwards—whatever may be the reason for it. I think that was the crux of the matter. Secondly, had we pulled out, it would have led to internal and external attacks on the government, and on the country, on a very much larger scale. I cannot say that our intelligence information was wrong as you suggest. This notion that their warriors were superior is not correct; actually, fighting numbers apart, they were not. It is like a man standing on top of a house dropping bricks on you. Now the question arises, in those circumstances should one have fought there? However, the whole thing was forced on us and there was no alternative. On the one hand, national feeling was then in favour of fighting. There are times when you have to resist such pressures. But at the same time a country must be emotionally prepared to take a setback and fight again. We were not prepared for a war on our soil like the Battle of Plassey or something of that kind. But the Chinese retreated before there could be any second round.

B Recently, Mr. Menon [March 1965], there has been a storm in a teacup because of remarks made by a member of the Rajya Sabha [Sudhir Ghosh] about an alleged U.S. aircraft carrier in the Bay of Bengal in November 1962 and the Chinese withdrawal from NEFA. There are various aspects to be explored here. It is now generally known that Mr. Nehru requested in writing the use of American planes as air cover for Indian cities. Was this act taken by the Prime Minister himself or did he, whether formally or informally, consult his Cabinet colleagues about it?

M Panditji did not make this request. It has been denied by the Government [of India] and by U.S. sources. In any other country such a wild statement would never be allowed to go unchallenged on the spot. But owing to the fact that Panditji was not there to answer it, from first-hand knowledge, it took time for the Government to discredit it, after checking with the U.S. You are a Canadian and you know the Americans, probably not as well as I do, but almost as well as I do. And do you think the Americans would want to become involved in a direct clash with China or any great power which may escalate into a world war? Have you found any desire in the American people to get involved in a major war or to start a world war? Their leaders play at brinkmanship which, of course, is a dangerous game and may lead to catastrophe. This is another matter. But so far as I know there is not an iota of truth in the story. There was one thing about Panditji—whatever the cost to himself, he would not do a thing of that kind.

B I should like now to conclude this supplementary discussion on China by asking about the most important phase of that relationship, that is to say, the late summer and autumn of 1962. I know that this is not a very happy period in the life of India but I think it is important to understand just how India was thinking, in terms of the attitudes which you, the Prime Minister, and the Delhi leadership in general adopted from 8 September 1962, when Chinese troops came over the Thagla Ridge into NEFA. It was just about the time that the Prime Minister left Delhi to attend the Commonwealth Prime Ministers' Conference in London, to be followed by his journey to Nigeria and elsewhere in Africa. He returned early in October. I should have thought that during the entire month of September, as Defence Minister you would have been in charge of the main area of India's policy towards China, both in the military and diplomatic spheres. Would you be good enough to reflect upon that period, from the Thagla Ridge incident of 8 September onwards, and simply recount to me as much as seems relevant and important for an understanding of the Sino-Indian conflict from September to November 1962?

M China crossed the frontier on 8 September 1962. She committed an act of aggression and we did everything we could to point that out to her. But she continued in that course and we were already committed morally and mentally as any independent country is, strong or weak, to defend ourselves against aggression. And so we tried to keep our ground, that is to say, we prepared to defend posts in these areas on Indian territory. Apparently, their strength proved to be much more than ours. The country had a shock. It was rather impatient and anxious to meet force with force. I do not feel that I have the right nor will my sense of propriety allow me to go into details of that period because, as a Minister, when I resigned I had the opportunity to make a statement in Parliament, but I did not, and it was not a lapse. I refused to do that deliberately. I abstained for reasons that I set out in my two letters of resignation to the Prime Minister on 9 November when I said I should not say anything that would help the Chinese, anything that might reflect on my colleagues in the Government, anything that might affect the morale of the army, or anything that might affect the position of the Government as a whole. I have no desire to say anything else. I regret neither my resignation nor my silence. I hope I shall maintain this position even under provocation.

Therefore, I resigned quietly. I want, now that you have asked me, to tell you quite candidly that my resignation was of my own volition, initiative, and insistence. The Prime Minister never asked for my resignation. Except for the Prime Minister I never told anybody I was resigning, because I think it was a matter between him and me. It was not a hurried decision. For a long time I had been trying to get out of the Defence Ministry because of the conditions that obtained. That much may be said now since it is not too well known, though the Prime Minister was good enough to tell this to Parliament after my resignation.

As for the rest of it, there have been no changes in policy in mid stream as you seem to imply. The policy was to defend our frontiers as best we could, not to wage war. Certainly no one would say, except people who had no sense of responsibility, that this country could have taken on a major war and been successful, placed as she was and her defence policy being what it was. At the same time, there comes a stage in a country's life when, whether you have the strength or not, you fight. It is like a man who lives with his family in a house and then an intruder comes and tries to violate his women folk or attempts to kill his children or himself. He puts up a fight. That was the position. I think it is to our credit that we did put up a lot of resistance. We decimated a lot of Chinese. In the end they went back.

I think history alone will decide why an advancing army, which according to themselves were carrying everything before them, should have withdrawn. There are only three or four reasons one can think of. One is that we inflicted enormous casualties on them. The second is they realized that while they could gain pyrrhic victories in this way with enormous numbers and a great cost in lives, they really could not conquer India. A third reason is that they found the temper of India, the unity of India, the vast area of this land a staggering revelation. A fourth reason is that on account of our foreign policy China found no sympathizers; she stood isolated even in her own Warsaw bloc. We didn't make any cease-fire arrangements with China. They withdrew as 'unilaterally' as they had come. When they had withdrawn, we said if they would go back to the previous position [that they had held before 8 September] we would talk with them and we have maintained this position ever since. They have not gone back to the previous position. They have not stopped their propaganda against us. They have been taking more territory than the Pakistanis have done since. But I cannot say that if something else had been done, things would have been any different. We did the best we could at the time.

B Mr. Menon, in your assessment of the NEFA campaign of 1962 you said at one point, 'Because of certain factors which I am not prepared to talk about at the present time we ran helter-skelter.' Could you now elaborate on what you had in mind?

M I think if you turn your tapes back you will find that I didn't use the words 'ran helter-skelter'. If I did then I am entirely wrong. I feel quite sure I didn't say it but my memory may be playing me false. We were certainly up against enormously superior numbers in a very bad terrain. The climate was also against us with the snows melting on their side and not on ours. The Indian army fought every inch of the way and there was no running away at all. This was all propaganda. The effect of it is clear from the phrase you used, not with malice, but conditioned by propaganda. And even today I am not in a position to tell you the number of our casualties. It has been widely exaggerated both in this country and abroad; you will have to get these figures from someone else. I think that, with very few individual exceptions, the armed forces fought very very bravely. When a division or a unit of an army is surrounded on all sides by a great superiority in numbers then it's very difficult to advance! By the time I had left the Government there was a great deal of talk about lack of equipment—I don't think that played any part in it. The only equipment we could have used after the fighting had assumed large proportions was the kind of equipment which would have escalated the whole thing into a major war. I am glad this did not happen. I cannot go into details.

B Mr. Menon, at one point in the earlier discussions you referred to a possible military strategy towards China today. I wonder if you could elaborate on this?

M What did I say? Well, I think I would like to leave it like that because strategies by people who do not have to actually deal with them are too academic. All I said was that we had to settle our relations with China by militant defences, that is to say we cannot surrender to her. We have to—internally. If there are major internal changes in China, then it should be possible for us to talk with them and they with us. Both now realize that we have to live side by side. But this cannot be done at the cost of the surrender of our territories.

B Mr. Menon, after the reverses in NEFA and Ladakh the Indian Government conducted an inquiry which has come to be known as the 'Henderson–Brooks Report'. I have not seen this Report, but there have been various summaries of what it contained. I would like to get your views here. First of all there was the observation that the training of Indian troops did not take into consideration a possible war with China. Why was this? Secondly, was war with China ruled out in the thinking of the Indian leadership right up to the autumn of 1962? Lastly what are your views of the conclusions of the Henderson–Brooks Report as they were discussed in Parliament in 1963?

M I have not seen this Report—and I have not seen the summary to which you refer. I understood that there was a Report and that it was private; I had not heard that it was discussed in Parliament. I don't think this Report could have any objective value because I was never called to give evidence, neither was General Kaul nor some of the officers who might have told the truth.

The Indian army was not at any time conditioned, nor did they attempt to wage war against China, but we had troops who had been trained for mountain warfare from a much earlier date than people imagine. It was largely a question of numbers, and to a lesser extent a question of some equipment. After all, the Indian army was the British army. I am not in a position to say what will happen in a future contingency. The circumstances are always different; for example, today we have trouble in the Rann of Kutch—it could be said that the logistics are against us. You can't say that we are not prepared to meet Pakistan. Again loyalties come into it. It is quite true that certain levels of our armed forces and administration are conditioned against changing the conventional ways of doing things. But whatever we do I think it is a question of superior weight of numbers and also the unwillingness of our people to do what Chinese people do, because people to them don't matter. It is well known that they don't need much equipment because only their front line is equipped—however many are decimated, there are more people behind. Our troops fought extremely well for the most part. I will not make any more comments on the Report you mention or on the things implied. I said this much because of the 'helter-skelter' phrase of yours and as a small tribute to the men who fought so gallantly although small in numbers and in inhospitable terrain. All I will say about General Kaul is that the Indian army is poorer without him. He was not an armchair commander and he functioned with great courage and daring on those incredible heights—some day the country will recognize it.

B I have just one more question on China, Mr. Menon, and it concerns public opinion. Amongst other things I am trying to explore the role of public opinion and pressure groups on India's foreign policy, and China strikes me as an important illustration. After the incident at the Kongka Pass in October 1959 and the Prime Minister's disclosures in Parliament about earlier tension with China, Indian public opinion, the Press, and certain pressure groups began to call for a strong line. You referred yourself to its influence at the time of the Nehru–Chou En-lai talks in Delhi in April 1960 and after. How would you evaluate the role of public opinion in India's Chinese policy in general?

M Well, public opinion or a great part of it had a sense of humiliation or of being betrayed. But there is no doubt that groups who were antagonistic to the Prime Minister, who are against our social policies and against non-alignment, utilized this position. At that time American influence in this country was anti-Indian. These groups exploited the Chinese invasion in order to influence opinion against the Prime Minister, against me, and against others. We should not have yielded to that. But they zealously cultivated the view that America came to the rescue of India.

Now it is true that not a matchstick was used against the Chinese that came from abroad or that we did not have ourselves. Whatever did come came after the Chinese withdrawal. There was no time for newer supplies and even less for their being 'converted'. Therefore, to cultivate the idea that when we were in difficulties the Americans came to our rescue is entirely wrong. Public opinion was shocked at the idea that we had incurred this reverse. In war time that kind of thing happens.

B I had in mind the restraint on the Indian Government's freedom of action in coming to a political settlement with the Chinese between 1959 and 1962. That is the essence of my question. Was the freedom of Mr. Nehru and the Cabinet limited by this constant pressure of public opinion in general, the Press and other kinds of interest groups, which in effect said, 'Do not pursue any policy which involves any kind of concessions?'

M We could not and would not make unilateral territorial concessions; they would mean surrender of sovereignty. The Prime Minister should perhaps have been left with more room for manœuvre. I don't say he didn't have it, I cannot say that, and I would not like to shift the burden on to anybody else. I am not prepared to say to you what freedom of manœuvre I had or what freedom of manœuvre the Government had or anything of that kind. Basically the action of the Chinese was such that it helped every anti-progressive element inside India and obstructed the reasonable progress of India and its peace policies. That was probably China's motive—to throw us into confusion. This country stood the ordeal well and will do so again if the need arises.

13. Indian Foreign Policy and World Politics: a Potpourri

B Today I would like to turn to a related theme, namely the proper foreign policy for India in the light of changes that have occurred in world politics since you left the Indian Cabinet [November 1962]. I am thinking of three things: the *détente* between America and the Soviet Union, the emergence of Africa as an important factor in world politics, and the Sino-Soviet split. What in your view should be the proper Indian response to these changed circumstances?

M We are going through a period when there are no final solutions to anything. Sometimes a deadlock is a solution, in other words trying not to arouse matters or to allow the situation to worsen. When a man is in terrible pain, he cannot always be cured of the cause of the pain but if he can move about a little that gives him a certain amount of relief; that is the position of the world at the present time. And when people tell me about a deadlock I ask them what problem of international tension has been solved in this world since the war apart from Trieste?

B That is a highly pessimistic view.

M It is not a pessimistic but a realistic view of things. In certain conditions you have to do certain things; you cannot expect a person who is suffering from typhoid to get up and run a hundred yard race.

B But cannot one argue that since the end of 1962 the cold war between the U.S. and the Soviet Union has moved into a stage of *détente*—almost indeed of friendship?

M That is what you say; I don't feel justified in thinking so.

B Then what is your view of that relationship?

M Until the U.S. is able to give up the idea of running the world—and not use the words 'racial and national superiority' or 'world dominion'—there is little hope for the world. I think that by electing a Labour Government the British people opened up an opportunity. If the Labour Government of 1945 had not chosen to take on the mantle of Churchill the world would have been a different place. Later Canada belied our hopes; I had hoped and expected that Canada would become a non-aligned country even though close to the West. She did to an extent, but unfortunately Lester Pearson took on this NATO business. And it must be remembered that Canada is European. Also they have a very powerful neighbour.

Britain today exerts little influence with the U.S. Recent events have highlighted this. In 1946 Britain could have asserted herself and she would have become a kind of Western type of non-aligned country which would have been effective in Europe and the world instead of being a satellite of America. I have the French in mind here: however, the French president had not the political approach to capitalize on the situation. He was tied up with imperial war in Algeria and all kinds of other things helped to spoil his position. At that time it was touch and go for Britain. She could have adopted her own kind of non-alignment.

B You still see that as a hope for the world?

M Of course.

B I think we have come to the end of that phase.

M I don't know. Of course, you can say 'who are you to say all these things; you may not be right'.

B But this represents a point of view.

M Mr. Brecher, I don't represent any point of view as you say, meaning the view of India. I just look at these things [as an individual]. If in seventeen years we have not only made no progress towards peaceful living as nations but have made things worse, in the sense of the increase in the quantity and destructive potential of armaments and their proliferation—now we have moved away from the position of limited disarmament—then it's a great mistake to think that we have passed the stage of world war.

B The danger undoubtedly still exists. The question is whether the dangers are greater now than they were five or ten years ago.

M They are not greater, and I think there have been slight improvements in the sense of what happens on either side of the bloc when there is slight provocation.

B Hasn't the leadership in both America and the Soviet Union been educated to understand the menace of nuclear weapons and the danger of using them?

M What the world is concerned about is not their education! The existence, the development and the stockpile [of nuclear weapons], the speed of their use, problems of proliferation, radiation from tests, and the continuing tensions, these are what worry and menace the world.

B Didn't Cuba prove this?

M I don't know what Cuba proved. It has proved that the Monroe Doctrine no longer works!

B Do you agree that both the super powers now have a more mature kind of leadership?

M Yes, but the situation has become very complex. This mature leadership might have dealt with the situation ten years ago but the maturity has not been proportionate with the increase in complexity.

So far as the *détente* is concerned, I think the contribution of the late President Kennedy will be found, historically, to have been much exaggerated. In India we felt he made a great contribution because we liked the idea of a young President who fought his way up and he spoke well. My Prime Minister thought that just as being friends would bring strength, this would give strength too. It was a break from the past, like the Labour Government in Britain. We cannot say what would have happened had Kennedy not died.

In my opinion American policy has basically changed very little towards us, towards the Soviet Union, towards anybody. I think that the failure at Vienna [1961] was an indication of this. All that has happened between the Americans and the

Soviet Union, in terms of actual advance, has been: (1) the limitation on nuclear explosions—although the fact that the Americans won't give way on underground tests has also been an indication; (2) some sort of agreement with regard to outer space—but there again it is very limited; and (3) the voluntary agreement of each side to limit the production of fissile material. These are the only three things on which there has been agreement. There has been no agreement, not even an approach to an agreement, on Korea, on Germany, on colonialism, on disarmament as a whole, on world policy. The United States and the Soviet Union have not come to any agreement about not competing for influence in Africa, Latin America, or elsewhere, which might justify the hope of a world free from fear of war and tensions.

B But there has been a substantial easing of tension and propaganda.

M I don't think it's deep enough to make a change amounting to a *détente*.

B Let me put it this way: has it been deep enough for Indian policy to respond?

M We have responded since de-Stalinization [1956] because we believe that Russia has become 'liberalized', added to which were the late Prime Minister's hopes of the Kennedy regime; Kennedy did not live long enough to reveal whether those hopes were justified. The trouble was that we preferred to ignore the terrible significance of the situation in Vietnam. We gave the impression that we took a rather different view about what was going to happen in South Vietnam than the situation and the facts warranted. We took a different view of the Laotian question after 1962 because of our conflict with China and the impact of China's betrayal. I think that this is where we are wrong. Foreign policies cannot be pursued in the way Pakistan pursues them: that is, the enemy of your enemy is your friend. The Soviet Union has not made the same mistake.

Our policy in Indo-China should be governed by the Geneva principles, by our reaction to intervention, by our special position both as an Asian country and chairman of the I.C.C., and not least by anti-colonialism and by humanitarian sympathies!

In the old days this country would have been shocked and would have expressed this strongly and would have taken steps to make the co-chairmen of the Geneva Conference take action. We would have used our relations with Britain and the past history of the Geneva settlement to urge Britain to do her duty as a co-chairman. We could also have helped to get Britain and the Soviets to work together.

It's shocking, Mr. Brecher, it's shocking that a great and powerful country should go and bomb a little country to smithereens—even if we assumed that the American case is sound, which they admitted was not so even in Congress. The great American Fleet had no business to go into the Gulf of Tonkin [August 1964]. I myself wish that the North Vietnam-ese had let well alone, but they were within their rights. They were also apprehensive of bomber raids or a blockade by the Seventh Fleet. Tonkin Bay is no more the open sea than Hud-son's Bay or Spencer's Bay in Australia or the Gulf of Cambay in India, and therefore the Americans had no business to send their warships there. Secondly—I say it because nobody else seems to have said it—American concentrated bombing des-troyed two islands completely; they destroyed the best part of four cities. Vietnam had probably asked for it by torpedo-ing the *Maddox*, but a big and great country like the United States has no business to go knocking a little State like that. And anyway, God didn't give the right to the English and the Canadians and the Indians and the Americans to police the world. If it were really such a bad matter [the attack on U.S. torpedo boats], she should have gone to the U.N. or she should have agreed to the calling of a Geneva Conference immediately. It's not that America was invaded or threatened.

I saw Kennedy [in 1962]; unfortunately the whole of the discussion was on Vietnam. It was not of my choosing; I put forward our point of view and he didn't like it. He took the view, 'Whatever we do, you think we are wrong.' I said to him with regard to South Vietnam, 'The only position that we can hope you will take is to withdraw.' Actually, though I didn't tell him this, is it not the case that the Americans have no business being in Vietnam [in the first place]? They went there on their basic supposition that they have to stop communism by force. You cannot stop communism by war-making. They do not try to stop communism by waging war against Russia and China.

Therefore in spite of the big effects or changes that you allege have reduced world tension, in my opinion few of these changes are real. This is indicated by the attitude of the United States in regard to U.N. dues. Leaving aside the legal and other questions, if there is a *détente* of any kind the Americans would not push the point as far as the near break-up of the U.N., and I am telling you from my own personal knowledge that the Russians would not have stayed in the U.N. under the condition that the U.S. thought they could impose. They seemed to have made up their minds that anybody could do very much what they liked—'We will not pay, we will not agree to this principle.' And I had to do the best I could, as far as a person can in retirement, to make our people understand this. The Americans would not have gone into the Congo [Stanleyville, December 1964] if there had been a *détente*. I don't believe for one moment this sob-story about saving every white man or woman; it does not wash. I talked to Dulles and Eisenhower and everybody else in 1955; they didn't care too much about those American prisoners in China, certainly not enough to allow the prisoners' relations to go to see them. I cared more for them than they did; I did my best with both President Eisenhower and Mr. Dulles; they were quite prepared to make them a kind of pawn in the political game. I have very strong feelings about this.

Now we come to Africa. Personally, our Government and the Prime Minister [Nehru] have been more than happy about the resurgence of African countries and their sense of national pride and confidence. They speak out. They commit themselves to bold measures by the U.N. They speak out and don't care whether those who have ruled them in the past are pleased or not. I say the very best of luck to them. They would do the same thing with regard to the Russians too, the same as we did when they were opposed to us on Korea. If they are hobnobbing with China or with Israel and it doesn't please the Americans or the Russians they say, 'Well, that is our policy.'

It is not understood that Africa is a continent with a large number of national States. Nationalism is a strong factor in Africa. African freedom is built in the context of the imperialism which the Africans resisted. The Empire took Indians to these places in Africa either as labour or as private traders. Some day there will have to be some working arrangement with those successor States. But African decisions will be what matter.

Unfortunately for some of our people, largely taking our cue and our terminology from the West, we thought of Africa in the same way as the West had thought of it. Speaking to students today I always say that we must study African history and recognize that these people, like ourselves, spring from ancient civilizations. They contributed to the building of the world from at least 4,000 years ago, not in an anthropological sense, but, for example, in the development of mineralogy. Very recently, until 500 years ago, European nations would just laugh at all this. Not viciously but in ignorance they thought of subject people as inferior races born to be ruled. Unless we understand this, unless we think that a Hottentot or a Bushman was not just taken and 'washed' by a missionary and given 'civilization', we won't get anywhere. That is the problem of the older nations. We lacked understanding [of Africa]. And unfortunately for us, our Prime Minister's health became bad [1962] and the best he could do was to prevent things getting any worse.

After the Prime Minister's death we made a mess of Ceylon.[1] In terms of foreign policy it means this: the talk that became current after Panditji's death about nuclear guarantees and nuclear umbrellas has not helped us to ensure protection as indeed it cannot. On the other hand, it has adversely affected our diplomatic capacity and prestige. If this talk had not come to a halt, the British would be talking of nuclear clubs into which we would be drawn. It's a fact that our Government did realize this quite soon. I believe we still have prestige despite all this talk. Cairo [the Non-Aligned Conference, October 1964] was not in the same class as Belgrade so far as India was concerned. We did not make much of an impact. But, of course, conditions were different.

Policy has not changed. The present Prime Minister [Shastri] has repeatedly said so. We are still non-aligned but non-alignment must be evident in action. You saw how badly the

[1] Indo-Ceylon Agreement on persons of Indian origin, October 1964.

Prime Minister was advised at Cairo in the proposal about sending a delegation to China from the Conference—there was no preparation or consultations with other non-aligned States or even with Nasser. What is more, we may not only be inconsistent but rather immature. I fear it will be found that the loss of our prestige will not even help the U.S. What is the use of India to them? Just as a country it is no use to them whatever. It's only one vote. India was valuable to them only because we had a position in the world and took initiatives and were in good standing with the principal non-aligned nations.

B And that has been dissipated?

M I would not say that. Time will tell.

B Has it been dissipated because of the tarnished image of India in the world after October 1962 or because of the manner in which policy has been implemented in the last six months?

M It is not a question of image alone. Since the late Prime Minister's time we have been functioning less potently or not at all. At the Eighteen-Nation Conference [in Geneva], together with Brazil we were holding a key position. We supplied what was required for the Committee of Eight [the neutrals on disarmament] and that group was holding the conference together. Harriman or Rusk should be aware of this. There have been occasions, as in the case of the nuclear guarantee, where it appeared to me that we were losing our position.

B And that has changed?

M Somewhat. On the 'plus' side this Government, this Parliament, this country has not said and dare not say that we are departing from the position of non-alignment.

B But, as you say, it is far more important that one implement this properly rather than cling to the words.

M That may be so but the end of the world has not come, has it? Furthermore it is important that the 'words' as you call them are not dropped. They are the indications that we cannot lose sight of non-alignment. In spite of all this India has very considerable prestige in people's minds; they know that we have suffered a setback on account of China's aggression and on account of the death of the Prime Minister [Nehru]. I will not do anything to embarrass the Government. It would not be in the country's interests. Also it would not help or change policies. When I have the opportunity, as when Shastriji frequently talks to me, I tell him what I know and what I believe.

B I am curious to know why you should be so solicitous of a Government which has failed to implement the policies associated with non-alignment.

M I fear the way you state it does not represent the facts. I am not in opposition. The right thing to do is to do what can be done by friendly and constructive reactions and approach. It is best to help our people and politicians understand that if we do not correct ourselves this may lead to changes in policy. The talk of the nuclear umbrella has finished; the Government has decided it will not make nuclear bombs. Responsible people should not act as if they were frustrated. It is important to remember that such impact as I could bring on the Government and others would practically disappear if I behaved as a critic. Had I acted like that I would not have been able to help the reversal on the question of Chinese representation at the U.N. or on the nuclear club issue and things of that kind. I believe that it is not my job to deal with government policy. The Government must be free to act and as far as I can I should help our people seek socialism and peace. It doesn't worry me personally as I am not an office-seeker.

You say the world has changed. How? According to you there is a *détente* between the United States and the Soviet Union. This is of a limited character. In fact there was a possibility of a *détente* which has not flowered. The emergence of Africa is a very welcome fact and if policy were properly handled and our relations carefully nursed we would be a force for good at the U.N.

I must accept some responsibility. I should have occupied myself more with files and records. Some people used to tell me that I was not fair to posterity and that I should not suffer from undue modesty. Some time before the end, when discussing a particular matter with the Prime Minister, I told him, 'there is only one thing I reproach myself for, that I should have stood up to you more', and, generously, he agreed. I did not always contribute what I could because I preferred or thought it more appropriate not to be insistent. But Pandit Nehru often sensed these things and he reacted to them in his own way afterwards. He was wonderful in that way—as in so many other ways. You may say, 'Why didn't you, was it cowardice?' Perhaps; it is not for me to judge. To a certain extent it was due to the special kind of personal relationship we had; I could not bear to disagree with Nehru beyond a certain point. In small matters, yes. I felt he had the responsibility and I never tried to 'persuade' him. I argued and stated my position. He was amenable to argument.

There was also the Sino-Soviet complication. This was the result of an outworn world trying to force itself on a newer one. China is in the Stalinist period; the U.S.S.R. is in the post-Khrushchev period. The Sino-Soviet complication also arises from the out-of-date expansionism of China and from the regrettable fact that the policies of the Soviets and their influence in the U.N. have served to isolate China. Further, it arises from the fact that people like Ronning [the former Canadian High Commissioner to India], who are friendly to the Chinese, are not sufficiently outspoken in their dealings with them to tell them that it would be to everybody's advantage if they changed their methods. It also arises from the fact that China's economic condition is not as good as it might be. China's attitude too is partly responsible.

China believes that the United States is set on humiliating her. No big nation will accept humiliation. This I think briefly sums up the world's troubles where China is concerned. The approach in the past, ever since the new China emerged, of treating China as though she had misbehaved like a little schoolgirl has not helped. China in return has behaved like a bully and has threatened weaker nations. This is my opinion for what it is worth. My view is not cynical but realistic. At the same time there have been no basic changes of policy in India.

I always tell students that you cannot negotiate unless you are yourself prepared to be persuaded—that was part of India's armoury. It accounts for some of our modest contributions and achievements. I think it was largely brought about through the personality of the Prime Minister—not in the sense that the world accepted him as a great Solomon or Plato or Aristotle or anything of that kind, but he was a man who had behind him the love and support of vast numbers of people. He was accepted as a man who was responsible and who was respected by other countries. The Americans may have disliked him sometimes but they knew the Russians liked him; the Russians may have been irritated and suspicious but they knew about his influence with America. Foreign policy in this country soon grew into a matter of pride and the population was behind it. The idea that we were a new nationalist country, a pioneer in the forefront of liberated countries, that we were prepared to raise our voice for Morocco, Algeria, Indonesia, or Egypt, was a spontaneous thing. It should be remembered that we produced something in a difficult situation. More than that—apart from Adlai Stevenson—practically everyone I dealt with would say that we had integrity and convictions. We were often ridiculed on the grounds that we held them to excess. Men like Harriman, Cabot Lodge, Eisenhower, Dean Rusk, Dulles—particularly Dulles, I believe—basically held this view. The latter, in my opinion, was a very honest man, but honesty can lead to all sorts of strange consequences. Dulles was frank; maybe that frankness came from arrogance, or from the knowledge that he was virtually the President of the United States.

All these people believed that we had integrity. We were perhaps the one country at the U.N. that could speak separately to the Russians and the Americans on a problem which concerned them both and learn both their closely held views. I have known of no instance, whether in Geneva, New York, or anywhere else, where the Americans were unwilling to speak to us. Contrary to what you read in some of their papers, I received both affection and trust from them. The same applied to the Russians. It is my belief that neither felt we would tell tales.

The United States were quite willing to push us into trouble or castigate us as trouble-makers. For example, take the troika business. The Russians feared that we were really Westerners in our approach—although to them we were at least the best of the Westerners. Even today they have this feeling, and I think with some justification—the English language contributes to a certain extent—despite our integrity and the fact that in the early days we carried Afro-Asia with us. They used to say sometimes, 'If Krishna Menon doesn't agree, we cannot do anything in the U.N.' This was no doubt a great exaggeration although it was not said sarcastically. Then came the influx into the U.N. of the new countries. We never thought of this as a catastrophe or as a disturbing or upsetting phenomenon. Indeed it was a very good thing and led to the feeling of greater equality. We promoted it ourselves. A country like ours ought to recognize quite consciously that sometimes centres of power shift.

B May I intrude for a moment? The analysis that you have given of these three factors, the emergence of Africa, the *détente*, and Soviet-Chinese tension, suggests that there has not been a basic change, though there have been some changes. Now, if that is so, it would follow that Indian policy towards the world powers in 1965 and beyond ought to be the same as India pursued in the middle and late 1950s.

M Policies can never be the same; it depends of course what you mean by policies.

B Not specific policies, but the Indian posture in the world should be the same as in 1950.

M The Indian posture in the world is one that should always reflect India's national independence, respect for the nationhood of others, and a dedication to peace.

B Mr. Menon, am I right in saying that in your opinion there ought not to be a change in Indian foreign policy?

M No, no. You are putting words into my mouth which would qualify me to be described as an obscurantist.

B No, no. If the setting has not changed then the policy response ought not to change.

M No, the external setting has continued changing even in the last fifteen years.

B In marginal terms.

M In marginal terms, yes. But basically there is no alternative to what is called non-alignment. I would go further and say that it would have been a good thing for the countries of Western Europe and Britain to have pursued non-alignment.

If the Labour Government hadn't fallen prey to the craving for imperial trappings, if Ernest Bevin had not thought he was a Winston Churchill, then conditions in the West and the world might have been different. That is why I blame Britain and Canada.

B But take specific issues of policy that have arisen in the last six months since the Shastri Government came to power. You pointed out certain errors, certain weaknesses. Has the failure of Indian policy on the Gulf of Tonkin incident or at the Cairo Conference or any of the other issues been due mainly to ineptitude or to unwillingness to implement the policy of non-alignment?

M It's very difficult to give a simple yes or no to such questions. It's partly because of the mesmerism of the United States and partly because even the late Prime Minister didn't appreciate what I warned him of so many times: 'It is no use saying we can deal with it; you won't be here.' He could not have been more generous about the large-scale entry of American experts, Peace Corps, and so on spreading themselves out all over the place. I was totally opposed to the Peace Corps. There are good individuals among them, no doubt, but we have enough people in this country and to my mind the whole conception is wrong as far as we are concerned. I would say the same about a large influx of any foreigners into key positions. They have got into the administration of our economy, they have got into the nerve points of our administration and our developmental efforts and cultural life. The effect of this is not good either for us or for them. The Africans didn't take them the way we did. During the Chinese aggression we should not have allowed so many foreign personnel to come here and move around in our forward areas. They knew no more than our people yet they lectured us. Some people expressed resentment. But most of the others kept quiet or adjusted themselves to this 'patronage'.

B The question is whether it was due to subservience or ineptitude?

M To subservience arising from our economic dependence. Our economic policy has changed. They don't understand that what comes from the United States is their taxpayers' money.

In a democratic country, the expenditure must ultimately be for the good of the people. I am not saying that there is no idealism in America; but the Administration and Big Business measure things by the dollar. We don't seem to grasp the fact that contributions should be made from both sides. When he was in control the late Prime Minister kept a balance. He said that for every dollar we get from outside we should provide eight dollars ourselves. However, T.T.K. [T.T.Krishnamachari, the Finance Minister] and Morarji Desai put forward and implemented the idea that a large influx of technicians and collaborators is a good thing. I myself don't mind collaborators on an equal basis, but marketing control and planning control should not be allowed as they lead to the domination of our economy. We have to be aware of economic imperialism.

B Does that mean that in your opinion Indian foreign policy has become subservient to Indian economic policy?

M In the twentieth century economic considerations condition foreign policy to a very considerable extent, particularly in underdeveloped and aid-reclaiming countries. It isn't correct to say that economic policy totally dominates foreign policy but economic factors are often the determining ones.

B It means that India's foreign policy at the present time has to be viewed against the degree of foreign investment and foreign involvement in this country.

M That is not an appropriate way of putting it. What I said was that economic factors tend to condition foreign policy. If the recipient of benefit or aid is not careful and firm, the party that pays the piper will call the tune; we must be careful to see that the nation's integrity, strength, and dignity come first. Economic dominance can lead to political dominance.

SUPPLEMENTARY INTERVIEW—MAY 1965

B I think it is generally acknowledged that India's role and prestige in world affairs have declined considerably in the past year or even before. When would you date the beginning of the decline? And what reasons would you cite for the decline?

M I don't think I can answer the question, nor is there any useful purpose served by doing so. I have been out of government since 7 November 1962.

B I am merely asking your opinion, Mr. Menon, as an eminent public figure.

M I think it might be argued that we have become 'aligned'. It had basically been our policy not to become tied up to dependence for arms. I suppose there might have been other mistakes too. I do not think, however, that our position has declined in the sense that we are written off as a nation without an independent policy and approach. When I went to Cairo recently, I didn't see anything of the kind. At the United Nations we don't perhaps play the same role as we used to. On account of our preoccupations, there is bound to be an emotional reaction against involvement in controversies. We may appear rather passive at the moment. But really you know the answers yourself.

14. Partition, Pakistan, Kashmir, and Indo-Pakistan Relations

M Technically it was wrong to call the Kashmir issue before the Security Council the 'India–Pakistan Question'. It was a tactical error to agree to it. But in our idealism we thought that the United Nations would set it right. We went to the Security Council under Chapter 6 and not Chapter 7 for this reason.

There is some historical truth about it, although I myself may not have agreed to this inscription. I would have thought it best to localize the question on the agenda and reduce it to the issue of the aggression that we alleged. Unfortunately during the earlier part of the Kashmir debate our representatives were new to the Security Council proceedings. In relation to the U.N. our Government was overlaid by idealism. When a man like General MacNaughton of Canada played the role that he did we were both sorry and shocked, but not cynical or petulant. When even Owen Dixon of Australia, who later became Chief Justice of that country and who should have known what he was doing, wrapped up what was a straightforward issue of aggression in circumlocutory phraseology, it was pathetic. But we have stuck to the U.N. Britain, ably assisted by the United States, is and always has been the villain of the piece. People here did not, however, quite accept my view that basically this is a cold war issue, not in the sense that the issue before the Security Council means a war between the Russians and the Americans, but that it is a consequence of the West's policy of bases and of 'standing up to be counted'. It's thus a cold war issue for the United States. I hesitate to tell you this. But do not go on thinking that all American statesmen are simple and naïve infants in world affairs as some people say and other people think; nowadays they certainly are not! Their attacks on me personally and their earlier attacks on the Prime Minister were largely an attempt to kill their main ideological opponent. Kashmir might have been another Congo today. Kashmir is a cold war issue; it's part of the desire to forge a ring round the Soviet Union, part of the policy of what is called 'containment'. I think that in the civilized world there should be no containment. I don't speak with bitterness; I am distressed to think that a country like Canada is, through NATO, a supporter of the containment doctrine.

To a certain extent the creation of Pakistan reflects our emotional not our political relations with Britain at that time. We wanted to get rid of the British at any price. Today, thanks to Gandhiji and later to the Prime Minister, and if I may say so without any lack of humility, to a certain extent thanks to smaller people like myself, we have decided to forget and not live in the past. There may be a scar but new tissues have developed. But to a certain extent even this is vitiated by various things.

In my opinion the emergence of Pakistan was not a diplomatic or political move; it was largely a reflex action against British imperialism, or part of the attempt to 'get rid of the British at any price'. Otherwise, can you imagine that a country in the throes of a national struggle, a country that afterwards was proud of its secularism, could accept partition as the price of independence? Would anyone otherwise have agreed willingly to partition? What is more, would anyone have agreed to a solution which the other side [Mr. Jinnah] propounded, an out-of-date obscurantist doctrine [the two-nation theory]? We did not accept it. We do not do so now.

It's the handiwork of Britain but, to their credit, I must say that at the very end they regretted it, but it was too late. And though it seems ungrateful, even Attlee could have prevented this because he was a good enough statesman to make a virtue of necessity.

Pakistan was created, however much we may dislike to say this, as part of a political agreement. It was a shock solution —that is the word for it. Ultimately it came to pass because we felt that if we had managed to keep them within the boundaries of India we would have had a confederal State rather than a federal one. This would really have meant a state of cold war within the State itself. We tried; we toyed with the idea of a confederal State. We even toyed at that time with the idea of making Bengal a kind of autonomous area, within the Confederation. Even that didn't work. What is more it was proved by the experience of the Interim Government [September

1946–August 1947]. The Interim Government was really two Governments working against each other. So that was the origin of Pakistan.

Basically it was Britain and no one else [who was responsible for Partition]. But as Gandhiji said, the outsider cannot create disunity unless the seeds of disunity are within yourself. To that extent we must accept responsibility.

My belief is that the Pakistani leaders looked upon Pakistan as a first instalment, thinking in terms of the English doctrine 'take what you can and fight for more'. They never seem to have accepted the Partition as final, as we did. Their main approach to the problem was that India was theirs; India was a Muslim country historically; the British had taken it away from them; now the British had gone away and it should be handed over to them.

Now if you look at the Pakistani leaders, not only the top leaders but lower down, few of them were involved in the National Movement; and even those few were not fully committed to it. This is to say, they got their independence because of India's national struggle. They may talk about a Republic now. But leaders of Pakistan are mostly former British officials and the kind of people who were opposed to Indian nationalism. Pakistan really was the result of the Indian national struggle led by the Congress. She is like Northern Ireland, a remnant of imperialism. So far as the British are concerned it's their classic imperial solution, and they can rely on the fact that they don't have to fight us any more than they need fight in Ireland.

Thanks to Gandhiji, and particularly to Nehru, and with the exception of some communalists, we agreed to Partition: we never tried to take their territory. We don't even want union with Pakistan; God knows what may happen in a hundred years but at the moment we have no ulterior motive here. It's not because we are virtuous, it's because we know why we did it. That is our position.

Pakistan will do anything and everything against us. The original Pakistan doctrine of Rehmet Ali, a Cambridge student, was that Bengal was Pakistan, Hyderabad was Pakistan, Kashmir was Pakistan, Punjab was Pakistan, and so on. Now, according to these ideas, what haven't they got? They do not have even half of the Punjab, they have not got Kashmir, they

have not got even half of Bengal, and they have not got
Hyderabad. So when we talk about Kashmir this is only part of
that Rehmet Ali map—and there is of course the larger map—
which could place almost all of India in Pakistan.

You may say, 'Why do they concentrate on Kashmir?' It so
happens that the folly of the Maharaja [of Jammu and Kashmir]
and our vacillation provided a golden opportunity for Pakistan.
It was one of those things like the inner tube of a bicycle where
the rubber is thin and a puncture tends to come at one particular
point although it might just as well have come somewhere else.
That is the basic proposition. This won't be written in a history
book; if I wrote it, it would be said that it was far-fetched or
fanatical or unrealistic. I don't say that this is necessarily right,
it is merely my analysis of it, and this analysis may have no
relation to the politics of today or tomorrow.

So long as there are nation-states in the world, in the absence
of total world disarmament an independent nation has to be
armed to protect itself. Pakistan's aggression is not for a place,
not for Kashmir alone; the aggression is against India, against
secularism. What has Pakistan claimed since we partitioned?
They claimed various parts of what was then India. On account
of the partition arrangements, we agreed to plebiscites in the
North West Frontier Province, Sylhet [District of Bengal],
certain villages, and so on. We lost them. In the North West
Frontier Province the Nationalists adopted non-co-operation
in the election, with the result that those who were in favour
of a United India stood out without voting for India.

B Are you suggesting that had there not been non-co-operation
in the North West Frontier Province it would have voted in
favour of India?

M Of course. How much did the Pakistan supporters get?
They won by a majority of 5 per cent with the bulk of the Red
Shirts[1] abstaining. Of course Abdul Ghaffar Khan's answer
today—probably he would not answer at all, but if he had to
answer—would be to say, 'I wanted to avoid bloodshed.'

---

[1] The pro-Congress party in the N.W.F.P., led by Khan Abdul Ghaffar Khan,
known as the 'Frontier Gandhi'.

Further, though I have no personal dislike for General Lock-hart,[1] I maintain that at that time the whole of the British administration was working in a partisan way. In the meantime the operation of the Boundary Force [in the Punjab] had created a situation which led to great violence. Auchinleck[2] was pro-Pakistani as subsequent history shows. You may turn round and ask, 'Why did you agree to all this?' That is where we perhaps miscalculated, or circumstances were against us. I wouldn't say that the Prime Minister or Patel or anybody was right or wrong, but one of the fundamental mistakes, as proved by events, was the acceptance of the Boundary Force. It was no boundary force but the imperial power on the boundary, and very much inclined towards one side.

Future relations between the Pakistanis and ourselves depend upon internal change inside Pakistan. But there will be no peace on this continent unless the United States, which in this context represents interventionism, retires from the Far East. Fortunately public and Congress opinion [in America] is moving in that direction. You take the world since the [Second World] War. Who has created all the wars? What is the difference between this and the situation in 1917 or 1918, except that there is now a twentieth-century temple of different languages, that is, the United Nations? Churchill said, 'I wanted to kill this baby [Soviet Union] in the cradle then but they would not let me.' The imperialists attacked the infant revolutionary Russia on twenty-two fronts; they promoted Denikin and Kolchak [White Russian Generals] and stirred up rebellions here, there, and everywhere. Now basically what is the difference between now and then? Please tell me.

You are a scholar; you will be writing about these things. Let us hope the world undergoes some change by the time you write. Let me hope that it is in a fitter state to reject Western imperialism—otherwise they will say that Krishna Menon is obsessed, and that he wants somebody to hate. These are difficult propositions in the context of five minutes or ten minutes or half an hour or two hours conversation. Observations become abrupt. They tend to convey hastiness and bitterness.

It needed a great statesman to anticipate all this. Therefore

[1] First Commander-in-Chief of the Pakistan Army.
[2] Supreme Commander in undivided India at the time of Partition.

the tragedy was the death of Roosevelt. For internal purposes Truman was a good President. But outside his country not only did he drop the Bomb [A-bomb on Japan in 1945] but he did other things too. I don't exonerate Truman in regard to atomic warfare. I have read some of the material in connection with this. United States governmental policy after the war is not based on anti-communist activities or ideological war. I don't believe that ideological conflict is the essence of it. Behind it instead are self-interest, fear, and false prestige. The Soviet Union had emerged as a mighty power. Only two great ones! What more is needed for conflict? At the time Russia lent support to America through her own domestic and foreign policy.

B Mr. Menon, you said that the only way one could have peace in the subcontinent would be if the United States withdraws from the Far East. More specifically, do you mean the withdrawal of the Seventh Fleet and the withdrawal of U.S. troops from Vietnam?

M All these are small parts of the bigger picture. What is needed is the withdrawal of a Mind, of the assumption that they are born to police the world, and abandonment of the hypocritical idea that the security of the United States requires a fleet in the Indian Ocean. It may well be that if they go away people will call them back. If they do it will be a different matter.

B But since it is highly probable that this withdrawal will not take place in the foreseeable future, one must deduce that you will not have peace in the subcontinent.

M No, there is the possibility of an American withdrawal. Ultimately I think that if the economic burdens are too heavy and the people get to know the results of the commitments of war, they will induce or compel their government to revise their position. The danger is that the American Proconsul today has become very much like the British *Sahib*.

I am laying myself very wide open to criticism by talking to you like this. It's my conviction that American imperialism is to blame—and this for me is not Russian phraseology. By their maladroit responses the Russians have often enough aggravated the situation. If the reversion from Stalinism had taken place in 1946 or 1945 instead of 1954, maybe the world might have been a different place; I don't say it would have been, just might have been. I don't say it was wholly due to Stalin or Stalinism, but when provoked they responded tit for tat. Perhaps they shared many of the same ideas, I don't know. At any rate the effect of it is a world sorely conditioned by what we call the Cold War.

B Even if the withdrawal of the U.S. from the Far East were to be achieved, in your opinion an inherently expansionist Pakistan which looks upon Kashmir or upon Partition simply as the first stage, would no doubt remain.

M No. That inherent expansionism may remain psychologically but it would have no arm, no teeth, and perhaps no body. There is no Pakistan *simpliciter* today; it is Pakistan plus the United States so far as the Indo-Pakistan issue is concerned.

B You mean that this inherent expansionism would still remain a source of resentment which would weaken any chances of an Indo-Pakistan reconciliation.

M No. Pakistan would know that if they sought to confront us we would deal with them. The Pakistani people wouldn't stand for the suicidal adventurism of their leaders now. Look at it another way: with American tradition, the general humanity of its people, and their earlier attachment to India (for India has had a kind of 'Swami' place in their minds, as China had at one time), American influence in the East might have been used for co-operation and toleration. But what happened instead? They took Pakistan into a military grouping [SEATO] knowing that a non-military country [India] would not join such groupings, didn't they? I think you [Canada] are better than some others. But you are part of NATO, and NATO arms were used against us.

B I would hardly think that the record shows Canada's policy towards India to have been one of hostility.

M I am not talking about Canada's general policy towards India. What I mean is that Canada has bloc politics.

B That may be, but in the Commonwealth, for example, I would think that over the years India has considered Canada to be a very close colleague and friend.

M They were not helpful to us on Kashmir. I myself have helped to promote that feeling [of friendship] because I do not think that Canada has any imperial policies. But they were not helpful to us on Kashmir.

B If I understand your position, Mr. Menon, it is that Kashmir is an issue that involves the possible dismemberment of India.

M We will come back to the question of Kashmir afterwards. It is the Pakistani background that you made me talk about. We have to understand it in the context of imperialism and the aftermath of imperialism.

B So the equation is that peace between India and Pakistan is dependent upon American policy.

M No, upon world policy.

B But that, in your view, means the withdrawal of America.

M No, there again you are subconsciously accepting the presence of the United States in the way the Pentagon does, accepting the presence as normality, the withdrawal as abnormal.

B No, not at all. I am saying that you cannot conceive of an Indo-Pakistan settlement without some prior action taken by the U.S.A.

M No. An Indo-Pakistan settlement has to be seen in the context of the general South-East Asian difficulties created by the policy of the United States. The U.S. policy is part of the whole of the aftermath of imperialism, of Western policy, fear of communism, and so on. To a certain extent that position was aggravated by the Stalinist policy of the Soviet Union.

B What in your view are the necessary conditions for American withdrawal from South-East Asia?

M One has done something by diagnosing the situation but I personally have nothing to prescribe. I do not prescribe for another country. I am not an imperialist. In my opinion we need world disarmament, not in the sense the Russians and Americans want it but total Gandhian disarmament where there are no arms at all.

B You think this is realistic?

M It is. In fact in the long run it is the only realistic proposition, unless war intervenes. Then atomic destruction will have made the question irrelevant. You know that I am not a pacifist or burning Gandhian of any kind. Some say I am a crypto-communist or a materialist or whatever you call it! I think that unilateral disarmament would be fatal but that full and total disarmament is the only possible road.

I often said [at the U.N.] that disarmament is not our ideal, we want the outlawing of war. I don't believe that war will disappear if disarmament means only the limitation of arms. I don't say that a limitation of arms may not be a step towards the other. It may or may not be, depending on the way it's done. I didn't mean to say all this. I have kept much of this to myself. I wanted these things to take shape in my mind.

Would you have believed—now tell me honestly—would you have believed that ten or fifteen years ago the open oceans would be used for atomic test explosions? And what did the rest of the countries in the West do? They didn't raise a finger. India's voice stood out alone at the Trusteeship Council. Bikini may be only a bucketful of sand but it was the Trustees' business to administer it, not to destroy it. It created a bad precedent for the expulsion of population. Now they have done it in Tonkin also [1964]. Two islands have disappeared completely as a result of air bombing. If it were anywhere in the Western world the world would have been shocked. Even if it were in Africa the thing would be regarded as shocking; the West cannot get away with such things in Africa today because the Africans speak Western languages.

If opinions are stated after having been thought out, if they arouse great passion in oneself, then they have to be expressed emphatically. Passions are justified once the ground has been dispassionately considered; then we must have passion, otherwise what is the use, it just becomes academic. Therefore I say emphatically, perhaps with passion but not with rancour or bitterness, that what is necessary is the withdrawal of all foreign bases, of all foreign troops, including ships. Secondly, there should be a refusal to give arms to people who cannot make them, even to us; those who traffic in arms are all merchants of death. Thirdly, we should not bank upon the policy of pitting one against the other. And the United States has to abandon the Monroe Doctrine, just as other countries have to abandon their 'spheres of influence' and their colonies.

B May we return to the future of such localized issues as Kashmir?

M Kashmir is not a localized issue. It is the Cold War that makes Kashmir an issue. Internationally Pakistan put this forward because they know that we will not surrender over Kashmir.

B Let me move off to a different track.

M No, no, let us stay on this track. The fact is that with great facility you asked, 'Why is Kashmir vital to India?' Supposing I said to you, 'Why is Ottawa vital to Canada', what would you say?

B But that analogy doesn't hold, Mr. Menon.

M Why not?

B Because, for one thing, the way Partition took shape in 1947 · · ·

M You are a scholar; may I ask you to read the documents?

B I have read them, *all* of them. While Kashmir went to India in terms of the Maharaja's decision and the Instrument of Accession, the fact of the matter is that as one of the successors to the former British Indian Empire, Pakistan didn't accept the way in which Kashmir was disposed of by means of that Instrument of Accession.

M Just a minute, just a minute. Pakistan is party to a tripartite agreement. You see Partition, as stated by Attlee in the House of Commons, had nothing to do with the Indian States.

Now the accession of Kashmir [to India] was probably more 'democratic' than anything else. Jinnah was the person who stated that accession must be by Heads of States. Furthermore, we did the best we could at that time by consulting the local organization, which was like our Congress. Now forget all this; assume that we had no rights and assume that we didn't ask for

Kashmir. Assume all that. Mountbatten was asked to tell the Maharaja of Kashmir, 'If you want to go to Pakistan then for heaven's sake go—but do not remain unattached.' We would not have minded; we would have thought that, like half of Punjab, it's lost. But Kashmir had no intention of doing this. There was no question of the accession of Kashmir [to Pakistan].

B I should like to ask a related question: what in your view is the relationship between the continuance of a dispute over Kashmir, the continuing problems of communalism, and the threat to secularism?

M Pakistan not Kashmir is the key here.

B Do I understand you to say that as long as Pakistan continues to exist there is bound to be communal tension?

M No, no, I never said that. We have no desire to wipe out Pakistan.

B I understand that. But you are saying that Pakistan is the key to the continuance of communal tension, that is, as long as Pakistan is there there will be communal tension.

M No, no, no. I said, Pakistan is not the result of a satisfactory settlement; it's only the first instalment. But I never said that Pakistan is the key to communal problems. It uses the communal problem for its own ends and in its own interests. That is a very different point. There is no reason even today why these two countries should not live together, even with [the] Kashmir [issue]. After all, we agreed to a cease-fire in 1949 but we did not count on their making use of that to take over our territory.

B But in your view it would be possible to continue the relationship between India and Pakistan indefinitely on the basis of the *status quo* in Kashmir?

M There is no other way except war. No settlement that would surrender Indian territory to Pakistan is constitutionally acceptable in India. There are many millions of people who feel this way. Kashmir is the one thing on which feeling is united. If I ask anyone, 'What do you want me to talk about?', they say, 'Kashmir'.

B Is this true in South India?

M Oh, certainly. There is even more feeling about this in South India than here. The fundamental mistake lies in speaking and talking to outsiders as though Kashmir is another country! As for this two-nation theory, we never accepted it. We accepted the Partition and Pakistan merely as an *ad hoc* practical arrangement. It was a political settlement.

B Yes, but that distinction is a very thin one. You may make the distinction in your own minds, but in accepting Partition you have virtually accepted the two-nation theory.

M No, no, not at all. We made it very clear. If we had agreed to the two-nation theory then we would have exchanged all populations immediately. Some sixty millions of Indians are Muslims by faith—they are constituents of the Indian nation. Meanwhile, you ask 'why is Kashmir vital to India', as if they were separate countries!

B Let me set the record straight, Mr. Menon. Of all the writings that have appeared on Kashmir in the past fifteen years, it is probably true that my own book on the Kashmir problem[1] is one of the very few that has been said to understand the Indian case sympathetically.

M I am merely asking you to accept the facts of history. It's a historical fact that India has perhaps not handled its side of the Kashmir case well. This does not alter the facts. You are not the first or the only person to do this you know—some Indians also say 'India and Kashmir' as though they are two separate countries. We swallow other people's propaganda and their terminology often without thinking about it. These are the things that happen to subservient people. I am not questioning your honesty or sincerity. What I am saying is that erroneous ideas gain currency and even we, not to speak of our friends, become victims. That is my point. It comes out in the way that Kashmir is said to be 'disputed' territory. We do not accept that. Part of Kashmir is illegally occupied. That is the fact. Now for argument's sake let us assume for a moment that our title in regard to Kashmir is 'disputable'. Do you think Pakistan

[1] *The Struggle for Kashmir* (1953).

has any right to assert what she regards as rights by invasion? We didn't invade, did we?

B No. I don't dispute that at all. I merely raised the question that in 1964 or 1974 or '84—this is or will be the position. We are realists. Here are two countries involved in a conflict over a particular territory; one can restate the background endlessly but that doesn't solve the problem.

M Realism? Do you mean by that we accept the fact of occupation and surrender? We *are* realists. That is why we urge them to abjure force and do not wage war ourselves. I think that once the Western Alliance came here it became more complicated.

B Why should the West be so keen to harass India, if that is what you mean?

M Because we are the greater country and are likely to be somebody in the world. If we propose to be independent it does not fit into their scheme of things. Secondly, they dislike the very idea of non-alignment; we have had to stand up to American ridicule in the past.

B But you yourself have said to me that in the past few months India has become virtually a vassal of the U.S.A.

M Yes, that is so, increasingly we have become an economic vassal. But they perhaps fear that the vassalage will not continue for long. And also it has come at a time when America does not regard vassalage as a comfortable proposition. The Americans are allergic to all this agitation [in India] for the Bomb; some of their responsible people came and saw me about it to make sure that my opposition to the Bomb was firm.

B So in this sense you are an ally of the Americans?

M I am not an ally of anyone. I am an ally of realism and, I hope, of common sense. But America has come to the realization of the danger of bombs rather late. They don't think as fast as some others do.

Here is a country that has material wealth and a peace-loving people with a lot of affection. But apart from a few individuals in the top echelons, they think in terms which do not correspond with this age. I would include Dulles among them as a knowledgeable person. He knew what he was doing and he was an honest man, though his policies were sinister. With a few exceptions they don't know about the world and are concerned not even so much with local problems as with local applause, votes, and wealth. You must not forget that for all practical purposes America is a confederate State. As I used to tell Cabot Lodge, they are more concerned about the Republican Convention in Texas than with the world.

B You are linking the Indo-Pakistan problem with the broad pattern of . . .

M Your difficulty is this: you are isolating the Kashmir problem and you have put it in a frame that is not of our making nor one of historical fact.

B At a certain stage one has to isolate it for the purpose of analysis.

M No. You have isolated Kashmir as though it were not part of the greater world politics of the Cold War, the play of imperial forces, and so on. The problem of Kashmir is in the same category as divided Korea, divided Germany, or divided Cyprus.

The moral, legal, and every kind of right to the whole of the territory that was under the suzerainty of the Maharaja lies with India. But in the interest of peace in the world we should not try to change the situation [partition of Kashmir] by armed action. This is different from the idea of dividing Kashmir across a cease-fire line. If we divide across a cease-fire line we won't get anywhere or improve anything. Also our people would not accept it. Moreover, it would be yielding to aggression.

So the interim solution is for Pakistan to behave, but she will not behave as long as she has arms and money. Now what you forget is this, that between 1954 and 1960 the Americans have given the Pakistanis as much as a billion dollars' worth of equipment which in real as distinct from money book-value terms is probably about two and a half billion dollars' worth of equipment.

B And that you see as the root of the perpetuation of the problem?

M You put it that way to put me in the wrong!

B That is not my intention.

M At the root of the problem is the world situation. Now why is America interested in Pakistan? She wants to complete the symmetry of the circle [the encirclement around the Soviet Union]. It's a foolish doctrine. To be charitable, we may interpret it as part of American giantism. The Americans make themselves believe that the Pakistanis will help them against the U.S.S.R.—with Sherman tanks they are going to fight Russia! No, they will use these tanks against us in order to defeat our position of firmness and non-alignment.

SUPPLEMENTARY INTERVIEW—MAY 1965

B Mr. Menon, when you discussed Kashmir and Indo-Pakistan relations earlier, you said that when Mr. Attlee was British Prime Minister he could have prevented Partition and you added, 'Some day when we talk about Indian independence we will talk about that.' Would you be kind enough to elaborate on this particular theme now? Perhaps there are other themes about the coming of Independence that you would like to comment on?

M Normally when you talk about these events the talk is speculative, but what I meant is something like this. Attlee is a socialist; he was Prime Minister of Britain, and they found themselves in the position of having to leave India. It is to Attlee's credit that he was quite clear about it at this stage. But they started off on the wrong foot by putting the question to us as a conundrum—that is, 'We are prepared to go but who are we to hand it to?' It was really an incitement to other people to make claims to share the spoils. What should have been said was, 'Pax Britannica is our great pride; we are going to hand it over as a united country on a democratic basis and recognize that the majority will have to accept responsibility. If you are not willing to take it then it is your own fault. It is

up to you to make the minorities agree.' If it was a question of
'blood baths' or trouble afterwards, well, we had it anyway
in spite of or because of Partition.

My own analysis is that when they started the negotiations
and missions they did not envisage that the thing [end of
British rule] was really to come so soon. They probably thought
it was going to be just a newer session of a Simon Commission
and would mean more protracted negotiations, and that
gradually our difficulties would lead to a partnership with
England or something of the kind. This was how it appeared
to them in 1943–5. That situation soon changed. I would like
to think that a man like Mr. Pethick-Lawrence made a big
contribution towards abdication, saying, 'We have to go.'

But my own feeling is that if Attlee had had the imagination
to realize in 1945 that it would happen in 1947 he would have
worked it another way. The British had sufficient power at
that time to see that it happened. The same thing could have
been said to the Princes. It must be remembered that as
a socialist Attlee had certain limitations. He had not understood the character and the passions that went into nationalism
at that period. In his mind socialism and nationalism posed
a contradiction. Having fed the Muslim League for half a century
with separatism, the British created a Frankenstein monster;
they should have laid it low, at least when leaving. Instead they
used it as a spectre and to create pressure against Indian
nationalism. Yet after all it was a great achievement for Mr.
Attlee. I think that Pethick-Lawrence was a much greater
man than most people thought at the time. He was the Chairman of the Cabinet Mission. He was really the functioning
member. He had a good grasp of things.

B Among the controversial questions connected with the
Partition of India, Mr. Menon, one concerns the reasons which
finally led the Congress leadership to accept the Mountbatten
Plan in 1947.

M I don't think Mountbatten is particularly responsible for
Partition. I believe he came here when the Partition question
had been more or less settled. I wouldn't think that he
himself was very enthusiastic about Partition. He came at
the time when his main job was to speed up the departure

and his main contribution was that he finished inside the time and his prestige with the ruling classes in Britain helped it along. Mountbatten's contribution therefore lay in speeding up Partition, creating a degree of confidence on this side, preventing the Indian Civil Service from playing tricks, and in not telling the British Government that the Hindus and Muslims would massacre each other if Independence came. I am not for a moment minimizing his contribution but I would say that history would finally say that what he mostly did was to save the Labour Government from embarrassment at the other end.

15. Succession to Nehru

B May we turn now to the succession to Nehru last June. I would appreciate your reflections on what happened, how the process was accomplished, and the implications for the future working of Indian parliamentary democracy, the Congress Party, and the leadership.

M The so-called 'succession' is not the kind of term you would use in Canada or England. This idea and terminology was largely the result of the general feeling which had arisen because of the personality of the Prime Minister that this was a vacuum which could not be filled. Some people thought and said 'After him—what? Anarchy?' American propaganda and the Prime Minister's own relative unwillingness to withdraw into retirement, as well as what appeared to be an axiomatic indispensability, added to the talk of succession. The Prime Minister's departure was a great and horrible blow. When it finally came a special and artificial atmosphere was created over the succession.

During Nehru's lifetime some of the people in the hierarchy whom he had trusted had died. Things might have been different had Maulana Azad or Pantji [Pandit Pant] still been alive. It's not for me to say whether the situation would have been better or worse. A situation arose in India where problems were becoming increasingly complicated. The Government was no longer a Congress Government in the old sense. In my opinion Nehru probably realized that he would not live for ever, yet there was a streak in him which made him say, 'I am a bounder', meaning that after a time he would resignedly say, 'What can I do, I have done the best I can.' I believe he had reached that stage during the last year or so. It was quite visible that he was working against time and that the work was not adding up to very much or helping to lengthen his life. No Prime Minister in the world worked harder or at more problems whether great or small or spoke to so many people as Nehru did. There came the question of 'succession', 'After Nehru—who?' People like me used to say, 'After Nehru, Nehru', meaning thereby the democratic processes.

When he died there was no question as to what should be the interim arrangements because the Home Minister was next in rank in the hierarchy in the Cabinet. In my opinion, the numbering of Ministers is very far from being a Cabinet-government procedure. But Nehru had not been in any government except his own! He was not very familiar with the theory or conventions of constitutional government. In a sense he may have been right; after all, we can create conventions like other people, but I don't think this is a good one. Very often it led to many incongruities; I was Minister of Defence but I used to sit next to the Minister for Commerce and all sorts of people who had less impact on Government or had less to do. One could understand a person like Maulana Azad, whatever we may think of his personal qualities for government, a doyen, a tradition, all kinds of things like that; the same with Pantji, and so on. But these things [the ranking of Ministers] went on in an illogical way—it was neither the term of office nor the seniority of portfolio; there was this kind of, what shall I say, disorder. I would not call it anarchy, but disorder or something less than order in the whole scheme of things.

Normally speaking, although the Deputy Leader of the Party would not necessarily be the successor he would be the Party boss. But a few years before [1961], because of differences inside the Party [Morarji Desai had wanted to become Deputy Leader], there was strong opposition to this in the Party. In short, there was no number two [when Nehru died]. Inevitably, Nehru never appointed a Deputy Leader or a Deputy Prime Minister after the death of Patel [1950].

B What was the reason for this?

M There was nobody. The obvious person in terms of rank and prestige would have been Maulana [Azad], but apart from his reputation as a scholar and so on he had a lot of fixed notions and very little political experience. I had a great respect for him and I always spoke highly of him. I knew his value in government. His right place in a Cabinet, however, would have been something like the Lord President of the Council in England—a minister without portfolio.

B What about Pantji? Might he not have served as Deputy Prime Minister?

M No. That would have created difficulties because both Pant and Azad were there. Pantji was made Deputy Leader but then he died [1960]—if he had lived he would certainly have succeeded. He probably would have been more of a Party boss than Nehru was. He had sturdy common sense. Some of the things that now happen might then have been prevented, some of the seesaws, hit-and-run, and doing things without considering the consequences. He would have been much more conservative and there is no doubt that vested interests would have felt safer with him. He had a prominent streak of liberalism, not radicalism. Unlike the Prime Minister he had very personal opinions.

Nehru died. Obviously there had to be an interim arrangement. The President appointed Mr. Nanda as Prime Minister [on 27 May 1964]. It was understood of course that he would be acting Prime Minister, although he was not called this; he was appointed Prime Minister. Whether he was not called acting Prime Minister because of the constitution or inadvertence I do not know; it might have been a better arrangement simply to call him *pro tem.* or something of that kind! But somebody invented the constitutional theory, which in my opinion is quite wrong, that there was an obligation to have a permanent Prime Minister. And then the constitutional process was thought to have been correctly followed when Nanda was nominated by the Emergency Committee of Cabinet and his name submitted to the President. Constitutionally it has no precedent as far as I know. It is really the Cabinet and not the Party choosing a leader.

B Wasn't that a novel process?

M Yes, it was; it was perhaps unconstitutional or at any rate contrary to democratic ways.

B Because the Emergency Committee of the Cabinet has no formal place in Government?

M In my opinion, even for the President to exercise his extraordinary [emergency] powers would have been more constitutional. Or they should have called an emergency meeting of the Party or the Party Executive and there could have been no objection raised. I believe it was T. T. K. more than anybody else who was responsible for this particular procedure [the Emergency Committee recommending Nanda]. It is very difficult for me to talk to you about it. But I think that in modern times, without some knowledge of comparative government and contemporary politics, I would not say constitutional theory, you cannot work a parliamentary system. This applies to all parties here including the more theoretical parties, like the Communist Party.

The moment his last breath was drawn the question of succession arose. And I want to say this—I would have said it some time before I die in any event—that none of the people who proclaimed their loyalty to him, who prided themselves on coming from his State, in whose interests he has sometimes disregarded people really closer to him to keep the peace, none of them, I won't mention names, had the decency to keep their mouths shut about succession until he was cremated.

One or two people spoke to me about this in the house where he lay dead. I said: 'I will in no circumstances talk about this matter until the Prime Minister's funeral rites are over. It's a parliamentary tradition; even in London they won't mention a by-election until the dead person is buried. It is not decent, it is most unfitting, and I certainly won't participate in it.' I was not in a fit state anyway; I was not demonstrative but I was in a very bad way, and I suffered much strain in trying to suppress it. I have not spoken about it so far. I am not yet reconciled to his absence.

I didn't make any contribution to the succession gossip. It was put out by interested parties that I had intrigued or come to some arrangement with Morarji Desai. I think it was largely American propaganda, to discredit both me and Morarji Desai. The Americans felt I had a certain hold on the radical sections and the young people in this country, and nothing would have discredited me more than to say that I had made an opportunist alliance! It was also, I believe, partly intended to discredit Morarji Desai because they would have said, 'Here he is, in order to have a job he is going to ally himself with the "Leftists".' At that time the Americans didn't approve of Morarji Desai,

There had to be a process of selection or more accurately of 'choice'. Nanda was in the seat [of Prime Minister] already and I believe that in the first few days he nursed the hope that it would be permanent. But then it went to the Working Committee; the high-ups talked among themselves. In so far as the Morarji business is concerned, I never saw him and I never talked to him openly or privately about this or indeed about anything else. I never met him. On the day I was supposed to have sat at night intriguing with him I had come back from the funeral [28 May], was almost carried back; I had nearly collapsed in the grounds because of the heat and everything else after the fire was set up. Somebody kindly brought me home. The physician, Dr. Mathur, was sitting with me until 1 o'clock in the morning because they said I was not too well and could not be left alone. That is not a matter of historic interest but comes into your query about 'succession'.

B It does indeed because I was told about a breakfast meeting which Mr. Malaviya[1] had at his home.

M Malaviya called a meeting at breakfast; I believe that it was two or three days later. As often happens in India the hospitality came first, and the greater part of the time was spent in arranging the breakfast! The only contribution I made to the conversation was to say that in the present circumstances Parliament should be in session; if it were not sitting it should be recalled. I was not discussing succession at all; it was a question of conditions in the country. I said I had reasons for saying so, and that we should all now agree that in no circumstances should Parliament be dissolved, or rather prorogued. That is the only contribution I made. I had no interest in the succession issue. Quite bluntly, cynically, at that time as far as the country was concerned I thought what is the difference between tweedledum and tweedledee? What is more, even then I felt that it was too early to discuss this matter. At no time did I mention the question of the Prime Minister's succession. Looking back on it, if I had known what was going to happen I would not have gone to that breakfast. I went because if

---

[1] K. D. Malaviya, former Minister of Oil and a leader of the Congress Left Wing.

I had stayed away Malaviya would have felt hurt; there were only seven or eight people there and I would have been missed.

B To go back if I may: after Mr. Nanda was sworn in as Prime Minister, you said that the issue went to the Working Committee. But in the interim period [four days] surely there was a good deal of lobbying, formation of coalitions, groups, etc.?

M But I sat here [at home]. I don't, even today, join a group; I don't discuss anybody in Parliament [Central Hall]. During that period candidates emerged. People talked about Shastri, and whatever propaganda Shastri made, he did it quietly with his own group or other people did it for him. Morarji was an obvious candidate; he had announced himself. Jagjivan Ram[1] said, 'I too am a candidate.' There were no candidates exactly, there were people in the offing, people who were being talked about. And everybody thought Jagjivan Ram would support Morarji and they would go as one force, but Jagjivan Ram apparently said, 'What are they talking about? I am, myself, a candidate.' So day after day went by and then the Working Committee was called. Personally I thought that the A.I.C.C.[2] should have been called but Congress has its own ways. I think that some had feared that this would have led to disturbance in the country.

B When you say 'Congress', do you mean the Party High Command?

M 'High Command' is a euphemism for the party caucus; who that is is difficult to say. At that time I believe it was Kamaraj,[3] his secretary Rajagopalan, who was a kind of faithful eye and ear, and Atulya Ghosh,[4] who is one of the powerful men in the Party today because he has control of the Bengal Congress and who is said to have good organizing ability; there was also Patnaik,[5] who believes in Madison Avenue methods in elections,

---

[1] Untouchable leader, who had served longer in the Indian Cabinet (1946–63) than anyone except Nehru.

[2] All-India Congress Committee, the parent body of the Working Committee.

[3] K. Kamaraj Nadar, President of the Congress 1964–8.

[4] Congress leader of Bengal.

[5] B. Patnaik, former Chief Minister of Orissa.

and there were two or three Southern leaders [Reddy[1] and Nijalingappa[2]]. All these people were in the leadership.

The first time I opened my mouth about the succession was when we met in the Working Committee [on 31 May]. I have no doubt that these elders or whatever you call them had already made up their minds. The first thing that was decided or rather put out in that atmosphere—an atmosphere conditioned by the almost universal desire for a speedy and unanimous decision and the avoidance of conflict—was that we should have a unanimous selection.

B Who put that idea out? Was it Kamaraj himself?

M Well I think it would be historically untrue to attribute the idea to him or to suggest that he prevented other ideas from being expressed. It is more true to say that he expressed the feeling of the meeting and the country. But he did say this. It is difficult to remember whether he said it after somebody else had articulated it in the Working Committee. There is often more than one person talking; shall we say that is what *emerged*. He pronounced it and it was confirmed as the agreed sense of the meeting. In the course of that discussion, I said that a unanimous choice is obviously a right choice but we should not say that it is absolutely necessary to regard a contest for the leadership as undemocratic. It was a purely theoretical thing so far as I was concerned. Whether that led to the inference that I wanted somebody in particular I can't tell you. It was purely theoretical; I left it like that, and nobody objected to the idea. Then I think Morarjibhai[3] took a very ill-considered step. He said that whatever anyone else did he himself was not going to withdraw.

B He said that at the Working Committee meeting?

M Yes, to the best of my recollection. The next stage of the meeting was that having agreed that there should be a unanimous choice, no names at all were mentioned. It was left to the Congress President to discover what the Party wanted. Instead

[1] N. Sanjiva Reddy, former Chief Minister of Andhra, Congress President, and later Minister of Steel; from 1967, Speaker of the Lok Sabha.

[2] Siddhavanahalli Nijalingappa, Chief Minister of Mysore, and from 1968 President of the Congress.   [3] Morarji Desai.

of having a party meeting the whole thing was almost spontaneously left entirely in the hands of the Congress President.

B May I ask whether, at that Working Committee meeting, there was any expressed opposition or doubt about the wisdom of this particular approach of consensus?

M Consensus and so on came afterwards. Let us take it step by step. It was not said that he might or should call a party meeting or that he might not or should not call a party Executive and so on. Meanwhile some people in the Congress Parliamentary Party expressed the view that they were being bypassed, and that this was a mistake. That idea was not encouraged. Some people said in effect, 'Who are they? After all, they have no one of the stature that we as a whole have [the Working Committee].' There were a couple of people in the Congress Parliamentary Party who would have liked to make a furore, but on the whole the Parliamentary Party Executive didn't want this. They were all anxious to have a unanimous choice. After all, at that stage there was the feeling that if one was against the likely winner, it would make it 'difficult for him after his election.

So the idea was that Kamaraj would use what methods he thought best. He said he would see as many people as possible. I believe he saw over 100 people. I was the first person to see him after the Working Committee decision; it so happened I had to go somewhere out of Delhi. I knew him well, I can understand his language [Tamil] though I cannot speak it nowadays. So I said to Kamaraj, 'I myself have no candidate and I think they are all equally good or equally not so good. At the present moment there are two candidates holding the field'—this was at 12 o'clock, the time is important—'and the Congress hierarchy think that Shastri has a majority. Other people say Morarji has a majority. I don't know who has a majority, but it's quite obvious that even if it were not a close contest the defeated person would get a substantial number of votes and things would be in a bad way afterwards. What is happening in the States would happen in the Centre too.' I said to him, 'Unless we are careful the Government of India is going to be like the Government of the U.P. [Uttar Pradesh].'

B By that you mean two factions?

M Not only two factions; big things being decided by group-ism. It would have become a government that was not fully supported and there would have been parish politics. Parish conditions and reasoning would have been applied to questions of foreign policy, such as the representation of China in the U.N., nuclear weapons, Vietnam, and so on.

'Therefore,' I said to him at 12 o'clock, 'the position is that there are two candidates whom we may presume to be equally strong. Then there is Jagjivan Ram, at present sitting in the wings, who will either stand himself or who may throw his weight one way or the other. So the situation is not ripe for a unanimous choice. In my personal opinion, the right thing to do is to allow Nandaji to continue on the definite under-standing that it's an interim arrangement. We don't want to make a permanent choice that would split the Party.' This was all in the context of two candidates in the field. 'And then, if you want to make it permanent it is necessary that he should be Prime Minister and, as in the Soviet Union and some other countries, there should be three or four Deputies representing the big groups inside the party and movement. They would be called Deputy Prime Ministers if you like or some such thing, and Nandaji could be allowed to carry on.'

I had no particular affection for Nandaji, though I had nothing against him. I believe he is somewhat of an obscurantist but with spurts of emotional radicalism. I also believe he is a person who has a big ego, despite professions and appearances, and a limited capacity to live up to it. I don't believe he would be a socialist either in governmental practice or in orientation. In his thinking, too, to my mind, he is not a socialist. You will always find that people who profess the same creed but who differ from you are more opposed to you than those who have a different approach. And so my suggestion was that he be allowed to continue for one month, two months, three months, or what-ever it was. In the meantime things would sort themselves out. Parliament ought not to be allowed to go away.

Another factor on which there was a unanimous decision—on which I didn't express an opinion—was that this matter should be decided by the 2nd or 3rd of June. I thought at the time that it was a mistake. I think the time limit was fixed in order to rush the choice through and not leave room for speculation and rivalry within the Party that would militate against national solidarity and unity. They had decided on Shastri because Shastri was supported by some powerful leaders of groups or States, largely I think because of antagonism to Morarji; Shastri was regarded as the lesser of two evils. Morarji is unpopular in large sections of the country because of his rigidity. The strongest henchman of Morarji was Patnaik, which did not help very much.

All this was at 12 o'clock noon. By 3 o'clock Morarji's supporters themselves had gone to him, saying, 'There is no use fighting.' In the morning [at the Working Committee meeting] he said that he would fight in all circumstances but he had lost ground when he didn't dissent against unanimity and consensus. There was speculation until 3 or 4 o'clock. By 4 o'clock the character of the question had completely changed. Although Morarji had made no announcement, he was out of the field. Who was going to vote for him in those circumstances? I believe that perhaps Jagjivan Ram also made it difficult. Nobody knows how many votes Jagjivan Ram would have mustered in a contest but everybody thought that the Scheduled Castes[1] members would vote for him. Anyway this was the impression, and he too is regarded by some of the 'Left' as being more than slightly left. Many other people would think that it's a good idea for India to have a Scheduled Caste Prime Minister. So there was this uncertainty. By 4 o'clock then, the situation had completely changed. There was only one candidate in the field, so whatever idea I put forward in the morning had ceased to be relevant. I should have gone back to him at 6 o'clock and said, 'Please disregard my earlier advice [that Nanda should continue for a short period of time].' But I had definitely said that I had no candidate. I believe Mrs. Gandhi also gave the same advice [to allow Nanda to continue].

Kamaraj announced the next day that he had seen everybody concerned and his view was that Shastri should be the next leader. Shastriji was correct in his behaviour. He said he was not going to contest the leadership, he would not split the Party. He knew he was going to be the Prime Minister. He

[1] Untouchables.

knew the Party—and that was a great asset. When Shastri came to the [Congress Parliamentary] Party [2 June], there was a certain amount of solemn resentment that the Parliamentary Party was being overlooked. The Parliamentary Party itself is a caucus of the Congress. While there might have been a hundred people who felt that way even these people didn't bother. The whole question was settled and finished. In fact, there were not as many people at the big meeting [the formal selection of Shastri by the Congress Parliamentary Party on 2 June] as was put out, because you see the controversy had died down. Kamaraj came [to the rostrum] and announced that he had done what was asked of him. He gave the history of this, saying that he had sent for many people according to his ideas as to who could speak for various sections of opinion. He had sent for 100 people and he was convinced that the choice of the Party was Lal Bahadur Shastri. It was then a unanimous choice, for by this time there was nobody else in the field. He made the speech and it was seconded. And then [S. K.] Patil[1] intervened and made another speech in support. This was the end of that meeting. Shastri became Prime Minister.

After he became Prime Minister I told Shastriji that Parliament should be kept in being. 'If you go before Parliament now,' I told him, 'you will have a great deal of sympathy as the new Prime Minister; the old Prime Minister's glow is still warm and even the Opposition will cheer you. If you come [before Parliament] three months hence and do not recall it till then, on some spurious excuse about wiring the chamber [Lok Sabha], they will already be used to you as Prime Minister.' Actually that was what happened. He said he would consult his colleagues and ultimately they did nothing.

B Can you tell me, Mr. Menon, what role if any the President of India played in this drama?

M None at all, none at all. It is not his function to take a hand in party decisions. He could not do any such thing.

B Do you think that the fact that he simply adhered to the constitutional forms but did not participate actively in the succession is a healthy development?

---

[1] Congress leader of Bombay city.

M I don't think it is expected that the President choose a Prime Minister. He sends for the leader of the majority and that is what he did. He does not therefore come into it. He does not do any Cabinet-making. He can give advice if asked, but he would not seek to interfere with processes which are part of the conventions of parliamentary government.

B There was some talk both at the time and later of concern among some members of the Congress Party and even of the Civil Service about an active role that might be played in this crisis by the army. Do you recall any such concern?

M I have heard something about it. But it has no basis. People used to say that the army would take over. Nobody took it seriously because the army is not able to run its own business to start with! Secondly everybody knows—including the army I hope—that even small people can make a *coup d'état*, take over a radio station and all that, but how would they hold this country?

B Is there evidence to suggest that they tried?

M I cannot tell you. I was not afraid of it myself. The Armed Services in India, when I knew them, were under civil control. We are a parliamentary democracy.

B What do you think will be the implications of the manner of succession for the relations between the Congress High Command and the Cabinet in the months and years to come?

M At that time it was thought that the Party would be the main element. In fact some people even thought that the real Government was Kamaraj Nadar's and that Shastri was an appointee of Congress. Subsequently, this proved not to be the case; for example, when certain important appointments or arrangements were made [July 1964], nobody, not even his Party colleagues, it is said, knew about it. They all read about it in the newspapers.

B But this means that very soon after the selection of Shastri the domination of the Party, which was apparent during those first few days . . .

M You must see it in the context of there being no public information. First of all, our electorate, our people, trust the Congress; they are mature in a negative way if you like; therefore those who disagreed with these arrangements were not prepared to come and speak out against the Party decision. Those who were in opposition were timid; politics, as the cynics say, is 'joining the stronger side'. Then again, Parliament was not sitting for three or four months after the new Government was formed. I believe that what people call 'The Syndicate' perhaps had some part in it. I think that in this kind of politics of manœuvre and management, Shastriji had a very deft hand. I believe he asserted himself. But he didn't assert himself on policy; it was like some of our State politics; he understands that very well.

B What was the effect of the coming together of southern political leaders in the Syndicate on the relationship between the Centre and the States?

M These are all textbook ideas; the southern political leaders don't count all that much.

B There has been a good deal of speculation that because Shastri was the choice of a particular group the Centre becomes much weaker *vis-à-vis* the State Governments.

M I don't think that is the position; that has been going on for a long time. I believe that towards the end, the late Prime Minister perhaps took the State feeling too much into account. But I am not competent to judge. He could quite legitimately say, 'What do you know about it? I have to keep the country together.' I believe this country should have been a federation of the Canadian type, and in practice this was the case. With the emergence of some of these provincial leaders and with the size of these provinces, and with the Central Government and the Planning Commission playing chess with them, they have created centripetalism rather than the opposite. It was a process that the late Prime Minister allowed or had to acquiesce in. I think if it goes too far it will mean the ruination of India.

16. Policy in the Shastri Transition, Notably the Bomb

B You began a few moments ago, Mr. Menon, to comment on Shastri's role as Prime Minister and you remarked that he had not yet taken the leadership on policy questions. May we explore this a little by looking at the course of the last six months? What do you think of the record of the new Government?

M I think the new Government has to its credit the fact that in a certain sense it is keeping the country together. But in historical terms it is difficult to say whether this will be regarded as the period of the beginning of decay or of marking time, or of the reversal of policy.

B I wonder if you would spell that out.

M In economic policy I think we have become more and more subservient to the West. The domination of the Finance Minister varies. Any Finance Minister is powerful—and he doesn't very much care what resolutions you pass—he holds the purse strings. What in London is control of the purse by Parliament is here really control by the Finance Minister and Ministry. The Finance Ministry probably means largely vested interests and a few officials. I don't think that there is a consistent policy. It may be that I am mistaken in saying that, but I do not think we have ever had a well-thought-out economic policy. I don't think there is much understanding of these matters, and that is part of the reason why we are in this position. Finance Ministers have been left too much to their own and their officials' devices.

B You used the term 'growing subservience to the West'. But what about internal affairs? Is decay evident there too?

M Oh yes, it is evident in the rise of nationalism! Each province is rather too much on its own. Andhra is reluctant to give enough rice [to other States suffering from food shortage in the autumn of 1964]. Yet you cannot say that we have become anarchic or ceased to be a *Federal* Union. The Congress has great mystique; the people have a sense of holding together. I think it would be very wrong to say that all is lost or anything remotely like that. There is no doubt, however, that the States are asserting themselves. Even the late Prime Minister used to talk of 'My State', although he didn't imply the kind of thing some Chief Ministers now have in mind. I used to say, 'How can you say "My State"; you have no State', and he used to laugh.

The decline in policy can be seen, for example, in Cairo [the Non-Aligned Conference, October 1964]. In my opinion it is not a question of little matters; there is a basic deficiency in understanding. To go to an international conference and produce a proposal quite out of one's hat—to propose to send a mission to China! It's like a little schoolboy of fifteen being shown that litmus paper changes colour as it's put in alkaline; he goes home and takes any piece of paper and puts it in water without knowing why the change he has seen before took place. It was merely an attempt to imitate what we tried to do at Belgrade [Conference of Non-Aligned States, 1961] when Nkrumah and our late Prime Minister were sent as delegates to Moscow and Washington.

This showed a lack of understanding of political affairs in which you can rarely go by analogy or repeat things without taking different circumstances into account. We became camp followers there. And we didn't promote any improvement in relations with the Africans. The Conference moved away from non-alignment to anti-colonialism—not that we are not anti-colonialist but this should have taken a second place at the Conference. The same thing came up at Belgrade—but non-alignment had pride of place. There was no 'Bandung spirit' or 'Belgrade spirit' at Cairo. Our personalities did not make an impact on the Conference or on the delegates. With one or two exceptions, even the officials that the Government of India sent there were misfits.

B Do you ascribe this to the changed position of India in the world or more to the ineptitude of the Indian delegation?

M To both causes; but perhaps we should not speak about ineptitude—it is a strong word.

B You think the Cairo Conference marks a serious decline of India's role in Afro-Asia?

M No, no. Every country has its ups and downs. Now if anybody were to write about Indian foreign policy in a few years time, they would write of the place India occupied or created for herself in the context of world politics. But it was not a useful thing to explain things this way to the late Prime Minister—he was not much interested in what he would call theory. But to my mind so long as there are nation-states the position that has gone on from 1947 should continue. In other words, there should be a balance-of-power arrangement or strategy or whatever you like to call it. We are also part of the balance of power both because we are its victim and because we are seeking to create our own balance. We were not playing the game of Balance of Power. But we were creatures or part of the complexes that can be described in terms of the balance of power.

B You say that the Prime Minister was indifferent to the notion of the balance of power and India's role in it.

M I don't know. I didn't discuss it with him.

B In all those years?

M Not in such terms or in so many words. It was obvious. What was the use of lessons on political science? That was not my job. I would only have made myself guilty of being theoretical.

B But one would take it as self-evident that the practitioner of foreign policy had a rudimentary knowledge of this.

M He did have more than a rudimentary knowledge. Theories are often inferred from what statesmen do. He himself might have thought, 'Why should I go into theory?' What I am saying is that non-alignment is not a kind of advantageous policy; it's part of the inevitability of the situation.

B But it has a theoretical rationale.

M Of course it has, because bipolarization has taken place. Now the balance must be kept between them and it is being kept; this has prevented everybody from becoming absorbed; if it had absorbed more people the 'balance' would be easier to upset.

B Let me return to the present situation. Do you detect any significant changes in foreign policy since May 1964?

M Not as such. But the lack of understanding is revealed by the very debate which is now taking place on the atom bomb. We won't make a bomb even though we have nuclear power and capacity. The debate is doing us a lot of harm.

B Internally or externally?

M Both ways.

B Why should it be harmful for people to question the desirability of having certain instruments of national security? After all, there are five other powers who have the bomb.

M That is begging the question.

B You say that it would be harmful.

M Yes, it's harmful because it creates the feeling in the minds of other people that we didn't mean it when we said that we wanted the total prohibition of nuclear weapons, tests, and stockpiles. The debate whether we should build the bomb or not is in itself a departure from policy. We have signed this [Test Ban] Treaty; we have maintained our policy for ten years now; at Cairo we asked everybody to refrain from tests and we have talked all along about the abolition of the bomb. You say that in certain contingencies the nuclear weapon is a weapon of peace and of course you as a Canadian take that view—I don't. I don't think it's a weapon of war or a weapon of defence; it's a weapon of mass extermination. What is the use of having a couple of bombs or a greater number of small-sized bombs unless you have enough to annihilate China and are able to deliver them before they beat us to it? The bomb has no value; it has not even a deterrent value. This is quite apart from the futility of weapons of annihilation and all the consequences of atomic war.

B You mean it has no political value?

M What political value does it have? China gains politically from that damn bomb because it obtains for her an entry into international circles. We don't need that.

B It also helps her to acquire a position of pre-eminence all over Africa and Asia.

M If the Africans and Asians are foolish enough to accept that, but most of them are politically mature.

B But I think they are accepting it.

M I don't know. I think the West exaggerates. The whole issue is riddled with confused thinking.

B Mr. Menon, I am not saying that India should *build* the bomb; what I am raising is the question of why you feel so strongly that one should not even *debate* the issue.

M Why should I debate mass suicide? The debating of this issue means that we are showing the world that we are in two minds about it, that if the majority decides or if something happens we are prepared to use the bomb. Moreover, we are proceeding on a fundamental fallacy; just six months ago we signed an agreement, only to say now that we don't adhere to it. Only three or four months ago we made a declaration that under no circumstances would we use it. Who is going to trust us afterwards? We shall have shaken everybody's confidence. Lastly, this will start a debate in Pakistan, in Ceylon, and everywhere else. It gives people the idea that the Americans are going to help us with a nuclear umbrella. I can tell you that the Americans are not going to get into nuclear war for our sake or anybody else's sake. And they are right.

B But if one maintains these assumptions—firstly that the nuclear weapon is one of mass destruction and under no circumstances should be built or used, and secondly that neither the U.S., the Soviet Union, nor any other nuclear power is going to provide a nuclear defence for India—isn't this abdicating responsibility for the security of this country?

M Not at all. You are begging the question. You are saying that the nuclear bomb is a weapon of security. I deny that this is so even for the United States or the U.S.S.R.

B But the fact of the matter is that there are five States that do have nuclear arsenals.

M Therefore?

B You are not critical of those; you accept those as part of the reality of the contemporary world.

M No, no. I am critical of them and always have been. Our effort should not be in building another bomb but in trying to rid the world of the bomb. What power would we have to say that nuclear weapons should be banned if we are building one ourselves?

B Why cannot you do both at the same time?

M You cannot do that.

B But this is precisely what the Americans and the Soviets are doing.

M And see the result. There is no agreement on anything concerned with nuclear-weapons, except for a limited test agreement. Why have we spoken against proliferation all these years? How can we stop everybody saying, 'Let us all build it and then we will stop?'

B Mr. Menon, how would you define the fundamental national interest of India? Is it the survival of the country?

M The fundamental national interest of this country is not to talk of the use of nuclear power for destructive purposes. What is the new factor that has arisen?

B The new factor is the Chinese offensive capability, not of one bomb but the potential for creating a nuclear stockpile.

M The answer is twofold. We knew that China was making this bomb; it was public so no new factor has arisen. Secondly, China's offensive capability, in the sense of using nuclear missiles against us, is not immediate; it will take a long time.

B Five or six years at the most.

M Maybe five or six years; if China uses the bomb against us or against you then maybe neither of us has any defence against it. If others retaliate then there is world war and annihilation. Therefore the only solution is to end the bomb.

B But you are saying that no effort should be made to create such defences.

M Well, that is the way you like to put it but I have made no such observation. You see you have got a Canadian approach— a NATO approach to this.

B What has that to do with it? There are many Indians who think the way I do and many Canadians who do not.

M You believe in the atom bomb.

B No, I *don't* believe in it.

M Of course as a Canadian you do believe in the atom bomb. NATO is striving to get these weapons for each of its constituent nations.

B But the fact is that Canada could have produced the atom bomb long ago and has never done so.

M But why? Why has she not done so? Do you think that it is because of her moral virtue? No, it is because she can get the bomb from America.

B I don't think that moral virtue enters into discussion of international politics.

M Canada has not made the bomb for the same reason that the Americans are telling the British not to make it.

B Namely, that they will provide the defence.

M In 1945, the U.K. said that all atomic secrets are common on the grounds that 'We developed it together and we should share in it equally.' The Americans turned round and said, 'Nothing doing, whatever we might have agreed to is past; you don't know how to do it and you don't need to make it; we will make it.' That is now history. And the British went on to develop their own independent production.

B Mr. Menon, are you saying that the case for India not building the bomb is essentially a moral one—that this is an evil weapon?

M No, no, it's a common-sense view. Firstly, the net result of building it is that what resources we have are put into this instead of making guns or training soldiers or whatever it is. Secondly, you are subscribing to the view that you can kill your own people by radiation as a result of tests. Thirdly, we would have weakened our position because of proliferation to which we would then be a party. We would also have weakened our position because if ever there was a view held in the world that the neutrals should take charge of the stocks, we would no longer qualify. I mean, once you make the atom bomb you are no longer a non-aligned country. I am not now going into the question of whether India can make it; it's purely a theoretical calculation. What are they going to make it with, the Canadian reactor?

B According to the agreement between India and Canada they have no right to use the reactor for that purpose.

M Exactly. And I hope that Canada will stick to it. In that case where will they make it from? The very fact that Dr. Bhabha[1] has made some speeches, which in my view were improper, shows that he has no practical political sense.

B So you are saying that this is a weapon which is morally offensive, economically impossible, and militarily ineffective.

M You are trying to put words into my mouth. I never used the word 'moral'. I said it's a common-sense proposal. If we want to deter China from using weapons against us we must have such large quantities of them. Secondly, we must have the capacity to carry them. And thirdly, we must be willing to drop them before they drop them on us; that is to say, we must embark on preventive war. That is the position, and I think all this talk weakens us. You can say it morally weakens our capacity to remove the atom bomb from the world. Your argument is an argument for an arms race. When I spoke at the U.N. all those years it was not with my tongue in my cheek. I refuse to believe that complete disarmament is utopian. If I had been able to convert my Canadian friends to this view it would have made a lot of difference to the world.

[1] Dr. Homi Bhabha, Chairman of India's Atomic Energy Commission until his death in January 1966.

B That suggests that between them India and Canada exert great influence in the world.

M Oh, yes! Canada has a very important position because she is a Western power and she is on the American continent. She is not like us—we can afford to disarm, it will be said, because we have few if any arms. I think Canada abdicated her responsibilities to posterity by not playing the role we had hoped she would on the Disarmament Sub-Committee, and also by making NATO her special assignment. But they would have accepted that responsibility if they had known what would happen. I think it is fair to blame Canada for the failure to make progress at the Disarmament Committee [1953–9].

B That is a grave charge.

M It is a grave charge but that is the grim reality. I think that if Lester Pearson had not been tied up with NATO this would perhaps not have happened. Tell me, what has Canada to gain? Does she fear that she herself might become communist, following Russia or China? Canada has not even got a Labour Party worth noting so that really there is no question of her so-called liberalism being infected. There is no question of invasion from America. In most senses Canada is the safest country in the world.

B I am only questioning your assumption that the Americans and the Russians were prepared to disarm if only Canada had taken the lead in the middle 1950s. I don't think there is any evidence for this.

M I said nothing of the kind. Canada abdicated her responsibility by taking sides in the Disarmament Sub-Committee and joining one group. I think that in those days she might have made a bridge for the people who were between the two [superpowers]. The Western side had the more difficulties not only because of America but because of Britain—who had joined the Nuclear Club to put herself into the same position that you now want India to put herself into. There is little use discussing it as a moral issue. If morality has to do with reality, then morality becomes common sense.

17. The Indian Cabinet at Work

B Mr. Shastri, announcing India's policy on the bomb, re-marked that this decision had never been discussed in Cabinet. Is this not an issue that one would expect to come before Cabinet?

M What is a Cabinet?

B It is a group of people who formulate government policy and who exercise collective responsibility in the administration of Government.

M A group of people do not always sit together in a room! Are you discussing the present Cabinet or the former Cabinet?

B This Cabinet.

M I don't agree with your view at all. Shastri may not have discussed it formally within the large Cabinet. Why should he? Our policy on nuclear weapons is an established one. He must have discussed it with his senior colleagues—and when he makes such a statement he knows that Cabinet will go along with him. He also knows that the Congress Party has taken this line and that from the very beginning we have been against the use of nuclear power for destructive purposes!

B Was this exercise of Prime Ministerial discretion a frequent characteristic of Mr. Nehru's?

M Now you are going to the other extreme. I don't want to be dogmatic about it, but the essence of Cabinet Government is that it is flexible. But it is not in any sense spineless. You cannot say that Shastri has not consulted the Cabinet when he is carrying out established national policy, or when as the Prime Minister he says or does something which he knows his colleagues and the country will accept or approve. That is how Cabinets work. Prime Ministers have to carry their colleagues with them —they must do it their own way and take the consequences. This happens in the English Cabinet as well.

B But, Mr. Menon, he has said, 'This issue has not come before Cabinet.'

M This issue probably didn't come before a Cabinet meeting in the sense of being on a Cabinet Agenda. I am not prepared to disclose what comes on a Cabinet Agenda but the greater part and often the weighty part of business which is discussed in Cabinet is often not on the Agenda. The late Prime Minister would discuss either with those who were most concerned or the discussion would be more general. Unfortunately, however, each Minister was coming to govern his own department and making a private agreement with the Finance Minister if he wanted money or seeking and receiving the Prime Minister's agreement or blessing privately. The Prime Minister would then have to carry the burden; that is more or less how it was. There are certain matters, indeed many matters, which are discussed formally by the Cabinet. But even so, the Cabinet never takes votes.

B No, but one can at least expect that the Prime Minister has found a consensus of opinion among his senior colleagues.

M But he has found that in the Congress Party, and his senior colleagues are not against it; if they were against it they would have gone and talked to him; they would have discussed it before the formal Cabinet meeting. In any event if there is a real difference of opinion which cannot be bridged the composition of the Cabinet will change. But most differences are ironed out.

B Isn't there the danger, then, that as a policy-making organ the Cabinet becomes subservient to the Congress Working Committee?

M There again you are speaking in 'schematic' terms.

B You say 'schematic' but I have never been a member of this Government and can only judge it by the working of its institutions, by the processes of government.

M No, no; even in England policy-making doesn't take place in the way you seem to think. Of course it varies with countries, Prime Ministers, and Cabinet compositions.

B But in England there isn't the relationship that exists here between the Congress and the Indian Government.

M Isn't there? When the Labour Party came into power [1945] there was a Consultative Committee between the Parliamentary Party and the Cabinet.

B But the President of the Congress here holds a position of influence and authority with respect to the Indian Government which the Chairman of the British Labour Party has never held.

M It depends. When there was a strong chairman or strong man in the party like Nye Bevan, Harold Laski, the late Arthur Henderson, or Arthur Greenwood, then it did.

B Even on policy questions? Surely the tradition of this country is rather that the Cabinet is almost the creation of the Congress —because of the National Movement?

M There is this difference. There is no doubt that the Government is a Congress Government. But it's not true to say that Kamaraj [Congress President from 1964 to 1968] knows or tries to know all that goes on in the Cabinet. As far as the atom business is concerned, I don't think he knows what is being discussed. But he knows what government policy is likely to be for it is Congress policy. The Prime Minister is not a replica or shadow of the head of the Congress; they work together— but not in the sense of offering approval or exercising vetoes.

B Isn't the degree of consultation between the Prime Minister and the President of the governing party far greater here than in Great Britain?

M Oh no, not on certain matters. I should imagine that there would be consultations if it were a question affecting voting which reflected serious differences between the leaders of the Government—as has occurred in the States. I should imagine that there would certainly be consultations and prior agreements if, for example, the Prime Minister were going to recommend that the President dissolve Parliament and face new elections. There is some talk going around about the constitutional position in regard to the elections in Kerala; I don't know whether the Congress President has been consulted on this. These are all political and not constitutional questions and turn on per-

sonalities and circumstances and particular friends. Cabinet
procedures and the way Cabinet works in each country or in
a country at different epochs are not governed by statistics!
They are based on conventions and the adjustments to large
and small changes brought about by different personalities and
circumstances.

B What about changes in the Planning Commission or economic policy?

M I don't think there is prior consultation on these matters.
I would imagine the matter would go to the Prime Minister
after the Finance Minister had dealt with it. Yet this is not
always the case. The Prime Minister is chairman of the Planning Commission while the Finance Minister is only a member.
The active functionary is the deputy chairman. There is no
cut-and-dried rule about these things; it all depends on what
you can get away with, or what you can get carried out.

When I wanted to get something done, and when I knew
there would be difficulties or personal inhibitions to be overcome, I would speak to the Prime Minister [Nehru] first. He
carried the burden of conciliation and persuasion among his
colleagues. That was his job. Sometimes he would express his
own views strongly and even say how some issue or other had
to be decided in the larger interest. The Prime Minister did not
steam-roll, but my experience has been that he got his own
way or got one or other of his colleagues to give way. Sometimes he spoke to the Home Minister, not because he was Home
Minister but because Pantji had a marked personality of his
own and had a great deal of experience. Panditji, at the time
Pantji was in government, looked on him as an elder statesman.
He once described him to me as a 'mountain of a man'. Or he
would get another Minister to talk to the colleague who didn't
agree. Or he has been heard to say, 'Here it is, let's agree on
this.' And in each case, usually at the end of a Cabinet meeting,
he mumbled that everyone was agreed. Cabinet does not
function by Resolutions and Amendments and Standing Orders.
Government functions according to 'rules of business' to which
the Cabinet largely adheres.

B What more does the Cabinet meeting perform in India?

M There are certain matters on which the Services would make the decisions. There are certain matters about which the Prime Minister himself would decide. Panditji never avoided discussions. Also there are certain matters which a member of the Party may bring up in regard to some State decision on, say, food, and all kinds of such questions. A Union Minister cannot be effective in the Cabinet unless he is supported by the Prime Minister or unless he carries the Prime Minister with him. It is not a question of opposition but lack of support from a team of 'equals'. The Prime Minister, when somebody says, 'Please, Sir, I want this and this done', might well reply, 'Yes, bring it to the Cabinet; we will raise it in Cabinet and see what they have to say.' This would not be done as a challenge or to expose the requesting member. It would be genuinely done to obtain a more or less collective view.

B Doesn't every Member of Cabinet have a right as a Member of Cabinet to request and expect that an issue which he or his department wishes to raise before Cabinet will be put on the Agenda?

M Sure.

B And the Cabinet Secretariat prepares the Agenda?

M Yes. Any member of the Government can ask for an item to be put on the Agenda. When matters have to have Cabinet sanction it may take place through comment at the official level, or the Minister may take the matter to the P.M. and he will have it put down on the Agenda. Normally the Prime Minister sees the Agenda before it is circulated. If there is a Ministry or more than one Ministry concerned, the Ministries and the Ministers are informed. This again is a formality. Unless members have been informed, the discussion in the Cabinet will lack the necessary documentation.

B The Agenda is then dispatched to every Member of Cabinet before a Cabinet meeting?

M Yes.

B And at the Cabinet meeting, time permitting, all those issues will be discussed?

M At the Cabinet meeting sometimes issues which are not on the Agenda will also be discussed.

B So it's a very live, vibrant body?

M Naturally.

B But a good deal of consultation takes place outside?

M Yes, yes, prior to the Cabinet meeting, and at the meeting.

B Is there an Inner Cabinet within the Indian Cabinet?

M I imagine that even an 'Inner Cabinet' is not a thing with fixed boundaries.

B It will depend on personalities?

M Yes. There are matters which Cabinet might refer to a committee for detailed consideration, for implementation, or even in order to reach a final decision. Supposing the Cabinet appoints a committee to discuss whether Mr. Brecher, being a biographer of Panditji and so on, should be allowed to come here; the decision of that committee would have to come before Cabinet. But if it's a question of the Standing Committees, then, whether the matter comes before the Cabinet or not depends upon the Prime Minister. In a sense the Prime Minister is both chairman and 'Director General' of the Cabinet. Of course there is a Cabinet Secretary who is the head of the Cabinet Secretariat. The Cabinet Secretary would largely advise on procedural matters. He has easy access to the Prime Minister. He also has to do with questions involving different ministries which are about to come or are already before the Cabinet. He is a civil servant; he sits at Cabinet meetings. An Armed Service officer, a General, may sometimes be called to a Cabinet meeting. A Junior Minister, a Minister of State who has Cabinet rank but who is not in the Cabinet, may also be invited. It used to be a convention in my time that if a Minister of State who is not in the Cabinet has an item on the Agenda, he can come and attend the meeting. He usually retires when the discussion of that issue is over. But unless there are special reasons, he would not be asked to leave.

B Was that true during your period in Cabinet?

M Yes, yes. For that reason some Ministers [of State], it was said, placed a little item on the Agenda in order to be present at Cabinet meetings. Some of them appeared to attend almost always. On the other hand, some Ministers of State, whose charges were also very heavy, were rarely present at Cabinet meetings. A Minister of State has ready access to the Prime Minister.

B You seem to put great stress on the Finance Minister. Is he almost a super-Minister?

M To a great extent that is true in India.

B Are there any special reasons for this?

M Everybody wants money! Both allocation and expenditure have to have financial approval. The Finance Ministry can hold up anything they like.

B Isn't that true in every government?

M I know. In England too the Chancellor of the Exchequer is a superior person. The Finance Ministry here also has other powers over such things as internal economic affairs and exchange control. In a controlled economy like ours there are so many checks and balances. Add to this a general inability of Members of Parliament to appreciate financial issues and questions—all these things come into it. And Finance Ministers, whether or not they have been very able, have very often been assertive men and have been very powerful.

B Has the unique role of the Finance Minister had any impact on the way in which foreign affairs have been conducted?

M I would not say a unique role; no, I don't think so; perhaps we might call it a substantial one.

B . . . In the sense of withholding funds which would limit the expansion of the Foreign Service or the establishment of new missions?

M That would be a matter between the Prime Minister and the Finance Minister. The Finance Minister could not exactly veto it; he would say that there is no foreign exchange available, and the Prime Minister, being the Head of the Government and

Foreign Minister at the same time, would say, 'If there is no money, then. . . .' There would be a compromise; there would be some kind of workable arrangement.

B Having sat in Cabinet for six years, Mr. Menon, how would you describe the way in which Panditji treated Cabinet?

M He treated it with great respect but he knew that he could obtain the decision he wanted. This isn't to say he expected the Cabinet to rubber-stamp his decisions. He would try to carry the persons concerned—either they would shrug their shoulders or else they would be persuaded and sometimes (and not infrequently) they would persuade him too! In his best days he was quite amenable to argument. He was not allergic to others telling him their views on anything. He was not a person who sought consultation, but you could 'force' consultation upon him, do you see. But 'consultation' in the usually understood sense was not his normal way. Towards the end he had too much to do and this inhibited his coming forward to seek the views of other people. But still, it worked.

B On the whole was the discussion frank and free among the senior Members of Cabinet?

M There you go again. You are theoretical because you are a professor! You think the British Cabinet worked the way Jennings wrote about it. Who was 'senior' for a given purpose depended on the particular circumstances.

B No. Professors are concerned with the way in which the Cabinet functions, not only with the way it is structured.

M I agree. Professors get to know this only by questioning people. They don't sit in Cabinets. If they did, they would relinquish their professorships. They would begin to function differently.

B They don't have that privilege. In your terms, how would you refer to the processes of discussion in the Cabinet?

M I think there is the Prime Minister on the one hand and on the other the more forceful Ministers—who often carry their points or get a reasonable decision in their favour. The Prime Minister usually gravitates towards the man who is in charge of the job. Much also depends on the Minister or the department which has the prestige. But if something is done against the declared constitutional policy, you could not but bring it up. But even before that stage the late Prime Minister would see what it was all about—I don't know what the position is like now.

Cabinet meetings take a long time sometimes, usually because there is no rigidly ordered discussion. There is a lot of cross-talk; you cannot sometimes get things over in a short time.

B Then, in my terms, it is frank and free.

M Not necessarily. In my opinion, cross-talk always suppresses the man who has something to say generally because he is not willing to say it. If there's a fight and if he joins in, he is likely to get lost in the 'noise'. This is generally true and not only in the Cabinet.

B Was the discussion focused, as it were?

M The Prime Minister would turn round and ask, 'What do you say about it?'—he would go around the table. Focused? Yes—that is what the chairman of the meeting does, if he is effective. Panditji achieved a great deal in this way. He was patient, contrary to what he might have appeared.

B But the special knowledge of the particular Minister would be respected and to that extent there was a kind of autonomy?

M Sometimes the Prime Minister would make it very obvious that he was asking somebody and sometimes he would not make it obvious at all; that was his particular tact and his particular privilege. Similarly, if the other person wanted to get something decided or have things his way, he would say so and the usual kind of discussion would take place. There is no particular kind of sanctity about these meetings. They are like other committees which are bodies of more or less equal persons and where there are no rules or standing orders and no voting. At the end the Prime Minister would dictate to the Cabinet Secretary in more precise language what had been decided. He was very good at that; he would tell the Cabinet Secretary that this is the decision and set it out in detail. This is what went into the minutes. Since he was the man who dictated he was more or less sum-ming up the discussion. So that if the discussion were referred to at any time it would be what he had dictated. He had a great deal of tact in that way although he was not a conjurer or anything. He was more methodical than people like me—he could always make notes—but still he was not methodical in the usually understood sense.

B Did Members of Cabinet have the feeling that if they had something to contribute to a Cabinet discussion it would be welcomed or at least listened to with the respect that was due to their special knowledge? In other words, they were not simply schoolboys waiting for the Prime Minister to pronounce judgement on issues that concerned their own ministry?

M It depends. When you say Cabinet Ministers do you mean all of them?

B I mean all of them, not just the senior ones.

M Well, anyone could talk; there was no senior or junior minister [in that sense]. I know one 'junior' minister who always talked about everything under the sun! You put up with it; and then someone would say, 'We would like to hear someone else.' It was just like any other meeting. But then, of course, it's the Indian approach.

B Apart from yourself and the Prime Minister, when foreign policy questions came before Cabinet did other Members of Cabinet participate in the discussion?

M Oh yes, certainly; they would join in and then the Prime Minister would talk in an informing rather than a debating manner and he would explain that 'we cannot do that because that would have this effect or we should do this, or we should wait', and so on. On the majority of questions they were in agreement with him from the beginning and if some query was raised he would explain it. He would never say to anyone, or even imply, 'This is none of your business!'

B So he was a patient educator?

M Partly, yes; sometimes impatient and sometimes patient. In Canada it would be different because your Prime Minister would not be able to expect the kind of almost reverential attitude or response that both the present Prime Minister and the previous Prime Minister could expect from their colleagues.

B In that sense you put the present Prime Minister on a par with Mr. Nehru?

M No, I am not doing that. There was only one Nehru—men like him have a uniqueness, a comprehensiveness of mind and wisdom. But the present Prime Minister is increasingly influential with his colleagues. A Prime Minister soon acquires a sense of the possible. If he is a sensible chap, he says, 'I cannot press things too far; either I will break or they will yield; there will be trouble'; very often the meeting is adjourned and the subject is referred to a committee. Sometimes it comes up two years afterwards!

B During your period in Cabinet from 1956 onwards who were the people who stood out?

M That is a difficult question.

B Surely Maulana Azad was one?

M He actually said very little and that not too often.

B And Pandit Pant?

M He didn't speak very much either, because he would have had discussions with the Prime Minister beforehand—unless it was a question on which it was desired that he speak; sometimes Panditji would say to someone, 'Will you please explain this to them.'

B Surely a man like T. T. K. would have a good deal to say on many issues?

M None of these people talked much more than was necessary. There were one or two people who talked a great deal on every subject. I don't think they had much effect.

B On defence policy, were there other people who participated?

M I hardly spoke on defence matters in Cabinet.

B Even though you were Defence Minister?

M Yes, but there was a Defence Committee of the Cabinet which met separately. Often it was a question of the Prime Minister's responsibility—as in the British system the Prime Minister has special responsibilities for foreign affairs and defence.

The question is to determine how far the working of Cabinet conforms to textbook ideas and how far it doesn't. In a parliamentary system of government, by which I mean practically all governments in the Commonwealth, the way a Cabinet functions and the number of its meetings is very largely *ad hoc*, informal, flexible. There are no set rules, no voting, not even a strict adherence to an agenda. Whatever is done is mostly done merely for functional reasons. In any Cabinet the practice would vary according to its age, the time during which its members have sat in it without change, the period during which its principal person, the Prime Minister, has presided over it, and so on. A kind of gearing-in takes place and its own conventions get set up and its own disregard for conventions also becomes a convention.

I had no practical experience of the Indian Cabinet in its earlier days. I didn't come into the Government until 1956, but I had been at Cabinet meetings before then. Although perhaps it would be wrong to call the earlier Indian Cabinets composite Cabinets, they certainly contained persons who were not Congress Party members, or even if they were, they were very new entrants. There was Dr. Ambedkar,[1] Shyama Prasad Mookerjee[2] of the Hindu Mahasabha, and Mr. John Matthai.[3]

While every Indian had a kind of regard and awe for the Prime Minister, ministers outside Congress had no particular affiliation to the Congress or their colleagues. Panditji could not take liberties with them in the way that he could with the others, although each of them respected his personality. Those Cabinets, therefore, may be regarded as more formal. It's even probable that, on ticklish questions, the people closer to the Prime Minister might have thought things out so that they faced the whole Cabinet with a brief they had already prepared. I don't say with a made-up mind, not in the same way

[1] B. R. Ambedkar, Untouchable leader from the 1930s until his death in 1956.
[2] Bengal Hindu communal leader and founder of the Jana Sangh (People's League) in 1950.   [3] Minister of Finance, 1948–50.

that the Western powers made up their minds and met the Soviet Union as four to one at the Disarmament Sub-Committee of the U.N. in the early fifties, not in that sense. They were not persons who would add to the confusion by differences amongst themselves within the Government. Or it might be that Sardar Patel or someone else went to speak to some of these people and said, 'These are our difficulties, these are our problems', and would bring about as much harmony or acquiescence as possible. I have no direct knowledge but I have reason to think that this was more or less how it worked. Yes, you may call it my inference but it's not just an academic inference.

Cabinet meets any time it likes. But the Prime Minister [Nehru] was a comparatively orderly person and he tried to make Cabinet meet on a fixed day, although it often didn't work out. Sometimes he found there was not sufficient give and take among members because there were not enough informal discussions before meeting. I very well remember that at one time it was suggested that each Member of Cabinet should ask the whole Cabinet to tea once a week, and that was done. But then in the Indian way that became not just a tea but a feast! And so the whole thing collapsed after a time because it became a kind of ritual; it didn't achieve the purpose for which it had been designed. It faded out. In these parties the Prime Minister did go around and sit down and speak to people and move from seat to seat. But somehow or other on account of his big personality, on account of the fact that people trusted his wisdom or his ultimate judgement, debate in the accepted Western sense did not take place. But that doesn't mean that there was no exchange of ideas or that no one felt able to take the initiative.

The other factor is that, whether in England or here, the term 'collective responsibility' covers many sins and excludes some virtues. Collective responsibility doesn't exist anywhere today. It's not even as though for the sins of one ministry or minister the whole Cabinet would resign. If this were so the resignation of certain individual members would not have taken place: the whole Government would have resigned.

There is little collective responsibility, in the sense that decisions largely concerned with an individual department about actions which may afterwards prove important do not necessarily come before Cabinet. They would do if the Prime Minister thought it was necessary; indeed any member could raise them. But you must appreciate the fact that while in certain circumstances, provided he has the consent of the Prime Minister, one minister may call for the papers of another ministry, this is not usually done. First of all, each man has his own troubles. Secondly, he doesn't want to antagonize his colleagues or create difficulties for himself. There are many matters on which more than one ministry is concerned, but the right position would be that those so concerned should discuss these among themselves or resolve their difficulties by talking to another colleague or to the Prime Minister. So collective responsibility, in the sense that a decision once made is everybody's, is very largely a myth— certainly in the Indian Cabinet. Even today one Cabinet member speaks almost like a Swatantra Party[1] man, another member speaks more with the emphasis of Gandhi's philosophy, a third one speaks perhaps as a socialist, and so on. That is the actual situation of the Cabinet—I could almost say of all Cabinets.

The Cabinet met about once a week—sometimes it met more often—and meetings usually took from two to three or four hours, largely depending on the number of people who were present. There are a certain number of items on the Agenda; these are matters which either require formal sanction, in the sense that Government orders have to be issued, or it may be some matter, such as the sending of delegations abroad, about which there has been a general desire to see that the thing is kept in restraint and therefore it has been thought best for it to come before the Cabinet as a kind of check. Though the discussion on such a topic in the Cabinet was limited, its purpose was clear; the fact that it came before the Cabinet meant that it was scrutinized minutely beforehand, and very often the numbers of the delegation would be cut down.

In the meetings of the Cabinet the way of recording these things was not for somebody to move a resolution that had to be written down. Discussion took place and ultimately, whatever decision was made, the Prime Minister, as Chairman of the Cabinet, mentioned it at the meeting to the Cabinet Secretary who was beside him. He practically dictated it and the Cabinet Secretary took it down. There was no question of the phrasing being left to civil servants: Nehru dictated it.

---

[1] Right-wing secular party founded in 1959.

It ensured that the decisions were brief, that they included the essentials, and that they were regularized. Whatever the variations this was the normal procedure.

In a Cabinet the Prime Minister is not an overlord. The usual idea is that he is *primus inter pares*, the chief among equals. In practice it depends on how many are really his equals and how many of these equals are not so equal. Secondly, being with equals, he can talk to them openly.

The fact that a matter is not referred to the Cabinet cannot for outside purposes be regarded as depriving it of any sanctity, because if the Prime Minister doesn't refer a matter to the Cabinet it is his own decision. In any case the responsibility is his, even if anything goes wrong. The theory is that he would carry his colleagues with him. I remember very few occasions when there have been sharp cleavages of opinion or expression —where in a Cabinet or a Cabinet Committee the Prime Minister has made certain propositions and where some of his senior colleagues, having arrived at a different view on account of extraneous circumstances, have failed to agree with him. Such issues had to be put off in order to avoid embarrassment. If the difference is sharp and there is no ultimate agreement the person will resign.

B I wonder whether these issues are sufficiently remote in time for us to discuss them now?

M No. Nothing is remote in current history if it occurred less than thirty or forty years ago. Besides, most of these people are living. And I believe myself that if Panditji had a difference with one of his senior colleagues, shall we say with Maulana Azad, it would not be brought to the Cabinet. The late Prime Minister had sufficient common sense and a sufficient sense of propriety either to solve it beforehand or to tell his colleagues, 'I am very sorry but this has to be like this'; and that was his own business, do you see. I cannot remember more than two instances where in the Indian Cabinet people resigned on principle. Having resigned for other reasons, some would invoke principle. This is not uncommon elsewhere too.

B In that setting, Mr. Menon, what was the function of Cabinet Committees?

M The Prime Minister set up a number of committees long before my time. There was the Economic Committee of the Cabinet, for example; this was a sub-committee of the Cabinet. But the Defence Committee of the Cabinet is the Cabinet itself; that is to say it does not include the whole Cabinet, but it functions as the Cabinet. Decisions taken by the Defence Committee are tantamount to decisions taken by the Cabinet, unless of course the Prime Minister, who is chairman of it, should say that it is a matter which should be considered by or mentioned to all our colleagues. But even so, certain questions are referred to the Defence Committee alone; normally this only happens if the Defence Minister or the Prime Minister desires it or if it is a matter involving large sums of money. Usually the Defence Minister prefers that things should be referred because he knows he can get them through. So the Defence Committee met more often than almost any other Committee of the Cabinet.

Again, with the Foreign Affairs Committee, usually no issue of policy arises. But when serious matters take place, for example a very considerable raid by Pakistan, it is necessary to meet. Usually the Prime Minister mentions it to the people concerned; he must carry his colleagues with him and by implication it is a decision of Cabinet.

There are some people who might have said, 'I was not consulted'; responsible members should not say that, and by responsible members I don't necessarily mean senior members. It depends upon their sense of propriety. So far as I know I never did that sort of thing at any time—there were large numbers of matters about which I knew nothing; I didn't bother about them. I never said, 'That is not my decision.' Sometimes one heard about a decision through newspapers or in Parliament; I didn't feel hurt about this because why should you carry unnecessary things in your head, especially when you knew what the decision would be even if you did happen to be there! The main thing was whether you could make a contribution. And then, even if the matter was over, you could still go to the Prime Minister and say, 'This and that has been done; I would like to say this.' But we were all committed to it whatever the issue. There has been no case that I know of where things were not examined or modified or corrected if one mentioned it to the Prime Minister. Sometimes Nehru would say, 'Yes, it could have been so but I am afraid the decision has already been made', in which case people would not press him any more.

B Are there other Committees of the Cabinet that fall into the same category as the Defence Committee?

M The others are sub-committees of the Cabinet. The Economic Committee doesn't make any decisions; matters are referred to it or it can even take up something and study it if it wants to and then theoretically it comes before the Cabinet. The Foreign Affairs Committee is in rather the same position but it is more like the Defence Committee of the Cabinet. It is largely a matter of practice that has grown up.

The Foreign Affairs Committee consists of members whom the Prime Minister nominates. In the early days it consisted only of myself and two or three others as well as the Prime Minister who is always the chairman of committees. But in India when you have decided to have a committee of three someone says 'Oh, this other fellow has been left out'. Later the Foreign Affairs Committee became larger and larger mainly because feeling began to arise that foreign affairs was a kind of private preserve which nobody looked into. So far as I know the Foreign Affairs Committee of the Cabinet is an Indian invention; and in my opinion it only arose because the Prime Minister was himself Foreign Minister; otherwise there would have been no necessity for it. It didn't meet very often; it met, for example, before delegations were finalized for the U.N. —the decision would already have been taken and members would be informed of it. Members of the Foreign Affairs Committee might mention to the Prime Minister that so and so should go. How much should be said and what should be discussed was a matter for the Prime Minister, both as Prime Minister and as Foreign Minister. The sub-committees have functioned for some years. There were also sub-committees of inquiry, *ad hoc* committees, and so on.

B Mr. Menon, as you look back on the working of the Cabinet and these committees, particularly in the realm of foreign affairs, would you regard them as being in any sense participants in decision-making or in shaping policy, or were they not really crucial to the decision-making process, but more organs of consultation in the very broad sense?

M By and large they did not shape policy although they did at times. I remember no case where proposals before the Defence Committee had to be postponed *sine die*. In some committees it took years to get a decision. As for the Economic Committee of the Cabinet, in the later days it certainly did not have much impact on the Government because economic affairs are largely considered by the Finance Minister, the Economic Affairs Committee, the Planning Commission, by public discussion, and so on. In the early days, I believe, it was very much more important. It all depends on the maturity of the Finance Minister, the composition of the Cabinet, and that sort of thing.

In my opinion, as time went on people with less and less experience and lower and lower stature became Members of the Cabinet. They have not been as important in the country as, say, Maulana or Patel were. I mean in the old days there was a giant national movement. The Prime Minister, Maulana Azad, Patel were three giants from that point of view—from the outside you may regard them just as ordinary home politicians but at home they had a very big place. But it's a mistake to think that a Cabinet is a body of delegates representing either communities or States, although no doubt the Prime Minister had in mind the fact that there should be a woman in the Ministry, that certain States should not go unrepresented, and so on.

B Isn't this essential in a federal State?

M Not constitutionally but in practice, yes. For example, you would not think of having a Cabinet in Canada without a Minister from Quebec. Apart from the Secretaries of State for Scottish Affairs and Welsh Affairs, the British Cabinet always includes of some Scotsman and Welshman, because they are the people concerned. I came from Kerala, I was born there; but nobody regarded me as being a Keralite or South Indian or anything like that. On the other hand, I can think of members who are mainly regarded as coming from their States, either because they thought like that or because they were associated with local politics for a long time. In the Cabinet there have also been two or three people who had a very international outlook who would be able to take their place in almost any Cabinet in the world. Equally there have been people who were more 'parish' politicians, who were very efficient in a limited kind of way. There were some members about whom no two people would agree; these are usual in any government and a certain amount of ballast is always carried.

B May we explore two other aspects of this? Firstly I am interested in the day-to-day relationship between the Cabinet and the Congress leadership. How would you describe the relationship?

M It varied. In the early period [1949] the Congress bosses, even local ones, tried to interfere with government officials and the Prime Minister made it quite clear that Government was Government and Party was Party, and that the Party had no business to interfere in State Government. But as time went on the Party has had more effect. That was largely achieved by statements at Party meetings which were often seminars led by the Prime Minister. It boils down to the fact that he felt he had his hand on the pulse of the people. Further, until the time of his death, he could find support for whatever he wanted, And he did not lord it over anybody; sometimes he might shout and say, 'What do you think this is—not a grown-up country?' Sometimes he would throw a fit of anger but it didn't add to or subtract from the situation. He never nursed ill feelings.

B You do not regard the Party as a pressure group in any sense?

M No. The Congress President counts sometimes; Nehru would say, 'I will consult the Congress President'. A private discussion could be held in the Cabinet; after all it is a Congress Cabinet. But there was no question of the Working Committee passing resolutions [on governmental issues] though there are some members who say that this did or should happen. In fact, even now it doesn't happen. Furthermore there is no reason to think that all the points made in the Cabinet are made after consultation with the Congress President. This might or might not be the case.

B One would assume, though, that in the changed circumstances of the present the Party would play a more significant role than it has done in the past.

M This is both true and not true.

B I don't know what you mean.

M In some cases it can be very difficult to exclude X, Y, or Z because he is an important man in the Party; that might be his only qualification. But certain important appointments have been made in the last few months which, it is said, were known to the Congress President only through the newspapers! I cannot vouch for this, but it seemed like it. And there is nothing constitutionally wrong in this. According to convention the appointment of a Cabinet colleague both in this country and elsewhere is ultimately the responsibility of the Prime Minister.

18. Pressure Groups, Parliament, and Foreign Policy

B I want to turn to the question of pressure groups, or interest groups, that have an effect on foreign policy. As you look back over the last seventeen years of Indian foreign policy, Mr. Menon, would you say that there exist groups which are highly organized and effective, which make demands on Government, and which put a point of view before Government which influences decision-making? Are there any instances in which such pressure groups operate effectively on foreign policy?

M On foreign policy?

B Such groups certainly affect domestic policy.

M Domestic policy and foreign policy too. I think that the 'American lobby' is powerful and active in this country.

B How do you define the 'American lobby'? What does it comprise?

M I would not like to define it in detail.

B What I have in mind is the presence or absence of pressure groups. For example, could it be said that in the discussions between India and Ceylon [1964] there was an organized Tamil or Madras group which attempted to influence the way in which Delhi negotiated with Colombo on the question of the treatment of people of Indian origin?

M I am too involved in this matter to discuss it. Normally speaking the late Prime Minister was always aware that there were large numbers of people in southern India who were affected, but this never dominated his calculations. He knew the burdens that we would have to carry but what worried him more was the impact on world opinion. The fact that these people had contributed economically and in all sorts of ways [to Ceylon's welfare] and that they were suddenly declared stateless worried him. How could a person become stateless by a declaration of another Government? They might have said that these people were Indians—that one could understand—but stateless means that by their domicile or by their contributions to relations [in India] from Ceylon they have recognized their connection with India, do you see. Nehru knew their problem very well; he would not have made the present Agreement [October 1964].

B Were there other questions in India's foreign policy where the presence within the country of local groups which felt strongly weighed heavily with the Prime Minister? For example, during the Tibetan revolt in 1959 there was a great outcry in this country. Would you say that influenced Mr. Nehru's policy?

M I think so. Certainly this was the case as far as policy towards China was concerned. But the main reason for this was the fact that China betrayed us.

B What about public opinion?

M I believe that in the beginning he could have controlled it —not only public opinion but the opinion of his entourage. His position was weakened by the fact that China had betrayed him. But even in the most difficult moments [pressure of Indian public opinion] he never gave in on the question of Chinese sovereignty over Tibet or on non-alignment.

B Mr. Menon, you have mentioned Ceylon and China. Would you say that public opinion has also played a powerful role over the years in restraining or stimulating Indian policy towards Pakistan?

M Do you mean that the Government has been restrained by public opinion?

B Yes, that public opinion has played a significant role.

M No. I don't think that there is very much difference between the Government and public opinion on this except that public opinion is in advance of the Government, particularly of this Government.

B Are there any other areas in which public opinion has played a role?

M Public opinion plays a role in everything. But the way you put it, it would only be thrown into relief when there are sharp cleavages. The fact that the Congress Party is still a great national movement as well as being a political party, the effect of the personality of the Prime Minister, the effect of the Federal Constitution on a Congress Government and all the States, and all our problems there, our nation-building programmes and problems which are largely in the States—all come into it. Public opinion does play a part through inhibition, fear, tradition, and pride.

B What about the public opinion that expresses itself in a very articulate way in the press—in editorials and columns by a dozen or so journalists? Are these considered seriously?

M Yes. They are effective in a negative not in a positive way.

B But you would not consider them important in affecting policy-making?

M No.

SUPPLEMENTARY INTERVIEW—MAY 1965

B In our earlier discussion, Mr. Menon, you touched upon the influence of pressure groups and public opinion on policy towards Ceylon, China, and Kashmir. Could you now discuss the business community's influence on foreign policy? Four questions come to mind: (1) How much influence did it have under Nehru's leadership? (2) On what issues, if any, was business pressure attempted? (3) What are the channels through which it is expressed—correspondence, personal contacts with officials and politicians, threats of one kind and another, or a combination of all these? and (4) What is the position today?

M I may be very naïve about this but I don't think that foreign policy has anything to do with the business group or that they had much to do with foreign policy. It was largely decided by those whom the Prime Minister took into his confidence. And I think myself that if the business group had been consulted it would probably have been against a Republic, against non-alignment, and so on. I am not saying that the national papers, which are controlled by business interests, supported the Government to the full, but that these ideas of independence, non-alignment, and so on have become a kind of accepted policy. As for non-alignment, after all, what else could we have done at the time we became independent? One has always to remember that.

B In some countries like Canada, the United States, Great Britain, perhaps others, the business community and other interest groups do weigh heavily in the shaping of foreign policy; that is to say, the National Association of Manufacturers, the Chamber of Commerce, trade unions, bring great pressure to bear on foreign policy. No government in the United States or in Canada can ignore the explicit or subtle pressure of these groups. Would you say that in Indian politics the business community was without any influence on foreign policy decision-making?

M As everyone knows, foreign policy here was shaped by Panditji. He guided it and so far as the public was concerned the presentation and handling were his. I don't think our businessmen realized that it was going to affect them in any way. I can't say the same today. Also you have to take another factor into account—that basic nationalism brushed away many obstructions and pressures. In the first flush of independence all these things were there: the personality of the Prime Minister, the fact that there was no other alternative for us, the fact that foreign policy itself was new to everybody. These factors combined to make foreign policy largely non-controversial.

You asked me about the Civil Service. On the whole in the earlier days, even if the Civil Service didn't implement policy as well as it should have done, this was largely through ignorance. I cannot say anybody tried to sabotage it or anything like that. It isn't fair for me to criticize the service personnel because they cannot defend themselves. There are notable exceptions and not small exceptions either.

B I appreciate the point you make about India being a new and under-developed nation in which the business community doesn't play the same role that it does in economically more developed States in other parts of the world. I appreciate too the fact that in your experience the tendency was simply to

accept Panditji's leadership and the leadership of those whom
he took into his confidence. But it seems to me natural that,
whether or not the business community was fully aware of
international affairs, it would be inclined to be more pro-
Western than pro-Soviet or pro-Chinese and that it must have
had some doubts about India's China policy, India's non-
alignment, and the tendency to equate the West with the Soviet
bloc. Did they ever express these views, and if so, how did they
do it? What I am trying to find out is whether the business
community was totally passive in respect of the stand India took
on a wide range of issues in the United Nations and elsewhere.

M So far as I know they didn't show evidence of much knowledge. There are some people in the industrial and business
community who thought it all wrong, who spoke in British and
later in American terms. They probably influenced the newspapers, they probably interviewed or exerted influence on some
Members of Parliament, but they have not carried on a campaign about it. Naturally all Indians irrespective of community
were happy that India had a position in the world. I am not
talking about how things are today.

B Could you say something about one aspect of how things are
today. Given the departure of that élite group which dominated
the Indian scene for seventeen years, and given the new political
constellation of the last ten months, the business community is
now in a position to exert far greater and far broader influence
in domestic and external policy than it ever could before. Is
there any evidence that since last year this has been the case in
the field of foreign policy?

M The way you put it the question is rather over-simplified.
What has happened is that in the last ten months our economic
policy has begun to influence our foreign policy. Also, with the
greater number of people in contact with foreign countries,
everybody thinks they know more about foreign affairs. Furthermore, people are also being consciously conditioned by Mc-
Carthyism. Broadly speaking, this section of our society is
anti-socialist, anti-communist, and perhaps some are even
against non-alignment. There are one or two individuals who
want us to follow the American line, but by and large I must

say that basically the Government's foreign policy doesn't come under too much criticism.

B There is one question I would like to ask about the Civil Service Establishment. I am not concerned here with their efficiency. It seems to me that the Civil Service, trained largely in the British tradition and with a strong intellectual and emotional affinity to Great Britain, would direct India's non-alignment towards the West and more particularly towards Britain and the Commonwealth. There is a highly anglicized élite which conducts day-to-day affairs in the embassies abroad and in the Ministry of External Affairs at home. Do they represent a pressure group in the sense of directing policy towards pro-Western non-alignment?

M They might have done so but to start with their numbers were small. It was the Government that made policy. I would not say they sabotaged it so much as that they didn't understand it or were inefficient about it. They were not makers of foreign policy. There were one or two individuals who would have liked to have done this, but it wasn't possible and then they accepted the position as it developed. But more recently I think that what you say has become increasingly relevant. The feeling is not so much pro-British as pro-American. It is not fashionable now for vested interests to be pro-British.

B There is a type of pressure group which often plays an important role in foreign policy, especially in Asian and African countries which have become independent in the last two decades. Time and time again we have seen that the Army Officer Corps or the Army Chiefs and the Army Establishment exert a major pressure on policy. One of the ways in which this happens is by demands for a larger military budget. Another is for a particular kind of foreign policy. Now that the budget for the Armed Forces in India has been doubled, trebled, quadrupled, is it not likely that the army becomes a major factor in the shaping of foreign policy?

M Well, I don't think they would influence us with regard to Pakistan and China; they could say that militarily speaking we could not take a particular step—but they would not argue about foreign policy with the Government. I don't know what the position is now but I don't think the Armed Forces have a great deal of say about the Government. Up to the time I dealt with it, the army was under civil control.

It is wrong for the army to try to make policy; their business is to be concerned with military tactics. Military planning and arrangements and things of that kind must remain in the hands of the Government, and even inside the Government these questions are largely conditioned by finance. I believe the statement that was made recently, that strategy was left with the army, was due to a misuse of terms. The Government is not going to say that it wants one company here or two companies there, but the Government will certainly say, 'we should attack Pakistan' or 'we should not attack Pakistan' or 'we should accept trainees from Indonesia and Malaysia', or things of that kind; these are all matters of policy. Since we use more Hindi words than English, sometimes English words are used in the wrong context. Even if it wanted to, I don't believe the Government would be allowed by Parliament to leave such matters to the Military. Of course, military matters are merely questions of expertise; strategy includes considerations that are related to our political orientation.

B Let me spell out more concretely the sort of thing I had in mind about the army's influence on foreign policy. During the last few months as tension mounted over the Vietnam war, particularly over the American use of gas in Vietnam, the Government of India was conspicuously slow in taking a stand. Some people saw in this the influence of the army, in the sense that India, feeling dependent on external aid for its armed forces as well as for economic aid, viewed any criticism of the U.S. in Vietnam as likely to slow down the aid programme. Does this not become a restraint on India's foreign policy?

M Sorry, Mr. Brecher, but I think you are trying to fit facts into your theory. It is quite true that a great many of the armed forces' officers prefer to think that America is the last word; this is largely because of their social life and that sort of thing. There is no doubt that after the Chinese affair they made greater demands and influenced some factors which in turn affected foreign policies. The army was conditioned to be like the British service, not for political but for economic, techno-

logical, factual, practical reasons, and because of the fact that
the top-brass officers are all Sandhurst men. The majority of
them are patriotic enough—but I don't think they are particularly brilliant or abounding in passion for the indigenous!
They are like everybody else; they go to an institution or college
and by and large they accept the policy of the Government.

The question of buying equipment from the communist
countries did not arise until very recently; I don't think the
first piece of such equipment came in until about four or five
years ago. At one time even the politicians were against it, not
from prejudice but because they felt they had to go cautiously.
The bulk of our goods came from Britain, for money of course.
We don't want to create difficulties for ourselves technologically,
nor do we want the army to use pressure to drive us in one
particular direction. Therefore, the two questions of yours about
the business community and the army are perhaps more appli-
cable to Canada. These things happened in Burma, in Indonesia,
and elsewhere, but here conditions are a little different.

B Apropos of your remarks that conditions are different here,
may I ask one other question about the army? During the last
fifteen years in a great many States all over the world we have
seen the increasingly important role played by the army in
politics; India has been a rather striking exception. But as the
army becomes more important, as national security issues come
to the fore in India, and as a large proportion of the budget is
allocated to the Military, is it not possible that the political
role of the army will become more important? What do you
think are the conditions in which the army would become a
major—if not the dominant—factor in the political life of India?

M Now this is very much in the realm of speculation. Certainly
all the time I knew it there was no question of the army making
decisions of national policy as regards foreign relations. The
army may resent something or other, they may limit our action
by what would appear to be technical considerations; however,
they are soldiers. This is the British pattern too. It is true that
the army has become more important, but economic factors
are the only explanation. The army has become more important
but it is the Government that has to provide the food, the guns,
the education, and keep up the morale.

Just suppose the army took over; they would still have to sort out all the economic problems, educational problems, and things of that kind; and if an army genius could do it, then the army would naturally carry greater weight than it does.

B What would you regard as the principal barriers to the army assuming power in the country?

M First of all both the problems and the country are too big; I don't think there are Napoleons in our army. I think the bulk of the army are good patriotic Indians; there may be some odd, politically ambitious men among them. So far as I know it would not be easy for them to carry the rest of the armed forces with them and erode their loyalty and their allegiance to the Constitutional Government. If ever the army were to form a government they would have all the problems other governments have. As a Government we have not tried to humiliate the personnel of the armed forces or to put them in their place; we have treated them as they should be treated. Even the Army Headquarters here is under the Ministry of Defence. I cannot talk about the future as anything is possible.

B Would you care to comment on Parliament's influence in shaping foreign policy? Each year there are about half a dozen debates on foreign affairs, apart from Call-Attention motions, the weekly Question period, etc.

M On the one hand, Parliament has an educative impact. In my opinion discussions in Parliament have the result of showing the world what we think and that we do think. On the other hand, it shows the limitations of our position since Parliament is often dealing with a *fait accompli*. This is not peculiar to India although there are certain differences here. I think it performs a very useful function. There are speeches made. Some of the speeches made are a kind of routine opposition and often strong views are expressed. This enables the Prime Minister and Government to feel that even if a thing has to be done for diplomatic or other reasons, Parliament should at least be told about it. Sometimes this may mean that the wise thing cannot be done or has to be delayed—but this is so in all politics.

As for general policy, these debates have been occasions for the assertion of the basic policies of the Government. With the large majority the Government has in Parliament and with the Prime Minister being an acknowledged pundit in international affairs, the debates could not materially affect issues. But Nehru's attitude to Parliament was one of great respect. In that sense the late Prime Minister never used the fact that the Government had a very big majority.

B Are you aware of any direct effect of the debates in Parliament on Panditji's thinking about foreign policy?

M Yes, but on all these matters he convened meetings beforehand. On big matters, like the Chinese invasion, he called meetings which included Opposition Members as well. He learned a lot of statecraft as he went on, and after all, he didn't think that the country was his private property. There was even freer discussion at these meetings than there was at Party meetings. It had, however, a two-way effect. There were some matters, in my opinion, in which he should perhaps have been much more the Prime Minister and less the chairman of a committee or leader of a party. However, I cannot say that the contribution of Parliament in foreign affairs has not been valuable.

B At all times during your experience?

M By and large. The Opposition would say that it was they who drew attention to the Chinese danger and so on. This is entirely wrong. When a Government appreciates or knows about certain things it doesn't always talk about them. The Opposition would perhaps say that 'non-alignment' was kept from being pro-Russian by their intervention. This again is not the case. But the importance of foreign affairs debates is mainly foreign [for the outside world]! Secondly, it educates our own people. Thirdly, it helps to make foreign policy acceptable in many ways—you can see that from the results. It's always the same; there are speeches, but all ends well.

B But the results were determined by the massive majority of the Congress in Parliament and the consensus of the majority of the people in the country?

M No. Only a few amendments are even pressed by the other side; of fifty or sixty amendments only one or two are pressed and that is largely for their own electorates, the Opposition electorates.

B Can you recall any issues in which parliamentary pressure was effectively exerted to alter or influence a particular policy?

M Well, all decisions are influenced by parliamentary pressure in the broad sense but I could not imagine the Government being defeated on a policy issue. In that case the Government would resign. I don't think our previous Prime Minister made any bones about it. He used to say, 'You can do it yourself' and he even shouted against the Opposition when his informed convictions were criticized. That you can see from the debates.

I never got any hostile reception from Parliament in regard to foreign affairs—even today I am happy to feel that they listen very attentively—even if one made speeches that were critical or contained repartees. Once or twice Kripalani[1] behaved offensively, but I did not respond in the same way. I believe that Nehru was more sensitive to the Opposition than almost any other Prime Minister in the world that I know of. I think it was largely because he knew that the people who were on his side did not represent all opinion. He liked to know what the Opposition felt.

B There is an institution in Parliament, Mr. Menon, which I think is called the Consultative Committee on Foreign Affairs. Was that of any importance?

M I don't know because, as a Minister, I found it was more akin to a conference! Unfortunately, a few people tended to monopolize the time. You give information but are more or less forced into the position of being on the defensive. I think that there should be more consultations and that members should be able to become better informed. And there should be more orderly discussions. It is only a poor Minister who avoids interrogation or the sharing of views.

---

[1] Acharya J. B. Kripalani, long-time Congress leader who went into opposition in 1950, and was later leader of the Praja Socialist Party and thereafter an Independent M.P.

B So there is not a vigorous give and take between Ministers and Members of Parliament?

M There is but it may not always add up to very much. The average Member of Parliament has not got the knowledge or the time. But if a Minister wants something carried it's a useful instrument. You answer a lot of questions; they are practically the same each time because the problems are the same. These meetings have their value. Apart from odd individual Ministers who have a greater sense of parliamentary responsibility, one doesn't have to depend on it or anything of that kind. And compared to Opposition members in any part of the world, I think ours are just as good. Perhaps the fact that there is no tradition of reading and organization behind them does limit the quality of debate. There are no Fabian Societies, no P.E.P.s and that sort of thing to provide the material. The Opposition, I am told, have some ways of informing members. But I do not know about this at first hand.

19. Economic Development

B I want to turn this morning, Mr. Menon, to one of the greatest problems confronting all the States in Asia and Africa—the problem of economic development. For the past thirteen years India has been involved in a major experiment of economic development within the framework of democracy. There are many who have come to the conclusion that the experiment has not achieved the success anticipated in the early 1950s. What do you think are the critical factors explaining the relative decrease in Indian economic growth in recent years?

M This is not my appraisal, it is the appraisal of the Planning Commission. The standard reached or even aimed at cannot be regarded as very high. The First Plan [1951–6] overshot the set targets for two reasons: they fixed the targets so low that it was impossible not to exceed them, and so there was the first flush of enthusiasm. I believe Panditji's personal attention counted for a great deal, and V. T. Krishnamachari was a very efficient and persistent administrator. I also believe that at that time it was more of a national plan, it was received with awe, and the response was largely one inspired by dedication. On the other hand, there is the general slothfulness of the nation, in other words they are not working hard enough. I do not mean to say that most of our people are slothful. The choice to work or not does not depend on them.

Now what are the reasons why people as a whole are not working hard enough? I think that social justice has not proceeded as fast as it should have. I am practical enough to know that these things take time, but apart from a few people like Panditji, I am sorry to have to say that people who have been in the Government have not always been fervent enthusiasts. Also we accepted the Public Sector and the Private Sector as matters of fact. The term 'mixed economy' now covers many social sins, and much economic and social regression and injustice. It was not intended to be like this. We were writing on a clean sheet. Before the departure of the British we were pretty well advanced industrially. From the point of view of the aggregate output and in relation to other countries, we were sixth or seventh in the world, although in relation to our size, resources, and population we were under-developed and backward. Therefore we allowed a considerable amount of private development here. We all took the view, I think the right view, that whatever resources we had, there was little point in shooting sitting birds. We should develop a public sector in other things such as capital goods because industries are necessary, and generally speaking when the quick rate of return becomes slower private industry is less anxious to come forward. It was thought that the public sector would act as a fillip to the private sector. But I notice now, and I have protested against it publicly, that people think there is a competition between the public and the private sector as to who should get there first! Now this is an impossible race because the public sector is badly handicapped. It cannot afford to ignore well-established administrative connections, it cannot buy material in the black market, and it cannot buy people at a high price—they must come forward in the official cadre. All State enterprises have these difficulties. At present, then, the advantages are very much in favour of the private sector.

Moreover it is an error to speak of a total dichotomy between the private and the public sectors. This is one of those illusions sedulously cultivated by the supporters of the private sector who want the public sector to close down. They would like to pretend that the public sector leaves them very little to do or that they are dispossessed. I will tell you how it works. How public is the public sector? Take the Bhakra Dam as an example. The bulk of the work was done by private contractors, foreign or Indian. It's no more the public sector than our roads are. The bulk of the work goes to the private sector and therefore the cost goes up. Efficiency depends very much on control and the project as a whole progresses at the pace of these contracts. To a very great extent it is the contractors who decide how long the project will take. In the old days the Prime Minister used to step in and, whether his choice of people was right or wrong, he would still do something and say, 'This cannot be; you must do something about it'. So in the first two Plans most of the projects got finished according to target.

The next question to ask is how private is the private sector? Who provides the foreign exchange? The answer is that it comes on government guarantees, on government negotiations; the only thing that is private is the profit! So these names [public and private sectors] cannot be taken too seriously. Also I believe that very considerable gains and profits are made from the Managing Agency system and various other things which we inherited from the past. When goods come to the consumer their price is high. Furthermore, I believe that the approach in this country in regard to scarcity is wrong. I think that they have interpreted the Gandhian outlook by extolling scarcity. I believe that economic and social justice must aim at plenty and not be content with scarcity.

I believe that the Planning Commission and planning are twentieth-century ideas. The Prime Minister [Nehru] brought them into our thinking from the very early days of our national movement [1938]. Today, however, the Planning Commission is run by people who are antediluvian in outlook. What is more, their methods of consultation are lavishly wasteful! I have sat at the Planning Commission's meetings week after week until the time came when I didn't know what meeting to go to because there were so many of them. One of them might be important, another might not be. Meetings sometimes consisted of 100 people. Also I believe that successive Finance Ministers have been allergic to the Planning Commission and have treated it as something which should take orders from them. As time went on, foreign affairs, our internal difficulties, and personnel difficulties all became more demanding. The Prime Minister's energy naturally became more and more taxed, even long before he was sick. No man has an unlimited amount of energy. So he gave less and less time to planning. And without realizing it, the efforts of some of the senior officials of the Planning Commission have led to the defeat of planning. I think they are good people, but the Planning Commission requires complete overhauling. I don't know what the position is at the present but I fear it is even worse.

Then we come to the last factor—our nationalism has declined. It shows itself in different ways. In the beginning, when we took foreign aid the idea was that for every rupee that came in we should produce seven rupees here. Instead of that we have now become an aid-receiving country with a vengeance. I believe that the receiving of aid has to be done with care in order not to compromise our economic and political interests. With the aid come experts; these experts are not always the best that the aiding country can provide. In many cases they are people who are dumped on us—of course there are exceptions—because we get this kind of assistance for nothing. In the later days the Prime Minister used to say, 'We may expect aid and take it if we are offered it but even if we get no aid we must still go ahead. We must find ways and means of continuing development.' He was saying that we should not allow ourselves to be put under pressure by other countries or by industrial agencies and foreign cartels which often work through indigenous monopolists and other profit-seeking individuals.

There have been two ideas floating around the Planning Commission. They call them 'quantity planning' and 'perspective planning'. Neither has been effective because in both cases planning is thought of in terms of money and currency. It saves them the effort of planning in terms of the actual labour and goods required. This is what was partly meant by 'quantity planning'. If implemented, it would lead to effective import substitution, the use of indigenously available material and talent. The lack of concern with the indigenous partly arises from foreign pressure and partly from the pressure of profit motives from within. We have found ourselves allowing other people to say what we should have and where it should come from. The aid-receiving country is also inhibited in the choice of the carrier, thus adding to our foreign commitments. Often we have to procure goods which place the least strain on the dollar or on sterling 'sale possibilities'! We could serve our own interests better by buying in the cheaper markets, by barter arrangements, and by the production of export goods specially required by the aiding country. We should not take 'aid' if it restricts our choice of buying markets, our choice of carriers and 'experts'. It will be found that the real value of such aid is much smaller than appears at face value.

Now we come to the question of the large numbers of 'experts'. They have the result of depreciating the value, the prestige, and the confidence of our own people, not only of our experts. They foster a sense of inherent inferiority. These experts are for the most part very expensive, not only in respect of their high individual salaries. Everything suffers a disproportionate rise. Costs become higher because of the inordinately high overheads.

We have talked a great deal about agriculture but we have not achieved very much in the way of considered scientific advance. We have done little to germinate a better seed, and even when we have done this it has not got down to the cultivator. We have been very slow in the way of land reform, so much so that today, if a reform comes, it has less meaning, population having far outstripped the availability of land. Over and above that comes the fact that the introduction of scientific and technical equipment which small people can buy has always been frowned upon by the vested interests and by the administration. The State has shown little initiative in introducing small-scale implements. I myself have tried several times in various ways, but objections have been made.

In my opinion, the fact that the Planning Commission continues is a good thing. Without it, we would certainly be in a much worse position. But the big industries and the banks are still in the hands of the cartels. Until we nationalize the banks, by which I mean credit and the source of capital formation, there is little use talking about social justice. Furthermore, we have not looked into the question of the extent to which new projects make us independent. Even if this steel plant [Bokaro] goes up we would still be importing steel.

As the Prime Minister and all his colleagues recognized, our Administration is out-dated and in many ways it is self-defeating. It takes months for a file to move from desk to desk. Stories of corruption don't quell corruption, and the use of the term 'corruption' as a weapon to denigrate certain ministers and officials does not help. Word gets about and frightens away honest people, and the dishonest individual finds a way of getting around it. The result is that the Administration is so slow that in the Planning Commission or in a Ministry you can hear discussed something that was described as urgent three years ago! The main reason why planning has endured is that it was the Prime Minister's own idea and he put drive into it. It has become established, I hope, and established enough to prevent the breaking away from all planning back to free enterprise. It was a very necessary idea—an essential one. The Prime Minister put in some competent men who shared his ideas and were dedicated—but they got short shrift in the new regime! The Prime Minister thought that the Planning Commission was trying to become a second or super Cabinet. That also didn't help. There was a failure to realize that the future was getting mortgaged, that our markets were being restricted, and the character of our people was being suppressed. It isn't the Planning Commission's fault. The private sector has increasingly become a scramble between different interests. In my opinion, in the early days the late Prime Minister was very sensitive to all this, but vested interests wormed their way in everywhere until he even thought they had the same idealism as he had!

B Mr. Menon, you were in Cabinet and in the Planning Commission during the years when India had three Finance Ministers, C. D. Deshmukh [1950–6], T. T. Krishnamachari [1956–8], and Morarji Desai [1958–63]. Looking at the Planning Commission and its relationship to the Cabinet and the Finance Ministry, how would you compare the attitudes of these Finance Ministers?

M The common factor was that each one tried to make the Planning Commission an adjunct of himself. I believe that, but for the fact that it was in existence from the beginning, that the Prime Minister was always Chairman of the Planning Commission and attached great importance to planning, and that we have something of a planned economy, each of the Finance Ministers would have tried or would have preferred to do without it. And ultimately all Finance Ministers —especially Morarji Desai and T. T. K.—used to say, 'That is all [the money] I can give.' T. T. K. used stronger language than the others; Morarji was more dogmatic, and Deshmukh was probably more suave; but he gave the impression that he was thinking, 'What do you people know, I am the expert and the judge.' Fundamentally he was the person who was most in agreement with the Planning Commission. Deshmukh did get on well with it. He was then and is now a civil servant; his whole mentality and approach is that of a civil servant. He also had certain advantages because he was not very much moved by Party considerations or public opinion. In fact, the Cabinet had sometimes to tell him that public opinion wouldn't stand for what he proposed.

B Are you saying, Mr. Menon, that a basic problem in Indian economic planning is that the very concept of planning simply has not penetrated into the minds of a large enough proportion of the administrators and decision-makers who wield authority?

M I am not saying that they are not intelligent people. They know what we want—that is part of the reason why they are opposing it! Professor Laski used to say, 'What is the Tory Government but a sub-committee of the Federation of British Industries'; you see the implication! The impact of Big Business on policy is far greater than people realize.

B Let us go back to some of these barriers to economic growth. You have made no reference to the argument that given the magnitude of the problem of transforming the economy of a country as large as India, change is virtually impossible within the framework of political democracy, unless one is prepared to wait such a long time that the whole political fabric itself changes.

M I don't believe it. I don't think that democracy is standing in the way of planning or transforming our economy. If by democracy you mean the wishes of the people, there should be no resistance [to planning]. You can say that planning has been interfered with by accounting and auditing, by red tape, and anti-social practices. We have kept some of the English system in form but without its spirit. And in a country like ours—it has been under Imperialism for 300 years—the man who is placed in authority exercises it quite unconsciously in his own interests, to show his power.

B What I am asking is whether an efficient totalitarian system could implement large-scale economic planning more effectively and more rapidly.

M It may or may not, but to me it is not a question, it's a conundrum. What would a totalitarian system which overthrows a democracy plan for? Surely it would plan for anti-democratic ends—for the maintenance of itself in power. Where do the people come in?

B I am not asserting it; I am merely trying to see the link between the political system you have here and economic planning.

M You are arguing or implying that a feudal system or an authoritarian system is more efficient than a democracy—and this is not the case. After all, what is democracy? Four hundred million people don't sit down together and say we shall have a refinery here. In these matters a democracy boils down to some Secretary or some Minister; it is very easy to blame democracy. It is true that somebody may make a hullubaloo in Parliament or on a platform which proves to be simply obstructive to progress. We have a sufficient majority in Parliament and if we exercise it we should not have any difficulty in planning more purposefully or efficiently. Besides, planning is popular in the country.

B Let me cite some other obstacles. First of all, there is the dispersion of interests among the States and the Union with the result that you get incredible competition—particularly evident in the preparation of the Fourth Plan—where each State uses the Plan almost exclusively in terms of its regional needs and interests.

M Why do you call it democracy alone? It is true that the competitive demands of the States may well be the result of democracy, but so too might be the interest and unity of the nation as a whole. Democracy has and should have elements of internal combustion which is what should make it dynamic.

B No, let us leave democracy alone. I am saying that the States vie with each other to satisfy their needs.

M Yes, that is certainly there; it is inherent in the context of scarcity and aspiration for better things.

B No, I think that it is a characteristic of federal politics.

M No, not at all. The insistence on States' rights against the Centre is an American not an Indian phenomenon.

B But you also have it in Canada, in Australia, and in many other countries. You are not being realistic.

M You have it in Canada mainly in regard to Quebec.

B Not so, Mr. Menon. There is a clash between British Columbia and Ottawa over the Columbia River project; there are clashes between Ontario and the Federal Government. It seems to me that this is an inherent by-product of a federal system of government.

M I do not agree. Neither democracy nor federation need be an obstruction to progress. Instead it can be argued that democracy makes for initiative and purposefulness; federation permits a great amount of decentralization and yet creates the unity of the nation! Ours has not been a federal system of government in this way because some people have been allowed to run away with it, although this is now changing.

B In the disclosures about the preparations for the Fourth Plan, I have been struck by the degree to which the States have looked upon the Plan as a pie to be divided among themselves.

M That may be so. The Plan is only in preparation. Part of its purpose is to reconcile conflicts and demands peacefully.

B Isn't this a barrier to economic development?

M But what I am trying to tell you is that this has not been so and need not be so although there is a tendency for it to become increasingly true. Supposing, for example, we had no democracy and no federalism but we had an emperor in each State, a viceroy like in Tipu Sultan's[1] time. The position would be more or less the same. Yet I want to reiterate that we would not have been able to do even as much as we have done without planning. Some of our major achievements, not the least of which is the greater awareness in the country of the need to develop, are at least partly due to our having planned our development.

B I don't question this, Mr. Menon. I am not questioning the value of planning. I am merely trying to explore the barriers to effective growth.

[1] A Muslim ruler in South India in the eighteenth century.

M I know. What I mean is that all my criticism is about the way it actually worked; it could have been better.

B Apart from the obstacles which you noted, it seems to me that there are a number of obvious major political and administrative barriers to economic growth. I want to concentrate on these a little more, if I may. One is the role of the States. Another is the absence of a sufficiently large administrative cadre, devoted to the idea of implementing the Plans. A third is the conflict within the Congress Party over the ideology underlining the Plan, over the extent of the public sector. And most important of all, it seems to me, is the deep-rooted inertia of the rural population, about which virtually nothing has been done by the Planning Commission.

M It is very easy to say all this, but tell me, what are we to do about it?

B May I ask what are the reasons for the agricultural crisis in this country? Why has production of food been stagnant in the last few years?

M Agricultural production is far from stagnant. Unless the Government's statistics are entirely wrong there is enough food grain in the country to feed our people. I believe that the food problem of this country can in the short-term only be solved by a truly national policy and approach, including monopoly procurement of food grains and the control of the wholesaler. I have no objection to the wholesaler being employed as a producing agent, but he must be the buyer for the community. The elimination of profiteering must be achieved by making hoarding by consumers, farmers, and merchants impossible and by doing away with State-compartmentalization [State food zones]. I would set up a central National Food Authority which Parliament would endow with powers of monopoly procurement. I believe we shall never be self-sufficient as far as food is concerned so long as there is profiteering, and so long as the cultivator is not offered an attractive price. If there is a shortage it is far better for us to tighten our belts now. There is no evidence that importing food has staved off shortages which, if Government figures for the whole country are right, are only local scarcities.

There is no famine in India. I don't want to go into the figures, but if you look at them you will find that the average amount of available food grain *per capita* has been sufficient over the years. The long-term problem depends upon land reform on the one hand and industrial development on the other. By industrial development I mean gearing the masses of our population, as in Japan, towards the requirements of industry. People so engaged would enjoy larger money incomes, higher standards of living, and the hope of a new dignity arising from wage earning instead of being unemployed for the greater part of the year. At present the food position is improving because of the elimination, however limited, of small bottlenecks, and because of the pressure of public opinion against anti-social practices; some hoarders have been put in prison in Bengal. But these are only palliatives.

In this country the only way to deal with food in the next five years or so is by mass and monopoly procurement and by the establishment of distribution centres large enough to distribute to the entire body of consumers. I am not saying that the Government can do all this at once; the idea of fair-price shops has been started and they sell large numbers of things. I think India will be able to feed herself by water-grown crops at least 200 or 300 per cent more efficiently. Views about clinging to familiar types of food will have to be revised. Nutritional education will have to become a part of school education.

I don't think that we need panic about the food situation, for the next hundred years at any rate. Although it is much less than people think, there is an induced shortage of protein foods which is the result of sentiment and of custom. There is no shortage of protein materials in India. We have to use scientific knowledge in order to produce proteins out of all kinds of wild growth which is now being wasted. The food problem today is not merely a question of rationing. We have to proceed at several levels: (1) you cannot stop food imports tomorrow because of the Government's publicity about food shortages; (2) we need to conserve all kinds of fertilizers and eliminate rodents; (3) we have to start to grow food seriously in every bit of land as it has to be done in wartime; (4) we need large-scale irrigation which would encourage food substitution and which would make the substitute foods more palatable and less costly in terms of processing; (5) we need to ensure that more adequate quantities of food are getting to the consumer through more efficient, speedy, and direct distribution. The fiscal resources and facilities that are now used for hoarding purposes should cease. And credit facilities, as well as saving for a purpose, should be allowed to become generally available and should be kept free from bottlenecks and from the intervention of middlemen. This requires national control of the channels of credit and the use of present sources of savings, such as general insurance, for development.

B Do you think that the absence of effective co-operative farming in the rural areas is an obstacle to increased production?

M We won't go into the question of co-operative farming; I don't think we understand co-operation well in this country. Much of it is not co-operation in the sense that I understand it.

B It is not that complex.

M Not at all, but they make it so. Co-operative farming cannot be run as a Government Department. Co-operation requires a voluntary *élan*. Governmental organization, departmentalism, and the Agricultural Institutes have tended to kill all that. If I want to register a co-operative society for my servants, shall we say, the first thing they want to know is, 'Are they *all* servants or not?'; they make so many difficulties. Red tape and the officiousness of small men dressed in brief authority also inhibit both the quantity and the quality of co-operation.

B You are saying that the problems of economic planning arise when planning is implemented, rather than when it is formulated.

M That is a major part of it. As I have already said, this is the case when perspective planning and quantity planning are ill-understood and not properly implemented. I believe that this country will never really build itself up except by its own efforts; there are so many people here and we don't have to do everything everyone else does. All I want is that our people should be happier and more comfortable.

B How do you bridge the gap between the urban planners and the countryside?

M You are over-simplifying the problem.

B But I am considering what I think is one area of importance, the gap between the city and the village.

M The problem is not 'urban planners'; it is more to do with imperfect or erroneous ideas or our own lack of experience.

B All right, the planning is ignorant. What I want you to talk about is the problem of communication between the man who plans and the man who has to implement the plan.

M You can do more about it when the problem is appreciated. There should be more public education about it and more participation of voluntary bodies in education for planning. We do a certain amount but I fear it is not enough. With notable exceptions, there are too many in this enterprise who are only interested in keeping their jobs.

B That means you are taking a totally pessimistic view about your ability to overcome this problem.

M No, not at all, indeed the contrary. But certain things have first to be recognized. To begin with, the relationship between the Government and the Planning Commission has been too nebulous. What does the Planning Minister do? I don't even know who he is just now; oh, yes, Bhagat is the Planning Minister. He has to be a very senior man in the Party with a great deal of enthusiasm and few fads. He should not merely be a look-out man for the Finance Minister.

B Is it not your impression that the emphasis on planning has declined in recent months?

M Oh yes.

B And what is the reason for it?

M Special private interests . . .

B . . . that have penetrated into the thinking of Government itself? If that is so, then I should think that progress in planning is stagnating, perhaps even declining.

M Who can say?

B It follows logically from your remarks. You have been saying that planning is the pre-condition for growth and that the whole planning mechanism is now becoming less and less efficient.

M You are painting too dark a picture. I talked about the side of things that you do not find in print. The best thing is to read the mid-term appreciation of the Third Plan. It is a much more candid document than most government publications.

B I have read it; it's a very pessimistic report.

M Yes. If we had avoided foreign dependence we would have been in better shape; I am not anti-foreign, but only against dependence and domination. I hope I am not giving you the wrong impression. Without being isolationist, introverted, or ultra-nationalistic, a new country has to be apprehensive and cautious about any return of imperialism.

B It is easy to attribute all these problems to the coming of the foreigner, but surely it is not as simple as that?

M Your question justifies my fear that a brief discussion of these matters gives a distorted picture. But still, perhaps it is simple because if you rely upon somebody else how can you expect to be strong? This is a realistic and honest view to take.

B I agree that self-reliance is a virtue but that in itself is not likely to produce economic growth. I am still left with the basic question of how one overcomes these problems; do you think they can be overcome within the present governmental framework?

M Of course they can be overcome—if the planning is vigorous enough, if Finance Ministers do not have an empire-grabbing approach, if planners and Finance Ministers co-operate, and if all the members of the Government recognize that planning is essential even if only because we are a country of poor people.

B What you are really saying is that if one could persuade the leadership of the Congress Party to accept planning then many of the practical difficulties could be overcome. But the chances of that happening are so remote that one must look elsewhere.

M That is true in many spheres but we have to remember that Congress is and always has been committed to planning. I do not think there is any other instrument in India with which to carry out national and progressive policies. We will overcome our difficulties.

B This raises the question of whether with a relatively stagnant economy your political system can survive over a long period of time?

M That is a challenge to anybody's political system; no political system survives for long unless it yields results; it may collapse in ten years or a thousand years, but when it doesn't deliver the goods it collapses.

B Don't you think this is already true in India?

M No, not yet, because our very low standard of living calls forth aspiration, pressures, and effort.

B Do you mean that the political system is likely to survive for a long period simply through inertia and the absence of opposition.

M No, the political system is likely to improve. It will meet problems. The chances are that the States will try to exert themselves more but at the same time they will also find it necessary to co-operate over larger issues.

B Suppose you have a recurring food crisis for three or four years, what then? It is not unlikely, after all.

M Not unlikely at all. But there is no food crisis now.

B Well, there is a shortage of food.

M A shortage for the consumer, yes.

B The net result is a crisis.

M No, if it is a crisis it is a crisis of prices and purchasing power.

B It's a crisis of prices which reflects itself mainly in an inadequate supply of consumer goods in the urban centres: this leads to the growth of dissatisfaction.

M It is not yet an agricultural problem—that will come in a year or two. At the present moment it's a problem of reorganizing the economy in such a way that what is produced by the earth gets into the market and to the consumer.

B You see this essentially as a distribution problem?

M No; the problem is essentially one of the stranglehold of monopoly interests and of administrative deficiencies.

B I am using the term distribution here to mean the capacity to move food from the earth to the consumer.

M No, the distribution problem is not only one of logistics. The basic problem of the Indian economy concerns the person who brings food to the market—the wholesaler. He is the money-lender and he is also the agent of the retailer; he decides everything about food—the time, the priority, the quantity, the place, and everything else.

B May I ask why during the last six months the present Government has not taken more stringent measures against this wholesaler complex?

M How can I tell you that?

B What is your view of it?

M Well, they say they are going to take action.

B But they haven't done so.

M According to them they have.

B I don't think the record supports that.

M They have taken or attempted to take certain steps. But there are powerful interests involved. They make too much cheap money available for these hoarding [storage] purposes.

B Isn't the real reason the fact that this group represents the bulwark of financial support for the Congress Party in the country as a whole?

M That is exaggerating this community's importance. I suppose there is a capitalist outlook in the country; everybody wants to be like them, making easy money by short cuts. And I think all this idealistic hypocrisy about scarcity adds to it.

B In trying to predict the political consequences, Mr. Menon, do you think that continuing economic stagnation of this kind in the future is likely to be reflected in declining support for the ruling party?

M I couldn't say for certain. But I think the Congress has the support of the people, certainly in rural India. The General Election is still two years ahead. There is no other Party. The Congress has its own mystique for the people. We have to live up to it.

B It still has that?

M Oh, yes; after all, the Congress got rid of the British.

B Isn't that wearing a bit thin after eighteen years?

M Oh I don't think so. And you would not think so if you were an Indian. What is the alternative?

B Well, in the whole of South and South-East Asia India is the only country in which the Party that brought Independence is still in power.

M Yes, that is so. It only proves the point I made.

B Are there special reasons for this?

M Yes, there are. Here there is no other party as large as the Congress and no other party in South-East Asia has accomplished as much.

20. Education and Language

B Earlier, Mr. Menon, you talked about the present deplorable state of Indian education and you said that you expected that educational standards would decline over a period of time. What do you think are the reasons for this?

M There is a lack of planning in education; there is inability to use what I call a multi-pattern, that is to say, you cannot have the same thing in Quebec as in Ontario; there is political interference; there are language controversies and fixations; lastly, the administration of universities is often in the hands of men who have spent their lives doing something else and some have little understanding of education. In certain parts of India there have been conflicts between student bodies and Vice-Chancellors although there are some good administrators too. But universities are not the main problem of education. The main problem is adult education. At the beginning of Independence we hoped that we would make this country literate within sixteen years; unfortunately, more than sixteen years have passed without this happening. The problem is too large and our effort has obviously been inadequate. We need to be more imaginative about it.

B Countries like Mexico have adopted an adult literacy campaign which produces wonders, a campaign in which every literate man teaches an illiterate one. Why can't such a scheme be adopted here?

M We have not done anything like that yet, although some people have talked about it. The Mexican pattern calls for certain social changes. There are a lot of people who come to tell us what to do. That itself has had a bad effect. One person even talked about projecting a film on a tree as though our main trouble was not being able to provide enough screens! In this country the simplest thing to do is to spread a lot of sand on the floor and write with your fingers. That is how I learned when I was just over two years old. And now we are inviting Mexicans,

Argentinians, and Welshmen to teach us about adult education! Ours is a social and not merely an educational problem. We cannot afford to ignore either the time element or the extent of our economic resources.

B But what is there about the Education Ministry or the group that dominates education that prevents them from taking the initiative?

M First of all education is not a central subject. Secondly we have had no Education Minister who has understood education! I tell every university audience that I speak to that so long as the community around the university contains a large number of illiterate people, to that extent the university has failed because the integration of student and faculty with the community around is a basic ingredient of university life and education.

B And yet the tradition in this country is for university students to avoid the illiterate community, to avoid the countryside.

M This is all very recent.

B Do you think the gradual abandonment of English as one of the main languages in university teaching has helped to cause the decline?

M I think so. It means turning one's back on progress. I am not saying that regional languages and Hindi should not have pride of place.

B Do you think that the South will accept Hindi in the foreseeable future?

M No. Probably there will be sustained agitation for everything to be in Tamil or Telugu. They regard this as a problem of linguistics, but English will be in greater use in the South.

B It is regarded as a linguistic rather than a social and economic problem?

M Yes, the whole question is beset by politics and the desire for power. In India regional languages are major languages spoken by tens of millions of people. I don't know how it will sort itself out. But the three-language formula, if effectively implemented, would be a workable solution. Hindi will not be forced on South India.

B What do you consider to be the major consequences of the linguistic agitation?

M Some provincialization, more domination of the Central Government by the Hindi-speaking States, a lowering of the standards of education and of the judiciary. Take a Hindi M.A. and let a Hindi-speaking man talk to him; he knows Hindi but often little else! Please don't ask me anything more about education; I have very definite views and feelings about it.

B You have given me the impression this morning that in various crucial spheres of Indian public life there is either stagnation or decline—in the economic system, in the Administration, and in education.

M I wouldn't say that there had been a decline in the quantity of education. On the contrary.

B Let me make my point. In India we are now seeing the beginning of a long period of stagnation in the political and economic system.

M That we cannot say.

B We are predicting here on the basis of the present trend.

M There is no stagnation. If there were perhaps the people wouldn't put up with it. The quantity, quality, and speed of advance may be leaving much to be desired—but we will get by.

B You yourself say that the Indian people have a capacity to wait and accept slow changes.

M It may be that people who are normally conservative will be forced in their own interests to accept change and progress. After all, men from palaces have sometimes been revolutionaries.

B But this is not a revolutionary society.

M I am not sure. Anyway I am glad to hear you say that.

B You don't agree?

M You may be right. It depends on what you mean.

B I am saying that India is not a revolutionary society.

M Yes and no. It is not a revolutionary society in the usually understood sense. We have a political democracy based on adult suffrage. We have equality and social justice written into our Constitution.

B That is on paper. But deep inside the society there is inertia, apathy, and an absence of the desire for change.

M Those factors are certainly there but this is not the whole of the story.

B What has gone out of the Indian society?

M I suppose it is something to do with the incidence of growth, personal jealousies, the interference of foreign interests. You may think that I am exaggerating this last factor, but as a scholar you would be very wrong to take that view. I am repeating this point several times because hardly anybody else will tell you about it. You have first to read back into history to see how Romanization affected people.

B Do you believe that there are no inherent barriers to change in Indian society?

M There are inherent barriers everywhere, but we are not a people whom it is difficult to change. Barriers have to be overcome and that is what we will do. After all, look at the big changes that have already taken place. I think the country today needs a big personality or personalities. The country has been overtaken by the power of money. We have to work for social change. It is a large country and there are many dimensions to the problems that we have to face.

B Have the people's values become more modern in some sense?

M I think so. The struggle in this country is a struggle between obscurantism and modernism; at the present moment obscurantism is a little ahead.

B That is the point I am raising.

M A nose ahead; but I would not say that that is true of the masses of the people. They are not apathetic, and they can no longer be taken for granted. This is what Gandhiji, Panditji, and adult franchise have done for our people. However, our masses are still reverential.

B To tradition?

M Not only to tradition but to individuals too.

B But the change is in the direction of the revival of tradition.

M Tradition itself can only be changed by a movement or by individuals. The great strength of the Congress Party is that they have a place in the hearts of the people. There is nothing to take its place. I mean, you cannot compare it to a Western political party; it's not strictly a 'party'. It has got a mystique; it's a *Movement* still.

SUPPLEMENTARY INTERVIEW—MAY 1965

B Mr. Menon, I would appreciate your observations on the language problem. I would like to know what you think of the way in which it was handled and more particularly how you yourself would handle it. What do you consider is a possible and reasonable language policy in a society as complex as the present Indian Union?

M I think it has become a political controversy. Now that it has been promoted into political dispute the only possible solution is a 'political' one. Since the Constitution makes Hindi the official language of India, it should be taught to everybody. I think the whole idea of what is called the 'medium of instruction' is an idea used to bolster up political demands and positions. I believe that the 'three-language formula', which I was the first person to talk about at a Convocation Address at Madras University some years ago, and which I had been talking about to the Prime Minister for years previously, is the basic solution.

It is mistaken to talk about 'English for international purposes' for on the international level you can speak in any language and get translations. It is not for international purposes but for reasons of modernity that one needs a developed, modern language. If, because of prejudice, it is not to be English, let it be say German or Russian, at least for a long time to come. I think we should get over our inhibitions about these things and implement the three-language formula conscientiously. It would be a good thing if all the universities in India had as many language facilities as possible and languages were encouraged and taught. A knowledge of several languages in addition to Hindi and English should be encouraged in the Administrative ranks.

Our politicians, I am sorry to say, don't appreciate the fact that a baby of two or three years of age can learn many languages without effort—why, that little fellow who came here speaks Punjabi, Hindi, and English and he is only two years old. He speaks these without difficulty, whereas if he were twenty years old it would be very difficult to teach him three or four languages. Whereas our people say, 'Oh, no, we cannot impose these burdens on children.' I think we should be recognized as a multi-language country and that we should mix up these languages, and ultimately our mother tongue would become a very impure kind of Hindi, as it would be receptive to all kinds of things. But it would take a very long time to be a language that is widely used in the world. English is not any longer the language of the English alone. Today one out of every six Russians learns English. A great many French people speak English today and English is even the second official language of Ethiopia. In the United States, amidst so many languages, English is the main one. More than any other, it has gained the status of an international language and has exhibited wonderful and complete flexibility.

21. Nehru

B You have been very candid, Mr. Menon, on all topics that I have raised except one, namely your reflections on Pandit Nehru. I would like once more to ask whether you would consent to think aloud about your friendship with Panditji from the early 1930s onwards.

M It is not because of humility or of an inferiority complex that I avoid the subject. The whole question is too large for me to understand it. As for speaking about nuances of a relationship of a personal nature—since you referred to an obligation to posterity—I would reply that in my mind it could not rise above my own ideas of loyalty in personal relations. I don't discuss these matters with anybody. You may say that the world is poorer for my silence; I cannot help it. I think I should keep quiet.

Panditji was not a superman; he was not a god or anything like that; he was a human being like all of us and very much of a full-blooded individual. He was impulsive; he came into Government very much as an amateur, and the first day that he went to Parliament he was Leader of the House. Though I have been close to him in many ways, I have lived abroad for many years. I think that the wisest thing for me to do is to keep my mouth shut. That is how I feel. I am sorry that I cannot be more helpful, but what can I do?

I do not think that Panditji's affection for me or my relationship with Panditji affected him in the way you imply. I was neither a buffoon nor a Rasputin. I understood his mind, or rather he thought I did, even if this may not have been the case. I do not believe in what is called autobiography; that is what it really comes to. Autobiographies tend to portray the world in a distorted way; you think you made everything because that is all you know! It really seems to me somewhat inappropriate that I should speak about my relations with Panditji.

If you go round to the Prime Minister's house you won't see any photographs of mine over there. If you look at his *Bunch of*

Old Letters[1] you won't see any letters of mine there. He made very few public references to me. That was how our relationship was. Even when I resigned, in explaining it to Parliament Panditji did not discuss any personal aspect of the matter. I am not resenting it; that was the type of relationship we had. With me being the kind of person I am it does not lend itself to the kind of treatment you suggest. I can't explain it myself and I don't want to. If I did you would only get a distorted picture of it.

B I agree, Mr. Menon, that no one relationship can exhaust the personality of any individual. But it is also true, I think, that your relationship with Panditji was unique and, while one must talk to many people in order to get inside a man's mind, his personality, his philosophy of life, it simply seems to me appropriate to round off these discussions with your reflections on a relationship which was important not only to India but also to the world. You knew Panditji not only when he was in power and you were in power but also when you were both intensely involved in the Indian Freedom Struggle—Nehru in India, and you in London. And you maintained that intellectual and emotional link for fifteen to twenty years before India attained independence. It seems to me that there are not many cases in the world today where two men have been so closely associated for such a long period of time both before and after Independence. It is really for this reason as well as because it was a very special kind of mutual understanding that I wanted to hear your reflections, thoughts, and comments on this association.

M Well, I thought I had explained all that; I have said all I had to say about it. From what you have just said it is evident that you have learned something about our friendship from your association with India in the past ten years during which you have had access to the Prime Minister. You know a great many people; you do not belong to an imperial country and you have no axe to grind. There is no reason why you should doubt my reasons for preferring not to discuss it. I am afraid that you must try to complete your picture as best you can. I am not being obstinate about it; even if I had the material at

[1] Published in 1958 under that title.

hand or had worked it out in my mind, I am sure I would not want to talk about it.

B We come, then, Mr. Menon, to the end of these discussions. I want to thank you both for letting me ask these questions and for answering them at considerable length, for a period of some seventeen hours. I would also like to thank you for allowing me to use this material for a book which I have in mind. May I then say farewell, Mr. Menon, and thank you once more for all your help.

PART II

ANALYSIS

KRISHNA MENON'S VIEW OF THE WORLD[1]

Framework

FOREIGN Policy may be viewed as a system of action. Like all social systems it comprises an environment, a group of actors, structures through which the units of behaviour respond to challenges and initiate decisions, and processes which sustain or alter the flow of demands and products of the system as a whole. It is possible—indeed it is necessary for rigorous analysis of foreign policy—to explore the content and interrelations of these key variables: environment, actors, structures, and processes, all placed within a framework of demands on policy or inputs, and products of policy or outputs.

The complexity and yet comparability of foreign policy behaviour emerge from a brief exposition of the construct of a Foreign Policy System, universally valid in time and space. This will be elaborated and explored in depth elsewhere.[2] The essentials may be noted here in order to relate the empirical data of the Dialogue with Krishna Menon to a theoretical frame of reference. This will not only enrich the value of his recollections and reflections as a primary source; it will also enable us, through an analysis of one facet of a Foreign Policy System, to illustrate the kind of research which is now essential and possible if the study of foreign policy is to progress beyond the bounds of historical survey and to induce rigorous comparative analysis and efforts at prediction worthy of a discipline.

[1] The concepts 'World View' and 'View of the World' are not synonymous. A World View comprises an Image of both the external and internal variables of the Operational Environment. A View of the World is confined to the external segment. This essay is limited to Menon's 'View of the World', and the Appendix has been structured in the same manner in order to provide the quantitative parallels to the qualitative analysis of Menon's Image of his external environment. An analysis of the internal variables of the Indian élite image and of the total World View is being undertaken in a separate research project by Janice Gross Stein, Assistant Professor of Political Science at Carleton University and a Ph.D. candidate at McGill University.

Krishna Menon's words as quoted in this section are from an early editing of the original tapes and are not always identical with the printed text.

[2] In a forthcoming paper on 'A Model of Foreign Policy Behaviour'.

A Foreign Policy System may be likened to a flow—into and out of a network of structures which perform certain functions and thereby produce acts or decisions or outputs. These, in turn, feed back into the System in a ceaseless flow of Demands on Policy (Inputs), Policy Process, and Products of Policy (Outputs). In all systems of foreign policy there are six basic components, which can be related to the three broad classification categories of a system, as follows:

I. INPUTS

OPERATIONAL ENVIRONMENT (E_o)

External—Global (G), Subordinate Own (S_1), Subordinate Other (S_2), Dominant Bilateral (DB), and Bilateral (B).

Internal—Economic Capability (E), Military Capacity (M), Political Structure (PS), Competing Élites (CE), and Interest Groups (IG).

COMMUNICATIONS—the transmission of data about the operational environment by press, radio, TV, face to face, etc.

PSYCHOLOGICAL ENVIRONMENT (E_{ps}) or ÉLITE IMAGES —of the operational environment and of the competing élites' images of the operational environment, as well as of their pressure potential.

II. PROCESS

FORMULATION—of strategic and tactical decisions in four Issue-Areas: Economic Development (ED), Political-Diplomatic (PD), Military-Security (MS), and Cultural (C); includes Authorization or legitimizing of decisions.

IMPLEMENTATION—of decisions by various structures: Head of State, Head of Government, Foreign Office, etc.

III. OUTPUTS

The substance of acts or decisions flowing from the implementation function.

All data regarding foreign policy can be ordered in one of these components and their sub-components.

The notion of flow and dynamic movement in a system which is constantly absorbing demands, channelling them into a policy machine which, in turn, transforms these inputs into

decisions or outputs, can be most effectively conveyed by means
of two figures:

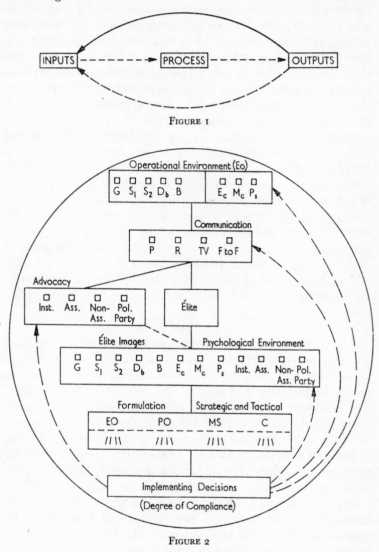

FIGURE 1

FIGURE 2

A general analysis of India's Foreign Policy System is beyond
the scope of this essay and will form the substance of a separate
volume. Our task here is more limited—to explore part of

Krishna Menon's place within that System. Like Nehru, his roles were multiple and intense, with influence of a high order on the policy flow. He possessed and articulated a comprehensive image of the operational environment. He advocated policy. He communicated ideas and decisions. He helped to formulate decisions and he was prominent in their implementation. Yet like Nehru he was subject to restraints, both environmental and constitutional. Despite appearances to the contrary, the views and acts of these two leaders were something less than the totality of India's Foreign Policy.

Krishna Menon impinged on the Foreign Policy System and through it on World Politics at three crucial points: as a member of the élite with a well-constructed Image forcefully articulated; as the principal aide of Nehru in the formulation of policy from 1953, perhaps earlier, until 1962; and as roving ambassador *par excellence* during the same period. In short, he occupied a key position in three of the six components whose interaction constitutes the Foreign Policy Flow. His roles in decision-making and implementation will be explored elsewhere; here we shall concentrate on his View of the World. By so doing we shall be able to assess its impact on policy choices.

The rationale for including élite images among the inputs of a foreign policy system is a simple truth: decision-makers act in accordance with their perception of reality, not in response to reality itself. Image and Reality may coincide or may diverge. To the extent that they differ, policy acts will be 'irrational'. They will also be less successful than the theoretically possible—in the measure that the decision-maker misconstrues, distorts, or deviates from the reality of the environment within which he must act. His image may be partial or general. It may be subconscious or consciously stated. It may be based on carefully thought-out assumptions about the world and his own state, or it may flow from instinctive perceptions and judgements. In any event, all decision-makers may be said to possess a set of images and to be governed by them in their response to foreign policy problems. Indeed, élite images are no less 'real' than the reality of their environment and are much more relevant to an analysis of the foreign policy flow.

The term 'élite image' is a creation of scholars—and few practitioners of foreign policy think and act as scholars do. They have neither the time nor the inclination to formulate an elaborate and integrated View of the World. Menon, for example, talking about Non-Alignment and the Balance of Power, remarked about Prime Minister Nehru: 'He was not much interested in what he would call theory but he did have more than a rudimentary knowledge of these things. Theories are often inferred from what statesmen do. He himself might have thought, "why should I go into theory?" [And then the interesting disclosure] I didn't discuss it with him in all the years—not in such terms or in so many words. It was obvious. I would only make myself guilty of being theoretical.' Yet Nehru—and Menon—often expressed a partial View relevant to the problem requiring action at that point in time.

The task of the foreign-policy analyst is to construct from words and deeds the operative élite perceptions of their environment, along with their views of the desirable or proper roles for their state within that environment. The environment, however, comprises three levels, that is, states operate in three distinct fields or zones of foreign policy interaction—global, subordinate, and bilateral. Thus the Élite Image comprises six closely related perceptions: of the external environment—global, subordinate, and bilateral—and of the proper or desirable role which a state should play in each of these three fields. The six sets of images, taken together, constitute the View of the World.

Once the decision-making élite is known, it is possible to discern and crystallize this View, which conditions policy acts and provides a key to foreign policy behaviour. In the case of India the élite was very small—Krishna Menon occupied a position second only to Nehru from 1953, some would say earlier, until late 1962. A structured analysis of Menon's View of the World, then, will also cast light on the View of the World held by the Indian foreign policy élite during that period. Our task is made easier by Krishna Menon's intellectual flair and agile mind, his carefully nurtured images of his environment, and his tendency to state these in a brilliant and often passionate flow of words. Both the Dialogue in this book and an array of speeches at the United Nations and elsewhere enable us to clarify and to integrate the content of his View.

Image of the Global System

There are several points of concentration in Krishna Menon's perception of world politics. One is the struggle between the two power blocs. Another is the notion of 'area of peace'. A third is the United Nations. There are also lesser themes in his image of the setting in which India's policy had to be made—though he never linked environment formally to decision-making. All these points emerge from the Dialogue.

Like most observers in the late 1940s and 1950s, Krishna Menon saw world politics as dominated by *two power blocs* led by the United States and the Soviet Union, in sharp and continuous conflict with each other. They shared responsibility for the high level of tension and the danger of a holocaust, but the weights, for Menon, are strikingly unequal. The Western bloc is invariably the greater culprit; this part of his image can be traced to his acceptance of the Leninist theory of imperialism as a phenomenon of expansion linked to the stage of 'Monopoly Capitalism'. The term 'Imperialism' is a favourite in his lexicon, frequently recurring in speeches at the United Nations and in India's Parliament, as well as the public forum, and in extemporaneous reflections, as evident in the Dialogue. Whether or not explicitly identified, 'Imperialism', for Menon, refers to the Western bloc, more specifically to those States which control or controlled territories overseas; it is the policy designed to enlarge, perpetuate, or prevent the dissolution of colonial empires—and colonial is by definition restricted to overseas lands and peoples.

The twin epithets 'Imperialist' and 'Colonialist' are never used with reference to the Soviet Union or China; these designations are inconceivable to Menon, for the two Communist powers do not possess colonial, i.e. overseas, empires. Thus, even in a mood of regret and sadness over China's 'betrayal' of India's trust and friendship, through its 'invasion' of 1962, Menon finds solace in the discovery that China has always been 'expansionist'—a lesser order of iniquity. The harsher epithets are reserved for Western States. Indeed, one detects an unexpressed racial bias in the curious treatment of Japan, whose behaviour from the 1870s to 1945 would justify the terms 'Imperialist' and 'Colonialist' in Menon's theory. Yet Japan

is never mentioned in the references to imperialism in the
Dialogue and rarely in any published remarks. Menon did
castigate Japanese militarism and expansionist policies in the
inter-war period but he appears to regard them as aberrations.

The central place in Menon's assault on Imperialism is given
to the United States, despite its modest record as a 'colonial'
power. In fact, he displayed a strange indifference to American
colonialism before the Second World War, when the United
States did exercise direct rule over an overseas territory, the
Philippines, and an intense hostility to 'American Imperialism'
during the past twenty years, when the classic Marxist criterion
of imperialism no longer applied to the United States. Of course,
Menon was never an unqualified adherent of the Marxist
creed; it was, rather, Laski's neo-Marxism of the thirties that
shaped this part of his Image. And, like all radical socialists of
the contemporary era, he does not regard formal colonial rule
as necessary to the policy of 'Imperialism' or 'Colonialism'.
The characteristics of 'Capitalist' and 'Interventionist', whether
overt or covert, direct or indirect, political, economic, cultural,
or military, justify, in Menon's eyes, the designation 'Imperialist' for the United States. Similar patterns of intervention
by the Soviet Union escape this symbol of condemnation,
though not the substance of criticism.

The tone and sweep of Menon's derisive comments on
'American Imperialism' suggest an intense emotional antipathy,
as well as intellectual disdain. Typical of the far Left is his
distinction between the 'American people', for whom he shows
friendliness, if not affection, and the 'state of mind' of the
United States political élite which expresses itself in a foreign
policy of intervention wherever possible on the assumption of a
'God-given right to police the world'. Towards the latter he
shows relentless hostility. A passionate *J'accuse* is rarely absent
from his reflections as he moves from one problem or issue of
international politics to another.

He begins with moderation: among the reasons for Non-
Alignment, 'we would not go back to the West . . . because to us
the West meant Empire' (ch. 1). In recalling the decision to
remain in the Commonwealth, 'it was probably a way of
keeping out intruders. Looking back, I didn't think about it at
the time; at least at that period American infiltration into

India was less' (ch. 2). He blames American intransigence for the delay in ending the Korean War on the basis of his proposals, especially regarding prisoners of war (ch. 3). So too with the Geneva Conference on Indo-China in 1954 (ch. 4). In explaining the Bandung Conference of 1955, he remarks: 'The Americans were against the idea; they tried to kill it— until it emerged and succeeded. Then they simulated enthusiasm about it. They sort of "came to scoff and remained to pray"— the same as with the Korea Resolution' (ch. 5). Apropos of the Korean War, Menon castigates Dulles and Eisenhower: 'They didn't care too much about those American prisoners in China. I cared more for them than they did. They were quite prepared to make them a kind of bond in the political game' (ch. 13).

In recalling the Suez Crisis of 1956, Menon shifts his attack to the lesser 'imperialist' powers, Britain and France. The Soviet role in terminating the invasion—through its threat to bomb London and Paris—receives high praise, while the U.S. contribution is treated as innocuous (ch. 6). In a passionate defence of his attitude and his voting at the U.N. on the Hungary issue, Menon displays bitterness at what he terms the U.S. exploitation of this unhappy episode for Cold War purposes and American indifference to the human aspects of the problem. On the Congo, too, he is harsh, particularly when referring to the landing of Western troops in Stanleyville in December 1964: 'I don't believe for one moment this sob-story about saving every white man or woman; it does not wash' (ch. 13). And on the Congo tangle generally, 'the Western group are basically responsible' (ch. 9). On the Goa issue, Menon's criticism of American behaviour is severe; and the roles of Ambassador Galbraith and U.N. Representative Stevenson are the objects of a searing attack. The long discourse on China is typified by a mood of sadness about Peking's strange actions, with much of the blame apportioned to Indian 'reactionary circles'; and, once more, America is brought into the discourse—for claiming to have come to the aid of India; Menon emphatically denies this (ch. 12). Indeed, he suggests that the United States urged India to take a forceful initiative regarding China; had Delhi yielded, 'we would have been bombed' (ch. 1). As for American pledges to aid India, he declares emphatically that a nuclear

umbrella was a myth; the United States would never resort
to nuclear war merely to defend India against aggression (ch. 16).

Menon's image of the two blocs is also illuminated in the
discourse on Pakistan, Partition, and Kashmir (ch. 14): 'You
take the world today, since the Second World War. Who has
created all the wars? What is the difference between this and
the situation in 1917–18? The imperialists attacked the infant
revolutionary Russia on twenty-two fronts. Now what is the
difference between now and then, basically?' In the same stream
of words, 'let us hope that (in the near future) the world will be
in a fitter state to reject Western Imperialism. Otherwise they
will say that Krishna Menon has it on the brain, they will say
that he wants somebody to hate. . . .' On Kashmir proper, 'the
villain in all this is and always has been Britain, ably assisted
later, not initially, by the United States'. And, on the possibility
of an Indo-Pakistani settlement, 'there will be no peace on this
continent unless the United States retires from the Far East.
It's a withdrawal of a state of mind, that is to say, the withdrawal of the assumption that they are born to police the
world.'

Even on purely domestic themes Menon pursues his *bête
noire*. Three examples will suffice. The first concerns the succession to Nehru: while dismissing reports of his alignment with
right-wing leader Morarji Desai, he remarks: 'I think it was
largely American propaganda, to discredit me partly and, at
that time, Morarji Desai too. The Americans at that time
didn't approve of Morarji' (ch. 15). A second instance is
Menon's immediate reply to a general question about interest
groups in the Indian polity: 'I think that the American lobby
is powerful and active in this country' (ch. 18). The third illustration relates to economic development and foreign aid. Menon
is harsh on foreign experts: 'In many cases they are people who
are dumped on us. In many fields they are persons who are
inferior in ability, experience, and wisdom to those whom they
are "advising" or presuming to "guide" or "direct" here.'
In a similar vein, 'foreigners have brought an atmosphere of
opulence which is followed by corruption. . . . The British are
more correct in these matters in their dealings with us. The
Eastern European countries do not fall into this category.' The
culprit is easy to discern. Finally, Menon denigrates the benefits

of massive American PL 480 food aid. He denies a food shortage and notes, rather, the danger of U.S. control of counterpart rupee funds: 'one third of our currency is in foreign hands and it is indirectly diminishing the volume of the entry of foreign exchange' (ch. 19).

The evidence is overwhelming: Krishna Menon equates the United States and the Soviet Union in the global power hierarchy; they are the two great powers; but he distinguishes very sharply their responsibility for the world's ills: 'American Imperialism' is unquestionably the pre-eminent evil force. In fact, criticism of the Soviets is rare and invariably mild. There is acknowledgement that Moscow, in the last years of the Stalin era, *aggravated* the tension but not the slightest intimation of blame for the conflict. There is a frequent expression of 'regret' at the Soviet resumption of nuclear tests at different times; and both powers are held responsible for the impasse on disarmament, though, ironically, the United Kingdom and Canada are singled out for failing to break the deadlock (ch. 16). In his United Nations speeches, too, the glaring discrepancy in Menon's assessment of the role of the bloc leaders in world politics is evident, though the language is somewhat more restrained; but the thrust and content of this part of Menon's Image are unmistakable.

Menon's image of world politics is not confined to the two power blocs, though he acknowledges their dominant role in shaping events. There is a third world, a vast and amorphous community of States which cross the boundaries of geography, race, and culture. Like Nehru, he calls this an *'area of peace'* to distinguish if from the arena of bloc politics which is, by inference, an 'area of war'—though the latter term never appears in Menon's speeches or statements.

'Area of peace' is a value-charged concept. It has a superficially positive aura, but the basic criterion of membership is negative—non-association or non-alignment with a power bloc. Most, but not all, of its constituent units are new States, the former European colonies or trust territories in Asia and Africa which have acquired independence since the Second World War. Those which have joined bloc-sponsored alliances, like SEATO and CENTO (the Philippines and Pakistan), are *ipso facto* excluded from the club. So too are States which have accepted the military protection of a bloc or bloc leader, such as Japan, the Koreas, the Vietnams, and Malaysia. Beyond these precise negative categories, however, the concept is riddled with anomalies which permit, indeed facilitate, highly subjective judgement. Thus one European State which eschews bloc affiliation, Yugoslavia, is an honoured member, while four others equally unattached—Austria, Sweden, Switzerland, and Finland—do not qualify, this despite the fact that the first and third have been neutralized by international agreement and the second has pursued a policy of non-alignment for two centuries. More pointed is the exclusion of a neutralized Austria and the inclusion of a neutralized Laos in the 'area of peace'.

There are other inconsistencies. China, which has had a network of treaty arrangements with the Soviet bloc since 1949, has participated in conferences of non-aligned States. With similar illogicality, Cuba entered the non-aligned group and the 'area of peace' after it disaffiliated from the U.S.-led American security system and became attached to the Soviet bloc, at least to the extent of accepting Soviet military protection. And, in Menon's eyes, some Latin American States, like Mexico and Brazil, are quasi-non-aligned and therefore potential recruits to the 'area of peace' while others are not; yet all are bloc-affiliated through the military and related networks of the O.A.S. One other illustration will suffice. Israel is barred *a priori* from this nebulous community despite the absence of an alliance with any other State in the world, while the former French African States belong to the 'area of peace' despite the presence of French troops and military missions on their territory. In short, one is confronted with a maze of conflicting criteria, some of which are determined by emotion or whim.

Menon might well counter that these comments obscure the real meaning of the concept, 'area of peace'. Yet he has displayed reticence about this key part of his Image, a strange lapse for a man so voluble and articulate. There is a brief, almost passing, reference to the idea in the Dialogue and very little in his United Nations speeches. Thus, in the context of non-alignment, he remarks, 'there must be something, an "area of peace" I called it, not territorially, but politically, diplomatically, morally, etc.' He reacted sharply to a question about the possible affinity of 'area of peace' to 'third bloc': 'third bloc, never. The third bloc is a foolish idea. My understanding of non-alignment is it cannot be a third bloc, for a bloc means power. Non-alignment is a policy of independence and peace, that is, materially speaking, a weak man's policy. In a sense, now that I think of it, it is like Gandhi's non-co-operation' (ch. 1).

Despite its brevity, this passage is revealing. It reveals the fuzziness of Menon's concept, 'area of peace'. It reveals, too, his emotional antagonism to the term 'bloc' and its connotation of power. There is, as well, a curious equation of non-alignment and independence, with the implication that participation in a military alliance results in the loss of independent statehood. Yet he later rebutted the charge that Hungary, a member of the Warsaw Pact, was a 'colony'—because it was a full-fledged member of the U.N.; Canada, by contrast, was described as a colony of the United States. Most importantly, though perhaps unwittingly, Menon shatters the myth, fostered and sustained by proponents of non-alignment, Indian and other, that this is a policy of superior morality; rather, as he declares with candour, it is 'a weak man's policy'. And finally, there is a facile interchangeability of non-alignment and 'area of peace'; yet these are not really synonymous. The former is a policy, the latter a loose metaphysical communion of those States which remain aloof from inter-bloc conflict.

From these and other remarks of Menon it is possible to delineate the indexes of an 'area of peace'. Most of them are negative: non-affiliation with a bloc-sponsored or bloc-led military alliance; the withholding of consistent support for a bloc's policies in the U.N. and other forums; non-dependence on either bloc for economic and military assistance; aid from both, which is not only beneficial but also strengthens the claim to non-alignment, hence membership in the 'area of peace'; military weakness and, especially, the absolute repudiation of nuclear weapons—that is to say, States in the 'area of peace' are atom-free zones; and opposition to the 'Cold War'. There is only one positive feature—active, purposeful pursuit of a foreign policy of 'peace', i.e. non-alignment. This is aimed at creating a cushion between the blocs and reducing the likelihood of overt conflict and, ultimately, the transformation of a bipolar system to a polycentric or multi-power system. (These are not Menon's terms but they denote his intent.)

The use of this frame of reference makes possible an explanation of some of the anomalies noted above, but not all. Thus the exclusion of the four European neutral or neutralized States may be attributed to their passive role towards the bloc struggle; they are not actively involved in the attempt to reduce inter-bloc tension. 'Non-alignment, in a sense, is an ugly word; it's negative, but becomes positive when you use it in the way we do!' The exclusion of Israel, to which Menon shows an undisguised hostility by resort to the stereotyped ideological clichés of the thirties, might be attributed by him to its dependence on States and communities in the Western bloc for economic and military aid. But there remain the inclusion of Soviet-bloc-affiliated Cuba and the French-dependent States of Africa, as well as Cyprus, with its multi-dependence on three NATO States, and some of the Arab States, like Jordan, Saudi Arabia, and Libya, no less dependent on the West.

These discrepancies, however, would be dismissed as 'a professor's view'. Indeed, it is an instructive commentary on the metaphysical concept, 'area of peace', that Menon has never systematically clarified its meaning and content. He has made high claims for non-alignment as a policy (ch. 1)—'it established India as an important quantity in world affairs; it prevented us from becoming a satellite State; it has on several occasions put a brake on war; it also showed a way for the newly-independent countries'—but he has not bothered to elucidate the meaning of 'area of peace'. It is 'one of those things that the world requires' as a counterpoise to the bloc struggle. And there is a strong emotive connotation to his terms. An 'area of peace' is inherently good, just as 'Imperialism', from whose control most of its members have escaped, and, to a lesser extent, the 'blocs', whose goals and values they reject, are evil. In Krishna Menon, more than most, emotion and reason are indissolubly linked in word and deed.

The third major component in Menon's image of world politics is the *United Nations*. His view is favourable but not without reservations. Indeed, one discerns ambivalence to the institution and the men who direct its affairs (ch. 10). The most important contribution of the U.N. is 'that it survives'; and this is crucial 'because things get debated; it's better to talk at each other than to shoot at each other; in that sense the U.N. has been a good safety valve and often delays crises'. He praises it as the central vehicle of decolonization and as a cushion against 'a head-on collision between the super powers', as well as a stimulus to aid for economic development. At the same time, he terms peace-keeping 'a dismal failure, except for UNEF. It can be a reality only when the world is disarmed and by disarmament I mean real disarmament.' He criticizes all innovations designed to enlarge the ambit of U.N. activities, seeing them as an intrusion into the sacrosanct realm of sovereignty. Thus Hammarskjöld's notion of a 'U.N. Presence' is dismissed as merely an expansionist idea; 'the U.N. was pushed in everywhere'. In the same way he opposes all suggestions for a standing United Nations Peace Force and all efforts at U.N.-directed plebiscite tests of popular opinion—in Hungary, Kashmir, and elsewhere. His rationale, repeated frequently in speeches to the General Assembly or one of its committees, is that, until the establishment of World Government and the effective rule of International Law, about which he was surprisingly optimistic, the core principle of the U.N. as presently constituted, namely, sovereignty, must not be violated or undermined. An expansion of U.N. powers in the political and military spheres would merely facilitate 'Imperialist' intervention in the affairs of weaker States.

Menon's image of world politics conforms in its essentials to what Professor Morton Kaplan calls a 'loose bipolar system': the flow of events is viewed as clustering around three sets of actors—the power blocs, notably the bloc leaders, the United States and the Soviet Union; the uncommitted States; and the universal organization, the U.N. But practitioners, even those as intellectually acute as Krishna Menon, do not engage in rigorous formulation of 'essential rules' of behaviour, 'transformation rules' of a system, and other paraphernalia of international relations models. Nor is this necessary to the decision-maker's role. What is pertinent, however, is the degree of *objectivity* in his perception of reality and the measure of *flexibility* in adapting his image to changes in the environment.

In both of these critical variables Menon's view of the global setting for India's foreign policy reveals distortion.

His assessment of non-alignment in the past—its benefits to India and the world—is plausible, even convincing, and is certainly reasoned and reasonable. But there is a disquieting intrusion of faith and metaphysics in the assertion that non-alignment is a Constant Good and is Constantly Viable as a basis of foreign policy; in this realm the 'scientific spirit' is nowhere evident. More important is the gross distortion of United States and Soviet responsibility for the ceaseless flow of tension in global politics since the Second World War. To ask, 'who has caused *all* the wars' since then and to answer by analogy with the assault on the embryonic Soviet regime is to cast grave doubt on Krishna Menon's ability to define the real situation of the global environment.

The contrast between derision, disdain, accusation, and denunciation of the United States role, and rare, mild regret with reference to Soviet actions reveals an enormous bias in Menon's image of this key component of world politics. It is deep-rooted and pervasive, an extension of his political philosophy and his emotional propensities—bitterness towards 'the West', a compound of colonialism, imperialism, and racism, with a specially intense hostility to the United States' 'state of mind', and a predisposition to approve, explain away, forgive and forget the Soviets and their bloc. The result is a glaring discrepancy between what the Sprouts have termed the 'operational environment' (reality) and the 'psychological environment' (image). This disconsonance, in turn, led to 'irrational' behaviour in foreign policy, that is, to non-objective choices of possible alternatives, leading to deficient decisions. Examples abound; two will suffice. Menon's image of the bloc struggle led him to an inordinate—and unproductive—alienation of the United States at the U.N. and elsewhere from 1952 to 1962. He also bears a large share of the blame for the creation of a no less distorted American image of non-alignment as a variant expression of Soviet bloc interests. In short, his perception was counter-productive in two respects. It contributed to deficient choices of policy in Delhi and portrayed non-alignment in a distorted light, thereby reducing the potential power and influence deriving from India's non-alignment posture; Menon's inability to apply the doctrine of 'equidistance' from the blocs was costly for India's foreign policy.

The same flow effect is evident in India's China policy. Menon's image (shared by Nehru) was widely at variance with Peking's real posture towards India. The gap continued until it was too late (1962). And the perception of China as a good neighbour with peaceful intent, indebted to India for championing her cause at the U.N. and elsewhere, and as co-equal leader of the Asian political renascence, led to a policy of unrestrained friendship, 'do-nothing' on the quiescent but unsettled frontier question, and indifference to security along the vast, 2,500-mile border with China. The introduction of a 'Forward Policy' came too late, in 1961. And even as late as 1965 Menon revealed strong traces of his inaccurate perception of China's intentions towards India. There is also a surprising touch of *naïveté* about decision-making in China's political system: 'I cannot imagine that a man who appeared to be so sensitive to argument [Chou En-lai] would be the Prime Minister of a country that invaded India' (ch. 12).

Menon's view of the outer layer of his external environment —the global system—reveals rigidity as well as bias. He discerns no basic change in the two-bloc relationship. More specifically, he rejects the notion of declining conflict and growing affinity between the U.S. and the U.S.S.R. He focuses on the tangible and sees only three modest agreements: limited test ban; outer space; and the production of fissionable material. But the easing of tension 'isn't deep enough to make a change amounting to a *détente*' (ch. 13). He ignores the polycentric trends in both blocs, the role of the Sino-Soviet conflict as an inducement to American-Soviet *rapprochement*, the more mature behaviour of the two super powers, and their implied assumption of joint responsibility for tranquillity and aid to developing areas (the Vietnam war notwithstanding), and a host of other indexes of change. As so often with committed practitioners of foreign policy, there appears to be a divergence between a rigid, static lens and a constantly changing reality.

There is some flexibility in his image of colonialism but far less than the process of decolonization would justify. Like Nehru, at the Belgrade Non-Aligned Conference in 1961, he gives higher priority to the maintenance of peace than to the elimination of the remnants of foreign rule. Yet he continues to regard colonialism as a vital force in world politics. More important in his image, as with many Asian and African leaders, is the idea of neo-colonialism, which he identifies exclusively with American economic penetration—and possible domination—of the new States. The Soviet Union is never mentioned in this context; its aid cannot be so identified because it was never a colonial power.

Prominent in his image of the 1960s is the lurking danger of a 'return to Empire', as revealed in his analysis of the Congo, Vietnam, and Malaysia. There is, too, a distinction between the 'progressive' U.K. policy towards parting with Empire and the behaviour of other colonial powers. The former French territories in Africa are regarded as less than independent; though France was commended at the United Nations for her withdrawal from Algeria. The Dutch were subjected to severe criticism for trying to retain control over Indonesia and West Irian; so too were the Belgians for their Congo policy; and the Portuguese received the most searing assault. The British, however, are spared, with few exceptions; their decolonization policy is the recipient of one of Menon's rare encomiums to the West. As might be expected, the granting of independence by the United States to the Philippines in 1946 is ignored.

The special regard for British decolonization must be set in the context of Krishna Menon's *ambivalence to the United Kingdom*. The long lean years of struggle against British rule in India had bred an intense hostility to the ideology and the substance of colonialism. Yet the India League phase of Menon's life, 1929 to 1947, was not without compensation: a higher education at the London School of Economics, then at its peak of intellectual vitality; friendships with men who helped shape the climate of opinion for what Menon would consider Britain's 'finest hour', some of whom were to guide Britain in the first crucial phase of withdrawal from Empire; a special attachment to Harold Laski, *guru* of the Left and inspiration for a whole generation of students from Asia and Africa; and a feeling of freedom, political and personal, so different from his earlier life in India. In short, Krishna Menon went through the indelible process of political socialization in England. Along with an intellectual commitment to Laski's neo-Marxism, he acquired an admiration for some of the values and traits of the 'British way of life': the liberal values of free speech, free press, and free assembly; respect for the individual; tolerance of opposition; safeguards for minority opinion and rights; decision by consent and conciliation; the central place of Law; and the system of parliamentary government with all its ramifications—theory, institutions, conventions, and pragmatic spirit.

The impact of these two parallel strands of 'the British connection' in Menon's life is evident everywhere, in deed and word. He felt strongly about India's continued membership in the Commonwealth and acted accordingly; in fact, he played a crucial role in devising the formula to 'square the circle' (ch. 2). And during the past seventeen years he has exercised a moderating influence during the periodic demands for withdrawal, over Kashmir, Suez, and the like. The essence of his diplomatic technique, as displayed in the Korean War, the Indo-China conflict, Bandung, and other areas of disagreement, namely the patient application of conciliation, may be traced to his familiarity with British party politics. A notable lapse, as in the Suez crisis, was almost certainly due to instinctive, reflex-like antagonism to what he perceived as the colonialist-racialist syndrome, combined with an ideological blind spot on the question of Israel (chs. 6 and 7). Yet even on this issue he tempered a sharp attack on Britain's Suez adventure with reiteration of the value of India's association with the U.K. Similarly, in many debates before the Trusteeship Council he paid tribute to the magnanimous manner of Britain's dismantling of her empire. It was, perhaps, his personal experience with the British form of colonialism and the relative ease of the transfer of power in India which induced a partisan attitude. In the domestic sphere, too, Menon's role and attitudes reveal the positive aspect of his British experience: his plea for the retention of English as the medium of higher education and as a window to the world; his attachment to the parliamentary system and his conviction that democratic planning is the proper path to development in India; and his respect for Law and constitutional procedures.

The Dialogue on *nuclear weapons* (ch. 16) reveals Menon at his intellectually most brittle and irrational. It also points up

an important admixture in his personality and outlook—
—militancy and pacifism or non-violence. The first is inherent
in Menon the man; the second derives partly from the pre-
valent attitudes of the British Left in the thirties and partly
from Gandhi's practice and creed. Not by chance is non-
alignment, in Menon's mind, the counterpart in foreign policy
to non-violent non-co-operation—both are weak men's policies.
Yet Menon has not adhered to the pacifist creed and has
justified the use of violence, as in Kashmir (so did Gandhi),
Goa, and elsewhere. On the Bomb, however, Menon is emotional in the extreme, and his image of nuclear weapons in the
global environment is fuzzy.

His comments begin—and end—with the same purist and
self-righteous assertion: 'Why should I debate mass suicide.
A nuclear bomb is not a weapon of offence or defence; it is a
weapon of mass extermination.' That may satisfy Menon's
penchant for virtue but it is a gross distortion of reality. Menon
knows that five States have already produced nuclear weapons,
one of them a danger to India's security. He also knows that at
least half a dozen others have the capability and that some of
them at least may have concealed programmes in motion. He
should know that India's decision to produce or abstain from
nuclear weapons is not the sole or even the decisive factor in
proliferation. Yet he dismisses such facts as irrelevant. He
could have made a plausible and possibly even a persuasive
case against India joining the nuclear club—in terms of exces-
sive cost, the higher priority of economic development, and the
doubtful political value of the Bomb. Instead, he retreated to the
comfortable realm of 'common sense', a synonym for rectitude,
except to urge that trust in India's reliability would suffer irre-
parably if she violated her commitment to the Test Ban Treaty.
Irrationality is evident not only in his categorical refusal to *debate*
the issue or even in his attempt to elevate this to a First Principle
of statecraft: 'The fundamental national interest of this country
is not to talk of the use of nuclear power for destructive purposes.' More disquieting is the facile dismissal of all options to
safeguard India's security. In no circumstances should India build
or acquire nuclear weapons; nor should India seek—or accept—
a nuclear umbrella from one or more nuclear powers, for this
would undermine non-alignment; and, in any event, he is

certain that such protection would never be offered or provided. Apart from a passionate distaste for nuclear war, a feeling not unique to Krishna Menon, there would seem to be an unstated belief that no State would use nuclear weapons against India. There is little evidence to support this optimism. And since Menon's image of China's intentions towards India proved to be so tragically wrong in the past, a rigid posture on the nuclear question would seem to be at least a doubtful basis for India's security. There is, finally, a striking discontinuity in Menon's line of argument. He does not propound a doctrine of pure pacifism. He accepts the necessity of conventional weapons until total disarmament and effective World Government are achieved. But nuclear weapons are rejected out of hand, on grounds of 'common sense'. In his frequent speeches on disarmament at the U.N., Menon was fond of applying his sardonic wit to the debate over 'clean' and 'dirty' bombs. It is, he said, like 'asking a fish whether he prefers to be fried in butter or margarine'. Reason seems to desert him at this point, for he never asks whether men prefer to be killed by conventional or nuclear weapons. His emotional predispositions govern his perception and an irrational image dictates his choice.

Image of the Subordinate System

A statesman's image, like that of any person, is characterized by varying degrees of stress on different levels of his environment and problems for decision. In the case of Krishna Menon there is a glaring omission, an almost total indifference to the broad regional setting of India's foreign policy. Menon's view of global politics is comprehensive and articulate, as noted earlier; so too with India's neighbours. But *Southern Asia*, as a distinctive area or system of international relations, is conspicuously absent from his perception. One searches in vain for such awareness in the wide-ranging Dialogue and in his U.N. speeches.

The only parts of this (his own) 'subordinate system' to which he devotes attention are Vietnam and Indo-China as a whole, Pakistan, and Ceylon. The first is dissected solely in the context of world politics, without reference to Southern Asia as such. The second is treated primarily as a subcontinental problem arising out of Partition and the complications resulting from the intrusion of Great Powers, outside the region. And the third is analysed as a marginal dispute with a neighbour. But the remaining States in the vast arc of Southern Asia—Burma, Thailand, the Philippines, Malaysia, Singapore, and Indonesia—and the region as a whole rarely enter his focus. Even when they do occasion remarks, as with West Irian or the conflict between Indonesia and Malaysia, they are viewed as expressions of colonialism, a global phenomenon. It is as if Southern Asia does not exist as a legitimate area for the pursuit of India's foreign policy; certainly it is not within Menon's mental horizon.

This striking lacuna was evident in Nehru's View of the World as well. It was reflected in India's policy of inaction and indifference in the region during the fifteen years following her initiative in the Dutch-Indonesian colonial struggle at the Delhi Conference of 1949. No efforts at regional integration worthy of the name were made by India. All States in South-East Asia were classified as category 'C', the least desirable and important in the Diplomatic Service hierarchy, with the result of inferior diplomatic representation. Apart from the Asian-Arab Group at the U.N., there was no forum or form of regional diplomatic co-operation, apart from the short-lived Colombo Powers group in 1954. And the one important conference in which India played a major role, Bandung, was organized on an ideological principle, non-alignment, and was far broader in geographic scope than Southern Asia. India abdicated from any role of leadership or catalyst in the area and exerted her influence only in negative terms, to prevent intrusion by the great powers, as with the emphatic rejection of SEATO. In short, Southern Asia was a backwater for India's foreign policy. And the key to that policy vacuum was precisely the vacuum in Nehru's and Menon's image of the region as part of India's external environment.

Krishna Menon's defence of this vacuum in thought and deed would probably run along the following lines. The concept of subordinate system, especially when applied to Southern Asia, is a 'professor's outlook'. The region rarely posed challenges to India's foreign policy, and when it did, as with Indonesia's struggle for independence, Indo-China (1954), and Vietnam, Delhi responded. The region is under-developed and its member-States wish to be left alone; their main function, in terms of India's interests, is to enlarge the 'area of peace' free of intervention by any powers. Finally, India's natural perspective for external policy must be the global system, where the issues of war and peace and colonialism, so vital to India, were being decided, and the narrow sphere of her neighbours, with whom problems for decision constantly arose.

There is much merit in this except for two shortcomings. To view Southern Asia or any region exclusively in terms of 'challenges' would be to deny the no less valid focus of foreign policy, namely, to utilize existing assets and to take initiatives and to build friendships. The cost of inactivity was brought to Delhi's attention forcefully during the conflicts with China (1962) and Pakistan (1965). Moreover, India's decision-makers may have recognized the importance of their neighbours but they did not bring to bear on disputes with Pakistan, Ceylon, or China anything like the energy, initiative, and ingenuity that was evident in their global involvements. And Menon's penchant for formulae and conciliation was never applied to Kashmir or the problem of persons of Indian origin in Ceylon, and only when it was too late in the case of China.

Despite his indifference to India's 'natural' subordinate system, Menon did perceive an intermediate level of interaction, linked to the global and the bilateral. This was an ideology-oriented, inter-continental *world of non-alignment*, embracing most of Asia and Africa, as well as pockets in Europe and Latin America. To him, as well as to Nehru, this was a far more important zone or theatre for foreign policy than Southern Asia. It provided a framework for concerted action which could cushion the inter-bloc struggle and thereby reduce the likelihood of global war, always the first concern, even in terms of India's narrow national interests. It could also hasten the process of decolonization and enlarge the scope of foreign aid for economic development, two other major policy goals. Finally, it provided India, in the United Nations and elsewhere, with a lever for the exercise of influence in global politics far beyond her real power. Membership of the Commonwealth complemented the non-aligned group as a forum for influence. Indeed, these two communities served as the institutional bases of this intermediate level of India's external environment.

This perception and the behaviour which ensued was rational and successful, as is evident in India's prominent role for a decade or more. Yet it did not require aloofness from and denigration of Southern Asia or the relegation of disputes with neighbours to a marginal place in the foreign policy nexus. It was only when the peculiar conditions of India's global role in the fifties began to undergo change, notably the softening of the bloc conflict and the shift from bipolarity to polycentrism, that the importance of these neglected levels of the external setting came to the fore. By then the accumulated cost was great, and the need to refashion the image and to restructure policy penetrated the Indian foreign policy élite.

Image of India's Neighbours

Krishna Menon's image of India's neighbours is no less pronounced than his perception of the global environment; if anything, it is more sharply articulated. In the case of Pakistan there is an element of passion akin to his aversion to the United States; the two are frequently coupled and serve as Menon's *bêtes noires*. Towards China there is respect and a feeling of Asian and anti-colonial kinship tempered by a sense of betrayal in 1962. And Ceylon is perceived as a cousin with deep cultural and historic ties who has behaved less than gallantly towards her large, peaceful community of Indian settlers who have contributed much to the island's welfare.

Menon's outlook on *Pakistan* (ch. 14) is derived from an ideology acquired in the twenties and thirties; both have remained constant over the decades. The point of departure is a commitment to the secular ideal and a rejection of the idea of religion as the legitimate basis of nationalism. Seen through this lens, Pakistan is antediluvian, a throwback, in a modern guise, to the retrogressive notion of a theocratic State. 'Would anyone', he asked rhetorically, but for 'the reflex action against British Imperialism—get rid of the British at any price—would anyone have agreed to a solution which the other side propounded, an out-of-date obscurantist doctrine [the two-nation theory]? We did not accept it. We do not do so now.' But this is only one component in his negative image of Pakistan.

Menon vehemently denies animosity. This may be taken as genuine conviction, in the sense of acceptance of the reality of Pakistan and the absence of a desire to undo Partition. But given his emotional propensity in political behaviour, one would expect disdain and antipathy in his outlook. There is, indeed, a complex web of ideological, political, and emotional strands which underpin the anti-theocratic theme. Taken together they explain why Menon has always regarded Pakistan as the principal threat to India's security, values, and institutions.

The 'anti-Imperialist' syndrome looms large in Menon's image of Pakistan. To begin with, 'it was the handiwork of Britain'. Once created, her function 'is like Northern Ireland, a remnant of imperialism. It's the British classic solution of empire and they rely on the fact that they don't have to fight us any more than they need to fight in Ireland. The Six Counties wage their fight against the rest of the Irish. More or less, it's the same position as Pakistan.' And then there is the link between traditional imperialism and the contemporary variety: Pakistan is decried as an imperialist stooge, tied to the United States through SEATO, CENTO, and large-scale military aid. 'There is no Pakistan *simpliciter* today [1965]; it is Pakistan plus the United States, as far as the Indo-Pakistan issue is concerned.'

Closely related to this perception is a contemptuous view of Pakistan nationalism as hollow and her national movement as artificial. A corollary is the provocative judgement that Pakistan was the recipient of independence by proxy: 'it really was not the result of a nationalist struggle of Pakistan leaders, but the result of the Indian struggle led by the Congress'. It follows, for Menon, that Pakistan's political élite consists of pro-British politicians and civil servants, without any apparent allowance for changes in eighteen years. In the same context Menon gives expression to a democrat's contempt for Pakistan's authoritarian regime with its alleged denial of the people's rights; no real elections have ever been held in Pakistan, he declares, yet her leaders dare call for a plebiscite in Kashmir. In short, Menon hurls a formidable ideological indictment: Pakistan is theocratic and authoritarian; it was created by a dying imperialism and is sustained by another, on the basis of a retrogressive and illegitimate principle of nationalism.

In Menon's eyes, Pakistan has committed grave political
sins as well. By accepting U.S. military aid from 1953 onwards
she weakened the 'area of peace', brought the Cold War to the
subcontinent, and opened the gates to the 'return of empire'.
All this was compounded by her hostile behaviour in India's
time of troubles, her collusion with China, and the consequent
accentuation of a massive burden on India's resources for
defence and economic development. These and other acts, says
Menon, reveal the enormous gap between India and Pakistan.
But they do more: they create profound mistrust of Pakistan's
intentions.

Other members of India's political, intellectual, and communications élites share this image of their neighbour in a
sundered subcontinent. Some may also share, but few articulate, an even deeper component in Menon's perception, indeed
the very core to which everything else is related as a superstruc-
ture of ideas. It is a thesis tinged with suppressed fear or at least
concern and is derived from Menon's reading of Indian history.
Briefly stated, it is that the Muslims once ruled the subcontinent;
that the British, the foreign successors to the Moghul *Raj*, have
now departed; that the Muslims assume a natural right to
restored authority; that Pakistan is the agent for the pursuit of
that historic goal; and that Kashmir is but the first stage on the
road to reconquest.

Menon states this view baldly in the Dialogue on Partition,
Pakistan, Kashmir, and Indo-Pakistan Relations: 'My belief is
that Pakistan leaders looked upon Pakistan as a first instalment,
"take what you can and fight for more", the English doctrine.
They never seem to have accepted Partition as final, as we did.
Their main approach to the problem was that India was theirs.
India was a Muslim country historically. The British had taken
it away from them. Now the British had gone away, and it
should be handed over to them.' Among other things, this
challenges the oft-stated Pakistani view that it is Indian leaders
who have not adjusted to 1947. On this point Menon is emphatic: 'We professed, and I think we did and do so honestly—
with the exception of some communalists—that, good or bad,
we agreed to Partition, and we don't want any of their territory.
We have no *arrière pensée* about it. It's not because we are
virtuous; it's because we know why we did it.'

It is only in this context, Menon insists, that the Kashmir issue can be properly assessed. Referring to the 'original Pakistan doctrine', he asks, 'what haven't they got? They have not got half of Punjab, Kashmir, half of Bengal, and Hyderabad. So when we talk about Kashmir, this is only part of that map, and [once more the core image] there is of course the larger map, which could place almost all of India in Pakistan.' To the Pakistan contention, widely shared in the West, that a solution of the Kashmir problem would lead to harmony with India, Menon takes the strongest exception: it would only encourage those who are dedicated to the 'Grand Design'—re-establishment of Muslim rule in the subcontinent. Why then the Pakistani stress on Kashmir? 'It provided a hurried step for Pakistan to take, one of those things like the inner tube of a bicycle where the rubber is thin, and therefore a puncture tends to come there.'

In a rare expression of doubt and modesty, Menon adds: 'It may be said that this is a far-fetched or fanatical or unrealistic or academic doctrine. I don't say that this is right; it is my analysis of it.' Nor is it important, in this inquiry into Menon's View of the World, whether or not he is correct. The crucial fact is that he believes it to be so, that he sees Pakistan in this untrustworthy and aggressive light, and that his behaviour flows logically, indeed inevitably, from this image. The policy choice is clear, and Menon has adhered to it consistently: India must stand fast on Kashmir and not yield an inch. At the same time, there is no display of revisionism, as with some right-wing Indian nationalists: 'There is no reason even today why these two countries should not live together, even with the Kashmir issue.' More specifically, he accepts the *status quo*: 'There is no other way except war.' Yet Menon is not optimistic about genuine peaceful coexistence between India and Pakistan, for Kashmir is in the same category as divided Korea, divided Germany, etc.: 'It must be understood in the context of world politics as they are.' And this is interwoven with his image of American imperialism, which attempts to use Pakistan as part of the containment of the Soviet Union. Thus is Menon's image of a neighbour integrated with his image of the global system.

Krishna Menon's image of *China* (ch. 12) differs from all other components of his View in two respects: it reveals the impact of unanticipated behaviour on thought and attitudes; and it lacks the rigidity displayed in his perception of global politics, notably of 'American Imperialism', and of Pakistan during the past two decades. There are, indeed, constant and variable elements in his outlook on China, the break-point being the trauma of 1962.

From the outset Menon viewed the New China as a progressive State, secular, socialist, and modern. It was a revolutionary movement in the best sense, pursuing with vigour the noble ends of economic development and social change. As such, it was worthy of encouragement. But Menon never praised the ruthless totalitarian means employed by Peking—nor did he criticize them, for this would be unwarranted interference in the internal affairs of another State. In fact, he remains a steadfast adherent of democratic planning, as is evident in the Dialogue.

Menon is drawn to the New China for other reasons, which lie in the realm of spiritual kinship. He perceives a natural affinity to India—two great civilizations that have asserted their national independence after a century or more of alien rule. They share as well a secular outlook and a commitment to anti-colonialism. Their paths may be different, but their ends are the same. Hence the foundations for co-operation between the two peoples and regimes. There is, too, a great respect for China's historic role as a Great Power, rightfully restored after an era of humiliation by Western Imperialism. It is that interplay of China and the West, paralleling India's subordination to Great Britain, which adds an emotional dimension to Menon's empathy with China. And, as so often, in U.N. speeches and elsewhere, the Dialogue on China begins with a lengthy discourse on history, with its stress on imperialist perfidy.

It is difficult to measure the relative importance in Menon's mind of antipathy to imperialism and empathy with a fellow Asian State with assumed common goals. The joint thrust, however, is to create a positive perception of China, unqualified until 1962 and retained in its essentials thereafter. The outcome, in policy terms, has been remarkable consistency. Menon has never wavered in his conviction that Peking has the inherent right to represent China at the U.N. Nor has he ever doubted its claim to Formosa as an integral part of Chinese territory. He defended China's intervention in the Korean War, applauded Chou's role at the 1954 Conference on Indo-China, and finds no fault with China's behaviour in the Vietnam war. He has steadfastly declared that Tibet is part of China; as late as 1964 he decried Delhi's shift in policy on this issue at the U.N. He does not seem to be disturbed by China's acquisition of a nuclear capability, apparently content with Peking's assertion that China would not be the first to use these weapons of mass extermination. And on the prolonged U.S.–China conflict his sympathies remain clearly with the latter. As he remarked on one occasion, 'China feels humiliated by the United States'; the tone and context indicate his sympathy for her grievance.

It bears mention, indeed emphasis, that Menon's fundamental orientation to China, as to Pakistan, has a strong emotional flavour rooted in his experience and ideology of the thirties. This emerges frequently in a long, discursive, defensive, and painful dialogue on China in 1964–5. One example will suffice: 'Our idea about China—this is quite true—is that she never invaded us in the past. I myself was one of the active people in the China Campaign Committee in London in the 1930s; and that has its roots in our hostility to Western intrusion into China, extra-territorially. The emotional base was there.' The powerful grip of another intangible—history—on Menon's image is also acknowledged: 'Our relations with China and everything that has happened, and everything that will happen in the future, are rooted in our past approaches to China.' In that context there is the first intimation of partial change in Menon's image: 'Equally now they are affected, and are bound to be, by the betrayal of our friendship and good faith.' That indeed was the cause, for Menon and for Nehru, of a reluctant redefinition of China after 1962.

The pervasive tone of Menon's revised image of China is regret, not anger as displayed in his comments on Pakistan and 'American Imperialism'. It is, rather, a feeling of hurt, a sense of dismay, even of surprise, a mood of disenchantment. India had championed Peking's claims at the U.N., had introduced her to Asia at the Bandung Conference, and had defended her interests in Korea, Vietnam, and elsewhere—and now the reward was betrayal. Menon takes great pains to deny the element of personal affront and to place the idea of betrayal in a broad context. Speaking of Nehru's reaction to the events of 1962—one may read his own response into this as well—he remarked: 'I think it affected him deeply; it had a very bad effect on him. It demoralized him very much. Everything that he had built was threatened; India was to have a militarist outlook which he did not like.' On the theme of personal betrayal: 'I think that is a wrong way of looking at it—he was far too big for that. But he felt that the Chinese action betrayed the world, betrayed, in the sense that it broke faith, the cause of Afro-Asian solidarity, etc.' In defence of Nehru (and perhaps himself as well), he added, 'but it was not as though he was mesmerized by the Chinese before the invasion; he was too realistic for that'.

These extracts point up two facets in the altered image of China. India had befriended her northern neighbour, and Peking had simulated reciprocity—but had then betrayed Delhi's trust and friendship. No less important, China had shattered Asian solidarity and had undermined the non-aligned 'area of peace'. The result was to strengthen the forces of imperialism in world politics and the forces of reaction within India. He recalled the descent into conflict: 'That is what I told Chou En-lai when he came here [1960]; "you may hurt us but you hurt yourselves more; you have hurt the world even more; you have strengthened every reactionary element in this country and the forces of tension in the world".' Yet he cannot bring himself to include Chou among the culprits: 'I don't think he had much freedom of action himself.'

There is a third element of change in Menon's perception of China—the sad reflection that a victim of imperialism had herself penetrated into the territory of other States, Burma, India, Nepal, and, in intent, the Soviet Union: 'I am not talking about Ladakh but about the whole world; they moved into Burma—they have made a treaty with Burma now in order to shorten their front—the same with the Soviet Union, just like the way the Russians tried to claim Alaska.' Along with this is the 'discovery' that China has always been expansionist: 'Basically they are expansionists—they have always been—and you have to put this side by side with their expansionism in the Soviet Union.' This belated recognition—he dates it to the Chinese incursions into NEFA in the autumn of 1959—suggests a disastrous misreading of the Chinese mind during the preceding decade or a strong dose of wishful thinking. On this the Dialogue is full of contradiction, which leads to the inference that both strands were and are present in Menon's image.

On the one hand, China was 'basically expansionist' and this had 'certainly become pointed' in 1959. Yet, in a later reference, 'at that time we certainly had no idea that the Chinese were going to wage war on us'. This disbelief in China's hostile intent appears side by side with the view that she is inherently expansionist, though the epithet 'imperialist' is avoided. The mixed feelings emerge, for example, in the remark, 'on the 8th September 1962 China invaded us—not invaded us—they intruded'. There is also the painful effort to find some rationale, however distorted, for China's perfidious acts: 'They could say to themselves that we had taken American aid; and they say we behave like Americans.' More to the point, 'I am not even now sure that the Chinese did not think we were much more powerful than we were in 1962, that the whole of America would be behind us with the threat to invade China from its underbelly. It may have been a foolish idea, but there it was. Therefore they were going to deal us a deadly blow'; as if the Himalayas were the ideal place for an invasion of China! Finally, he reflects the ambivalence on responsibility for the 'tragic conflict', which could have been avoided: 'If the Prime Minister [Nehru] had been able to leave himself alone, without unmodern [Indian] minds and China's own mistakes, it would have probably been different. We could have got, not a settlement, a kind of Korea business, a kind of no-war situation.'

All these gyrations merely reflect the feeling of anguish that China had misbehaved. In the context of this inquiry into Menon's View of the World, the Chinese did not act in accordance with his preconceptions. The gap between image and reality was too great for someone as sensitive as Menon to ignore. And so he revised his view of India's most powerful neighbour, but only reluctantly and in part. The will to believe that this was atypical Chinese behaviour, aggravated by America's presence in Asia, prevented a transformation of Menon's deep-rooted image of China. Given the traumatic experience—the autumn of 1962 was a turning-point in his political life—this is not surprising.

Ceylon occupies a marginal place in Krishna Menon's View of the World. This is typical of his relative indifference to the lesser States of South and South-East Asia. It is also a reflection of the Indian foreign policy élite's preoccupation with Pakistan and China, and with the global political system. Indeed, it is noteworthy that he seems more concerned with events in Africa, despite the infinitely greater direct Indian 'national interest' in her southern neighbour. He is aware of the delicate —some would say tragic—problem of the 1,000,000 persons of Indian origin in Ceylon but treats the issue in a perfunctory manner. It is as if, like everything else that does not impinge on the great issues of war and peace, colonialism, and racialism, Ceylon's treatment of her Tamil minority does not merit serious attention. Menon reacted violently to the Suez War, and not primarily because of the dangers of escalation; rather, it touched the sensitive chord of anti-colonialism. He has spoken with passion about apartheid in South Africa, much more so than about the discrimination against Indians in the Union. Belgian iniquities in the Congo inspired another of his ubiquitous assaults on imperialism and revealed an emotional identity with African victims of maltreatment. Yet the precarious position of a large community of India's kinsmen near by does not call forth a volatile response; at most, there is a restrained expression of disquiet. Perhaps this is due to a desire not to aggravate an already unhappy condition. It is almost certainly to be attributed in part to the absence of a 'colonialist' or 'racial' element.

There is no hostility in Menon's image of Ceylon; rather, he wishes the island and her people well. As with most Indian leaders, there is a thinly concealed 'big brother' attitude, a patronizing air towards a nation with strong cultural and historical ties to India. On the specific issue of Ceylon's treatment of people of Indian origin, he is critical, but the tone is tempered (ch. 18). International law and custom are invoked: 'How could a person become stateless by a declaration of another Government?' His real concern was conveyed by a reference to Nehru's attitude: 'He knew the burdens we would have to carry [their absorption into India's economy], but what worried him more was the impact on world opinion. Secondly, the fact that these people had contributed economically to

Ceylon's welfare, and that by a mere ukase they are declared stateless; things of that kind worried him.' In short, it was an unworthy policy for any State which considers itself modern, especially disquieting from a friendly neighbour of long standing. And once more the primacy of world politics in Menon's (and Nehru's) image was clearly articulated.

Image of India's Proper Roles

A View of the World, as defined at the outset of this essay, is a complex set of images: first, perception of the external operational environment in which decisions must be taken, in the global, subordinate, and bilateral systems of interaction; and secondly, advocacy, implied or explicit, of the desirable policy orientations within that environment. The image of the desirable should but may not bear a high correlation with a definition of the real environment. If it does not, policy choices and hence decisions and behaviour will be 'irrational' and, therefore, other things being equal, unsuccessful.

There are at least six strands in Menon's advocacy of India's *proper role in world politics*. Some of these are fully articulated, others less so, and still others may be inferred from his reflections. The most important is his unqualified and unvarying recommendation that India remain committed to a policy of non-alignment. Although he would deny the emotional implication, this is an article of faith which has not been shaken by events affecting the position of India or the character of international politics from 1950 to 1965. The basis of this policy is a simple equation: non-alignment is merely the external manifestation of national independence; alignment in word or deed would mean the reversion to a dependent, i.e. colonial, status. And, since dependence is the worst possible evil that could befall India, she must scrupulously avoid attachment to any bloc, whether by participation in a military alliance or even by consistent *a priori* support for the policies of a bloc or super power.

This posture is supported by Menon's reading of events. For one thing, he denies that there has been any basic change in global politics; bipolarization remains intact, and the *détente* between the U.S. and U.S.S.R. is a fiction or, at best, marginal

—'the external setting has continued changing in the last fifteen years, but in marginal terms'. For another, non-alignment was a distinct asset in the Sino-Indian conflict. Very few States supported China; even the Soviet bloc did not do so: 'In my opinion, apart from the national excitement, disappointment, and anger in India, the China clash, if anything, only reinforces non-alignment. Where would we be today supposing we were aligned with America?' Thus rigidity in the image of the external setting leads to rigidity in the policy posture. The intensity of his commitment is nowhere better revealed than in the remark, 'even in twenty years' time it would be wrong for us to join a war bloc'. There is no doubt in Menon's mind: 'There is no other alternative to what is called non-alignment, what is called independence of policy; this has to continue.' Moreover, this policy is desirable not only for India: 'I would go further and say that, in the present condition of the world, it would have been a good thing for the countries of Western Europe and Britain to have pursued non-alignment. This was my opinion in 1945, not only my view now.'

Is non-alignment possible for India in the late 1960s? The answer is an emphatic yes, for Menon; indeed it is essential. In fact, he does not acknowledge the shift from non-alignment to bi-alignment—that is, the change from 'equidistance from the super powers' to 'equal proximity to the super powers', the reality under Nehru's successors. This smacks too much of alignment and is therefore anathema.

A second strand, really a corollary of the first, is that India should continue to expand the 'area of peace' by enlarging the number of non-aligned States free of nuclear weapons and entangling alliances. More specifically, this involves pressure on the U.S. to withdraw from Vietnam and Southern Asia generally, support for the Rapacki Plan of denuclearization of central Europe and its extension to all States outside the nuclear club, and the withdrawal of bloc power—bases, alliances, and military aid—from the non-Western world. Is this feasible? In part, Menon would reply in the affirmative. Despite her decline in status after 1962 and, even more, after Nehru's death in 1964, India has adhered to this broad policy objective and has used her limited influence in this direction. But Menon also recognizes that the impact has been less, partly because of the lean years in her economic development, partly because of her preoccupations with hostile neighbours, and partly because of the lack of decisive leadership. All this has reduced, but has not nullified, the possibility of this inherently sound policy line. India must first recover her strength, confidence, and will to project this goal with vigour in the global arena.

India must also continue to cherish, and to play, the role of conciliator, using her good offices, when called upon, to ease the conflicts between blocs and States. For Menon, mediation is a natural extension of non-alignment. While it may not be a function unique to non-aligned States—'it depends on circumstances, on whom you are mediating with'—the evidence in cases of inter-bloc conflict is clear: 'it is history, isn't it?' This is not only a source of pride for Menon and India; it is a policy suited to India as the first and most consistent exponent of non-alignment, a policy which serves the interests of India and of world peace. Yet Menon acknowledges that it is not possible for her to perform this function now, at least to the extent she did in the 1950s. India's internal weakness and lack of confidence have reduced her capacity in this sphere.

A fourth strand in Menon's advocacy for India is continued identity with the forces engaged in the struggle against colonialism. For more than a decade, he stressed, India had taken the lead in the efforts to eradicate this curse of the modern world. And, despite the great progress in decolonization, he attaches greater attention to the remnants of alien rule. Intense feelings were expressed on Rhodesia as an evil mixture of racialism and colonialism, and India's task is to press for decisive action to eliminate the white minority regime. But the real danger is neo-colonialism, the masked return of empire. In both these spheres the proper policy for India is clear and feasible. Menon regrets the lapses from India's traditional policy, which he ascribes mainly to the growth of American influence in India in recent years. India had begun, even while he was a leading member of the élite, to adopt more moderate and conservative postures in foreign policy.

On no issue, perhaps, has Menon spoken more passionately and more consistently than on disarmament. His objective, as with most men, has been total disarmament, the precondition to abiding peace and World Government. But, unlike most practitioners of foreign policy, he has always declared this to be possible in the short run. Both in power and afterwards he has defined India's proper role as relentless pressure on the nuclear powers to reach agreement to cease tests, suspend the production of fissionable material, and begin the destruction of stockpiles. To the 'Non-Aligned Eight', including India, he gives the credit for whatever progress has been achieved. And India's obligation is to persist in this endeavour—until complete disarmament, conventional as well as nuclear, is attained. He admonishes those who advocate a nuclear capability for India or any variant thereof and notes with regret the diminished militancy and activity of Indian spokesmen on this issue at Geneva and New York.

The final strand of Menon's advocacy in global politics relates to the U.N. As in the past, India must strengthen the world organization as a forum for the expression of diverse views and conflicting ideologies. The rationale remains unchanged—'it is better to talk at each other than to shoot at each other'. Moreover, the U.N. performs valuable services in the fields of decolonization and economic development. It also constitutes the framework for progress towards effective international law and government. India's contributions have been of a high order and should continue in this vein. But her energies should also be directed in part to preventing the 'illegitimate' and unwise expansion of U.N. activities, lest it intervene in the internal affairs of member-States. Sovereignty must remain supreme in the transition period.

The policies advocated by Krishna Menon in *Southern Asia* may be treated with the utmost brevity, for they are mere extensions of India's proper role in world politics. As noted earlier, he does not recognize the region as a distinctive subordinate system and, in any event, he perceives it as peripheral to India's vital interests. India's policy must continue to be preventative and responsive—to the threat of penetration by the blocs and the super powers, especially to the danger of neocolonialism. In negative terms, the proper role for India is to help keep the region free from Cold War alliances and nuclear weapons. More specifically, it is to press for the elimination of U.S. power in Vietnam and the self-assumed 'burden' of protecting the entire area from Chinese expansionism. Stated more positively, India should aim at strengthening the non-aligned character of Southern Asia as an 'area of peace' and the preservation of the independence of States in the region. In his preoccupation with 'U.S. Imperialism' Menon is no longer in tune with Indian élite images and he expresses this indirectly by criticizing India's moderate and passive role in the Vietnam conflict.

Menon's policy preferences regarding India's neighbours reveal diverse traits. There is rigidity and extremism in the case of Pakistan, reluctant acquiescence in Ceylon's behaviour, and flexibility, combined with firmness, towards China. In all three his image of the proper role is consistent with his perception of the environment. Moreover, his prescriptions with regard to Pakistan and Ceylon are widely shared among India's élites and attentive public. By contrast, his view of the desirable in Sino-Indian relations sets him apart from the mainstream of post-1962 Indian thought.

The Menon line on *Pakistan* is as brittle and unyielding as that advocated by the Nationalist Right. India must stand firm on Kashmir and make no concessions whatever. She must reject Pakistan's claims and U.N.–Western bloc pressure for a plebiscite, which is no longer relevant and, in any event, was never pledged in the form assumed by most observers. Pakistan's aggression has never been decried, and India's legal rights to the entire territory of the former princely State remain unqualified. The full integration of Kashmir into the Indian Union is logical and right and should be consummated. Talk of an independent Kashmir is nonsense and should be squashed. The one point on which he departs from the extreme Right is his willingness to accept the cease-fire line of 1949 as the permanent *de facto* boundary—in the interest of harmony between India and Pakistan; the Right advocates force to incorporate the 'occupied territory'.

Menon has urged this policy on countless occasions, with the intensity of a true believer; it is, he proudly remarked, his favourite topic for public speeches in India and the one most sought after. Indeed, he seems to regard it as a personal mission to educate his people in the 'truth' about Kashmir and to instil a determination not to yield an inch. And to those who talk about concessions—or Kashmir's secession—he declares: 'No settlement that would surrender Indian territory to Pakistan, constitutionally, is possible in India. There are many millions of people who feel this way.' With supreme assurance in his cause, he added: 'Shastri [and, presumably, any future Prime Minister] would not do it. He knows public feeling on this matter. He cannot do it even if he wants to.' And, without elaboration, he cautioned, 'there are graver and more sinister implications in such surrender'. All this was said before the Indo-Pakistan War of 1965—which only confirmed this hard line as the proper policy, for Menon and almost everyone else in India.

Menon's advocacy on Kashmir is only part of his general posture on Pakistan. It is equally imperative that India avoid an alliance with what he terms a theocratic, imperialist-aligned State, for this would contaminate and ultimately destroy India's non-alignment. In the same vein, India must remain wary of Pakistan's oft-declared pledge of friendship—once the Kashmir problem is settled. Given the premiss that Kashmir is only the first step in a 'Grand Design' to re-establish Muslim rule over the subcontinent, this is logical advice. For the same reason India must maintain a 'Pakistan First' policy in her planning and organization; to do otherwise would be to jeopardize her most vital interests—security and territorial integrity. The only positive element in his Pakistan policy is that India try to establish a relationship of genuine peaceful co-existence based on the *status quo*.

Menon's policy recommendations concerning *China* are the most elaborately articulated. They derive from four interrelated elements of a complex perception of the past, the present, and the future: empathy with the Chinese revolution; an acute feeling of betrayal of trust and friendship; ambivalence about responsibility for the tragic conflict; and recognition of the geopolitical realities. His definition of India's proper role is equally complex, revealing a careful blend of friendship and firmness.

Despite the recent past, and in order to secure the future, India must renew the policy of a 'Good Neighbour'. It must eschew provocation of any kind—by word or deed. Responsible leaders of Government should set the tone, and the press should avoid angry condemnation and fiery talk of war. At the same time, India should not provide a pretext for renewed Chinese incursion by massing troops along the border or dispatching patrols to controversial points, where calm now prevails. This prescription is not set out in such clear terms but may be inferred from his criticism of India's behaviour in the autumn of 1962—including Nehru's statement in October of that year, 'I have given orders to the Army to throw the Chinese out'. In the same vein, he recalled: 'Shastriji went all round the country making similar speeches. There were lots of such speeches. I kept quiet—I had some knowledge of what strength we had and of what we were assuming at the time.' And, while the 'Forward Policy' of 1961–2 was defended by Menon, its revival now would only aggravate the tension.

India's 'Good Neighbour' policy should extend to global politics as well. She should continue to espouse Peking's claim to China's seat at the U.N. She should not aggravate the Tibet situation by a volte-face on her traditional support of China's rightful claim to sovereignty. To do so would be to cause ridicule and doubt about India's bona fides and maturity; it would also heighten Chinese animosity, with no compensation. In Vietnam, too, India must press for withdrawal of American power and influence and, by inference, acknowledge China's historic leadership in the area. In all these recommendations Menon is consistent with his pre-1962 views and acts; in 1964 he dissented sharply from the Indian Government's passive role on the U.N. China issue, its contemplated revision on Tibet, and its moderation on Vietnam.

A logical inference is that India should let it be known she is willing to resume negotiations with China on a reasonable basis. Menon has not publicly dissented from the official Delhi stand that China must accept, as India has done, the Non-Aligned Colombo Proposals, as clarified by the Ceylon and U.A.R. representatives. But his eagerness for a settlement would suggest his willingness to negotiate without any conditions. The inference is supported, too, by Menon's remarks, in 1964, that, had Nehru not been subject to pressures in India, 'we could have got to a situation from where we could have sought a way to negotiations. . . . Actually, the Prime Minister and I had talks on what could be done, but other people, some of them senior men, said, "why all this now, we will see when it comes". It was not understood that in diplomacy what you can do today, if you take the initiative, has far greater effect' (ch. 12).

Menon does not rely solely on conciliatory gestures towards China. As with Pakistan-occupied Kashmir, India must maintain a firm claim to the 'lost territories' overrun by the Chinese —but in both he opposes the resort to force. He regrets the belligerency of the Indian claim to Aksai Chin, in marked contrast to his own assertive claim to India's sovereignty over all of Kashmir. Perhaps this is due to a conviction that a formula associated with him in 1962, namely, a long-term lease exchange of Aksai Chin for the strategic Chumbhi Valley, is still an honourable way out of the Sino-Indian impasse.

In the military sphere, too, Menon's nationalism is not wanting. He advocates a rapid and sustained expansion of the armed forces, a process which he initiated as Defence Minister from 1957 to 1962; the glaring weaknesses, brought home so forcefully when the Chinese struck, must be overcome so that India's territorial integrity can be assured. But under no circumstances should India embark on a nuclear weapons programme. Indeed, it would appear that this recommendation for a military build-up, widely shared by India's élites, is directed more to the Pakistan 'threat' than to China: 'even today [1964], I say our main enemy is Pakistan. China, even if she came here, could not stay. Pakistan could invade and live here.' Along with growth in the defence establishment, India must extend her presence in the hitherto neglected frontier areas, but only to assert her sovereignty, not to provoke a renewed Chinese incursion. And, in the field of economic development, India should not abandon the democratic path; it is neither necessary nor desirable.

Menon has rarely articulated his thoughts on India's neighbour to the south. Given his volubility on virtually all aspects of public policy, this reticence suggests, as noted earlier, indifference. One may infer his view, however, from chance remarks. Three interrelated themes are apparent. He criticized the 1964 Shastri–Senanayake Agreement as an unnecessary and unprincipled sacrifice of the legitimate interests of people of Indian origin in *Ceylon*—but not so bitterly as South Indian leaders and not to the extent of demanding revision. He was content to remark for the record: 'Nehru knew their problem very much better and he would not have made that Agreement.' He is, in fact, much less sensitive to the expulsion of Tamils from Ceylon than of Hindus from East Pakistan. At the same time, he shares with most Indians the belief that, on humanitarian grounds, India must absorb the half million or more refugees from Ceylon. Nor does he regard this as a serious economic or social burden. As for future policy, the desirable course is to impress upon Colombo the need for fair treatment regarding the substantial assets of those who will return to India under the compromise terms of agreement. India must avoid the tactics of a bully but must be firm, lest the victims of ethnic, linguistic, and religious intolerance suffer material deprivation as well as forced migration.

Conclusions

At the outset of this essay a plea was made for greater rigour in the analysis of State behaviour. To that end the concept of a Foreign Policy System was suggested as a framework of inquiry. Among the six general components of this system, dynamically interrelated as Inputs, Process, and Outputs, was Élite Images. These, in turn, were defined as six sets of perceptions held by decision-makers in foreign policy; in their totality, these images constitute a View of the World. And, within that frame of reference, we have explored the View of an important member of the Indian élite, relating his images to the content of India's external behaviour. What conclusions emerge from this inquiry and, more important, what hypotheses arise about the concept of Élite Images and their link with policy acts?

A conspicuous fact about Krishna Menon's View of the World is the *varying intensity* of his sets of images. In the area of operational environment there is a strong perception of two levels, global and bilateral, but little awareness of India's own subordinate system. In the realm of response there is an equally sharp distinction. But most significant is his muted, virtually non-existent assessment of the possible. In short, he does not perceive restraints on policy implementation. This may be atypical but it may well be the norm. The following proposition suggests itself:

> Decision-makers in setting out foreign policy goals do not consciously articulate an image of the possible because they equate objectives with reality. This disposition is more pronounced in decision-makers with a high ideological motivation.

This in turn leads to a more basic hypothesis, namely:

> The criterion of success in foreign policy is the degree of congruence between the operational and psychological environment.

Another striking fact about Menon's View is that his image of the environment reveals a *Time Lag* in the adjustment to changing reality. This is evident in two important areas: his failure or unwillingness to recognize the basic change in Soviet-American relations from intense hostility to *détente* and the implications for a policy of Non-Alignment; and the persistence of a large part of his pre-1962 image of China after the border war. There is reason to think that this is not unique to Menon, for images are formed early in life and are deep-rooted in the psychology of decision-makers, as with all men.

Three propositions, all of which may be tested by further research, arise from this inquiry:

> The image of all decision-makers in foreign policy reveals a time lag in the adjustment to changing reality.
>
> The degree of error or failure in policy choices will bear a high direct correlation with the duration of the time lag and the proportion of the image of the environment that persists after the reality of the environment has changed.
>
> The rigidity of the image of the decision-making élite and the time lag will be greater than in the case of the attentive and mass publics.

The reason for the last proposition is that decision-makers have a commitment to their images and the policy choices they make in accordance with their images; it is far more difficult to admit error in either than for the public, which does not have such commitments to sustain and can therefore readjust more quickly.

A more general proposition arises from this inquiry. One objective, shared by many, is to make the study of foreign policy a rigorous discipline. It follows that this requires efforts at prediction of probable behaviour of States. In theory there may be various ways of achieving this goal. The submission here is that one viable and researchable key to prediction of future behaviour is analysis in depth of the images held by foreign-policy élites. In Krishna Menon's case, we have seen a high correlation of images and policy choices. If we can uncover the images of decision-makers we can project likely policy acts, for

> Policy choices flow inexorably from the composite images of the decision-making élite, modified only by the counter-images of competing élites within the political system.

While élite images will not provide the total data required for prediction, they can serve as the foundation for such projections.

It is recognized that this inquiry has been confined to one decision-maker's View of the World and that there are many types of View. Indeed, if the link between image and decision is valid, a more general hypothesis is indicated:

> There are various types of Views of the World. Criteria for constructing a typology include the degree of congruence between the operational and psychological environments, the degree of completeness, and the degree of persistence and flexibility. All foreign-policy élites' Views of the World can be grouped in such a typology and probable behaviour deduced from each type.

It may well be that further research will indicate one or more of these propositions to be inaccurate or to require modification. But these paths to empirical investigation will contribute to greater insight into the complexities of foreign policy, either for an individual State or, ideally, for the State as a unit of behaviour in the international system.

APPENDIX

KRISHNA MENON'S VIEW OF THE WORLD

A CONTENT ANALYSIS
BY
JANICE GROSS STEIN

Introduction

THE study of international relations has recently become more systematic. In the realm of foreign policy, however, there has been relatively little effort to explore behaviour with a view to making explanation and prediction more precise. This paper is an attempt, by the use of quantitative techniques, to suggest, elaborate, and refine hypotheses about the behaviour of those who have been instrumental in shaping Indian foreign policy.

Krishna Menon has been one of the key decision-makers in the Indian Foreign Policy System. The record of his discussions with Professor Michael Brecher[1] provide the raw data for the following study. From these data we shall derive Menon's perceptions of the environment. The framework for the analysis, as well as the basic organizing concepts, are provided by Professor Brecher, in his essay 'Krishna Menon's View of the World'.[2]

The technique of analysis which will be employed is that of content analysis—a method which 'aims at quantitative classification of a given body of content in terms of a system of categories devised to yield data relevant to specific hypotheses concerning the content. . . . Content analysis is a research technique for the objective, systematic, and quantitative description of the manifest content of communication.'[3]

Content analysis can be undertaken on three distinct yet mutually complementary levels. First, one can study the incidence of attention or the frequency of occurrence of those items judged to be relevant. Implicit in this focus is the assumption that the greater the interest of the decision-maker in a given topic, the greater the frequency with which items associated with this topic are produced.[4] We partially accept this assumption, and the first part of this paper will present the frequencies of occurrence for seventy-seven content categories.

A second level of analysis is the study of attitudes—'the average favourable or unfavourable loading of evaluative terms'.[5] The best technique for measuring and scaling the intensity of attitudes is the 'pair comparison' scaling method,[6] which permits comparison of

---

[1] See Part I of this volume, Dialogue.   [2] See pp. 295–336 above.
[3] Bernard Berelson, *Content Analysis*, 1952, p. 18.
[4] Charles E. Osgood, 'Representational Models and Relevant Research Methods' in Ithiel de Sola Pool (ed.), *Trends in Content Analysis*, 1959.
[5] Ibid., p. 20.
[6] Dina A. Zinnes, ' "Pair Comparison" Scaling in International Relations' in Robert North, Ole R. Holsti, M. George Zaninovitch, and Dina A. Zinnes, *Content Analysis, A Handbook of Applications for the Study of International Crisis*, 1963, pp. 80–9.

levels of intensity of expressed attitudes. From the data provided by this analysis, it is then possible to construct a 'pattern of variables' which represents an empirical model of the perceptual world of the decision-maker.[1]

It is also possible to analyse the 'association structure' of a decision-maker, that is, the ideas which tend to be associated by him. This can be done by the technique of contingency analysis,[2] which permits the charting of the co-occurrence of two items to a greater-than or less-than chance degree. An alternative method, which will be used in the third part of this paper, is factor analysis. Factor analysis uses the correlations of each variable with all the others to discover underlying factors or axes, around which a high proportion of the content categories will cluster. We are then able to isolate a smaller number of more basic variables which are crucial to the association pattern of the decision-maker.

This study is divided into three parts. The first will provide a frequency analysis or a charting of the occurrences of seventy-seven content categories. The second will measure the intensity of expressions of hostility, friendship, satisfaction, and change of *status quo*. And the third will use factor analysis to attempt to determine the underlying structure of association.

It is necessary at the outset to delineate our categories. After a preliminary reading of the material, approximately 100 content categories were selected. In the course of the analysis twenty-three were eliminated because of their low rate of occurrence. The interview data are those which deal directly with foreign policy, that is Interviews 1–14, and Interview 16 (numbered 15 in all graphs and tables of this paper).

Six broad categories of analysis are used. The first is Actors in the contemporary international system. The second is Symbols used by the decision-makers. The third refers to the various 'Levels of the International System': the Global system or the relations between the super powers with or without their attendant blocs, the neutral nations, and international organizations; Bilateral, which refers to all interactions of State A with State B, except the interaction with one or both of the super powers, which we term Dominant-Bilateral; the Subordinate system[3] which has been operationalized in this

---

[1] M. George Zaninovitch, 'Pattern Analysis and Factor Analysis' in North, Holsti, Zaninovitch, and Zinnes, op. cit., pp. 105–28.

[2] Charles E. Osgood, op. cit., pp. 54–78.

[3] The concept of Subordinate System used here is developed by Michael Brecher in 'International Relations and Asian Studies: The Subordinate State System of Southern Asia', in *World Politics*, xv, no. 2, Jan. 1963, pp. 213–35. It refers to a system which has the following characteristics: (1) Its scope is delimited,

paper to include Africa, Asia, Latin America, and the Arabs-Middle East.

The fourth category is Values of the decision-maker. The typology is drawn from Harold Lasswell,[1] and is grouped under two broad headings, welfare and deference. The welfare values include Well-being, or the health and safety of the person or group; Wealth, or income, material resources, etc; Skill, which is proficiency in any practice whatever, be it trade, profession, or art;[2] and Enlightenment, or knowledge, insight, and information.

The deference values include Power, which refers to both physical power and influence over others; Respect, which is status, honour, recognition, prestige, and glory or reputation; Rectitude, which comprises the moral values of virtue, goodness, and righteousness; and Affection, which includes the value of love and friendship.

The fifth category is that of Strategies. This refers to the strategies suggested by the decision-maker for use by his own State in relation to any international problem.

The sixth category is that of Issues—i.e. the issues in connection with which statements and assertions are made.

We will now turn to an analysis of the material which we have gathered from the precise counting of the frequencies of occurrence of our content categories.

Frequency of Occurrence[3]

Table I below provides a summary of the actual occurrences of twenty-two actors throughout the fifteen interviews.[4] The sixteenth

with primary stress on a geographic region. (2) There are at least three actors. (3) Taken together, they are objectively recognized by other actors as constituting a distinctive community or region. (4) The members identify themselves as such. (5) The units of power are relatively inferior to units in the Global system, using a sliding scale of power in both. (6) Changes in the Global system have greater effect on the Subordinate system than the reverse. (7) No super power can be a member of a Subordinate system.

[1] Harold D. Lasswell and Abraham Kaplan, *Power and Society, A Framework for Political Inquiry*, 1950, pp. 55–6.

[2] After preliminary analysis, the category of skill was eliminated, due to its low level of occurrence throughout the analysis.

[3] It is necessary to note the precise coding techniques used. One of the primary rules of content analysis is that no sentence can be left in a compound form, that is, each sentence can have only one subject, one verb, and one object. Where sentences appear in compound form, they are broken down and coded as two separate sentences. For example, 'India wants the U.S.A. and China to settle the Vietnam war', would be coded as 'India wants the U.S.A. to settle the Vietnam war', and 'India wants China to settle the Vietnam war'. India would thus be checked twice, as would the Vietnam war, under the heading 'Issue'.

[*Footnotes 3 and 4 continued on next page*

or last column gives us the total of occurrences for each actor, that is, its cumulative frequency. The cumulative frequency column reveals the preponderant occurrence of India. This is not unexpected since the focus of discussion is Indian foreign policy. What is surprising, however, is the high level of occurrence of the United States which far exceeds that of the Soviet Union. In fact, Menon refers to the United States almost three times as often as the Soviet Union. It is also striking that mention is made of the United States in every interview, regardless of issue. Looking along the spectrum of issues, the United States is consistently referred to more frequently than is the Soviet Union.

Total frequency occurrence of the United Nations is the only other content category that rivals the occurrence of the United States. Yet the pattern of distribution of occurrences indicates that more than half is accounted for within two units, one dealing with the United Nations itself, the other dealing with Hungary. Generally speaking, then, the pattern of occurrence of the United Nations is much less even throughout.

China follows the United States and the United Nations in frequency of occurrence. It does occur in twelve out of fifteen units but more than half of the references are accounted for in two units, Bandung and China itself.

The United Kingdom follows China in total occurrence. Interestingly, the United Kingdom occurs more frequently than the Soviet Union and is surpassed only by India, the United States, the United Nations, and China. Almost half of its frequency of occurrence is concentrated in the discussions on the Commonwealth and the Suez crisis. Nevertheless Britain is mentioned in all fifteen interviews. The only other actor which occurred in all fifteen units is the United States.

Secondly, the data have been tabulated from the interviews after they had been subjected to only one editing, that of Mr. Menon himself. After the initial transcription, they were submitted to Mr. Menon for editing. His version was then re-edited twice by Professor Brecher. None of these changes was taken into account in tabulating frequencies of occurrence.

Thirdly, the varying lengths of the interviews posed a problem of comparative analysis. The length and depth of questioning no doubt contributed instrumentally to the proportion of space devoted to any particular issue. For this reason, all interviews were weighted according to length, to make them comparable.

For all the above reasons, it will be impossible for the reader to check the tabulations presented in Tables I–VI.

[4] The interviews consist of questions asked by Michael Brecher and the responses of Krishna Menon. Only the words of Mr. Menon have been subjected to analysis. At no time were the remarks of Professor Brecher included in the analysis. It was found, however, that this collection of interviews provided much more meaningful insights than a comparable collection of speeches, which are more highly structured and less revealing.

TABLE I

FREQUENCY OF OCCURRENCE OF ACTORS

Actor	Non-Alignment	Commonwealth	Korea	Geneva Conference on Indo-China	Bandung	Suez	Israel, Arabs, and India	Hungary	Congo	U.N.	Goa	China	World Politics	Partition, Pakistan, and Kashmir	Bomb	Cumulative Frequency
North Korea	0	0	7	0	0	0	0	0	0	0	0	0	0	0	0	7
South Korea	0	0	16	0	0	0	0	0	0	0	0	0	1	0	0	17
NATO	0	2	0	0	0	8	0	0	0	2	2	3	1	2	8	28
India	107	89	72	18	46	82	68	64	43	45	190	131	98	63	48	1164
Indonesia	1	1	0	0	32	0	2	0	0	3	0	0	1	0	0	37
West	5	8	4	0	7	0	5	26	2	3	3	2	0	3	4	74
Pakistan	0	5	0	0	28	0	7	11	0	2	9	4	1	29	1	97
France	2	0	0	7	1	2	2	1	5	2	1	0	3	0	0	26
United Nations	10	3	27	0	10	8	25	105	49	107	12	1	17	5	1	380
Commonwealth	0	56	10	0	11	2	0	0	0	4	4	1	0	1	0	85
Burma	2	0	0	0	5	0	4	2	0	2	2	2	0	0	0	13
Britain	7	50	4	20	6	47	0	2	2	0	6	12	19	21	10	206
Japan	0	0	0	0	0	8	0	0	0	0	0	0	1	0	0	9
China	12	1	10	21	76	5	0	1	0	4	0	50	28	1	10	219
United States	33	10	23	19	13	36	5	44	15	20	49	9	74	17	12	379
Soviet Union	11	3	18	11	7	13	2	18	5	14	1	5	19	6	4	137
Canada	10	9	17	34	3	16	0	0	5	7	1	1	0	7	20	130
Ghana	2	0	0	0	1	0	0	0	0	5	0	0	0	0	1	9
Egypt	3	0	0	0	9	64	51	2	0	0	0	0	4	0	0	133
Australia	0	0	0	0	5	10	0	0	0	0	0	0	0	2	0	17
Israel	0	0	0	0	3	10	111	0	1	0	0	0	1	1	0	127
Portugal	0	0	0	0	0	0	0	0	0	0	77	0	0	0	0	77

The pattern of occurrence for the Soviet Union reveals the lack of concentration. It appears in all units except Goa. As noted, the United States, the United Nations, China, and Great Britain occur more frequently than the Soviet Union. Without equating frequency of occurrence with importance, this pattern is striking for a country such as India whose foreign policy is allegedly symmetrical, based on non-alignment between two super powers. It may be suggested that this symmetrical image does not in fact conform to Krishna Menon's image.

Almost the same level of occurrence is evident for the United Arab Republic, Israel, and Canada. A very high proportion of references to the first two is accounted for in the units dealing with the Suez crisis and Israel, the Arabs, and India. Both of these actors are mentioned in only one-fifth of the total interviews. The high level of occurrence of Canada is striking, but it must be noted that Professor Brecher is a Canadian and that this fact was known and alluded to by Mr. Menon. The level of occurrence of Canada may thus be slightly inflated.

More striking is the level of occurrence of Pakistan. It has often been suggested that Indian foreign policy decision-makers are 'obsessed' with Pakistan. Preliminary content analysis does not support this, at least in the case of Mr. Menon. Although a full interview is devoted to problems connected with Pakistan, its over-all level of occurrence is relatively low. A third is accounted for in the unit dealing with Partition, Pakistan, and Kashmir, and another third in the unit dealing with Bandung. The remainder is distributed throughout eight units.

In summary, then, we have noticed the strikingly high level of occurrence of the United States, relative to that of the Soviet Union; the high level of occurrence of Great Britain and of the United Nations; and the relatively high occurrence of China as contrasted with the low level of Pakistan. We know that these actors are important in the perceptions of Menon. It remains to explore the intensity of Menon's attitudes towards them, and the patterns of association in which they are significant.

Table II indicates the frequency of symbols throughout the fifteen units, with the last column providing the cumulative frequency. When we look at the cumulative frequency column, we notice the high occurrence of the symbol 'Imperialism'.[1] There is a considerable

---

[1] The absolute levels of occurrence should not be compared across the seven broad types of variables, but rather within each type. Given the various types of variables under analysis, it is only within each type that meaningful statements can be made. This is fully recognized when the factor analysis is undertaken, for each variable was scored only plus or minus relative to occurrence above or below its own median frequency in order to obtain the matrix of correlations.

TABLE II

FREQUENCY OF OCCURRENCE OF SYMBOLS

Symbols	Non-Alignment	Common-wealth	Korea	Geneva Conference on Indo-China	Bandung	Suez	Israel, Arabs, and India	Hungary	Congo	U.N.	Goa	China	World Politics	Partition, Pakistan, and Kashmir	Bomb	Cumulative Frequency
Two Blocs	8	1	3	0	0	0	0	0	1	2	0	0	1	2	5	23
Non-Alignment	32	0	2	0	0	0	0	0	0	0	0	2	7	1	8	52
Republic	0	22	0	0	0	0	0	0	0	0	0	0	0	1	0	23
Communism	2	0	0	1	0	0	2	0	1	2	0	1	2	0	0	11
Dominion	0	10	0	0	0	0	0	0	0	0	0	0	0	1	0	11
Independence	13	16	0	0	0	0	1	0	2	3	1	3	4	2	0	45
Imperialism	3	12	0	3	8	4	9	0	1	2	14	1	9	5	0	71
Nationalism	7	0	0	0	3	2	3	4	1	1	1	1	7	2	5	36
Economic Development	3	0	0	0	0	0	0	0	0	1	0	2	8	0	0	17
Balance of Power	2	3	0	0	0	0	0	0	0	0	0	0	0	0	11	16
Peace	2	0	3	2	0	1	0	1	1	0	3	1	3	1	1	22
War	0	0	0	0	0	2	11	3	5	3	29	4	7	3	3	70
Colonialism	5	0	0	0	12	1	0	0	3	9	6	0	5	1	4	46
Aggression	0	0	0	0	0	0	12	0	0	0	4	3	2	2	0	23

gap between this symbol and all others except 'War'. Moreover, its distribution is widespread—it occurs in twelve of the fifteen units. It is most heavily concentrated in the unit dealing with Goa but appears consistently throughout the interviews.

Following closely in absolute level of occurrence, is the symbol 'War'. Unlike 'Imperialism', however, it does not occur evenly throughout the interviews; almost half is connected with Goa. It is interesting to note that both 'Imperialism' and 'War' occur most heavily in the interview dealing with Goa, but 'War' occurs almost twice as often in that interview. 'War' occurs also heavily in the interview on Israel, the Arabs, and India, but the remainder of its occurrence is distributed thinly throughout eight other interviews.

'Non-Alignment'[1] follows both 'Imperialism' and 'War' in its absolute level of occurrence. However, more than one-half of its occurrence is accounted for in the unit dealing with non-alignment and it occurs only marginally in five other units. 'Non-Alignment' is followed closely by 'Colonialism' and 'Independence' whose total frequency occurrence is approximately equal. 'Colonialism' is heavily concentrated in the discussion of Bandung and occurs in eight other units. 'Independence' is concentrated heavily in the discussions on non-alignment and the Commonwealth and occurs in seven other units.

In the pattern of occurrence of symbols, then, 'Imperialism' and 'War' clearly predominate, followed by 'Non-Alignment', 'Colonialism', and 'Independence'.

Table III shows the frequency of occurrence of the various levels of the international system.[2] The pre-eminence of the Global system is striking. There are almost twice as many references to it as there are to Bilateral interaction. Although the Global system has a concentration in the unit dealing with non-alignment, there is a relatively heavy and even distribution in all fifteen units.

References to the Bilateral level of interaction are also widely distributed. Approximately one-third are concentrated in the units dealing with the Commonwealth, and Israel, the Arabs, and India, but references occur in all fifteen interviews.

The relative under-representation of Dominant-Bilateral, that is bilateral relationships with either of the two super powers, is striking. It has the lowest absolute level of occurrence, and a third of the references is concentrated in the units dealing with non-

---

[1] 'Non-Alignment' here is treated as a symbol. It is also coded as a strategy, when it is so used by Menon.

[2] See p. 347 below.

TABLE III
FREQUENCY OF OCCURRENCE OF LEVELS OF INTERNATIONAL SYSTEM

Levels of International System	Non-Alignment	Commonwealth	Korea	Geneva Conference on Indo-China	Bandung	Suez	Israel, Hungary, Arabs, and India	Congo	U.N.	Goa	China	World Politics	Partition Pakistan, and Kashmir	Bomb	Cumulative Frequency
Global	40	9	22	7	6	21	19	11	20	3	4	22	16	36	236
Dominant-Bilateral	20	0	12	3	1	13	3	0	9	1	3	15	3	7	90
Bilateral	4	22	5	3	11	13	23	0	20	1	3	10	12	5	132
Africa	7	4	1	0	9	1	5	11	28	1	1	24	2	3	97
Asia	0	1	1	2	24	10	7	0	4	3	3	3	1	2	61
Latin America	0	0	0	0	1	0	0	0	7	1	0	1	0	0	10
Arabs-Middle East	2	0	0	0	4	2	36	1	5	0	0	0	0	0	50

alignment and contemporary world politics. Moreover, it does not occur at all in four of the fifteen units.

References to Subordinate Systems[1] in totality are heavier than references to Bilateral interaction, and more than twice as heavy as Dominant-Bilateral. Africa predominates. Almost one-half of the occurrences of Africa are found in the units dealing with contemporary world politics and with the United Nations but Africa is mentioned in all but two units. References to Asia are concentrated in the units dealing with Bandung and the United Nations. Like Africa, however, Asia's occurrence is distributed among all but two units.

The total frequency of occurrence of Arabs-Middle East is not significantly lower than Asia; however, more than two-thirds of the references are concentrated in the single unit dealing with Israel, the Arabs, and India, and it does not occur at all in nine units. Finally, the low level of occurrence of Latin America is worth noting. Seventy per cent of the references to it are concentrated in the interview on the United Nations and in the same interview there are twice as many references to Asia, and four times as many references to Africa.

In summary, the Global system predominates, followed by the cumulatively high level of occurrences of Subordinate systems, with special attention paid to Africa and Asia. Reference to Bilateral interaction is third in frequency and there is a striking indifference to the Dominant-Bilateral level.

Table IV deals with the frequencies of occurrence of the seven values. Noteworthy is the pre-eminence of two deference values—respect and power. Respect is distributed quite evenly in all but one interview; power occurs in all but two units, but is concentrated in the discussion on the Commonwealth. These two values are followed closely by another deference value—rectitude—and by a welfare value—well-being. Rectitude occurs in all but three interviews, while well-being occurs in all fifteen units. Taken together, the deference values have a higher level of occurrence, but well-being is referred to in the context of all fifteen issues.

Table V sets out the frequencies of occurrence of strategies: these are strategies to be used by India in the international system. The most significant fact is the paucity of over-all references to strategies. In the interview dealing with the Geneva Conference on Indo-China, for example, there is no reference to any strategy. The

[1] Initially Western Europe and Eastern Europe were included as Subordinate Systems. The cumulative frequency was so low that they were later omitted from the analysis.

TABLE IV

FREQUENCY OF OCCURRENCE OF VALUES

Values	Non-Alignment	Common-wealth	Korea	Geneva Conference on Indo-China	Bandung	Suez	Israel, Arabs, and India	Hungary	Congo	U.N.	Goa	China	World Politics	Partition, Pakistan, and Kashmir	Bomb	Cumulative Frequency
Power	3	13	1	0	2	3	1	3	0	2	6	5	3	3	5	50
Wealth	1	2	0	0	1	0	1	0	0	1	0	2	1	1	1	11
Well-being	4	3	6	5	7	1	1	1	1	1	5	1	5	5	2	48
Enlightenment	0	0	0	0	0	1	0	0	0	0	0	0	3	1	2	7
Affection	7	4	0	0	0	1	4	2	1	5	1	4	6	0	0	28
Respect	7	5	1	2	4	3	7	1	0	8	3	4	10	1	0	56
Rectitude	3	2	0	1	0	5	5	0	1	1	7	3	8	2	8	46

TABLE V

FREQUENCY OF OCCURRENCE OF STRATEGIES

Strategies	Non-Alignment	Common-wealth	Korea	Geneva Conference on Indo-China	Bandung	Suez	Israel, Arabs, and India	Hungary	Congo	U.N.	Goa	China	World Politics	Partition, Bomb Pakistan, and Kashmir	Cumulative Frequency
Mediation	3	1	7	0	3	1	0	1	1	0	0	0	2	0	19
Negotiation	0	1	0	0	0	3	1	1	4	0	5	2	5	0	22
Dialogue	0	0	0	0	0	0	5	0	0	2	5	0	0	0	12
Recognition	0	0	0	0	0	0	7	0	0	0	4	3	0	0	14
Non-Alignment	15	0	2	0	0	0	0	0	0	0	0	0	0	0	17
Disarmament	0	0	0	0	0	0	0	0	0	2	0	2	2	4	15

TABLE VI

FREQUENCY OF OCCURRENCE OF ISSUES

Issues	Non-Alignment	Common-wealth	Korea	Geneva Conference on Indo-China	Bandung	Suez	Israel, Arabs, and India	Hungary	Congo	U.N.	Goa	China	World Politics	Partition, Pakistan, and Kashmir	Bomb	Cumulative Frequency
Bandung	0	0	0	0	54	0	4	0	0	0	0	0	0	0	1	60
Korea	7	0	25	4	2	1	0	0	1	1	0	0	1	1	0	42
Kashmir	0	0	0	0	3	0	3	0	3	1	4	0	0	8	0	22
Hungary	0	0	0	0	4	0	0	66	1	0	0	0	0	0	0	71
Goa	0	0	0	0	0	0	0	0	0	0	43	0	1	0	0	44
Colombo Plan	0	2	0	0	17	0	0	0	0	0	0	0	0	0	0	19
South Africa	0	3	0	0	0	0	0	1	0	2	1	0	0	0	0	7
Cold War	11	0	0	0	0	0	0	6	0	0	0	0	0	3	0	20
Racial Discrimination	0	4	0	0	3	1	10	0	0	2	0	0	2	0	0	22
Suez	5	0	0	0	2	15	15	0	1	1	0	0	0	0	0	39
Indo-China	1	0	1	24	4	2	0	1	0	0	0	0	7	0	0	40
Atomic Weapons	0	0	0	0	0	0	0	0	0	0	0	0	15	2	13	30
Congo	1	0	1	0	1	0	0	0	55	0	0	0	1	0	0	59
Tibet	0	0	0	0	0	0	0	0	0	0	0	10	0	0	0	10
Bomb	2	0	0	0	0	0	0	0	0	0	1	0	2	1	17	23

strategy with both the widest distribution and the highest frequency of occurrence is negotiation; it is followed closely by mediation, which occurs in eight of the fifteen interviews. Non-alignment, which has a relatively high absolute level of occurrence, is heavily concentrated in the interview dealing with non-alignment. What emerges from this table is Menon's low frequency of attention to strategy.

Table VI deals with issues, in which mention of actors, symbols, values, levels of interaction, and strategies occur. In interpreting this table, one must look not only at absolute levels of frequency but also at patterns of distribution throughout the interviews. Since the units of analysis themselves deal with issues, one expects heavy concentration of references with the units. The most significant issues, then, would have wider patterns of distribution.

The three issues with the highest cumulative frequencies, Hungary, Bandung, and the Congo, are heavily concentrated within their own interviews. Goa, with a lower absolute level of occurrence, is also heavily concentrated within its own unit. Korea, Indo-China, and Suez, occurring at approximately the same level, are relatively widely distributed through eight, six, and six units respectively. Finally, atomic weapons, with a lower level of absolute occurrence, occurs in three units. We notice in this case an inverse ratio between level of occurrence and pattern of distribution.

Thus far, our analysis reveals only the incidence of attention of Krishna Menon to the variables we have selected. The *kind* of attention he paid to them, however, and their *association structure* remain to be explored.

Measuring Intensity of Attitudes[1]

In order to measure the intensity of attitudes of the decision-maker, we selected the following four variables: expressions of hostility,

---

[1] The method of analysis used here is called the 'pair comparison' scaling method; Dina A. Zinnes, '"Pair Comparison" Scaling in International Relations' in North, Holsti, Zaninovitch, and Zinnes, op. cit.

A judge selects from the total amount of recorded data under analysis all statements expressing hostility, friendship, satisfaction, or demands for change in the *status quo*. These are not limited to statements which involve the decision-maker or his country; on the contrary, they include all such statements, for we are interested in analysing both the decision-maker's perception of each of the four variables and the degree of intensity.

From the statements which are selected, a random sample of eighteen is drawn for each of the four variables. These are listed on a separate sheet of paper, and all friendship, change of the *status quo*, and satisfaction.[1] We shall look first at absolute levels of occurrence, then at patterns of intensity, and finally at the actors and symbols involved in all four variables.

possible pairs of each of the eighteen statements with each of the others are drawn up. Naturally, this will not include pairs consisting of the same item twice.

Each pair is then considered separately, and the question is asked: which of the two statements represents the most intense expression of that variable, for example, hostility? The winner, or the most hostile statement, receives one vote. The votes are recorded and then the votes for each statement are tallied. Of course, both in the initial selection of statements and in the scaling, judges are checked for consistency by the usual statistical tests of reliability.

The eighteen statements are then hierarchically ordered, and collapsed into a nine-point scale by combining every two degrees on the larger scale. The remainder of the statements are then classified at appropriate levels of the scale by comparing it to the examples obtained. We have thus given scale values of 1–9 for the entire universe of hostility statements obtained from the interviews. These values reflect the statement's scale value relative to the entire set of statements. What we have achieved, then, is a relative scale without a forced distribution.

When we have completed this process for all four variables, we wish to organize the data so that we can interpret them. The measure we shall use is that of 'functional distance' (op. cit., p. 107). Functional distance represents a measure of the relationship between two variables, such as friendship and hostility. The measure of functional distance may be viewed as the deviation of two curves from possible congruence or perfect similarity. Any value for functional distance above 0·00 signifies some degree of difference between the expression of any two measurable variables.

The determination of functional distance is predicated upon two qualities which any two curves representing variables possess. The first is MVD, or mean vertical distance. The MVD is the index of closeness or discrepancy between two curves on the vertical plane which represents the intensity scale. The second of the two qualities is the MTD, or mean transitional difference, which serves as the measure to which two curves representing variables move in the same or in opposite directions. The degree of functional distance is computed by summing the values of MVD and MTD for a relationship between two variables.

It should be noted that the application of functional distance analysis does require a common differentiating scale for determining the behaviour of two or more variables. We have met this requirement by using pair comparison scaling and a nine-point scale.

When we have computed the functional distance for each variable with the other, we can then construct a pattern analysis, or the plotting of relationships among a set of variables in diagram form. Once the relationship between two variables is expressed by the measure of functional distance, this one relationship may be termed an 'empirical dimension'. A set of such empirically derived dimensions constitutes a pattern of variables.

The formula to compute MVD: $\text{MVD} = \dfrac{1}{n} \sum_{i=1}^{n} (x_i - y_i)$, where n refers to the number of time units in which the two variables are related.

The formula to compute MTD: $\text{MTD} = \dfrac{1}{2n} \sum_{i=1}^{n} (d_i - \Delta_i)$ in which n represents the number of 'transitional points'.

[1] Mr. Zaninovitch, in his use of 'pattern analysis', tested for a fifth variable, frustration. We found this variable extremely difficult to operationalize, and state-

Figure 1 provides a graphical representation of the absolute levels of occurrence of the variables of hostility, satisfaction, friendship, and change of the *status quo*, through each of the fifteen units of analysis. Immediately apparent is the very high incidence of hostility statements relative to those of friendship, satisfaction, and change of the *status quo*: 388 hostility statements were discovered, while only 130 statements of friendship, 127 statements of satisfaction, and 96 statements of change of the *status quo* were found. Hostility was by far the predominant attitude of Krishna Menon in this Dialogue.

By tracing the paths of the graphical lines, which represent the four variables, we notice the clustering of three of the variables, satisfaction, friendship, and change of the *status quo*, especially in the last eight units. Hostility, however, clusters with the other three only in the units dealing with the Commonwealth, Korea, the Congo, the U.N., and Policy in the Shastri Transition, notably the Bomb. At all other times hostility occurs with much greater frequency than the other three, and the distance between it and any one of the remaining three variables is greater than the combined distance between the three variables. Especially striking is the high incidence of hostility in the units dealing with Bandung, Israel, the Arabs, and India, Hungary, Goa, and Partition, Pakistan and Kashmir.

Friendship, occurring at the same absolute level as satisfaction, shows significant deviation from the graph of satisfaction. Statements of friendship occur prominently in the units dealing with Non-Alignment, the Geneva Conference on Indo-China, and in the unit dealing with Israel and the Arabs. Satisfaction statements occur prominently only in the context of Non-Alignment, Bandung, and the Commonwealth.

The total number of statements concerned with a change in the *status quo* is extremely low. The under-representation of strategies was noted earlier. There is a corresponding paucity of statements concerning change in the *status quo*. Hostility, the dominant variable, appears not to be translated into precise demands for change.

We are interested not only in absolute levels of occurrence, but also in the frequency of statements of high, moderate, and low intensity.[1]

The distinction among three levels of intensity is important because it provides a key to qualitative differences in probable

ments initially classified under this heading, with few exceptions, were later more suitably classified under either hostility or change in the *status quo*.

[1] High intensity refers to those statements on the 7–9 points of the scale, moderate intensity to those statements on the 4–6 points of the scale, and low intensity to those on the 1–3 points of the scale.

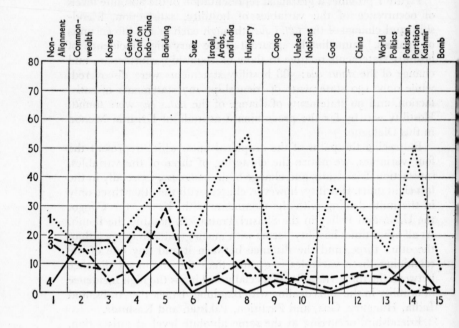

FIGURE 1. Graphical occurrences by unit of four variables.

Hostility 1
Satisfaction 2
Friendship 3
Change of Status Quo . . 4

behaviour. Thus, a concentration of high intensity statements of hostility and change of the *status quo* would suggest a high probability of violence in foreign policy acts. A clustering of low intensity statements by contrast would imply the probability of non-violent change.

Figure 2 presents a graphical representation of statements of high intensity. The most intense statements of hostility occur in the discussion of Partition, Pakistan and Kashmir, and then in the discussion of Bandung, of Israel, the Arabs, and India, and of Goa. In all three units the incidence of the other three variables is relatively low, except in Bandung; the units are dominated by intensely hostile statements. The highest occurrence of intense statements on change in the *status quo* relates to the Commonwealth. Here we notice a low level of occurrence of intensely hostile statements; there is no apparent relationship between intensely hostile statements and intense statements of change of the *status quo*. Intense statements of satisfaction are made only in the context of Non-Alignment, and of Bandung. Intense statements of friendship are made only in the unit dealing with non-alignment.

We turn now briefly to the graphical presentation of statements of moderate intensity. The highest incidence of moderate hostility occurs in the units dealing with Hungary, Pakistan, Bandung, and Goa in that order. In three of these four units we again find the other three variables clustered together, all at a low level of occurrence. Only in the context of the Geneva Conference on Indo-China is there a high incidence of statements of moderate friendship. In the discussion of the Commonwealth there is a high incidence of moderate satisfaction. Nowhere do we find a high level of occurrence of moderate statements dealing with a change in the *status quo*.

Figure 4 presents a graphical representation of expressions of low intensity for all four variables in the fifteen units. Here we find a high incidence of expressions of low intensity hostility in the units dealing with Israel, the Arabs, and India, Hungary, and the Geneva Conference on Indo-China; in the discussions of Israel and the Arabs there is also a relatively high level of low intensity friendship. Nowhere do we find a high level of low intensity statements dealing with either satisfaction or a change in the *status quo*. In general, at a low level of intensity, we find that hostility will cluster with the other three variables much more frequently than usual.

Having looked in detail at the three levels of each of the variables in all fifteen units, we can now return to the over-all picture presented in Figure 1 and make more significant statements about

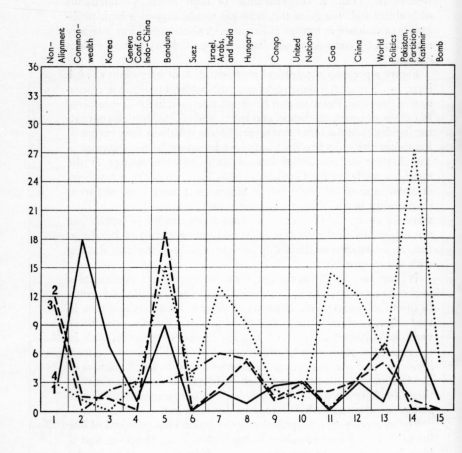

Hostility 1
Satisfaction 2
Friendship 3
Change of Status Quo . . 4

FIGURE 2. Intensity of High Hostility, Satisfaction, Friendship, and Change of *Status Quo*.

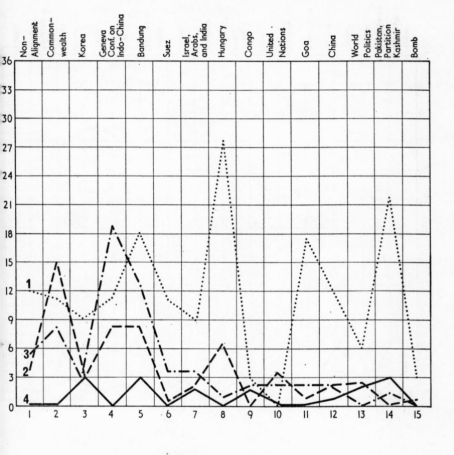

Hostility 1
Satisfaction 2
Friendship 3
Change of Status Quo . . . 4

FIGURE 3. Intensity of Moderate Hostility, Satisfaction, Friendship, and Change of *Status Quo*.

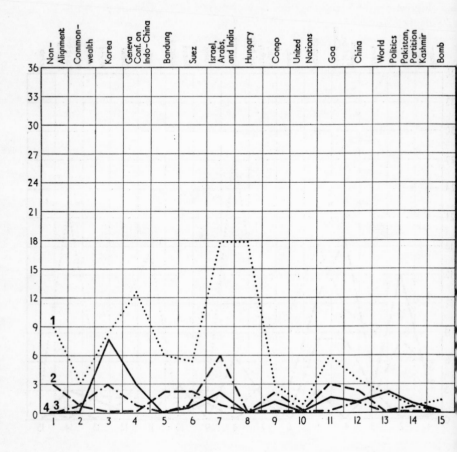

Hostility 1
Satisfaction 2
Friendship 3
Change of Status Quo . . 4

FIGURE 4. Intensity of Low Hostility, Satisfaction, Friendship, and Change of *Status Quo*.

the composite levels of intensity of each of the variables. From
Figure 1 we noticed that hostility occurred most often in the units
dealing with:

Hungary—the result of statements of medium and low intensity.
Bandung—the result of statements of medium and high intensity.
Israel, the Arabs, and India—the result of statements of high
and low intensity.
Goa—the result of statements of high and medium intensity.
Pakistan and Kashmir—the result of statements of high and
medium intensity.

From this compendium one can deduce the following probabilities of extremism in policy choices: high probability in the cases of
Goa and Pakistan–Kashmir; the possibility of extremism or moderation on the Arab–Israel issue; and moderation on Hungary. The
Bandung Conference is not an issue of the same type; it did not pose
continuing problems of policy choice.

Statements of friendship occurred most often in the units dealing
with:

The Geneva Conference on Indo-China—the result of statements
of medium intensity.
Non-Alignment—the result of statements of high intensity.
Bandung—the result of statements of medium intensity.
Israel, the Arabs, and India—the result of statements of low intensity.

Probabilities concerning India's identification with these issues
are as follows: very close identity with Non-Alignment, moderate
identity with the spirit of Bandung and the Indo-China settlement
of 1954, and relative aloofness from the continuing Arab–Israel
conflict—as contrasted with high identity with the Arabs in the
Suez issue.

Statements of satisfaction occurred most often in the units dealing
with:

Bandung—the result of statements of high intensity.
Non-Alignment—the result of statements of high intensity.
Commonwealth—the result of statements of medium intensity.

Finally, statements concerning a change in the *status quo* occurred
most often in the units dealing with:

Commonwealth—the result of statements of high intensity.
Korea—the result of statements of low intensity.

The evidence drawn from satisfaction and change in the *status quo*
statements leads to the following assessment of probable revision of

policy: very little likelihood with respect to Non-Alignment, Bandung, and Korea; and moderate likelihood of change regarding the Commonwealth.

Now that we have measured the level of intensity of expression we must modify the importance of absolute levels of occurrence. What is important for the prediction of foreign policy behaviour is not only volume of expression, but the intensity as well.

It is now possible to compute the functional distance values[1] for each of these variables with each of the others. Figure 5 provides us

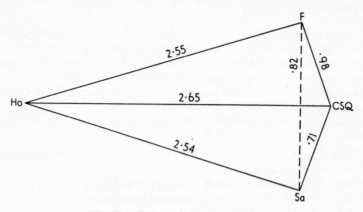

Hostility–Change of *status quo* = 2·65
Hostility–Friendship = 2·55
Hostility–Satisfaction = 2·54
Friendship–Change of *status quo* = 0·98
Friendship–Satisfaction = 0·82
Satisfaction–Change of *status quo* = 0·71

FIGURE 5. A Map of Functional Distances.

(Functional distances are computed on the basis of Average Scale Values.)

with such a diagrammatic representation. This diagram can only be properly represented in multi-dimensional space; inevitably there are some distortions.

Hostility is almost equidistant from the other three variables, and all three variables are closer to each other than to hostility. This may be described as an 'uncritical conflict system',[2] for both friend-

---

[1] See n. 1, p. 352.
[2] In a 'critical' conflict system the decision-maker perceives Fd–CSQ to be greater than Ho–CSQ, and Sa–CSQ to be greater than Ho–CSQ. In a healthy conflict system, one in which the participant benefits from a heightened but not destructive level of tension, Fd–CSQ is approximately equal to Ho–CSQ, and Sa–CSQ is approximately equal to Ho–CSQ. See Zaninovitch, 'Pattern Analysis and Factor Analysis', op. cit., p. 116.

ship and satisfaction are closely positioned to a change in the *status quo*. In times of intense crises, hostility will be closely positioned to change of the *status quo*. This reinforces our earlier suggestion that Menon, though hostile, did not focus his hostility on particular demands for change of the *status quo*; that is, he did not articulate strategies related to objectives.

An 'index of tension'[1] has been developed to measure the likelihood of the eruption of conflict and violence. The ratio is that of the satisfaction–change of *status quo* dimension to that of the hostility–change of *status quo* dimension. If the quotient is 1·00 then a conflict system is functional, that is, it serves to maintain the system. If it is above 1·00, the system is in a state of high tension and will tend toward disruptive conflict. In our case the quotient is only 0·25. The system, therefore, tends in the direction of low tension, which in its extreme form represents the danger of decay. We can suggest, then, that the pattern of the perceptions of this decision-maker is extremely unlikely to produce foreign policy behaviour which is violent or disruptive.

Although one cannot calculate functional distance values for any individual unit, one can look at the relative positions of the four variables and make certain predictions about foreign policy behaviour. In Figure 1 we noted the high level of hostility in the units dealing with Bandung, Israel, the Arabs, and India, Goa, and Pakistan. In the latter three, however, all other variables are closely clustered together as in Figure 5. For this reason it is extremely unlikely again that Indian foreign policy behaviour would be disruptive, with Menon in a key decision-making role. In the discussion of Bandung, hostility is closely related to satisfaction, a pattern also unlikely to produce violent behaviour.

When we turn to Figure 2 we find once more that incidence of intense hostility is never closely related to incidence of intense change of the *status quo*. Interestingly, where we do find high incidence of intense change of the *status quo*, as in the unit dealing with the Commonwealth, the other three variables cluster together. Although the likelihood of change is great, it is probable that this change will not be violent in nature.

In Figure 3, dealing with moderate intensity of expression, we noted high frequencies of hostility in four units. In two of these, Pakistan, and Goa, the other three variables were again closely clustered. In the unit dealing with Bandung moderate hostility is closely positioned to moderate friendship; in the unit dealing with Hungary, although the other three variables do not cluster together,

[1] Ibid., p. 117.

there is no incidence of moderate change of the *status quo*. In neither case is violence likely to erupt.

Finally, in Figure 4, we find that the incidence of low intensity hostility is not related to change of the *status quo* in either of the two units in which it occurs—Hungary, and Israel, the Arabs, and India. We do note a greater clustering of all four variables at the lowest level of intensity than at either of the other two levels. Foreign policy behaviour resulting from the clustering of the four variables at a low level of intensity will be more limited in scope and in direction.

The use of functional distance as a tool of analysis thus facilitates an estimate of the over-all pattern of variables of the decision-maker and the likelihood of violence. It also permits speculation about probable behaviour in any particular foreign policy issue.

Now that we have explored the relationships among all four variables, it remains to look briefly at the actors and symbols involved in statements of hostility, friendship, satisfaction, and change of the *status quo*. This will enable us to give added depth to our preliminary suggestions of salience based purely on frequency of occurrence.

In order to obtain these data we subjected all the statements of all four variables to analysis. For each statement we listed the main agent or actor of the statement, the symbol around which the statement revolved, and the target of the statement.[1] The data will be found in Tables VII–X.

The United States occupies the most prominent position as the actor in Krishna Menon's hostility statements. Half of these statements are of moderate hostility. India, also a key actor in this respect, is involved half the time in statements of intense hostility. China occurs twice as often as does Pakistan as the agent in hostility statements, and both occur predominantly in statements of moderate and intense hostility. It is also noteworthy that while Israel occurs as an agent in hostility statements, the United Arab Republic does not.

The predominance of the symbols 'War' and 'Imperialism' was noted earlier. We find that these are the two symbols which occur significantly in connection with hostility statements. The term 'American orbit' or American domination also occurs frequently throughout the range of hostility statements.

Krishna Menon perceives India as the principal target of hostile

[1] Various breakdowns of the parts of a sentence have been suggested in the literature. However, none of these was particularly suitable when analysing attitude sentences. For this reason we have employed a more simplified version.

statements. In fact, it is the target of more than one-quarter of all the hostile statements in the Dialogue. The Soviet Union, too, occurs as the target—not as the agent—of hostile statements. And the symbol 'Imperialism' is itself the target of hostile statements.

TABLE VII

FREQUENCY OF OCCURRENCE OF SUBJECTS, SYMBOLS, AND TARGETS OF HOSTILITY

	High	Moderate	Low	Totals
Subjects (agents) of hostility statements				
United States	17	66	43	126
India	64	37	22	123
China	56	43	8	107
Pakistan	23	26	6	55
Britain	15	15	14	44
Portugal	22	7	1	30
Israel	..	4	14	28
France	8	1	3	12
The West	1	8	2	11
Imperialism	9	1	..	10
Symbols around which hostility is centred				
Imperialism	11	4	..	15
United States orbit	1	11	2	14
War	9	2	..	11
Targets of hostility statements				
India	59	46	18	123
China	12	7	5	24
Egypt	5	5	2	12
Soviet Union	4	7	..	11
The West	2	3	4	9
Portugal	3	..	5	8
United States	1	..	7	8
Arabs	..	5	2	7
Menon	..	4	3	7
Imperialism	4	2	1	7

The evidence concerning actors of friendship statements is very striking. India again is the main agent, but there is a high proportion of personalities relative to States. Interestingly, Nasser precedes Nehru in the number of friendly references. We find also that, while Britain is an agent in hostile statements, individual British diplomats are agents in friendly statements. The only two countries or areas represented are the Soviet Union and Africa, neither of which was the main actor in hostile statements. By way of contrast, there were only two friendship sentences in which the United States was the agent.

The targets of friendship statements are relatively restricted. India and Menon himself top the list, followed by Africa and by Lester Pearson. There is then a high degree of association of Africa with statements of friendship.

TABLE VIII

FREQUENCY OF OCCURRENCE OF SUBJECTS AND TARGETS OF FRIENDSHIP

	High	Moderate	Low	Totals
Subjects (agents) of friendship statements				
India	18	9	13	40
Nasser	17	4	2	23
Nehru	12	7	..	19
British Diplomats[1]	6	10	1	17
Menon	8	1	2	11
Canadians	..	8	1	9
Chou En-lai	..	9	..	9
Hammarskjöld	3	4	..	7
Pearson	2	4	..	6
Soviet Union	1	4	..	5
Africa	2	3	..	5
Targets of friendship statements				
India	5	5	4	14
Menon	6	3	4	13
Africa	7	2	..	9
Pearson	2	2	..	4

The data presented in Table IX reveal, not unexpectedly, that India is the main actor. She is closely followed by Bandung, and then by Menon himself and the U.N. The single State which appears here is China—a demonstration of the fundamental underlying ambivalence in Menon's attitude toward China. Asia and Africa, as well as the category 'new nations', also appear as actors in statements of satisfaction.

The symbols around which statements of satisfaction revolve are 'Imperialism' and 'Non-Alignment'. At first glance it appears anachronistic that 'Imperialism' should appear in this context. It becomes understandable, however, in the light of the frequent references to the halting and defeating of Imperialism.

[1] Addison, Ismay, Eden, and Mountbatten.

The targets of statements of satisfaction are India, and then the symbols 'Independence' and 'Peace'. We find again that the two Subordinate systems of Asia and Africa are targets of satisfaction. The value of power, a deference value, is the only value which is the

TABLE IX

FREQUENCY OF OCCURRENCE OF SUBJECTS, SYMBOLS, AND TARGETS OF SATISFACTION

	High	Moderate	Low	Totals
Subjects (agents) of satisfaction statements				
India	18	13	13	48
Bandung	16	4	..	20
Menon	3	4	8	15
United Nations	3	12	..	15
Non-Alignment	8	2	1	11
China	..	10	1	11
Nehru	10	..	..	10
Commonwealth	..	9	..	9
Asia	5	..	..	5
Africa	5	..	..	5
New Nations	3	..	2	5
Goa	..	2	3	5
Symbols around which satisfaction is centred				
Imperialism	4	2	..	6
Non-Alignment	..	2	2	4
Targets of statements of satisfaction				
India	11	5	5	21
Independence	3	3	..	6
Peace	2	4	..	6
Africa	6	..	..	6
Commonwealth	..	5	1	6
Asia	5	..	..	5
China	..	5	..	5
Power	2	3	..	5

target of statements of satisfaction. Again, China is the only State other than India which is the target of statements of satisfaction.

Both the United Nations and the Commonwealth appear in Tables IX and X as actors in statements of satisfaction and in statements dealing with change of the *status quo*. This immediately points to an underlying ambivalence in Menon's attitude towards both these organizations. China, Britain, and the U.S.A. appear both as agents in hostility statements and in change of *status quo* statements. From our previous analysis we can deduce that it is in dealing with these three actors that Menon would be most violent.

The symbols which are associated with statements of change of the *status quo* are again 'United States domination' and 'Imperialism' (which occur in connection with hostility statements) and 'Republic'. Change in connection with 'Republic' would not likely be violent;

TABLE X

FREQUENCY OF OCCURRENCE OF SUBJECTS, SYMBOLS, AND TARGETS OF CHANGE IN THE *STATUS QUO*

	High	Moderate	Low	Totals
Subjects of statements dealing with change in the *status quo*				
India	22	8	7	37
The World	10	1	4	15
United Nations	6	3	2	11
China	3	3	2	8
Menon	6	..	2	8
United States	6	1	..	7
Commonwealth	7	..	..	7
Britain	1	2	2	5
Symbols around which change of the *status quo* is centred				
United States domination	3	1	1	5
Republic	4	..	..	4
Imperialism	4	..	..	4
Targets of statements dealing with a change in the *status quo*				
United Nations	5	2	4	11
United States	6	2	2	10
India	6	2	1	9
Disarmament	6	..	..	6
Asia	3	1	1	5
Bandung	5	..	..	5

change directed at 'Imperialism' or 'American domination' has a high probability of violence.

The targets of statements dealing with change of the *status quo*, with two exceptions, demonstrate again the low probability that change will be violent in nature. Only the United States and India are both targets of hostility and change of the *status quo*. It would appear that Menon perceives the danger of violence to India and desires violent change in connection with the United States.

Referring back to the initial analysis of frequency tables, we can make more precise statements about the relevance of the actors and symbols which had high frequencies. The United States and Britain are both prominent in statements of hostility and change of the *status quo*. China is prominent in statements of hostility, satisfaction, and change in the *status quo*. Pakistan and Israel are agents in hostility statements, while the Soviet Union, the United Arab Republic, and Canada are associated with statements of friendship. The United Nations is an agent both of statements of satisfaction and of change of the *status quo*.

We can also make more precise statements about the three most prominent symbols which emerged from the frequency tables. 'Imperialism' is associated with hostility, satisfaction, and change of the *status quo*, 'War' with hostility, and 'Non-Alignment' with satisfaction.

By analysing attitude statements we are able to determine precisely the attitude of the decision-maker towards the most frequently occurring actors and symbols. Wherever patterns of attitudes emerge it is also possible to predict the probable behaviour of the decision-maker towards these actors and the issues associated with these symbols.

Factor Analysis

The seventy-seven categories of content analysis were subjected to factor analysis. 'Factor analysis starts with a set of observations obtained from a given sample by means of such *a priori* measures. It is a method of analysing this set of observations from their intercorrelations to determine whether the variations represented can be accounted for adequately by a number of basic categories smaller than that with which the investigation was started. Thus data obtained with a large number of *a priori* measures may be explained in terms of a smaller number of reference variables.'[1]

The student of foreign policy can profitably employ the technique of factor analysis but not necessarily with the aim of reducing the

---

[1] B. Fruchter, *Introduction to Factor Analysis*, 1954, p. 1. To report a factor analytic study fully it is necessary to include a detailed description of the basis of the sample. The correlation matrix of all the variables, the data for applying the criteria for sufficient factors, and the table of residuals following the last extracted factor should be shown. Finally, the loadings of the variables on the factors should be given. Due to lack of space it is impossible to provide this material here. Correlations were based on product-moment correlations, and the centroid method of factoring was used. The complete report of this factoral study will appear in a later work.

The term 'loading' refers to the correlation of each variable with the common factor.

TABLE XI

FACTOR ANALYSIS OF KRISHNA MENON'S IMAGES

Factor	Actor	Symbol	Level	Value	Strategy	Issue
I Atomic War	..	'Aggression' 'War'	Bilateral	Respect, Rectitude, Affection, Enlightenment, Wealth	Recognition, Disarmament, Negotiation	Bomb, Atomic Weapons
II Problems of Nationalism	Pakistan	..	..	..	..	South Africa
III Cold War and the Universal Actor in Subordinate Systems	Israel, Egypt, Soviet Union, Indonesia, Burma, United Nations	'War' 'Communism'	Arabs-Middle East, Africa, Latin America	..	..	Suez, Korea
V Imperialism	United States, Portugal, India	'Imperialism'	..	Power	..	Goa, Indo-China
VI Colonialism	France	'Colonialism'	..	..	Dialogue	Kashmir
VII Cold War	Nato, Canada, Commonwealth, South Korea	'Two Blocs'	Global	..	..	..
IX United States and the Cold War	..	..	..	..	..	Hungary, Congo
X Independence	..	'Independence' 'Economic Development'	..	..	..	Tibet
XII Well-being	..	'Peace'	..	Well-being	..	..
XIII Non-Alignment	The West Ghana	'Non-Alignment' 'Nationalism'	..	..	..	Bandung

number of categories to more basic variables. Rather, we are interested in determining patterns of association along several basic indicators. Thirteen factors were extracted for this analysis,[1] only ten are immediately relevant, and only three merit detailed attention in this paper. The analysis of the factors will be done from a sharply focused perspective, namely, the relationship of images to policy choices.

As evident in Table XI, Factor I explained the highest proportion of the variance of several key variables. The values of respect, rectitude, affection, enlightenment, and wealth—five of the seven values tested for—clustered with the symbols of war and aggression, with the issues of the bomb and atomic weapons, and with the strategies of recognition, disarmament, and negotiation. The level of interaction is bilateral. We have decided to name this factor *Atomic War*.[2]

It is striking that the majority of values occur with respect to the problem of atomic war and disarmament. This is a crucial problem in the perception of this decision-maker; it involves highly negative symbols and is associated with positive values and rewards. Interestingly, there is a relatively high loading of strategies on this factor. As noted earlier, Menon was little concerned with precise strategies for realizing his goals. Most of the other factors include no reference to strategy. The problem of atomic war is thus linked with strategies and these are bilateral, that is, they are to be implemented at the bilateral level of interaction.

A high proportion of the total variables was heavily loaded on the third factor, which has been named *The Cold War and the Universal Actor in Subordinate Systems*. The actors are Israel and the United Arab Republic, the Soviet Union, Indonesia, and Burma; the symbols are War and Communism; the arena of interaction is the Middle East, Africa, and Latin America; the issues are Suez and Korea; and the universal actor is, of course, the United Nations.

Negatively related are the symbols 'Cold War', 'Two Blocs', and the actor, 'NATO'. It is interesting to note in this context that the U.S.A., the object of extreme hostility, does not occur here positively or negatively: there is no association of the United States with penetration of the Cold War into subordinate systems. Allied to this pattern of association is the absence of the subordinate system of Asia from the grouping of the three major subordinate systems. Asia has no significant loading on this factor, despite the fact that

[1] The aeigen value descended below zero after the thirteenth factor.
[2] Japan was highly loaded on this factor. This can be explained by its association with atomic warfare and with aggression. Due to its low overall rate of occurrence, it is included as an optional category.

it occurs more than five times as frequently as does Latin America throughout the analysis.

Factor V is one of the most suggestive. Its actors include the U.S.A., Portugal, and India; its issues, Goa and Indo-China; its value, Power; and its symbol, Imperialism. This factor has been named *Imperialism*.

A quarter of the variance of the content category—U.S.A.—is explained by this factor: it is as an imperialist power that the United States is most significant. Despite our predispositions to believe that Menon sees the world divided into two bellicose camps, we find that, while the Soviet Union is negatively correlated on Factor III to the symbol 'Cold War', the United States is highly positively loaded on the factor which we have identified as 'Imperialism'. It is also striking that the greatest positive variance of India, one-fifth of the total, is explained on this factor. Power, too, is highly loaded on this factor. In a significant pattern, then, India, Power, Imperialism, and the United States are most positively loaded on the factor of Imperialism.

Table XI presents a diagrammatic illustration of the ten factors. Several vertical patterns are apparent.

Although only slightly more than half of the coded strategies emerged as significant, those that did emerge are highly concentrated: three cluster on the factor of Atomic War, a factor which is not loaded significantly with any single actor. All seven values coded emerged as significant on these ten factors. Again, however, five of these are clustered along the first factor; the sixth is highly loaded on a factor, Well-being, in which Peace, the polar opposite of Atomic War, is a significant symbol. It is in relationship to the two issues of peace and war that almost all values occur.

We thus note a marked clustering of values and strategies on a single continuum. It is possible to hypothesize that such a pattern reveals no clear perceived relationship between objectives and means; rather, that the foreign policy behaviour of this decision-maker can be termed 'irrational', that is, there exists a large gap between image and policy choices in almost all the major factors of Menon's perceptions.

Krishna Menon's image may be summed up as follows: three factors deal with the cold war, one with the problem of atomic warfare, and one with non-alignment; four deal with nationalism, colonialism, imperialism, and independence; and the remaining one with peace and well-being. These then are the basic axes around which Menon's perceptions revolve and from which his foreign-policy behaviour flows.

Conclusion

The central thesis of Professor Brecher's paper was that Élite Image constitutes the key to understanding and predicting probable choices in foreign policy. Through an analysis of frequencies, attitudes, and factors, this paper has attempted to examine one important decision-maker's image and to predict behaviour on specific issues. Certain hypotheses were formulated regarding the probability of the occurrence of violence. Krishna Menon as a decision-maker functioned in an 'uncritical conflict system'. The relationship between images and strategies was also analysed, and the low salience of strategies was discovered.

Perhaps the most striking conclusion of the content analysis is the validity and multi-dimensional utility of Professor Brecher's thesis. An exploration in depth of the major categories of Krishna Menon's image illuminated many of the choices which he as a member of the Indian foreign-policy élite selected over the years. This has more far-reaching implications for the study of foreign policy. Empirical studies focusing on élite images and their spill-over effect on policy choices are now essential if accurate prediction is to be achieved.

These two papers were done independently. Nevertheless, the basic features of Menon's View of the World that emerged were remarkably similar. This strongly suggests the value of combining the two approaches to image analysis as a means of testing the relevance and accuracy of conclusions derived from each other. A series of such inquiries can only enrich our understanding and thereby our ability to predict probable State behaviour in the international system.

INDEX

PRINTED IN GREAT BRITAIN
AT THE UNIVERSITY PRESS, OXFORD
BY VIVIAN RIDLER
PRINTER TO THE UNIVERSITY